AN OUTLINE OF HISTORY OF ŚAIVA PHILOSOPHY

An Outline of History of Śaiva Philosophy

Kanti Chandra Pandey

General Editor
R.C. Dwivedi

MOTILAL BANARSIDASS PUBLISHERS
PRIVATE LIMITED • DELHI

First Published: Varanasi, 1954
Reprint: Delhi, 1986, 1999

ISBN: 81-208-0091-5

Available at:

MOTILAL BANARSIDASS

41 U.A. Bungalow Road, Jawahar Nagar, Delhi 110 007
8 Mahalaxmi Chamber, Warden Road, Mumbai 400 026
120 Royapettah High Road, Mylapore, Chennai 600 004
Sanas Plaza, 1302, Baji Rao Road, Pune 411 002
16 St. Mark's Road, Bangalore 560 001
8 Camac Street, Calcutta 700 017
Ashok Rajpath, Patna 800 004
Chowk, Varanasi 221 001

PRINTED IN INDIA
BY JAINENDRA PRAKASH JAIN AT SHRI JAINENDRA PRESS,
A-45 NARAINA, PHASE I, NEW DELHI 110 028
AND PUBLISHED BY NARENDRA PRAKASH JAIN FOR
MOTILAL BANARSIDASS PUBLISHERS PRIVATE LIMITED,
BUNGALOW ROAD, DELHI 110 007

GENERAL EDITOR'S NOTE

Īśvarapratyabhijñā-Vimarśinī, *IPV* in short, (Critique of the Doctrine of Divine Recognition) is the most important work of the Pratyabhijñā school of Kashmir Śaivism. This is a commentary by the great Abhinavagupta on the *Īśvarapratyabhijñā-Sūtra* (or *-Kārikā*) of Utpala, expounded by a commentary *Bhāskarī* of Bhāskarakaṇṭha. The original text with *Vimarśinī* and the *Bhāskarī* thereon was edited and published by my teachers, Dr. K. C. Pandey and Professor K. A. Subramania Iyer, along with English translation of the *IPV* by Dr. Pandey, in three volumes under the title, *Bhāskarī*, as the Princess of Wales Saraswati Bhavan Texts Nos. 70, 83 and 84 in the years 1938, 1950 and 1954 respectively. These works were out of print for long and are now being re-issued under the general title of *Īśvara-Pratyabhijñā-Vimarśini of Abhinavagupta*, in three volumes. *An Outline of History of Śaiva Philosophy* given by Dr. Pandey in Vol. III of the *Bhāskarī* will be issued separately for the sake of general readers and the scholars interested in the history of religions. Reprint of the rare and fundamental works of Kashmir Śaivism will be welcomed by the scholars concerned with the idealistic systems of Indian Philosophy.

It was in the mid-9th century A.D., when the whole of India was fired with the Advaita Vedānta of Ācārya Śaṅkara that the beautiful land of Goddess Śāradā, the Kashmir valley, produced a great ācārya, who systematized the philosophical postulates of the Śaiva non-dualism on the basis of the monistic Śaiva scriptures. His name is Somadeva, better known as Somānanda. He was an older contemporary of another great Śaiva ācārya, Bhaṭṭa Kallaṭa who wrote his *Vṛtti* on the *Spanda Sūtras* revealed to Vasugupta. The spanda system hardly differs in its philosophical thought from Somānanda. Their real difference lies in prescribing different means of realizing the philosophical goal. *Śivadṛṣṭi* or Vision from Śiva by Somānanda is the first systematic formulation of the philosophy of what is later on conveniently described as the Pratyabhijñā school of Kashmir Śaivism, following the term occurring in the *Īśvarapratyabhijñā* of Utpala. Somānanda in his foundational work, the *Śivadṛṣṭi*, consisting of seven chapters of 700 verses, declared (I. 2) that Lord Śiva is the essence and identity of all the beings. He shines in all the beings. He is bliss and consciousness whose free will nothing can impede and who manifests himself through his powers of knowledge and action. This concept of the highest reality is basically different from the Buddhistic idea of momentary *vijñāna,* from the *nirguṇa* (hence passive) Brahman of Śaṅkara, from the dualistic conception of *Puruṣa* and *Prakṛti* of the Sāṅkhya and from the later schools of Vaiṣṇava Vedānta. Somānanda not merely propounded his theory of the ultimate reality, he refuted the grammarians' theory of Śabda Brahman, the views of the Śāktas, the dualistic Śaivas, and the followers of the Yoga and demonstrated the lack of logic and consistency in their view of reality. Utpaladeva, Utpalācārya, or simply Utpala, built the great edifice of the Pratyabhijñā on the foundations laid by his teacher Somānanda. He wrote his famous *Īśvarapratyabhijñā Sūtra* or *Kārikā* by working out at great length the germinal ideas of the founder of the system (Utpala treats his Kārikā as the reflection of the *Śivadṛṣṭi*) and by providing a suitable fencing against the onslaughts of the counter systems of Indian philosophy.

Utpala advocates the permanence and universality of the self and criticises the Vijñānavādin's theory of momentariness and individuality. He asserts that freedom of will, thought and action is basic essence of being. Being must have innate power to become at will. He vehemently opposes the passive Brahman of Vedānta and lack of integrality between *Puruṣa* and *Prakṛti* of the Sāṁkhya. Vasugupta had recognized three ways of final freedom of human beings: *Śāmbhava*, *Śākta* and *Āṇava.* These ways required an ascetic life of complete detachment and austere practice of Yoga. Somānanda and Utpala show a new way to freedom and beatitude. The realization in the Pratyabhijñā system, to quote from the Introduction of Vol. II (pp. v-vi) by Dr. K. C. Pandey, "consists, not in the actualisation of the potential, nor in the attainment of something new, but in penetrating through the veil that makes the Maheśvara appear as the individual of which everyone is immediately aware and in recognising the Maheśvara in the individual." The followers of this system daily recite the following verse which sums up the attitude of a Śaiva:

शिवो दाता शिवो भोक्ता, शिवः सर्वमिदं जगत् ।
शिवो यजति यज्ञश्च, यः शिवः सोऽहमेव हि ॥

The following prayer for universal peace and happiness occurring at the end of the manuscript B of the *Vivṛtivimarśinī* of Abhinavagupta quoted by its editor in his Preface to Volume I explains the Śaiva's feelings for the world around him and for his fellow human beings :

शुभमस्तु सर्वजगतां परहितनिरता भवन्तु भूतगणाः ।
दोषाः प्रयान्तु शान्ति सर्वत्र सुखीभवन्तु लोकाः ॥

Utpala holds that the human being is essentially free; freedom is the very nature of the individual. However, the veil of ignorance covers this freedom of man and thus keeps him away from the God within him. Man must remove this ignorance; he must penetrate through the veil to recognize his real self, eternally free, omniscient and omnipotent. Recognition is the way to regain the lost freedom. Incidentally, it is significant to note that the philosophy of Utpala has intimate parallels in the *Dakṣiṇāmūrtistotra* of Ācārya Śaṅkara, as interpreted by his great disciple, Sureśvara (See *Abhinavagupta*, pp. 151-52) and the lyrics of the *Saundaryalaharī*.

According to the tradition, Utpala lived near Vicharnaga to the north of Srinagar and belonged to the end of the 9th and first half of the 10th century A.D. Many of his works are lost, those surviving include *Ajaḍapramātṛsiddhi*, *Īśvarasiddhi*, *Sambandhasiddhi* and the commentaries on the latter two works. His commentary on the *Śivadṛṣṭi* is available only in part. His devotional lyrics are collected under the title *Śivastotrāvalī* and quotations from his unknown works are found in the *IPV*. But he is justly famous for his *Īśvarapratyabhijñā Sūtra* or *Kārikā*. This reveals sharpness of his intellect, original thinking and masterly exposition, intimate knowledge of the monistic tradition of the Śaiva Āgamas and the recognitive Sādhanā to realize the Lord Maheśvara.

He wrote two auto-commentaries on his *Kārikā*: *Vṛtti* and *Vivṛti* or *Ṭīkā*. No complete MS of either of these two commentaries by Utpala has so far been discovered. The available portion of the *Vṛtti* upto the 20th *kārikā* of the third *adhikāra* was published in the Kashmir Sanskrit Series and the fragment of the

Vivṛti is in the personal collection of Dr. K. C. Pandey, which remains unpublished. The fragment of the *Vivṛti* begins with the 6th *Kārikā* of the *Jñānādhikāra*, *Āhnika* 3 and ends abruptly with the 3rd *Kārikā* of the fifth *Āhnika*. Utpala imparted his new doctrine to Lakṣmaṇagupta who transmitted it to his worthiest disciple, Abhinavagupta, an encyclopaedic writer on Indian aesthetics and Kashmir Śaivism. Abhinava wrote a commentary on the *Vivṛti* of Utpala, known as the *Vivṛtivimarśinī*. This was published in the Kashmir Series of Texts and Studies, Nos. LX (1938 A.D.), LXII (1941 A.D.) and LXV (1943 A.D.) in three volumes. Abhinava's direct commentary on the text of Utpala's *Kārikā* is also known as *Vimarśinī* and described as *Laghu Vimarśinī*, being shorter in length than the *Vivṛti-Vimarśinī*, which is described as the *Bṛhatīvimarśinī*. They are also known as *Catussāhasrī* and *Aṣṭādaśasāhasrī* respectively in accordance with the old method of calculation. The Sūtras or Kārikās of Utpala remain unintelligible without a commentary, like the Sūtras of Pāṇini or Bādarāyaṇa. Utpala's own commentaries are more in the nature of independent exposition of the Pratyabhijñā system than actual explanation of the text. Abhinavagupta's *Vimarśinī* offers explanation of the *Kārikā* and also reads like an independent work. It is available in full and it represents the systems comprehensively and correctly. Abhinavagupta's *Vimarśinī* is thus the most authentic commentary of the Pratyabhijñā system, which enjoys the reputation of an original work. However, in spite of its clarity and lucidy and comprehensive treatment of the system, it does require a guide to understand the full implications of the words and the ideas of the *Vimarśinī*. The commentary does not solve the problem fully particularly when the oral tradition of teaching the śāstras is lost and when we know that the original thinker like Abhinava will naturally make fresh points in promoting the tradition and in defending it against newly formulated counter-points in the philosophical circles of India in the 10th century A.D.

It was to obviate this difficulty that Dr. K. C. Pandey set on the search for a commentary on Abhinava's *Vimarśinī*. He struck gold in 1931 when he discovered a commentary *Bhāskarī* by Bhāskarakaṇṭha. He belonged to the later half of the 18th century A.D. According to the *Bhāskarī* he was of the Dhaumyāyona Gotra and the names of his grand-father and father were Vaidūryakaṇṭha and Avatārakaṇṭha respectively. It was to teach his son Jagannātha ('*svasutādibodhanārtham*') that Bhāskara wrote his learned commentary giving traditional interpretation of the *Vimarśinī* or the Pratyabhijñā school of Kashmir Śaivism for that matter, which was handed down to him through unbroken chain of ācāryas. Besides this commentary, he translated the mystic sayings of Lalleśvarī, *Lallā Vāk*, into Sanskrit, wrote a commentary, available in fragment, on the *Yogavāsiṣṭha* and composed a poem, named *Harṣeśvarastava*, in singing the glory of the Lord on the occasion of his visit to the temple in Kashmir.

Another anonymous commentary on the *Vimarśinī*, *Īśvarapratyabhijñā-Vimarśinī-Vyākhyā* procured by the late Dr. K. C. Pandey from the Government Manuscript Library, Madras and edited by him before his sad demise is under print and will be published before long by Messrs Motilal Banarsidass, Delhi.

According to Mādhava (15th century A.D.), the author of the *Sarvadarśana-Saṃgraha*, (i) *Sūtra* i.e. *Īśvarapratyabhijñākārikā* of Utpala and his two commentaries thereon, (ii) *Vṛtti* and (iii) *Vivṛti* and short and long commentaries of Abhinavagupta, namely, (iv) *Vimarśinī* and *Vivṛtivimarśinī* constitute the Pratyabhijñāśāstra which in essence is the exposition of the *Śivadṛṣṭi* (spoken of as a *prakaraṇa* of the Śaivaśāstra) of Somānanda:

सूत्रं वृत्तिर्विवृतिर्लघ्वी बृहतीत्युभे विमर्शिन्यौ ।
प्रकरणविवरणपञ्चकमिति शास्त्रं प्रत्यभिज्ञायाः ॥

(This verse also occurs in the *Śāstraparāmarśa* of Madhuraja where the last word reads as '*pratyabhijñākhyam*'.)

The *Īśvarapratyabhijñā* of Utpalācārya has four *Adhikāras*: *Jñāna-*, *Kriyā-*, *Āgama-* and the *Tattvasaṅgraha-*. The first volume contains the *Jñānādhikāra* which has eight *Āhnikas* or chapters along with the *Vimarśinī* of Abhinavagupta and the *Bhāskarī* of Bhāskarakaṇṭha. The second volume completes the text and the commentaries in the remaining three *Adhikāras*. This also carries an Introduction giving in brief the History and Literature and Philosophy of the Pratyabhijñā system along with various appendixes for Vol. I and Vol. II. Vol. III gives English translation of the *Īśvarapratyabhijñā* and the *Vimarśinī*. As these volumes are essentially photo-prints; the original edition has not been disturbed except in the formal matters where the change of title, publisher etc. is involved. In some cases it might create apparent difficulties. For example, the volumes, although now differently titled will still be found under the old title of the *Bhāskarī* in the contents, Introduction etc. of Dr. K. C. Pandey. In our desire to place these volumes in the hands of readers at the earliest, we did not think it proper to make changes warranted by new circumstances of the publication. I crave the indulgence of the scholars in this matter and hope the reprint of the classic texts of the *Īśvarapratyabhijñā* system of Kashmir, for which real credit should go to Shri J. P. Jain, the publisher, will help in further promoting the growing interest of Indologists in this branch of Indian Philosophy.

Department of Sanskrit, R. C. DWIVEDI
University of Rajasthan, Jaipur

CONTENTS

	Page
General Editor's note	(v)
List of Abbreviations	(xviii)
PART I HISTORICAL APPROACH TO EIGHT SYSTEMS OF ŚAIVA PHILOSOPHY	
ANTIQUITY OF ŚAIVAISM AS A RELIGION	
Śaivaism in the Veda	1
Śaivaism as known to Buddha ..	2
Śaivaism amongst kings	3
Śaivaism amongst great authors ..	4
Śaivaism and the Veda	5
Eight systems of the Śaiva Philosophy ..	6
Śaiva Āgamic Literature	7
(I) PĀŚUPATA DUALISM	
The Vaiśeṣika as a Pāśupata system ..	10
Haribhadra's basis of classification ..	10
Light on the Pāśupata, thrown by Rājaśekhara.	12
Identification of the Pāśupata system in Śaṅkara.	13
(II) SIDDHĀNTA ŚAIVA DUALISM	
Sadyojyoti	15
Bṛhaspati	16
Śaṅkara Nandana	17
Devabala	17
ŚAIVA DUALISM IN KASHMIR	
Rāmakaṇṭha I	18
Śrīkaṇṭha	20
Nārāyaṇa Kaṇṭha	20
Rāma Kaṇṭha, the author of the Sarvatobhadra.	21
Rāma Kaṇṭha II	22
King Bhoja of Dhārā	23
Aghora Śiva	24
(III) LAKULĪŚA PĀŚUPATA SYSTEM OF ŚAIVAISM	
Nārāyaṇopaniṣad	27
The date of the Lakulīśa Pāśupata system	28

	Page
Reference to Śaiva teacher Uditācārya	29
Identification of Kauśika	29
The probable shape of the memorial Liṅgas	30

(IV) THE ŚAIVA VIŚIṢṬĀDVAITA

Śaiva Viśiṣṭādvaita and Śrīkaṇṭha	32
Criticism of Śrī Kaṇtha's Viśiṣṭādvaita	35

(V) VIŚEṢĀDVAITA OR PURE DVAITĀDVAITA OF VĪRA ŚAIVAISM

The five teachers as historical personalities	X	39
Revaṇa Siddha and Revaṇārya		40
Marula		41
Ekorāma		42
Śrīpati Paṇḍita		43
Śrīpati Paṇḍita's date		43
His commentary		45
Aggressiveness of Rāmānuja		46
Some unfamiliar authorities referred to in the commentary		47
Śrīpati's Viśeṣādvaita	X	48

(VI) NANDIKEŚVARA ŚAIVAISM

Tradition about Nandikeśvara	49
The date of Nandikeśvara Kāśikā	49
Upamanyu, the commentator.	50

(VII) RASEŚVARA ŚAIVAISM

The cause of the rise of the Raseśvara system	52
Raseśvara as a Śaiva system	52
Probable time of Raseśvara Darśana	55

(VIII) MONISTIC ŚAIVAISM OF KASHMIR

PART II. PHILOSOPHICAL APPROACH

Preliminary	58
The basis of the arrangement of the systems	60
Śaiva dualism	62

(I) PĀŚUPATA DUALISM

Salient features of the Pāśupata Dualism	64

(II) SIDDHĀNTA ŚAIVA DUALISM

The Siddhānta Śaiva Dualism and the Vaiśeṣika.	66
The Siddhānta Śaiva Dualism and the Sāṅkhya.	67

	Page
The process	68
The Siddhānta Ṣaiva Dualism and the Vedānta...	69
The Pāśupata Dualism and the Siddhānta Ṣaiva Dualism.	70
The Siddhānta Ṣaiva Dualism and the philosophy of Grammar	71
The Categories of the Siddhānta Ṣaiva Dualism ..	72
The primary and the dependent categories ..	73
(I) Pati, the transcendental Ṣiva, the first primary category.	75
The difference in the conception of powers explained	77
Powers of the Lord (Pati)	78
(1) The power of knowledge	78
(2) The power of action	78
(3) The power of will	78
(4) The power of creation	79
The pure creation	79
The impure creation	80
(5) The power of maintenance (Sthiti Ṣakti) ..	80
(6) The power of annihilation(Saṁhāra Ṣakti)..	81
(7) The power of obscuration (Tirobhāva) ..	81
(8) The power of grace (Anugraha Śakti) ..	82
(II) Pāśa, the bondage, the second primary category.	82
(1) Mala	83
(2) Māyā	84
(3) Karma	84
(4) Nirodhaśakti or Tirobhāva.	85
(5) Bindu	85
Bindu as an impurity or Mala	85
Mysticism of the Śaiva dualism and Plotinus ..	86
Bindu as the first dependent category ..	87
THE REASONS FOR ADMITTING THE BINDU	
(1) Bindu as the material cause of the pure creation.	88
(2) Bindu and the impure world ..	88
(3) Bindu and individual self	89
Another view of the Bindu	90
Its refutation by the Dualists	90
Nāda as a substitute for Sphoṭa of the philosophy of Grammar	91
The criticism of the Grammarians' view ..	91
Vijñāna as the arouser of the meaning.. ..	92
Its criticism and a reply to it	93
The theory of Nāda	93

	Page
Nāda and philosophy of music	95
Bindu and Nāda	95
Bindu and the theory of Paśyantī etc, in the philosophy of Grammar. ..	96
The difference between Bhartṛhari and Śrīkaṇṭha	97
Nāda and the second dependent category, Śakti Tattva.	98
Sadāśiva Tattva, the third dependent category. ..	98
Īśvara Tattva, the fourth dependent category. ..	99
Vidyā Tattva, the fifth dependent category. ..	99
Bindu, subtle and gross	99
Māyā, the sixth dependent category.	99
Kāla, the seventh dependent category.	100
Niyati, the eighth dependent category.	100
Kalā, the ninth dependent category.	101
Vidyā, the tenth dependent category.	101
Rāga, the eleventh dependent category. ..	102
(III) Paśu, the third Primary category and Puruṣa, the twelfth dependent category. ..	102
(1) Two types of Vijñānākala	103
(2) Pralayākala	103
(3) Sakala	103
Puruṣa	104
Avyakta, the thirteenth dependent category. ..	104
Guṇa Tattva, the fourteenth dependent category. ..	104
Liberation or Mokṣa	105
The experience of the liberated	106
The Dualist Śaiva conception of Mokṣa and that of the Vedānta	106
Lakulīśa Pāśupata conception of Mokṣa criticised ..	108
Other conceptions of Mokṣa, criticised by the Śaiva Dualist.	108
(1) Utpatti samatā Pakṣa	108
(2) Samatāsaṅkrānti Pakṣa	108
(3) Āveśa Pakṣa	108
The teacher and the lower liberation ..	109
Fundamental identity of the Tamil Śaiva Siddhānta and the Siddhānta Śaiva Dualism	109

(III) DUALISM-CUM-MONISM OF LAKULĪŚA PĀŚUPATA

Lakulīśa Pāśupata and the Veda	112
The conception of Brahman or Pati	112
The conception of Mokṣa	114
Other points common or similar to the Lakulīśa Pāśupata	115

	Page
Sāyaṇa's interpretation of the text, the Vedic basis of the Lakulīśa Pāśupata	116
The distinctive features of the Lakulīśa Pāśupata system	117
The points of difference between the dualist Śaiva and the Lakulīśa Pāśupata	118
Lakulīśa Pāśupata as rationalistic voluntarism ..	118
The categories of the Lakulīśa Pāśupata ..	119
(I) The cause (Pati), the first primary category.	120
(II) The effect (Kārya) or Paśu, the second primary category.	124
The relation between the cause (Pati or Kāraṇa) and the effect (Kārya)	125
(1) Vidyā or sentiency	126
Vidyā-chart	127
Lakulīśa Pāśupata theory of perception ..	128
The theory of knowledge	129
Perception	129
Inference	129
Āgama	130
(2) Kalā	130
Kalā-chart	131
(3) Paśu	132
Impurities (Mala) of the individual subject (Paśu) ..	133
Paśu-chart	134
Eight Pentads (Pañcaka) of the Lakulīśa Pāśupata ..	134
(1) Bāsa	135
(2) Caryā	135
Caryā (Mode of living and worship) chart ..	136
(3) Japa-Dhyāna	137
(4) Sadārudrasmṛti	137
(5) Prasāda (Grace)	137
Siddha	139
(*III*) Yoga, the third primary category of the Lakulīśa Pāśupata	140
(*IV*) Vidhi, the fourth primary category. ..	143
Vidhi-chart	144
(*V*) Duḥkhānta (End of all miseries), the fifth primary category.	145
Yukta and Mukta	145
The characteristics of the united (Yukta) ..	145
The conditions of the union	146
Table of the categories of the Lakulīśa Pāśupata system	147

Page

(IV) VIŚIṢṬĀDVAITA OR QUALIFIED MONISTIC ŚAIVAISM

Viśiṣṭādvaita and Bhedābheda 148
The influences 149
Bhedābheda and Viśiṣṭādvaita distinguished .. 150
Brahman or Śiva 152
The individual subject or Paśu 155
Impurities or malas 156
Liberation or Mokṣa 157
Influence of Aesthetics 158
The nature of identification at liberation .. 159

(V) THE VIŚEṢĀDVAITA OF ŚRĪPATI

Vīra Śaivaism 163
Vīra Śaivaism and Śāṅkara Vedānta .. 164
Criticism of the theory of superimposition (Adhyāsa) 164
Criticism of the practically real (Vyāvahārika Satya) 165
Criticism of the illusory nature of the world .. 166
Criticism of the theory of reflection 167
Criticism of the Viśiṣṭādvaita 168
Bhedābhedavāda of Śrīpati 170
Bhedābheda and liberation 171
Sacred texts and Bhedābheda 172
Brahman, Para Śiva or Pati 173
Paśu, Jīva or Individual soul 175
Liberation or Mokṣa 176
Six ways to union (Ṣaḍadhva), and six forms of Grace (Ṣaḍvidhaśaktipāta) 177
Six sections of the sacred text (Ṣaṭsthala) 178

(VI) ADVAITA ŚAIVAISM OF NANDIKEŚVARA

The importance of Nandikeśvara Śaivaism .. 180
The main tendencies of the system 181
Monism of Nandikeśvara 183
The Theory of Manifestation 184
The categories 184

(VII) RASEŚVARA ŚAIVAISM

Contributors to the Raseśvara system .. 186
The persisting tradition 187
The value of the Rasa tradition .. 188
The scientific aspect of the Raseśvara system .. 189
Religious aspect of the Raseśvara system .. 190
Philosophical aspect of the Raseśvara system .. 191
Śaiva dualism as the basis of Raseśvara system 192
Liberation in life (Jīvanmukti) 193
The means to liberation in life (Jīvanmukti) .. 194

(VIII) MONISTIC ŚAIVAISM OF KASHMIR AS PRESENTED IN THE ĪŚVARAPRATYABHIJÑĀ VIMARŚINĪ

Author's motive and point of view ... 195
The introduction ... 195
Buddhism and Monistic Śaivaism of Kashmir 196
Bauddha Objections against Śaivaism ... 197
The reply of the Monistic Śaivaism of Kashmir 198
Epistemic basis of the Śaiva Metaphysics 200
The All-inclusive Universal Mind and its Omniscience 201
Omnipotence (Kriyāśakti) of the Lord and phenomenon of action 202
The Bauddha conception of action ... 202
The Śaiva conception of action ... 203
The last two Adhikāras ... 206
Appendix: Textual Authorities indicated by foot-notes ... 207
Index 249

LIST OF ABBREVIATIONS

Abh.	Abhinavagupta (An Historical and Philosophical Study).
A. In.	Ancient India No. 3 Bulletin of Archaeological Survey of India. (Delhi).
A. I. N.	Ancient Indian Numismatics (D. R. Bhandarkar).
A. P. S.	Ajaḍa Pramātṛ Siddhi.
A. Pra.	Aṣṭa Prakaraṇa.
Arch. S.	Archaeological Survey Annual report 1923-4.
Bh.	Bhāskarī.
Bh. Ka.	Bhoga Kārikā.
Car.	Caraka.
E. H. I.	Early History of India (Smith).
Ep. Ind.	Epigraphia Indica.
G. K.	Gaṇa Kārikā.
Hock	Hocking (Types of Philosophy).
H. Ph. E. W.	History of Philosophy Eastern and Western.
H. S. L.	History of Sanskrit Literature (Keith).
I. I. A.	Invasion of India by Alexander (J. W. M'Crindle).
I. I. Ph.	Introduction to Indian Philosophy (Chatterji and Dutta).
Inge.	W. R. Inge : The Philosophy of Plotinus.
I. Ph.	Indian Philosophy (Radhakrishnan).
I. P. V.	Īśvara Pratyabhijñā Vimarśinī.
I. P. V. V.	Īśvara Pratyabhijñā Vivṛti Vimarśini.
J. B. B. R. A. S.	Journal of Bengal Branch of the Royal Asiatic Society.
K. A. S.	Kashmir Sanskrit Series.
K. P.	Kūrma Purāṇa.
K. S.	Kriyā Sāra.
L. C.	Linga Dhāraṇa Candrikā.
M. Ka.	Mokṣa Kārikā.
Ma. Ka.	Mādhyamika Kārikā.
Ma. Tan.	Mataṅga Tantra.
M. U.	Mānasollāsa.
M. U. S. Bh.	Mahānārāyaṇa Upaniṣad Śaiva Bhāṣya.
M. Bh.	Mahābhāṣya (Patañjali).
Mr.	Mṛgendrāgama.
Mr. Vr.	Mṛgendra Tantra Vṛtti.
Mr. Vr. Di.	Mṛgendra Vṛtti Dīpikā.
N. K.	Nandi Kārikā or Nandikeśvara Kāśikā (Mysore edition 1936).

N. Ka.	.. Nāda Kārikā.
N. P.	.. Nareśvara Parīkṣā.
P. Hr.	.. Pratyabhijñā Hṛdaya.
P. K.	.. Paramokṣanirāsa Kārikā.
Pan. Bha.	.. Pañcārtha Bhāsya.
P. Su.	.. Pāśupta Sūtra.
P. V.	.. Pramāṇa Vārtika.
R. A.	.. Rasārṇava.
R. Hr.	.. Rasa Hṛdaya.
Rg.	.. Ṛgveda.
R. R. S.	.. Rasa Ratna Samuccaya.
R. T.	.. Ratna Traya.
R. U.	.. Rasopaniṣad.
R. Y.	.. Rudra Yāmala.
Ra. T.	.. Rāja Taraṅgiṇī.
Ra. Tan.	.. Ṛaurava Tantra.
S. Bh.	.. Śāṅkar Bhāṣya on Vedānta Sūtra.
S. Bha.	.. Ṣarvatobhadra.
S. C.	.. Śivārcana Candrikā.
S. Dr.	.. Śiva Dṛṣṭi.
S. D. S.	.. Sarva Darśana Saṅgraha. (Abhyankar's edition, Poona).
S. D. Sam.	Ṣaḍ-darśana Samuccaya.
S. K.	.. Siddhānta Kaumudī.
S. P.	.. Śaiva Siddhānta Paribhāṣā.
Sri Bh.	.. Srīkara Bhāṣya.
Srikam.Bh.	.. Śrīkaṇṭha Bhāṣya.
S. S.	.. Siddhānta Sārāvali (Mss).
S. Si.	.. Siddhānta Śikhāmaṇi.
S. Sri.	.. Śivādvaita of Śrīkaṇṭha. (Surya Narayan Shastri)
Sva. Tan.	.. Svāyambhuva Tantra.
T.	.. Translation of I. P. V.
T. A.	.. Tantrāloka.
Tai. A.	.. Taittirīya Āraṇyaka.
Thil.	.. Thilly. (History of Philosophy).
T. P.	.. Tattva Prakāśikā.
T. R. D.	.. Tarka Rahasya Dīpikā.
T. San.	.. Tattva Saṅgraha.
T. T. N.	.. Tattva Traya Nirṇaya.
Ueb.	.. Ueberbeg . A History of Philosophy.
V.	.. Verse.
V. A.	.. Vārtikālaṅkāra.
V. P.	.. Vākyapadīya (Banaras edition).
V. P. (Cha)	.. Vākyapadiya (Charudeva Shastri's edition).
V. Pari.	.. Vedānta Paribhāṣā (R. K. Mission edition).
V. S.	.. Vedāntasūtra.

Vi. S.	..	Vīra Śaivendu Śekhara.
Wint.	..	Winternitz.
Y. S.	..	Yoga Sūtra.

AN OUTLINE OF HISTORY OF ŚAIVA PHILOSOPHY

PART I

HISTORICAL APPROACH TO EIGHT SYSTEMS OF ŚAIVA PHILOSOPHY

ANTIQUITY OF ŚAIVAISM AS A RELIGION

The Śaiva Philosophy is an outgrowth of the religion, the distinctive feature of which is the worship of the phallic form of God Śiva. Śaivaism as a religion has persisted since the prehistoric time of the archaeological finds of Harappa and Mohenjo-daro. It has a continuous history of at least five thousand years. The phallic emblem of Śiva, as found in the ruins of the Indus valley civilizations, is even today an object of worship among the followers of Śaivaism. It is a living faith all over India. That there was a dominant element of religion in the Indus valley cultures and civilizations is now well admitted[1]. And the Archaeological finds at Harappa, (I) a Śiva Liṅgam, a conical terracotta object with a rounded top, which, even according to the statement of Dr. R. E. M. Wheeler, represents "probably a phallus" and (II) a large thick ring representing "probably" a Yoni (female principle), lead to a fair assumption that whatever other religion or religions may have been, Śaivaism, in its characteristic prevalent form of worship of Śiva and Śakti[2] in union in the symbolic form of a Liṅgam on Yoni, was there.

These finds lend some support to the view, expressed by Mr. R. D. Banerji, about a water reservoir, provided with narrow covered channel, found in Harappa, analogous to the one, found at Mohenjo-daro[3], that it was used as Caraṇāmṛtakuṇḍa, a receptacle for the holy water, used for washing the sacred image. For, such a reservoir is a common feature of temples of Śiva even today.

ŚAIVAISM IN THE VEDA

Worship of the Phallus of Śiva is referred to in the Ṛgveda (Śiśnadevāḥ)[4]. Various names of Śiva, such as Rudra and Paśupati etc. occur in all the four Vedas.

---

*1. A. In., 76.
*2. A. In., 129.
*3. Arch. S., 52.
4. Rg. M. VII, S. 22 RK 5

In the Ṛgveda, there are verses, which refer to Rudra and Tryambaka, e.g.

(1) Imā Rudrāya Tapase.
(2) Imā Rudrāya Ṣatadhanvine.
(3) Tryambakam Yajāmahe.

In the Sāmaveda also in the Sāmavidhāna, there is a Saṁhitā, collection of hymns, addressed to Rudra, e.g. "Āvorājānam tadvargādeva pravṛjyāto hani".

In the Śukla Yajurveda[1] section XVI of the Vājasaneya Saṁhitā and in the Taittirīya Saṁhitā of Kṛṣṇa Yajurveda section IV, 5: hundred names of God Ṣiva are enumerated. To this fact there is reference in the Mṛgendrāgama[2], to show that the Ṣaiva tradition goes back to the Vedic times.

In the Atharvaveda also there are many collections of hymns, addressed to Rudra and also dealing with the ways of worshipping him, e.g.

1. Kāṇḍa VI, Anuvāka 2, Prapāṭhaka 20.
2. Kāṇḍa VI, Anuvāka 4, Prapāṭhaka 1.
3. Kāṇḍa VI, Anuvāka 7, Prapāṭhaka 44.
4. Kāṇḍa VI, Anuvāka 7, Prapāṭhaka 57.
5. Kāṇḍa VI, Anuvāka 7, Prapāṭhaka 59.
6. Kāṇḍa VI, Anuvāka 9, Prapāṭhaka 90—93.
7. Kāṇḍa XI, Anuvāka 1, Prapāṭhaka 2.
8. The XV Kāṇḍa is devoted to Mahādeva.

In the Kalpa also, Ṣiva is well recognised. For instance, in Kāṭhaka Sūtrapariśiṣṭīya Rudra Kalpa the ritualistic way to the visualisation of Ṣiva as Pinākin, is given. In the Upaniṣads also the Ṣaiva philosophical doctrines are found. The Ṣaiva writers on the different aspects of the Ṣaiva thought were aware of the unbroken continuity of their religio-philosophic traditions from the Vedic time to their own days and very often refer to the Vedic and the post-Vedic texts in support of their views.

ṢAIVAISM AS KNOWN TO BUDDHA

Buddha refers to Ṣaivaism in his own way. In one of his sermons, he refers to it as Siva Vijjā, which the commentator Buddhaghoṣa (5th century A. D.) explains as Bhūta Vijjā or exorcism.

*1. Wint. Vol. I, 185. | 2. M. 19.r

ŚAIVAISM AMONGST THE KINGS

If we cast a glance at the early history of India we find that many kings and the members of the royal families were worshippers of Ṣiva and erected magnificent temples in honour of the deity, which stand even today. The temple of Paśupati in Nepal was already in existence when Ashoka visited the valley in 250 B. C. His daughter Cārumati,—who accompanied him, but stayed behind, when her imperial father returned to the plains,—built a convent to the North of Paśupatinātha[1]. Ashoka himself was a worshipper of Ṣiva in his early life. Jalauka, one of the sons of Ashoka, who was an active and vigorous king of Kashmir, was hostile to Buddhism and was devoted to Ṣiva. He and his queen Īśānadevī[2] erected many Ṣiva temples (one of them being called after his father "Ashokeśvara").

Āndhra became independent soon after the death of Ashoka (232 B. C.), under a king, named Simuka[3]. During the reigns of all thirty kings, who successively ruled for about 460 years, the worship of Ṣiva was popular[4].

The coin of Kadphises II, bears the image of Ṣiva on a Bull. He is supposed to have ruled[5] from 78 to 110 A.D. He is admitted to have been a devotee of Ṣiva. Kanishka I and Huvishka issued gold coins bearing the image of Ṣiva on the reverse side and the name of the deity has been given as "Oesho" (Umeśa). Huvishka also issued gold coins bearing on the reverse figures of Ṣiva and Pārvatī (Oesho and Nānā) (Punjab Museum catalogue vol. I, 197).

The coins of King Vāsudeva, the successor of Huvishka, who ruled from 182 to 220 A. D. which exhibit on the reverse the figures of Ṣiva, with or without Bull, Nandī, behind him and carrying noose and trident etc. are clearly indicative of the influence of Ṣaivaism.[6] That Puṣyabhūti, a remote ancestor of King Harṣa was an ardent devotee of Ṣiva and that Ṣiva was one of the gods, whom Harṣa himself worshipped, are well known historical facts.[7] Harṣa's contemporary, King Ṣaśāṅka of Gauḍa was an ardent believer in Ṣiva, as stated by Yuan Chwang and testified by his gold coins, bearing the image of Ṣiva on the obverse side.

---

*1. E. H. I. 170.
*2. E. H. I. 201.
and R. T. BK. 1 VV 108--52.
*3. E. H. I. 218.
*4. E. H. I. 224.
*5. E. H. I. 271.
*6. E. H. I. 288.
*7. E. H. I. 358--364.

The temples, built during the two centuries of the rule of the early Chalukya dynasty of Vātāpi (550 to 750 A. D.) though now in ruins, form magnificent memorials of the kings of this period[1]. King Krishna I (760 A. D.) the successor and uncle of Dantidurga, (a Chieftain of the ancient Rāṣṭrakūṭa clan who overthrew Kīrtivarman II, the son and successor of Vikramāditya II) was a great devotee of Śiva, as is testified by the most marvellous architectural freak in our country, the Kailāśa monolithic temple of Ellora, the most extensive and sumptuous of the rock-cut shrines[2].

Chola kings were great devotees of Śiva. Rājarāja (985 A. D.) built a magnificent temple of Śiva, which stands even today as a memorial of his brilliant career, architectural taste and devotion to Śiva[3]. And his successor, Rājendra (1023 A. D.) adorned the capital city, Gangaikonda-Cholapuram, built to commemorate his exploit, with a gigantic temple enshrining a Liṅgam of Śiva 30 feet high.

The Vīra Śaivaism, the Liṅgāyat School, arose or rather, was revitalized after the abdication of Bijjala in 1167. It was founded or rather upheld, as we shall show, by Basava, the Brahman minister of Bijjal. It has a very large following even to-day in South India

ŚAIVAISM AMONGST GREAT AUTHORS

Pāṇini was a Śaiva. The first fourteen Sūtras of his grammatical work are articulate representations of the inarticulate sounds, produced in fourteen sets by Śiva through his hand-drum, known as Ḍhakvā. Their grammatical importance has fully been brought out by Pāṇini. But they represent Śaiva philosophy also, which has been presented in the Nandikeśvara Kāśikā.

Kālidāsa was a Śaiva and followed the view of Nandikeśvara about the relation between Śiva and Śakti. He admitted that there is inseparable union between them, similar to that between language and meaning.

Nandikeśvara, while denying the separate being of Śiva from Śakti, cites two analogies (1) of the moon and her light and (2) of language and meaning, "Candra—candrikayoryadvad yathā Vāgarthayoriva"

(N. K., V. 11)

This idea seems to have been repeated by Kālidāsa in the very first verse of Raghuvaṁśa:—

"Vāgarthāviva sampṛktau".

•1. E H. I. 444
•2. E. H. I. 444—5.
•3. E. H. I. 487.

He very clearly refers to one of the twelve jyotirliṅgas, namely, Mahākāla at Ujjayinī, (Ujjain) in his Meghadūta:—

"Mahākālamāsādya Kāle".

Naṭarāja temple was famous in the time of Aghora Śiva (1158 A. D.). He refers to a distant ancestor of his, Śrīkaṇṭha, who came to worship Naṭarāja Abhrasabheśana[1].

ŚAIVAISM AND THE VEDA

Whatever may have been the Brahmanic antagonism towards Śaivaism in the early Vedic period, as some hold on the basis of reference to its followers as "Phallus worshippers", etc., this antagonism died out with the passage of time; and Brahmanism and Śaivaism got more and more reconciled, as testified by the inclusion of the hundred names of Śiva in the Śukla and the Kṛṣṇa Yajurveda, numerous references to him in the Atharvaveda and change in the conception of the god from "terrific" under the name "Rudra" to "the protector of cattle" under the name "Paśupati". Towards the end of the Vedic period, in the tenth book of the Taittirīya Āraṇyaka, we find the five Mantras, on which the Lakulīśa Pāśupata system is based. And two out of the six recognised Vedic systems, (I) the Nyāya and (II) the Vaiśeṣika, present the Śaiva Dualistic Philosophy, according to both Haribhadra Sūri and Rājaśekhara as stated in the two summaries of six systems of Indian Philosophy, called by the same name, "Ṣaḍ-darśana Samuccaya". Though most of the authoritative works on the Eight systems of the Śaiva Philosophy, now available, professedly follow the authority of the Śaivāgamas, yet almost every one of them quotes from the Vedic texts at least to show that the particular principle, propounded, is in agreement with the Vedic text. Thus, for instance, Somānanda in his Śiva Dṛṣṭi, refers to the Vedic passages, such as

"Eka eva Rudrovatasthe na dvitīyaḥ"

and

"Sorodīt" Ś. Dṛ. 122.

A careful study of the works on the various Śaiva systems shows that the attitude of the Śaiva Philosophy as a whole towards the Veda was not that of condemnation, such as was taken up by the Cārvāka : nor that of opposition, which marked the Buddhism. It was rather like that of a step-daughter, whose agreements and differences with the father are those which the mother has with him. Thus, Śaivaism owes its allegiance

*1. S. Sri, 73.

to, acknowledges the authority of, the Veda only in so far as the Veda agrees with the Śaivāgamas, some of which assert that the Śaivāgama is the essence of the Veda (Vedasāraḥ Śivāgamaḥ). It may, however, be noted here that some systems of the Śaiva Philosophy agree with the Veda more than others. This point we shall clarify when we deal with each Śaiva system separately.

EIGHT SYSTEMS OF THE ŚAIVA PHILOSOPHY

The available literature shows that there were eight system of the Śaiva Philosophy—

(1) Pāśupata Dualism.
(2) Siddhānta Śaiva Dualism.
(3) Dualistic-cum-non-dualistic Śaivaism of Lakulīśa Pāśupata.
(4) Viśiṣṭādvaita Śaivaism.
(5) Viśesādvaita Śaivaism (Vīra Śaiva).
(6) Nandikeśvara Śaivaism.
(7) Raseśvara Śaivaism.
(8) Monistic Śaivaism of Kashmir.

According to the classification of the Śaiva thought by Abhinavagupta in his Tantrāloka, however, there were three Śaiva systems (I) Dualism (Dvaita) (II) Dualism-cum-non-dualism (Dvaitādvaita) and (III) Monism (Advaita). And they were based upon ten, eighteen and sixty-four Śaivāgamas, respectively. Thus, logically the Śaiva Philosophy developed from dualism to monism, through dualism-cum-non-dualism.

These three groups of the Śaivāgama are known after three different names of Śiva. The dualistic, the dualistic-cum-monistic, and the monistic groups are called Śiva, Rudra and [1]Bhairava groups respectively. They are recognised to have emanated from different mouths of the five-faced (Pañcavaktra) Śiva. Dualistic Śaivāgamas are said to have come from three, Īśa, Tatpuruṣa, and Sadyojāta, the dualistic-cum-monistic from Vāma and Aghora, and the monistic from the union of Śiva and Śakti.

Each Śaivāgama represents a separate school. Thus, there were ninety-two Schools of the Śaiva Philosophy. They have all, however, been put under three heads as stated above. They are not opposite schools, but are essential parts of an organic

1. T. A., Vol. I, 37—48.

whole. They have to be followed in succession. Each of them aims at taking its followers up to a certain stage of the whole path to the final emancipation. They present reality as it shines at different stages. They recognise that multiplicity, unity-in-multiplicity and unity are equally real in succession. They deal with different aspects of the Reality as a whole.

A group is called dualistic, because it deals with such aspects of the Reality as pre-suppose diversity; namely, action, knowledge and will, (Kriyā, Jñāna and Icchā). Another is called dualistic-cum-monistic, because it is concerned with the self and the self-awareness (Cit and Ānanda) as essentially identical but logically and formally different. And the third is called monistic, because it presents a spiritual level, which is beyond the reach of will, knowledge and action, where logical and formal diversities disappear, where the Real shines in itself, by itself and to itself.

Each Śaivāgama is generally divided into four sections:—

(*I*) Jñāna, (*II*), Yoga, (*III*) Kriyā and (*IV*) Caryā. The first deals with the Philosophy, including metaphysics, epistemology and ethics. The second deals with the yogic practices, necessary for the realisation of the goal that the philosophy promises. It gives the necessary details of the yogic discipline such as are not to be found elsewhere. It presents an advance on the yoga tradition recorded by Patañjali in his Yoga Sūtra, not in its philosophical but in its practical aspect. The third is concerned with the method of building the temples and sculpturing the images of the deities, which are to be enshrined therein. It records the architectural and sculptural traditions, in accordance with which the temples were built and the images made. This section of the Śaivāgama seems to have been the basis of the treatises on architecture, e.g. the Samarāṅgaṇa Sūtradhāra by King Bhoja; who wrote many of the available works on the Śaiva Philosophy, such as Tattva Prakāśikā, etc. And the fourth deals with the rituals.

ŚAIVA ĀGAMIC LITERATURE

The Śaivāgama literature was very vast. Appayya Dīkṣita in his Śivārcana Candrikā states the number of verses in each of the twenty-eight Āgamas, which are the basis of the Siddhānta School of Śaivaism. According to him, the total number of verses in these Śaivāgamas was more than a Parārdha, a Śaṅkha and six Padmas[1]. Add to this the number

1. S.C. 104.

of verses in the sixty-four monistic Śaivāgamas, and there will be fabulous number of verses. Most of this literature is lost, probably beyond recovery. The Śaivāgamas, which have been printed in different scripts, such as Rudra Yāmala, Kāraṇa, Pauṣkarāgama, Suprabheda, Yogaja, Netra, Svacchanda, Mṛgendra, and Mataṅga, etc., and those the fragments of which are preserved in different MS. libraries, such as Ajitāgama, etc., represent a very small portion only of what actually once existed.

It may be pointed out here that Appayya Dīkṣita's statement about the number of verses in the Śaivāgamas of the Siddhānta School, represents a tradition which is found in the Ajitāgama, in the very first chapter, called Tantrāvatāra. A manuscript of this is found in the Madras Oriental Manuscript Library.

Whatever may be the time when the Śaivāgamas were written; the common opinion is that they are the products of the early centuries of the Christian era. It is clear that they were recognised as authoritative texts on the various aspects of the Śaivaism, before the time of Śaṅkarācārya (788—820 A. D.) For, he refers to the sixty-four monistic Śaivāgamas in his Saundarya Laharī : "Catuḥ ṣasṭhyā tantraiḥ ṣakalam abhisandhāya bhuvanam". That he had distinctive Śaivāgamic monistic doctrines in his mind when he wrote the Dakṣiṇāmūrti Stotra, admits of no doubt. This point has been dealt with in an earlier work[1]. Sureśvarācārya, a pupil of Śaṅkara, in his Mānasollāsa, distinctly refers to the thiry-six Śaiva categories :

"Brahmāṇḍādiśivāntāyāḥ ṣaṭtriṁśattattvasaṁhateḥ" M. U. 174.
"Teṣvakṣareṣu tiṣṭhanti ṣaṭtriṁśattattvasaṁyutāḥ" M. U. 168.
"Ṣaṭtriṁśattattvasaṁghātaḥ sarvatrāpyanuvartate" M. U. 154.
And Rāmatīrtha Yati, commenting on the last of the verses, quoted above, definitely says that the thirty-six categories are those which are well known in the Śaivāgama.

"Evaṁ ṣaṭtriṁśattattvāni yāni Śaivāgame prasiddhāni."

It may be pointed out here that these thirty-six categories are slightly different from those admitted by the Kashmir Śaivas. They may be stated as follows:—

Five vital airs, five elements, fourteen Indriyas, Mahān, Kāla, Pradhāna, Māyā, Vidyā, Puruṣa, Bindu, Nāda, Śakti, Śiva, Śānta and Atīta[2].

1. Abh., 80. | 2. M. U., 154.

(I) PĀŚUPATA DUALISM

In the Vedānta Sūtra of Bādarāyaṇa in Chapter II pāda II, section VII is called Patyadhikaraṇa. Many students of the Vedānta are under the impression that the system, that is criticised there, is identical with the Lakulīśa Pāśupata. Some support seems to be lent to this view by reference to the categories of the Lakulīśa Pāśupata system by Śaṅkara in the course of his commentary on the first aphorism of this section "Patyurasāmañjasyāt". There is no doubt about this that the categories, referred to by Śaṅkara, are the categories, admitted by Lakulīśa in his Pāśupata Sūtra in the very first Sūtra, according to the commentator, Kauṇḍinya[1]. They are as follows:—

(I) Kāraṇa (II) Kārya (III) Yoga (IV) Vidhi and (V) Duḥkhānta[2].

But the subsequent statement in the Śāṅkara Bhāṣya itself makes it clear that the system, which Śaṅkara is criticising, is a dualistic system, which asserts that Maheśvara is only an instrumental cause and that He depends on something external to Himself, as a material cause, for His creative activity; exactly as a potter does on clay. This statement raises doubt whether the system, referred to by Śaṅkara, is Lakulīśa Pāśupata or some other system, which preceded it and admitted the same categories as those of the Lakulīśa Pāśupata; but differed from it in its metaphysical theory.

That the system, referred to by Śaṅkara, is different from the Lakulīśa Pāśupata, is evident even from the colophon to this section in Śrīkaṇṭha Bhāṣya. It is called Pāśupatādhikaraṇa and not Lakulīśa Pāśupatādhikaraṇa. This difference becomes clearer if we take into account the metaphysical theory of the Lakulīśa Pāśupata. The Lakulīśa Pāśupata system, as presented in the Pāśupata Sūtra, with the commentary of Kauṇḍinya, is not a dualistic system. It is, on the contrary, dualism-cum-non-dualism (Dvaitādvaita). It holds that the effect, the Kārya, the triad of Vidyā, Kalā and Paśu, springs from the Pati. (Bhavodbhavaḥ)[3]. He is the origin, the abode, the Āsana, of the triad. The triad lies in His Śakti which constitutes his very being, the most essential nature, the principal attribute, the chief characteristic, Dharma or Guṇa[4].

1. P. Su., 6.
2. S. Bh., 488.
3. P. Su., 55.
4. P. Su., 58.

The objective world is in Him as the starry heaven is in Ākāśa or the ether. The cause and the effect have no confused being (Vṛttisaṅkara) like the water and milk. They have, on the other hand, distinct being like the light of the eyes and that of the sun or lamp that illumines the object at the time of perception.

That the Pāśupata system, under discussion, is different from the Lakulīśa Pāśupata, is evident from the three commentaries on the Śāṅkara Bhāṣya: (I) Ratna Prabhā, (II) Bhāmatī and (III) Ānandagirīya. For, commenting on "Kārya", the second category of the Pāśupata, every one of them says "Mahadādi". But we know that the Lakulīśa Pāśupata holds the triad of Vidyā, Kalā and Paśu to be the Kārya, but not "Mahadādi". Further, the conceptions of Mokṣa, as found in the two systems, are different. According to the Pāśupata, the end of all pains (duḥkhānta) is mokṣa. But, according to the Lakulīśa Pāśupata, not only the end of all pains but also the attainment of the supreme lordship (Pāramaiśvaryāvāpti) is Mokṣa, as pointed out by Mādhava[1]. We will deal with these and allied points in detail in the next section.

THE VAIŚEṢIKA AS A PĀŚUPATA SYSTEM

There are two summaries of six systems of Indian philosophy called Ṣaḍ-darśana Samuccaya ; one by Rājaśekhara (900 A. D.) and the other by Hari Bhadra Sūri (700-770 A. D.). The latter has two commentaries; one by Guṇa Ratna Sūri[2] (1466 Vikrama) 1409 A. D. called Bṛhatī, and the other by Maṇi Bhadra Sūri, called Laghvī. Maṇi Bhadra's commentary has a commentary on it by Vidyā Tilaka[3], who, according to his own statement, completed it in (1392 Vikrama) 1335 A. D. Both Rājaśekhara and Haribhadra are well known writers in the history of Sanskrit literature. Let us, therefore, see what light we can get from them on the Pāśupata system.

HARIBHADRA'S BASIS OF CLASSIFICATION

Haribhadra admits that there are hundreds of systems of thought in India. But philosophy is simply an outgrowth of religion and aims at pointing out the ways and means to final emancipation. Therefore, if we classify them on the basis of religion, the means to final emancipation and the essential nature

1. S.D. S., 171.
2. S.D. Sam. 118.
3. S.D. Sam. 154.

of it, and the categories, we find that there are only six systems of thought. On this basis he divides the systems of Indian thought under six heads[1] (I) Bauddha, (II) Naiyāyika, (III) Sāṅkhya (VI) Jaina (V) Vaiśeṣika and (VI) Jaiminīya.

Haribhadra, who is earlier than Śaṅkara and Rājaśekhara, asserts that both the Nyāya and the Vaiśeṣika are the systems, the founders of which followed the Śaiva religion and had a common conception of Mokṣa, which consists, according to them, in the freedom from all kinds of pain. And Maṇibhadra, in the course of his commentary, points out that they have a common metaphysical theory also, namely, both admit Śiva or Īśvara to be the instrumental cause only of the creation[2]. But Haribhadra states the reason for classifying the Nyāya as a separate system from the Vaiśeṣika and that is the difference in the philosophical categories. For, while Nyāya is primarily concerned with the logical categories; the Vaiśeṣika presents phenomenological or metaphysical categories.

If we look at the categories of the systems of the Nyāya and the Vaiśeṣika from the point of view of evolution of thought, the Vaiśeṣika system is nothing more than a more logical and essentially phenomenological presentation of the objective categories, hinted at by the Nyāya. The distinction, however, between the two systems in respect of the categories was recognised and is asserted by Haribhadra himself. But it appears that before the time of Haribhadra the distinction between Śaiva and Pāśupata was not emphasised. He, therefore, represents both Gautama and Kaṇāda to be the devotees of Śiva[3].

From the foregoing discussion, it is clear that the Nyāya and the Vaiśeṣika follow an earlier Śaiva tradition in respect of the metaphysical theory and the conception of Mokṣa. And from the reference to the Pāśupata system in the Śaṅkara Bhāṣya it is evident (I) that the system, referred to by Śaṅkara, admitted the five categories, which are retained in the Lakulīśa Pāśupata, which is a Dvaitādvaita system, as we find it in the available Pāśupata Sūtra, attributed to Lakulīśa; and (II) that the five categories belonged earlier to the Dvaita system, the dualistic metaphysics and the conception of Mokṣa of which were accepted in common by both the Nyāya and the Vaiśeṣika. This explains the reference to the Pāśupata as distinct from the Vaiśeṣika by Śaṅkara.

1. S. D. Sam., 4—9.
2. S. D. Sam., 25.
3. S. D. Sam. 121.

LIGHT ON THE PĀŚUPATA THROWN BY RĀJAŚEKHARA

Rājaśekhara in his Ṣaḍ-darśana Samuccaya deals with the same systems as those on which Haribhadra wrote, though he names them differently: for instance, he gives the Nyāya system the name " Yauga ". There are two interesting and important points touched upon by Rājaśekhara. He speaks (i) of the dress and the life of the followers of the Śaiva religion and (ii) of the line of teachers as follows:—

The Yauga school is otherwise called the Śaiva. The religious teachers of this school bear staffs, put on thick piece of cloth over the privities, cover their bodies with blankets, keep matted hair, smear their bodies with ashes and eat insipid food. They hold gourds in their arm-pits and live mostly in the forest. They are devoted to the duties of hospitality and eat bulbs, roots and fruits. They are of two kinds : (I) with wives and (II) without wives; but those without wives are the best. They practise austerity, exposing themselves to five fires. (Pañcāgnisādhanaparāḥ). They wear a consecrated liṅga on their arms.

Here Rājaśekhara (900 A. D.) is talking of "Prāṇaliṅga" which is one of the important "Liṅgas" admitted by Vīra Śaivaism and also of wearing it on arm, exactly as do Vīra Śaivas. Thus it appears that Vīra Śaivaism in its characteristic form existed before Basava (1169). It would, therefore, be better to refer to Basava, not as the founder but as a great upholder of Vīra Śaivaism (Prāṇaliṅga-dharāḥ kare). (G. K. Appendix II 35).

After cleaning their teeth and washing their hands, feet and mouths, they apply ashes to the body thrice, meditating on Śiva. The lay worshippers, with folded hands, recite the formula "Salutation to Śiva". Their God is Śaṅkara, who creates and destroys the Universe. Eighteen are His best incarnations and these are worshipped by them. These are: Nakulīśa, Kauśika, Gārgya, Maitrya, Kauruṣa, Īśāna, Paragārgya, Kapilāṇḍa, Mānuṣyaka, Aparakuśika, Atri, Piṅgalākṣa, Puṣpaka, Bṛhadācārya, Agasti, Santāna, Rāśīkara, and Vidyāguru.

Akṣapāda, being their preceptor, they are called Ākṣapādakas. Among them those who have attained the best state of Self-restraint, wander naked. In all their religious places Bharatas[1] conduct the worship while others bow from a distance. There is no restriction of caste for taking the vow of the Bharatas. Any one, who is devoted to Śiva, may take the vow and become a Bharata.

*1. G. K., (Intro.) III.

And Guṇa Ratna Sūri in his commentary on the Ṣaḍ-darśana Samuccaya of Haribhadra Sūri, gives the additional information about the similarities and differences between the Nyāya and the Vaiśeṣika as the followers of the dualistic Śaivaism and refers to the four sects as follows:—

The Vaiśeṣika school, which is otherwise called Pāśupata, is akin to the Naiyāyika. The outward characteristics of the pāśupatas are the same as those of the Śaivas and they adore the same Tīrthakaras. The difference lies in the Pramāṇas and categories.

The Vaiśeṣika is called Aulūkya Darśana because Śiva revealed the doctrines, incorporated by Kaṇāda in his system, in the form of an owl. And the Nyāya is called Ākṣapāda because it was founded by Akṣapāda. The former, on account of devotion of its founder to Paśupati, is called Pāśupata ; and the latter,, on account of devotion of its founder to Sadāśiva is called Śaiva.

And referring to the various sects among the Śaiva ascetics, Guṇa Ratna states, on the basis of an earlier authority, that on account of difference of their practices they are divided into four sects (I) Śaiva (II) Pāśupata (III) Mahāvratadhara and (IV) Kālamukha[1].

IDENTIFICATION OF THE PĀŚUPATA SYSTEM IN ŚAṄKARA

If we keep in mind the facts, referred to in the preceding two sections, and take into consideration what the commentators on the Śāṅkara Bhāṣya say in the context of the Pāśupata system, we can identify the system, referred to by Śaṅkara, with the one that served as a common basis for the Nyāya and the Vaiśeṣika. (I) Ratna Prabhā and Ānandagirīya refer to this system as the system of the Śaivas with matted hair (Jaṭādhāri Śaiva-mata). (II) All the three commentaries refer to four sects of the Śaiva ascetics. The last two names, however, differ. Instead of Mahāvratadhara and Kālamukha, in Haribhadra's work, we have Kārunika siddhāntin and Kāpālika in the commentaries on the Śāṅkara Bhāṣya. Abhinavagupta refers to Mahāvrata (A. Bh., Vol. I. 338). (III) Bhāmatī and Ānandagirīya refer to the metaphysical doctrine that the Maheśvara is only the instrumental cause of the creation. (IV) All of them refer to the effect as Mahān, etc. the products of the Pradhāna. (V) They refer to the conception of Mokṣa as freedom from all kinds of pain.

1. S. D. Sam., 59-60.

Now if we compare the points, stated above, with those brought out by Haribhadra, Rājaśekhara and the commentators, there does not remain much doubt about the system, referred to by Śaṅkara and his commentators, as the same, the fundamentals of which were the basis of both the systems, the Nyāya and the Vaiśeṣika. The common points may be stated as follows:—

(I) The followers of the system are represented to be ascetics with matted hair (Jaṭā paṭala śālinaḥ)[1]. (II) There were four sects among them: (1) Śaiva (2) Pāśupata (3) Mahāvratadhara (4) Kālamukha. (III) It is well known that the systems of the Nyāya and the Vaiśeṣika accept the Īśvara to be the instrumental cause only of the creation: and this view is maintained by all the writers referred to above. (IV) The categories, which are generally taken to be those of the Sāṅkhya, the twenty-three categories from the Mahān to the earth, are admitted under the Kalā, a subdivision of the Kārya, not only by the Lakulīśa Pāśupata, which arose subsequently as distinct from the Pāśupata ; but also by all the dualistic Śaiva thinkers. (V) The conception of Mokṣa as freedom from all kinds of pain is adopted by both the Nyāya and the Vaiśeṣika ; and it is improved upon by Lakulīśa in his Pāśupata Sūtra, where it is asserted, according to Mādhava's interpretation, that Mokṣa is not only freedom from all kinds of pain, but also the acquisition of omnipotence and omniscience.

There is, thus, very little doubt about this that there was a dualistic Śaiva system before the rise of the Vedānta, as presented by Bādarāyaṇa ; that it was followed by the founders of the Nyāya and the Vaiśeṣika ; that it is this system, to which Lakulīśa refers; that it was known as Pāśupata, which is distinct from the Lakulīśa Pāśupata; that it had the five characteristics referred to above; and that it was a leading school of thought in pre-Christian era. But unfortunately no independent work on this system has so far been discovered. It seems to have been a system that arose before the Śaiva tradition assumed a systematic form in the Śaivāgamas, which are generally ascribed to the early centuries of the Christian era. Some of the ten Dualistic Śaivāgamas seem to incorporate the dualistic Pāśupata tradition.

1. G. K. (Appendix III) 35.

(II) SIDDHĀNTA ŚAIVA DUALISM

From the discussion on Śaṅkara's attitude towards the monistic sixty-four Śaivāgamas, as interpreted by his pupil-commentator, Sureśvarācārya, in the section "Āgamic Literature" it appears that from the point of view of Śaṅkara, there was no antagonism between the Vedic and the Āgamic monism in the fundamentals ; and that, leaving aside the details, on which the differences are apparent, the Veda and the Śaivāgama constituted a common basis of philosophy, which Śaṅkara himself lived. We know that Śaṅkara advocated the worship of Śiva and himself used to put the characteristic mark of a Śaiva, the "Tripuṇḍra", on his forehead and a "Rudrākṣa" on his neck.

He identified the Śaiva Philosophy with Monism. But perfect monism does not fit in well with religion. In it logically there is no place for religion. According to this, the devotion to God is meaningless. For, the object of devotion is nothing but an illusion and, therefore, the cry of a devotee in trouble and distress is nothing but a cry in wilderness. It deprives the humanity of a hope of rescue from suffering, which the religion holds out. It strikes at the very root of religion. Sadyojyoti, who belonged to the close of the 9th century A. D., therefore, took up the task of justifying dualism on the basis of the dualistic Śaivāgamas, which had been ignored by Śaṅkara. He is the earliest of the pronouncedly Āgamic dualists, whose works are available so far.

It appears, however, that the tradition of the monistic Śaivāgamas, as reflected in some of the writings of Śaṅkara and his pupils and successors, lived side by side with the Dualistic Śaivāgama tradition, which acknowledged the authority of the twenty-eight Śaivāgamas; ten of the Śiva group and eighteen of the Rudra group, referred to above. For, Sadyojyoti, as is clear from his own statement, belonged to the line of the exponents of the Dualistic Śaivaism.

SADYOJYOTI

According to the statement of Sadyojyoti, at the end of his own Mokṣa Kārikā, as interpreted by his commentator, the tradition of Rauravāgama persisted unbroken from Ruru through Ātreya, etc. to Sadyojyoti himself[1]. He, according to the available literature, was the first man to start writing commentaries

1. M. Ka., 79.

on the Śaivāgamas, which formed the basis of the Siddhānta School of Śaivaism. There is definite information available in the existing literature that he wrote commentaries on the Rauravāgama[1] and the Svāyambhuvāgama[2]. He presented the fundamentals of the Dualistic Śaivaism in independent works, based upon the authority of the Śaivāgamas, such as Tattvatraya Nirṇaya, Bhoga Kārikā, Mokṣa Kārikā and Tattva Saṅgraha. He also wrote other works, in which he refuted the theories of the Schools of the opponents, such as Paramokṣa Nirāsa Kārikā. He, for the first time, used the word Siddhānta for the views propounded in the Rauravāgama[3]. This word "Siddhānta" was soon adopted as the name of the Śaiva Philosophy, based on the twenty-eight Śaivāgamas[4]. The name of the teacher of Sadyojyoti was Ugrajyoti[5]. He was an opponent not only of the Śaiva monism but also of the Lakulīśa Pāśupata system[6]. For, he criticises the Saṅkrānti theory of Mokṣa propounded by it.

Sadyojyoti was a recognised authority on the Dualistic Śaivaism at the time of Abhinavagupta (990—1015 A. D.). He was also known as Kheṭapāla or Kheṭakanandana. He is quoted by Abhinava and his theory of impurity (Mala) as a substance (Dravya) is refuted in the Tantrāloka, Vol. *VIII*, 36. His conception of the categories comes in for a detailed criticism in Āhnika IX of the Tantrāloka. In fact, the section of the Tantrāloka, dealing with the Śaiva categories, had as one of its aims to refute the Dualist Śaiva conception of Categories; and Jayaratha explicitly mentions the authorities by names as Śaṅkaranandana Sadyojyoti, Devabala and Kaṇabhuk[7].

BṚHASPATI

Bṛhaspati was as great an authority on Dualistic Śaivaism as Sadyojyoti. The two are coupled by Aghoraśiva in his commentary on the Mokṣa Kārikā[8], and are spoken of as the objects of reverence to the teachers. From this coupling it appears that they were regarded as contemporaries. Like Sadyojyoti, he is also quoted and referred to by Abhinavagupta in different contexts in the Tantrāloka in Āhnikas, first, eighth and ninth. All these references and quotations are from a single work, the Śivatanu Śāstra. Some of them are on the points of agreement; for instance, the etymology of the word "Deva" (T. A., Vol. I, 143—6), others are on points of difference; for instance, the conception of Mala, which Bṛhaspati regarded, in common with

1. T. S. 52
2. N. P. 216.
3. Bh. Ka., 2.
4. R. T. 5—6.
5. M. Ka., 79.
6. P. K. 27—32.
7. T. A. Vol. VI, 250.
8. M. ka., I.

the other dualist thinkers, as a substance (T. A. Vol. VI, 166). He is quoted as an authority by the Dualist writers, such as Aghoraśiva and Rāmakaṇṭha II. Thus, he may be said to belong to the 9th century A. D.

ŚAṄKARA NANDANA

We learn from Jayaratha's commentary on the Tantrāloka[1] that Śaṅkara Nandana was a dualist Śaiva writer. For, he couples this name with those of the other dualistic thinkers such as Sadyojyoti, whose views he professedly controverts. Abhinavagupta refers to one work of Śaṅkara Nandana, the Prajñālaṅkāra, in the Īśvara Pratyabhijñā Vimarśinī (Bh., Vol. I, 225) in the course of the refutation of the atomic theory of the Nyāya and the Vaiśeṣika. We know that the dualist Śaivas, in common with the Monists, reject the atomic theory and propound the Māyā as the material cause of the universe. It appears that this critical view was first put forward by Śaṅkara Nandana. For, Abhinava clearly states that for detailed criticism of this theory the reader should refer to the Prajñālaṅkāra by Ācārya Śaṅkara Nandana. The circumstantial evidence goes to show that he also belonged to the 9th century A. D.

DEVABALA

Devabala, as a dualist Śaiva authority, is known from the Tantrāloka. His views on the Śaiva categories are intended to be refuted along with those of the other dualist thinkers. He may have belonged to the 10th century A. D.

We know nothing about the places of births of the writers, mentioned above. But writers, with whom we are going to deal, definitely belonged to Kashmir. The most important thing to be noted about them is that they belonged to the Kantha family of Kashmir, the learned tradition of which was maintained by our commentator, Bhāskara Kaṇṭha, in the Bhāskarī.

ŚAIVA DUALISM IN KASHMIR

Sadyojyoti had strong following in Kashmir. He had a great commentator in Rāmakaṇṭha II who, according to his own statement at the end of the Nāda Kārikā belonged to Kashmir.

If we survey the literature that Kashmir produced during the 9th, 10th and 11th century A. D. we find two parallel Philosophic currents, the Śaiva Monism and the Śaiva Dualism. Both

---

1 T. A., Vol. VI 250.

seem to have been equally strong. Each was aggressive towards the other. The followers of each school tried to interpret the authoritative texts of the other school in the light of their own school. Thus, we find that Kṣemarāja, in the beginning of his commentary on the Svacchanda Tantra, refers to a commentary on the said Āgama from the dualistic point of view and asserts that such an attempt is unjustifiable. For, the very name of the Āgama, apart from its content, advocates the doctrine of Freedom, the monistic voluntarism. In a similar tone Aghoraśivācārya, at the beginning of his commentary on the Tattva Prakāśikā of King Bhoja, says that he is writing this commentary, because it had been commented upon from the monistic point of view by those who had no knowledge of the Siddhānta[1].

RĀMAKAṆṬHA I

Rāmakaṇṭha I is the earliest Kashmir writer on the Dualistic Śaivaism. According to Abhinavagupta, the different Schools of Śaivāgama were propagated at the command of the Lord, Śrīkaṇṭha[2]. This tradition seems to have been common to both the dualistic and the monistic schools of Śaivaism. For, Aghora Śiva also refers to it in his commentary on the introductory verse of the Ratna Traya by Śrīkaṇṭha. Rāmakaṇṭha I is spoken of as the incarnation of Lord Śrīkaṇṭha[3], at whose command the various Śaivāgamic schools were propagated, as stated just above. It appears, therefore, that he was an exponent of both the dualistic and the monistic schools of Śaivaism. If we accept this, it will not be difficult to fix the period of his literary activity. For, we know of a Rāmakaṇṭha, as the author of a commentary on the Spanda Kārikā, who talks of himself as a pupil of Utpalācārya, the author of the Īśvara Pratyabhijñā Kārikā. The colophon to his commentary runs as follows:—

> "Kṛtiḥ Śrīmad-Utpaladevapādapadmopajīvinaḥ śrīmad Rājānaka Rāmakaṇṭhasya."

He, therefore, belonged to the second half of the tenth century A. D.

Rāmakaṇṭha I is also referred to as the author of a work, called Sadvṛtti, by Śrīkaṇṭha in the concluding verses of his Ratna Traya[4]. This work, according to the author's statement,

---

1 T. P., 1.
2 T. A., Vol. I, 26.
3 Mr. Vr., 4.
4 R. T., 107.

is a mere imitation of the Sadvṛtti by Rāmakaṇṭha I. It was, therefore, a work on dualistic Śaivaism.

Rāma Kaṇṭha I is also referred to as his grand-teacher (Prācārya) by Nārāyaṇa Kaṇṭha, the author of the commentary, the Vṛtti, on the Mṛgendra Tantra[1]. And Nārāyaṇa Kaṇṭha also is referred to by Rāma Kaṇṭha II, as his father, in the concluding verse of his Nādakārikā. Here it may be noted that he talks of himself as belonging to Kashmir. Rāma Kaṇṭha II was a teacher of Aghoraśiva[2], who according to his own statement in his Paddhati, completed it in the Śaka year 1080 i.e. 1158 A. D.

Thus, we find that, Rāma Kaṇṭha I lived four generations earlier than Āghora Śiva. The names of the teachers, who came in succession between Rāmakaṇṭha I and Āghora Śiva are (1) Vidyākaṇṭha, (2) Nārāyaṇa Kaṇṭha and (3) Rāma Kaṇṭha II.

Thus, it is clear that Rāma Kaṇṭha I belonged to the close of the 10th and the beginning of the 11th century A. D. There is, therefore, some justification in identifying Rāma Kaṇṭha I, the author of the Sadvṛtti, with Rāma Kaṇṭha, the author of a commentary on the Spanda Kārikā. In view of the scanty literary evidence, however, this may still be treated as an open question.

The reason, why we assign the Sadvṛtti to Rāma Kaṇṭha I, is that the Ratna Traya by Śrī Kaṇṭha is commented upon by Aghoraśiva, who is admittedly a pupil of Rāma Kaṇṭha II. In the course of his commentary on the Kārikā 53, which deals with "Bindu"[3], he says:—

"This subject has been extensively dealt with by Rāma Kaṇṭha in his Nāda Kārikā". This means that the treatment of the Bindu in the Nāda Kārikā is of the nature of an elaboration of what was said on the subject by Śrīkaṇṭha in his Ratna Traya. Further, if we accept Śrīkaṇṭha to be a successor of Rāma Kaṇṭha II, and admit that the Sadvṛtti, referred to by Śrīkaṇṭha is the work of Rāmakaṇṭha II, we will bring him (Śrīkaṇṭha) down chronologically to a younger contemporary of Aghoraśiva, who has commented upon the Ratna Traya. But Aghoraśiva was too great a writer to write a commentary on the work of a younger contemporary. There is, therefore, sufficient justification to hold that Rāma Kaṇṭha I was the author of the Sadvṛtti.

1 Mr. Vr., 4.
2 Mr. Vr. Di., 1.
3 R. T., 24.

ŚRĪKAṆṬHA

If we accept the conclusion arrived at in the preceding section that the Sadvṛtti, which Śrīkaṇṭha imitates in his Ratna Traya, is the work of Rāma Kaṇṭha I, it will follow that he was a pupil of Rāma Kaṇṭha I and therefore, belonged to the 1st half of the 11th century A. D.

He quotes many verses[1] such as "Svarupajyotirevāntaḥ," dealing with the aspects of speech, admitted in the philosophy of grammar. These verses, it may be pointed out, occur in the commentary on the Vākyapadīyam by Bhartṛhari himself[2] on

"Trayyā Vācaḥ param Padam"

V. P. ch. I, 144.

But Bhartṛhari himself says that these verses are quoted from the Mahābhārata, Āśvamedhika Parva, Brāhmaṇa Gītā. However, though the first set of verses is actually found in the Āśvamedhika Parva, as stated by him, in Chapter XXI, with some minor variations: yet the other set, which is introduced with "Punaścāha" and begins with

"Sthāneṣu Vivṛte Vāyau"

is not found there. It is apparently a quotation from elsewhere.

About the time of the rise of the monistic school of Śaivaism in the 9th century A. D. for three centuries, there was intense discussion on the theory of Meaning in Kashmir. Somānanda, Helārāja[3] and Abhinavagupta are three great exponents of it from the monistic point of view. And Śrīkaṇṭha and Rāmakaṇṭha II are from the dualistic. All belonged to Kashmir.

NĀRĀYAṆA KAṆṬHA

Nārāyaṇa Kaṇṭha was a grand-pupil of Rāma Kaṇṭha I and a pupil of Vidyā Kaṇṭha[4], who was his father also, as it is clear from the colophon appended to each chapter. He was thus, a successor of Śrīkaṇṭha, the author of the Ratna Traya and, therefore, belonged to the middle of the 11th century A. D.

We know of two works of this writer (I) Mṛgendra Vṛtti, which has been published and (II) Bṛhaṭṭīkā or Śarannisā, a commentary on the Tattva Saṅgraha of Sadyojyoti, which

1 R. T. 32.
*2 V. P. (Intro. Cha.) 2.
3 V. P. (Ban.) 744.
4 Mr. Vr., 4.

we know from reference to it by Aghora Siva in an introductory verse to his own commentary[1]. It appears that many commentaries had been written on the Mṛgendra Āgama before Nārāyaṇa Kaṇṭha. He refers to them and points out their defects[2]. Following the text he criticises many systems of thought, such as Bauddha, Jaina, Cārvāka, Vedānta, Mīmāṁsā, Sāṅkhya, Yoga, Nyāya and Vaiśeṣika. He refers to Sadyojyoti[3], alias Kheṭaka Nandana and Bṛhaspati[4]. He also quotes the Tattva Traya Nirṇaya[5] and the Bhoga Kārikā[6]. He was the father of Rāma Kaṇṭha II.

RĀMA KAṆṬHA, THE AUTHOR OF THE SARVATOBHADRA.

The name, Rāmakaṇṭha, is very confusing in the history of the Śaiva philosophy. We have already dealt with Rama kaṇṭha I and have assigned him to the second half of the 10th century A. D. on the basis of his relation to Aghora Śiva, who, according to his own statement in the Paddhati, completed it in 1158 A. D.

But Rāmakaṇṭha, the author of a commentary, the Sarvatobhadra, on the Bhagavadgītā, speaks of himself (I) as a descendant of Nārāyaṇa who belonged to Kānyakubja, and (II) as a younger brother of Muktākaṇa. We know of a Muktākaṇa as a contemporary of King Avanti Varman of Kashmir (855-883 A. D.).

Is this Muktākaṇa, who adorned the court of Avanti Varman as a poet, identical with the brother of Rāma Kaṇṭha, the author of the Sarvatobhadra ? We can identify if we suppose that an ancestor of his, like that of Abhinavagupta, was taken over to Kashmir from Kānyakubja, by king Lalitāditya of Kashmir (8th century A. D.). On the basis of this identification we can assign Rāma Kaṇṭha, the author of the Sarvatobhadra, to the first half of the 10th century A. D.

There is, however, a clue to distinguish Rāmakaṇṭha, the author of the Sarvatobhadra, from both Rāmakaṇṭha I and II. For, this Rāma Kaṇṭha does not talk of himself as the son of Nārāyaṇa Kaṇṭha, as does Rāma Kaṇṭha II (refer just below) but as a descendant (Tadvaṁśe). Nor does he talk of

1 T. San., 1.
2 Mr. Vr., 3-4.
3 Mr. Vr. 80,
4 132.
5 Mr Vr., 229.
6 Mr. Vr., 331.

Nārāyaṇakaṇṭha as such. He simply refers to Nārāyaṇa, who belonged to Kānyakubja. He can, therefore, be easily distinguished from Rāmakaṇṭha II. He quotes from the Stotrāvalī of Utpala, referring to the author with great respect "Utpaladevapāda". He, therefore, seems to be a generation or so later than Utpalācārya, who belonged to the end of the 9th and the first half of the 10th century A. D. But Rāmakaṇṭha I was a contemporary of Utpala and hence cannot be identified with Rāmakaṇṭha, the author of the Sarvatobhadra. If, however, we do not interpret the respectful reference to Utpalācārya, as indicative of a later date, or hold that it is indicative of his being a pupil of Utpala; because Rāmakaṇṭha I, in his commentary on the Spandakārikā, refers to himself as such; we may identify this Rāmakaṇṭha with Rāmakaṇṭha I, the author of the Sadvṛtti, of which the Ratna Traya of Śrīkaṇṭha, referred to earlier, is merely an imitation as stated above. In this case we have to suppose that Rāma Kaṇṭha I was blessed with long life.

RĀMA KAṆṬHA II

Rāmakaṇṭha II, the son of Nārāyaṇa Kaṇṭha (11th century A. D.) was 'predominantly a dualist Śaiva thinker. He wrote commentaries on the Āgamas of the Siddhānta School and independent works, dealing with the various important philosophical problems from the dualistic point of view. He criticises the Lakulīśa Pāśupata conception of Mukti as attainment of similarity with Śiva.

A MS. of his commentary on the Mataṅgāgama is preserved in the library of the Government Sanskrit College, Calcutta. His commentary on the Svāyambhuvāgama, called the Svāyambhuvodyota, is known from his own reference to it in his commentary on the Nareśvaraparīkṣā, page 89.

By his time the dualist Śaiva School, based on the twenty-eight Śaivāgamas, was well established. He refers to its followers as the Siddhāntavādin. Following this school, he asserts the being of the individual independently of the Universal, the Īśvara.

The theory of meaning was hotly discussed by his predecessors, both the monists and the dualists. Helārāja,—who, at the end of his commentary on the Vākyapadīya Chapter III refers to himself as a descendant of Lakṣmaṇa, who was a minister to King Lalitāditya Muktāpīḍa of Kashmir (733 A. D.) and as a son of Bhūtirāja, to whom Abhinavagupta refers as his teacher in dualism and who, therefore, belonged to the later half of the 10th century A. D.—had already spoken on it from the monistic point of view. And Śrīkaṇṭha in his Ratna Traya had spoken on it from the dualistic point of view. Following the dualistic current of thought, he, therefore, wrote his Nāda Kārikā, refuting the Sphoṭavāda of the Indian grammarians.

The theory of liberation is an essential part of every system of Indian thought. Sadyojyoti in his two works had refuted the conceptions of Mokṣa, as propounded by other systems in his two works, dealing with this subject (I) Mokṣa Kārikā and (II) Paramokṣa Nirāsa Kārikā. Rāmakaṇṭha II in his commentaries on these works refutes (I) Utpatti Samatāpakṣa, the theory that the omniscience and omnipotence do not originally belong to the individual limited subject and that they arise at liberation: (II) Samatā saṅkrānti pakṣa of the Lakulīśa Pāśupata, which held that just as the fragrance of musk passes on to other things, so omniscience and omnipotence of Śiva pass on to the limited subject at liberation: (III) Āveśapakṣa, which asserted that just as a Graha, while at its own place, enters into a person so do the powers of Śiva into the liberated. He propounded (IV) Abhivyakti pakṣa.

Other two works of this author, which are known from references only, are (I) Mantra Viveka Ṭīkā (M. Kā. 4) and (II) Āgama Viveka (P. K. 49).

KING BHOJA OF DHĀRĀ

The preceding discussion has shown that Śaiva dualism was very popular in Kashmir during the four centuries about the rise of monism in Kashmir and that writers on it were descendants of Nārāyaṇa, who had migrated from Kānyakubja to Kashmir exactly as the ancestor of Abhinavagupta, Atrigupta, had. It is thus clear that the currents of the Śaiva dualism and monism were running in Kānyakubja and flowed from there to Kashmir.

Śaiva dualism was equally popular in central India also. It engaged the attention of no less a person than King Bhoja of Dhārā (1018-60 A. D.), who is a recognised authority on so many subjects, such as Alaṅkāra and Vāstu Śāstra etc. and who is considered to have been a great patron of Sanskrit learning. His available work on Śaiva dualism is the Tattva Prakāśikā.

Aghora Śiva wrote a commentary on it. Therein he maintains that the Siddhānta school is dualistic and that his commentary aims at refuting the monistic interpretation of the text by those who were ignorant of the fundamentals of the Siddhānta Śaivaism. Another commentary on it was written by Kumāradeva, who is recognised as an authority in the various Paddhatis. He is referred to as "Taduktam Kumāradevena".

The Tattva Prakāśikā is quoted by Vidyāraṇya Yatīndra[1] in his commentary on the Sūta Saṁhitā. It admits thirty-six categories and holds that Śiva with Śakti, which is inherently in Him, is beyond the categories.

The name of the teacher of King Bhoja in dualistic Śaivaism was Uttuṅga Śiva, who lived in Kalyāṇa Nagarī in Lāṭa or Southern Gujarāt, wrote a Paddhati and was recognised authority in interpreting the Śaivāgamas. This we know from the Paddhati of Aghora Śiva[2].

AGHORA ŚIVA

In the course of the preceding sections it has been shown that the dualistic Śaiva school had its exponents in Kānyakubja, Kashmir, central India and Lāṭa or Southern Gujarāt, during three or four centuries about the rise of the monistic Śaivaism in Kashmir. It has to be shown now that the south was not without an exponent of this system.

Aghora Śiva, a great commentator on the works on dualistic Śaivaism, according to his own statement, was an inhabitant of Cola country and belonged to the city of Kuṇḍina Kula[3]. He flourished in the middle of the Twelfth century A. D. For, he completed his Paddhati, as he himself says at its conclusion[4], in 1158 A. D. He was a great teacher and had no less than two Lakhs of pupils[5]. The name of his teacher was Sarvātma Śiva[6]. He was not only a great religious leader and commentator on the dualistic Śaiva works, but also a poet and dramatist. He wrote the following Kāvyas:

1. Āścaryasāra
2. Pākhaṇḍāpajaya
3. Bhaktaprakāśa

---

1 A. Pra. (Intro) 4.
2 A. Pra. (Intro) 4.
3 T. T. N. 22.
4 A. Pra. (Intro) 6.
5 T. P. 58.
6 T. T. N. 22.

He also wrote a Drama (Nāṭaka), entitled *Abhyudaya.* He commented upon the following dualistic Śaiva works:—

1. Tattva Prakāśikā of Bhoja.
2. Tattva Saṅgraha of Sadyojyoti.
3. Tattva Traya Nirṇaya of Sadyojyoti.
4. Ratna Traya of Śrīkaṇṭha.
5. Bhogakārikā of Sadyojyoti.
6. Nāda Kārikā of Rāma Kaṇṭha II.
7. Mṛgendra Vṛtti of Nārāyaṇakaṇṭha.

He refers to the last named commentary on the Mṛgendra Vṛtti in his commentary on the Ratna Traya[1].

It appears that before the time of Aghora Śiva commentaries on many of the Twenty-eight Tantras of the Siddhānta school had been written. For, he distinctly mentions commentaries on Svāyambhuva, Kiraṇa and Mataṅga Āgamas together and puts the word etc. at the end[2]. And referring to their authors he states the name of Rāma Kaṇṭha using the word, etc. (Ādi) at the end[3]. He also mentions a Vṛtti on the Kālottara Āgama by Rāma Kaṇṭha, in his Dīpikā, a commentary on Nārāyaṇa Kaṇṭha's Vṛtti on the Mṛgendra Tantra[4].

---

1 R. T. 8.
2 R. T. 105
3 R. T. 8.
4 Mr. Vr. Di. 421.

(III) LAKULĪṢA PĀṢUPATA SYSTEM OF ṢAIVAISM

In the foregoing pages we have dealt with a system of Ṣaiva Dualism, which,—in the light of (I) our conclusion on the identification of the system, referred to in the Pāśupata section of the Ṣāṅkara Bhāṣya on the Vedānta Sūtra, with the system, which served as the common basis of both the Nyāya and the Vaiśeṣika and (II) reference to the founder of the Vaiśeṣika as a Pāśupata,—may be called Pāśupata. There is no independent work on this system available so far. We can get an idea of the fundamentals of this system from references only.

The Lakulīśa Pāśupata is different from the Pāśupata. In fact, Mādhava, in his Sarva Darśana Saṅgraha, seems to have the distinction between the Pāśupata and the Lakulīśa Pāśupata in his mind, when he called the system, dealt with after the dualistic Ṣaivaism, Lakulīśa Pāśupata. The two systems differ from each other in so far as the one is dualistic (Dvaita) but the other is dualistic-cum-non-dualistic (Dvaitādvaita) : the one has no available independent literature, but the other has authoritative texts, such as (1) Pāśupata Sūtra by Lakulīśa himself with the commentary of Kauṇḍinya : (2) Gaṇa Kārikā of Bhāsarvajña with a commentary by a writer whose name we do not yet know: (3) Yama Prakaraṇa and Ātma Samarpaṇa by Viśuddha Muni: (4) Kāraṇapadārtha etc. The first two are referred to by Mādhava, who quotes the first aphorism of the available Pāśupata Sūtra and some verses from the Gaṇa Kārikā. There is, therefore, no doubt about it that these works are on the Lakulīśa Pāśupata system.

In dealing with the Lakulīśa Pāśupata we are on surer historical ground. For, there is epigraphical evidence to show that Lakulīśa, the founder of the system, flourished in the second century A. D. The Lakulīśa Pāśupata system is very closely related to the Veda in general and the Black Yajurveda in particular. In fact, the five objects of contemplation for the gradual attainment of the liberation, as stated in the Pāśupata Sūtra, are the five aspects of Ṣiva as presented in the Taittirīya Āraṇyaka in its closing sections.

The Taittirīya Āraṇyaka, in its last three books, from the 7th to the 10th, contains an Upaniṣad, which is divided into three parts: (I) Sāṁhitī (II) Vāruṇī and (III) Yājñikī. (I) Sāṁhitī is contained in the 7th Book. It contains prayers of different kinds and instructions, which have necessarily to be followed to attain fitness to tread on the path to Self-realisation. (II) Vāruṇī is the content of the VIII and the IX Books. It deals with Brahma Vidyā. It is called Vāruṇī, because it was promulgated by Varuna. (III) Yājñikī forms the X Book[1].

NĀRĀYAṆOPANIṢAD

The tradition current among the Vedic teachers represents the X Book of the Taittirīya Āraṇyaka, which constitutes the Yājñikī Upaniṣad and which is also called Nārāyaṇopaniṣad, to be a miscellaneous collection (Khila)[2]. It is so called because it is a collection of miscellaneous things, which are put together at the end, after all, that is of importance, has been said in earlier sections in regard to rites, contemplation, symbols and the Ultimate Reality. There are different recensions of this Book, in different regions[3]. They considerably differ from one another. The Draviḍas have sixty-four sub-sections, the Āndhras 80, the Karṇāṭakas 74, and others 89.

It appears that the closing section of the Taittirīya Āraṇyaka, the miscellaneous collection, belongs to a period when the antagonism between Brāhmanism, as represented by the earlier portion of the Vedic Saṁhitās, and Śaivaism, as represented in the subsequent Śaivāgamas, had completely disappeared. This becomes clear from the following facts :—

(I) The Mantras from "Sadasaspatī" to "Mānohiṁsīḥ" are found in the Karmakāṇḍa of the original Taittirīya Āraṇyaka. They are repeated in the Khila[4].

(II) In regard to the Mantras, beginning with "Puruṣasya vidma", Sāyaṇa says that from this point onward there are different readings in different places. He, however, follows the reading, as found in Draviḍa : because it was accepted by earlier compilers like Vijñānātma[5].

(III) The Mantras, as Sāyaṇa points out, from "Tatpuruṣāya" to "Nārāyaṇāya" state the forms of the various gods as found in the Āgamas. He also quotes from them.

And the similarity between the philosophical doctrines, presented in the Taittirīya Āraṇyaka, with those, propounded in the Pāśupata Sūtra of Lakulīśa, is so great that there seems very

1 Tai. A., 487.
2 Tai. A., 689.
3 Tai A., 690.
4 Tai. A., 698.
5 Tai. A., 699.

little doubt about it that the latter contains the philosophic tradition, presented in the former. Both present the Māyā to be the power of the Brahman and, therefore, as having no existence independently of the Brahman. Both talk of the Brahman as Māyin and, therefore, Saguṇa. Both present the monistic-cum-dualistic (Dvaitādvaita) philosophy. That the concluding section of the Taittirīya Āraṇyaka, the Nārāyaṇopaniṣad, presents such a philosophy, is evident from the fact that it is taken as an authoritative text by the Viśiṣṭādvaitins : it is commented upon from the point of view of the Viśiṣṭādvaita Vaiṣṇavaism also. We shall deal with the points of agreement between the philosophical doctrines, presented in the Taittirīya Āraṇyaka and the Pāśupata Sūtra of Lakulīśa, in detail in a subsequent section.

THE DATE OF THE LAKULĪŚA PĀŚUPATA SYSTEM

In determining the date of the rise of the Lakulīśa Pāśupata system, we have to take the following material into consideration:—

(I) Mathurā Pillar inscription of Chandragupta II.

(II) Stone slab inscription of Somanātha.

(III) References to the successive pupils of Lakulīśa, as found in (a) the Vāyu Purāṇa (b) Liṅga Purāṇa (c) Sūta Saṁhitā (d) Ṣaḍ-darśana Samuccaya of Rājaśekhara.

There is enough historical evidence to show that the Lakulīśa Pāśupata system was propounded in the 2nd century A. D. There is epigraphical evidence of the Mathurā Pillar inscription of Chandragupta II in support of this view. The inscription refers itself to the reign of Chandragupta, son of Samudragupta. The date of the inscription is 61, which for reasons, stated below, has to be referred to the current Gupta era. Though, unfortunately the part of the inscription, which states the era, is mutilated; yet the portion, stating the day, is well preserved and there is the indication of month also through the word "Prathame":—

"Ekaṣaṣṭhe 60 1 (Pra) thame Śukla divase Pañcamyām".

It means that in the year 61 there was an intercalary month. And on the evidence of Jain works, Dr. K.B. Pathak has proved that expired or current Gupta years can be converted into corresponding Śāka years by adding 241. Thus, if we add 241 to 61 Gupta year of the inscription, we obtain 302 Śāka which is equal to 380 A.D. The year of inscription, therefore, is 380 A.D. For, the year 61 in the inscription refers to current Gupta years. This becomes clear, if we refer to page 42 of Table X of the Indian Chronology by Swami Kannu Pillai. Therein we find that there was an intercalary month only in 380 A. D. and that this was Āṣāḍha. Therefore, the year referred to in the inscription, has to be taken to be current Gupta year.

REFERENCE TO ŚAIVA TEACHER, UDITĀCĀRYA.

Uditācārya, according to the inscription, was a Māheśvara, a pupil of Upamitācārya and grand--pupil of Kapila and great-grand-pupil of Pārāśara. Thus, Uditācārya was the fourth in succession from Pārāśara. The inscription also states (I) that Uditācārya was the tenth in succession from Kauśika: (II) that he installed two images, called Kapileśvara and Upamiteśvara. The second part of these two names indicates that these two were Liṅgas, one in the name of Upamita and the other in the name of Kapila, who were his teacher and grand-teacher respectively.

These images were installed in Gurvāyatana, the teachers' shrine, the place where the memorials of teachers were established. It was a shrine, similar to that of which Bhāsa talks in the third act of his Pratimā Nāṭaka. These images comprised the Liṅgas, set up in the names and to the memory of teachers of that lineage, to which Upmitācārya belonged. The Liṅgas were not only named after the teachers, but also bore the portraits of teachers, Upamita and Kapila, separately.

IDENTIFICATION OF KAUŚIKA

The inscription presents a problem. Though it mentions the two teachers, who preceded Upamitācārya in the lineage from Pārāśara; yet it does not state the names of the five teachers, who came in between Kauśika and Pārāśara. The problem, therefore, arises "Who was this Kauśika ?" We can fix the date of the Lakulīśa Pāśupata system, if we can correctly identify Kauśika. Let us, therefore, see what help we can get from the Purāṇas and other sources on this point.

A passage which is common to both the Vāyu and the Liṅga Purāṇa, shows (I) that Lakulī was the last incarnation of Maheśvara (II) that this incarnation took place in Kāyārohaṇa or Kāyāvatāra, which is identical with Kārvān in Baroda state : and (III) that he had four ascetic pupils: Kauśika, Garga, Mitra and Kauruśya[1].

*1 J. B. B. R. A. S. VOL. XXII, PP. 154 ff.

The statement, as found in the Purāṇas, is corroborated by a stone slab inscription, which originally belonged to Somanātha in Kāṭhiābād, but is now in Portugal. This was edited by Dr. Buhler in Ep. Ind. Vol. I, p. 271 ff. All the four names are found in it, though with slight variation. But the name Kauśika is unaltered. This belongs to the reign of Chalukya king Sāraṅgadeva.

The name, Kauśika, occurs as that of the first pupil of Lakulī, not only in the Purāṇas, referred to above, but also in (a) the commentary by Kauṇḍinya on the Pāśupata Sūtra as Kuśika[1] (b) Sūta Saṁhitā IV, section dealing with Lakulīśa Kṣetra, (c) Ṣaḍ-darśana Samuccaya by Rājaśekhara[2] and (d) Bṛhadvṛtti[3] by Guṇa Ratna Sūri. There is, therefore, very little doubt that Kauśika was the first pupil of Lakulīśa.

The stone slab inscription of Somanātha states also (I) that these four pupils of Lakulī, who came in succession, were founders of four lines among the Pāśupatas (II) that the three Ācāryas, mentioned in it (1) Kārtikarāśi (2) Vālmikirāśi and (3) Tripurāntaka belonged to the line of Gārgya; and (III) that the last was a contemporary of Sāraṅgadeva, in whose reign the inscription was incised[4].

Thus, the two inscriptions refer to two lines of teachers from the two pupils of Lakulī (1) Gārgya (2) Kauśika. The one, it seems, settled down at Somanātha and the other at Mathurā.

Uditācārya (380 A. D.) therefore, is the eleventh in the line of teachers from Lakulīśa, being the tenth from Kauśika, the direct pupil of Lakulīśa. If we allow 25 years for each generation, Lakulīśa may be said to belong to the first half of the 2nd century A. D.

THE PROBABLE SHAPE OF THE MEMORIAL LIṄGAS

The custom of erecting memorials of the outstanding personalities is very old in India. They were of different forms. From reference to one such memorial in the Pratimā Nāṭaka of Bhāsa, we understand that about the time of Bhāsa there was the custom of putting up images of the Kings, belonging to an important dynasty, in a building, which very closely resembled a Devakula. These images were so faithful reproductions

1 P. Su., 4.
2 G.K. (Appendix III) 35.
3 S. D. Sam. 59.
4 E. Ind., Vol, XXI, 6.

of the originals that the latter could be recognised in the former. The memorials of Upamitācārya and Kapilācārya, put up by Uditācārya, to which there is reference in the Mathurā Pillar inscription, do not seem to have been in the form of images of the teachers alone. Their images seem to have been carved out in the Liṅgas of Śiva. This is clear from reference to Liṅgas in the inscription itself. The conclusion that these Liṅgas had the portraits of the teachers carved out in them, seems to find support from the fact that there are two Liṅgas with portraits of Lakulī, sculptured in front. One of these is in the temple of Nakleśvara and the other in that of Rājarājeśvara, both at Kārvān in Baroda state. Thus, the custom of combining a Liṅga with a portrait of the person in the memory of whom it was put up, seems to have been prevalent among the followers of Lakulīśa. The Liṅgas, therefore, put up by Uditācārya, seem to have had the portraits of the teachers carved out in them.

(IV) THE ŚAIVA VIŚIṢṬĀDVAITA

The Viśiṣṭādvaitism is generally identified with Vaiṣṇavaism, as presented by Rāmānuja, who was born in Śrīperumbudūr in 1027, A. D. If we look at the history of the Viśiṣṭādvaita Vaiṣṇavaism, we find that it has evolved out of the Dualism-cum-non-dualism (Bhedābhedavāda). For, before Rāmānuja the Brahmasūtra of Bādarāyaṇa had been commented upon by two eminent authorities.

(I) Bhāskarācārya, who lived about 900 A. D. upheld the Bhedābhedavāda. He did not agree with the views of Śaṅkara or those of the Pañcarātra Vaiṣṇavas. He asserted that unity and multiplicity are equally real; that the Brahman is not an undifferentiated mass of pure consciousness, but possesses all perfections; that the causal state of the Brahman is a unity, but its evolved state is a multiplicity; that things are non-different in their causal or generic aspect, but are different as effects and individuals; and that non-difference does not absorb difference, as fire consumes grass.

(II) Yādavaprakāśa, who was for some time the Guru of Rāmānuja and lived in the 11th century A. D., wrote an independent commentary, leaning to advaita interpretation. His theory also is called Bhedābhedavāda. He holds that Brahman changes into Cit (Jīva) Acit (matter) and Īśvara (God). He asserts that both Cit and Acit are only different states of one substance and not different substances in themselves; that the Brahman, though it undergoes changes, yet it does not forfeit its purity; that there is no contradiction in saying that a thing can be different and at the same time non-different from itself[1]: for, every thing is unity from one point of view and multiplicity from another.

Thus, it is clear that in the history of the Vaiṣṇava thought, the Viśiṣṭādvaita has been preceded by the Bhedābhedavāda. And if we study the available literature on the Śaiva Philosophy, we find that the Śaiva Viśiṣṭādvaita also evolved in the same way.

ŚAIVA VIŚIṢṬĀDVAITA AND ŚRĪKAṆṬHA

One thing that can very definitely be said about the time of Śrīkaṇṭha is that he was a successor of Utpalācārya, the author

*1 I Ph., Vol. II, 670—1.

of the Īśvara Pratyabhijñā Kārikā, a recognised authoritative text on the monistic Śaiva Philosophy of Kashmir, on which Abhinavagupta has written a commentary, called Vimarśinī, an English translation of which is given in the body of the present volume. Śrīkaṇṭha quotes from the above work, a well known verse :

"Cidātmaiva hi devontaḥ" etc.

I. P. V. (Bhāskarī) Vol. I, 226.

He quotes it not less than three times in the course of his commentary on the Vedāntasūtra : Vol. I, 341, Vol. II 29 and 111. Utpalācārya belonged to the first half of the 10th century A. D. Śrīkaṇṭha quotes from the Īśvara Pratyabhijñā Kārikā with the following remarks:—

(I) "Tathā abhiyuktasūktiḥ" Śrikam. Bh. Vol. I, 341.

(II) "Tathā" āptavacanamapi" Śrikam. Bh. Vol. II, 29.

(III) "Ityādyāgamaprāmāṇyācca" Śrikam. Bh. Vol. II, 111.

From these it is clear that by the time of Śrīkaṇṭha, the Īśvara Pratyabhijñā Kārikā of Utpalācārya had already been recognised as an authoritative text on Śaivaism. We shall, therefore, be not wrong if we assign him to the 11th century A. D.

It may be pointed out here that the verse under discussion is quoted by Śrīpati Paṇḍitārādhya in his Śrīkara Bhāṣya on the Vedānta Sūtra and is said to be taken from the Vātulāgama. But this does not affect our position. For, the verse as quoted from the Āgama differs though slightly from the verse as we find in the commentary of Śrīkaṇṭha. Śrīkaṇṭha's quotation fully agrees with the reading of Utpalācārya's verse as printed in the Bhāskarī Vol. I, 226. And it is important to note that this is not quoted by Utpala but presents his view in the context of criticism of the subjectivist Bauddha.

Utpalācārya belonged to the first half of the 10th century A. D. This, therefore, is the upper limit of Śrīkaṇṭha's date. The lower limit, which can definitely be fixed is the 16th century, to which Appayya Dīkṣita, who has commented on the Bhāṣya of Śrīkaṇṭha, belongs. That Śrīkaṇṭha belongs to some distant period from Utpalācārya is clear from his respectful references, quoted above. He was probably a contemporary of Rāmānuja as the circumstantial evidence shows. Thus, in the 11th century both Rāmānuja and Śrīkaṇṭha seem to have propounded viśiṣṭādvaita. One from the point of view of Vaiṣṇavaism and the other from that of Śaivaism.

According to him, there is no antagonism between the Veda and the Śaivāgama. He recognises both to be of equal authority. He insists on the use of the word "Śivāgama" for the Veda also. He holds that Śivāgama is of two types, (I) for the twice-born only, and (II) for all, irrespective of the caste to which they belong. The Veda is of the former type and the Āgama is of the latter[1].

Śrīkaṇṭha refers to an interpretation of the Pāśupatādhikaraṇa, which seems to agree with our view, expressed earlier: (I) that the Pāśupata system, criticised by Śaṅkara in the Pāśupatādhikaraṇa of his commentary on the Vedāntasūtra, is not the system, as presented in the Pāśupata Sūtra by Lakulīśa, which is clearly a Dvaitādvaita system, and to which, therefore, the criticism does not apply; (II) that the system, under criticism, is dualistic, different from that presented by Mādhava, in his Sarva Darśana Saṅgraha, under the title "Śaiva Darśana". Śrīkaṇṭha, in the course of his commentary, says that the earlier authorities maintained that "Patyurasāmañjasyāt" criticises[2] "Śivāgamaikadeśa" which asserted that the material cause is separate from and perfectly independent of the instrumental, and that Śiva is the instrumental (Nimitta) cause only.

He is an exponent of the Viśiṣṭādvaita Śaivaism. He rejects the Bhedābhedavāda as impossible. For, unity and multiplicity being opposite in nature, cannot co-exist on the same substratum. It is against the fact of experience. He distinguishes his view from many others. He holds that the difference between the Ultimate Unity and the phenomenal multiplicity is not such as we experience between a jar and a piece of cloth: nor are they perfectly identical, as mother of pearl and silver, for which the former is mistaken. He asserts that he is a Viśiṣṭādvaitavādin[3], admitting the relation between the Śiva and the phenomenal multiplicity to be similar to that which exists between a body and a soul or between a substance and a quality. The non-difference of them is similar to that of clay and jar or of quality and substance, in so far as the two, being cause and effect or substance and quality, do not exist in isolation from each other. For, just as jar has no existence without clay nor does lotus exist without blueness; so the power to produce multiplicity cannot exist without Brahman or Śiva; nor can Brahman have being without the power. Just as we cannot

1 Srikam. Bh. Vol. II, 111.
2 Srikam. Bh. Vol. II, 111.
3 Srikam. Bh. Vol. II, 31.

know fire without heat, so we cannot know Brahman without the power. And the one, which is invariably experienced together with the other, is the attribute; and an invariable attribute constitutes the essential nature. The power to produce multiplicity is invariably in the Brahman. The Brahman, therefore, has the power as the invariable attribute. Hence, according to Śrīkaṇṭha, Viśiṣṭādvaita is the only sound metaphysical theory.

CRITICISM OF ŚRĪKAṆṬHA'S VIŚIṢṬĀDVAITA

THE above discussion reveals the weakness of the theory of Śrīkaṇṭha. He identifies an attribute with essential nature. He has no hesitation in admitting heat to be an attribute of fire. But the difference between an attribute and the essential nature has logically to be admitted. For, a thing does not necessarily have the same attribute. Lotus is not necessarily blue. It can be white or red; and blueness can and does belong to many other things, sky or cloth, for instance. But the essential nature does not belong to any other thing than that of which it is the essential nature. Warmth, for instance, cannot belong, as the essential nature, to any other thing than fire.

The fact is that he has put together the analogies, cited by the opposite systems, Advaita and Viśiṣṭādvaita, without distinguishing them from each other logically. He has also quoted the opposing authorities similarly. This becomes evident, if we take into account his quotation of Utpalācārya's famous verse:—

"Cidātmaiva hi devontaḥ"

I. P. V. (Bhāskarī) Vol. I, 226.

which presents the fundamental doctrine of the monistic Śaiva School of Kashmir. He also accepts the view of identity of power and its possessor, which is the basic view of the Pratyabhijñā system, as presented by Somānanda in his Śiva Dṛṣṭi[1]. He also quotes the verse, cited by Bhāskarakaṇṭha in the Bhāskarī in support of the monistic view:

(I) "Śaktayosya jagat kṛtsnam"

Bh., Vol. I, 266, 345.
Śrikam. Bh. Vol. I. 300.

(II) "Śaktiśca śaktimadrūpāt"

Bh., Vol. II, 153.
Śrikam. Bh., Vol. I, 300.

---

1 S. Dr. 96.

The monistic tendency of Śrīkaṇṭha was noticed by his great commentator, Appayya Dīkṣita (1550 A. D.) in the Ānanda Laharī and Sivādvaita Nirṇaya, wherein he inquired into the precise implications of Śrīkaṇṭha's system and established that, in essence, Śrīkaṇṭha is a monist[1]. Our inquiry from the point of view of the works of authorities on the monistic Śaiva Philosophy of Kashmir confirms the above view.

*1 S. Sri. 35.

(V) VIŚEṢĀDVAITA OR PURE DVAITĀDVAITA OF VĪRA ŚAIVAISM

The historians say that Vīra Śaivaism was founded by Basava, the Brāhmaṇa minister of Bijjala, in 1167 A. D. The word "Vīra Śaiva" seems to have a historical significance. It seems to refer to the heroic attitude of the followers of Śaivaism in defence of their faith and philosophy. The Chalukya dynasty is well known. After the death of Vikramāṅka, the hero of Bilhaṇa's historical poem, Vikramāṅkadeva Carita, the Chalukya power declined. And during the reign of Taila III (1156—62 A.D.) Bijjal or Vijjana, the commander-in-chief, revolted and obtained possession of the greater part of the kingdom. One legend says that Bijjala was a Jain and wontonly blinded two Śaiva ascetics. This led to a religious revolution. The revolutionaries, it seems, took to a kind of 'passive resistance'. In defiance of the attitude of Bijjala towards Śaivaism, the followers of the faith courted the wrath of the cruel king by wearing the phallic form of Śiva on arm, neck or head. They identified the life (Prāṇa) with the phallic form (Liṅga) so that they refused to part with it while they lived. Parting with it meant parting with life.

Śrīpati Paṇḍitārādhya seems to be referring to such a movement in the course of his commentary on "Jīvamukhya Prāṇaliṅgāt" (Sri. Bh., Vol. II, 91). He refers to the religious ceremony of identifying Prāṇa with Liṅga and quotes the religious instruction, given to the disciple at the end of it. It runs as follows:—

"Resolve to keep this phallic image of Śiva as if it were your very life. Do not part with it so long as you live" (Sri. Bh. Vol. II, 92.)

Thus, it seems that the wearers of the phallic image of Śiva were called "Vīra" (Hero), because of the bravery with which they faced the wrath of the cruel king Bijjala.

As a religious sect of Śaivaism, it is distinct from other Śaiva sects, (1) Sāmānya, (2) Miśra and (3) Śuddha. The followers of the first two worship both Śiva and Viṣṇu. And the followers of the last, worship Śiva exclusively as do the Vīra Śaivas. Vīra Śaivaism, however, is distinct from Śuddha Śaivaism in so far as the followers of Vīra Śaivaism wear Liṅga on the body, preferably on the head or suspend it from the neck[1].

Vīra Śaivaism follows the authority of Twenty-eight Śaivāgamas of the Siddhānta School. on which we have spoken earlier. The leading doctrines of the system are (1) Aṣṭavarṇa and (2) Ṣaṭsthala, on which we shall write subsequently. It is a living faith, particularly in South India. Its followers, because of their wearing the Liṅga on the body, are called Liṅgāyat. As a religious sect it emphasizes devotion to Śiva.

The religious tradition, current among the living Vīra Śaivas, however, says that Vīra Śaivaism was founded by five Ācāryas : (1) Reṇuka (2) Dāruka (3) Ekorāma (4) Paṇḍitārādhya and (5) Viśvārādhya : that these Ācāryas belonged to hoary past, and that Basava simply revived and popularised it. These Ācāryas are believed to have sprung from the Śiva Liṅgas (1) of Someśvara at Kollipaki, (2) of Vaṭa Vṛkṣa Siddheśvara (3) of Rāmanātha at Drākṣārāma Kṣetra (4) of Mallikārjuna at Śrīśaila and (5) of Viśvanātha at Kāśī. It is interesting to note in this connection that Maṭhas, associated with the names of these teachers, exist even to this day. They are found respectively at the following places which have been identified with those, mentioned just above:—

(1) Balehonnur (Rambhāpurī) in Kadur district in Mysore State : (2) Ujjain in Bellary District in Madras Presidency; (3) Himavat Kedāra in the Himalaya ; (4) Śrīśaila in Kurnool district in Madras Presidency ; and (5) Kāśi (Banaras) in U. P. The tradition about the five teachers of Vīra Śaivaism has the support of Suprabhedāgama[2].

The religious tradition, which says that Basava was not the founder of Vīra Śaivaism but only a great exponent and upholder of it, seems to find some support in Rājaśekhara's reference to the wearing of Prāṇaliṅga on arm by a Śaiva sect, as we have stated earlier. And Rājaśekhara belonged to 900 A. D. Śrīpati Paṇḍita quotes from the Sadānandopaniṣad, which belongs to the Sāmajaigīśīya Śākhā[3], in justification of wearing of Prāṇaliṅga on arm. He also quotes from other ancient texts including the Veda to support the wearing of Liṅga. And Liṅgadhāraṇa Candrikā by Nandikeśvara has as its sole aim as its title shows, to prove that wearing of Liṅga is enjoined by the Vedas, the

*1. Sri. Bh. Vol. I, 7.
2. Vi. S., 102.,
3. Sri. Bh., Vol. II, 92.

Purāṇas and the Śaivāgamas, such as Kāmika[1] etc. Thus the literary evidence makes us believe that the characteristic religious practices of Vīra Śaivaism go back to very much earlier period than the 12th century A. D. and that Basava was a great upholder and propounder of the Śaiva Religion and emphasized the wearing of Liṅga.

THE FIVE TEACHERS AS HISTORICAL PERSONALITIES

The mythical account of the earliest five teachers, given in the preceding section, in accordance with the religious tradition, current among the living Vīra Śaivas, should not lead us to think that these teachers have no historicity. Mythology of a religion has a propaganda value and contains the same amount of truth as does the propaganda literature of a political party. It needs verification just like the identification of the author of a particular work with that of another, because both have the same name. For, in the history of our literature we find many persons, belonging to distant periods, having the same name, and identification of one writer with another, on account of identity of the name, leads to very serious confusion.

Keeping these two things in mind, if we try to find out the historical element in the religious tradition of the Vīra Śaiva, we have to base our conclusions on the references to them in the available literature from the pens of those whose historical reality is beyond all doubts and who can be assigned to definite periods.

If we study the authoritative literature on Vīra Śaivaism; we get a fairly clear idea of the five teachers, referred to above, as historical personalities. We come across references to them in (I) the Śrīkara Bhāṣya of Śrīpati Paṇḍitārādhya and (II) the Śaiva Bhāṣya on the Mahānārāyaṇopaniṣad by Vṛṣabhendra Paṇḍita, who claims to be a descendant of Śrīpati Paṇḍitārādhya. Paṇḍitārādhya refers to at least three of the five teachers in the very introductory verses to his commentary on the Vedānta Sūtra of Bādarāyaṇa, (I) Revaṇa (II) Marula and (III) Ekorāma.

Revaṇa is the first historical personality that is mentioned in a long list of teachers, which is based upon the Śaivāgamas, and which gives the teachers as they came in succession :(I) Sadāśiva (II) Śaktidhara (III) Sukeśa (IV) Caṇḍīśvara (V) Bhṛṅgi riṭa (VI) Śilāda (VII) Kumbhodbhava(Agastya) (VIII) Vāmadeva (IX) Revaṇa.

---

1 L. C., 2.

Revaṇa is represented to be well versed in the rituals[1] and ceremonies of the Ṣaivaism, very popular among his pupils, a man of perfect self-control, who had become a Siddha, had attained spiritual greatness and, therefore, could grant any boon, like a Kalpavṛkṣa. He is said to have refuted the theories of the opponents, such as (I) Mithyādvaita (II) Ṣūnyādvaita, (III) Jaina (IV) Bauddha and (V) Lokāyatika[2]. He is said to have written a commentary, or at least to have expressed views on some important problems, discussed in the Vedānta Sūtra. Thus, he is said to have held that in the aphorism "Patyurasāmañjasyāt" (Sri. Bh. 232-4.) Bādarāyaṇa refutes the dualistic Pāśupata[3] (and not Lakulīśa Pāśupata, as we said earlier). He is said to have attained final emancipation, on account of his devotion, renunciation and faith in and practice of Ṣravaṇa, Manana and Nididhyāsana. He is spoken of as a great Vedic scholar, who had mastered all the Ṣākhās and written commentaries on the Vedāntic works. He is said to have held that all the passages in the Ṣrutis, which talk of Saguṇa Brahman, refer to the manifested state of the Ṣakti of Brahman; while those which talk of the Nirguṇa Brahman refer to the unmanifested state of the Śakti[4]. He[5] along with Vemana etc. is said to have held that the Puruṣa Sūkta, beginning with "Sahasraśīrṣā' etc. is to be interpreted as referring to Parama Śiva, though there are epithets in it, which are applicable to Viṣṇu only.

REVAṆA SIDDHA AND REVAṆĀRYA

Ṣrīpati Paṇḍita refers[6] to Siddhānta Ṣikhāmaṇi by Revaṇārya. But we have to distinguish between Revaṇa Siddha and Revaṇārya. For, the author of the Siddhānta Ṣikhāmaṇi in the introduction to his work, speaks of himself as Revaṇārya, son of Revaṇa Siddha and grandson of Vīraṇārādhya. He gives the names of two more of his ancestors, who came before Vīraṇārādhya in succession: (I) Viśvanātha and (II) Sarveśa Deśika. It is thus clear that Revaṇa Siddha was the father of Revaṇārya, the author of the Siddhānta Ṣikhāmaṇi and that Ṣrīpati Paṇḍita in the references, given in the preceding section, refers to Revaṇa Siddha but not Revaṇārya.

1 Sri. Bh., Vol. II, 1.
2 Sri. Bh., Vol. II, 193.
3 Sri. Bh., Vol. II, 234.
4 Sri. Bh., Vol. II, 382.
5 M. U.. S. Bh. 57.
6 Sri. Bh., Vol. II, 12.

Siddhānta Şikhāmaṇi is a very important work on Vīra Şaivaism. Hardly there is any work on this system, in which it is not referred to. It has a commentary by Bhoga Malleśa, a copy of which is preserved in the Madras Oriental MSS. Library (X no. 5119). It was translated into Tamil by Turaimaṅgalam Şiva Prakāśasvāmin in the 17th century A. D.

It may be pointed out here that Şrīpati Paṇḍita quotes from the Siddhānta Şikhāmaṇi[1] and attributes it to Reṇuka Bhagavatpādācārya. The question, therefore, arises : "Is it a work of Revaṇārya, as stated above or of Reṇuka, *alias* Revaṇa, whose descendant he claims to be ?". In view of the fact that in the introduction to this work, the author calls himself Revaṇārya and speaks of himself as a descendant of Renuka[2], Şrīpati seems to have used the family name of the author, instead of the personal name.

Revaṇārya, the author of the Siddhānta Şikhāmaṇi, wrote four other works, each of which is a commentary on the work of his grand-father, Sosali-Vīraṇārādhya. These are :—(1) Pañcaratnavyākhyā (or Tantrasāraprakāśikā), which is a commentary on the Tantrasārapañcaratna of Sosali-Vīraṇārādhya; (2) Tārakapañcaratnavyākhyā (or Tārakapradīpikā), which is a commentary on the Tārakapañcaratna by the same author; (3) Pañcaratnavyākhyā (or Şivatattvaprakāśikā), which is a commentary on the Şivaratnapañcaratna by the same author; (4) Pañcaratnavyākhyā (Şrutyarthapradīpikā), which is a commentary on the Şrutipañcaratna by the same author. This work is also called Şrutyarthaprakāśikā. In it, Revaṇārya mentions both his father's and grand-father's names, Revaṇasiddheśvara and Sosali-Vīraṇārādhya, which apear in the Siddhānta Şikhāmaṇi as Revaṇasiddha and Vīraṇārādhya, and his own name as Revaṇārya. This establishes the identity of the author of the above works with the author of the Siddhānta Şikhāmaṇi beyond all doubts. (MSS. of these works are in the Madras Government Oriental MSS. Library. *See* Madras D. C. X, nos. 5090.)

MARULA

Marula is the second of the five teachers of Vīra Şaivaism. He was a pupil of Revaṇa. He also was a Siddha and had attained spiritual greatness. He commanded the respect of the learned. He was well versed in various arts[3]. In many of the

1 Sri Bh Vol II, 15.
*2 Sri Bh Vol I, 54.
3 Sri Bh Vol II, 1.

references to Marula in the Śrīkara Bhāṣya his name is coupled with that of Revaṇa. Thus, he is said to have rejected false monism, nihilistic monism, Jainism and Buddhism, in common with Durvāsā and Revaṇa[1]. Similarly in common with Revaṇa he is said to hold (I) that the system, criticised in the Pāśupatādhikaraṇa of the Vedānta Sūtra, is the Dualistic Pāśupata, the principles of which are opposed to the teaching of the Śaivāgama; (II) that all the Śrutis, referring to Saguṇa Brahman, refer to the manifested state of Śakti and those which speak of the Nirguṇa refer to the unmanifested state of Śakti[2], and that the Puruṣa Sūkta refers to Parama Śiva.

EKORĀMA

Ekorāma was a grand-pupil of Revaṇa and pupil of Marula. The learned bowed to him because of his character. He had a large following. He was a great exponent of the twenty-eight Śaivāgamas. He was a keen controvertialist. He was master of Tarka, Vyākaraṇa Mīmāṁsā and the literature on monism. He was a great yogin and used the garb of a Vīra Śaiva Sanyāsin. He[3] was the teacher of Śrīpati Paṇḍita, the author of the Śrīkara Bhāṣya on the Vedānta Sūtra.

It appears that Ekorāma also wrote a commentary on the Vedānta Sūtra. For, Śrīpati Paṇḍita at many places in his own commentary refers to the views of Ekorāma on important points and says that he sticks to it, because it was held by Ekorāma. For instance, he refers to Ekorāma's view[4] on "Śrotavyaḥ" etc., in the course of the commentary on, "Tattu Samanvayāt". Similarly in the commentary on the word "Jijñāsā" of the first Sūtra, he prefers the interpretation that was put upon it by Ekorāma.

Very often Śrīpati refers to Ekorāma as Rāma. This is particularly so, when he couples Ekorāma with his predecessors such as Revaṇa and Marula because of their agreement on a certain point or something else that is common to them. Thus, he is represented to agree with his predecessors that the Pāśupatādhikaraṇa refutes dualistic Pāśupata School, and to have followed the same means to the final emancipation as did Revaṇa and Marula[5].

---

1 Sri. Bh., Vol. II, 193.
2 Sri. Bh., Vol. II, 382.
3 Sri. Bh., Vol. II, 1—2.
4. Sri. Bh. Vol. II, 23.
5. Sri. Bh. Vol. II, 26.

ŚRĪPATI PAṆḌITA

Śrīpati Paṇḍita, the author of the Śrīkara Bhāṣya on the Vedānta Sūtra from the point of view of Vīra Śaivaism, is a very important person in the history of the Vīra Śaiva literature exactly as Abhinavagupta is, in the history of the monistic Śaiva literature of Kashmir. For, it is in relation to him that we can fix the dates of other authorities. In fact, if we can talk of the dates of the five great teachers of Vīra Śaivaism with a certain amount of plausibility and certainty, that is because of his references to at least three of them. He occupies the central position among them, being the fourth, as a pupil of Ekorāma. Naturally, therefore, he does not mention the fifth of the great Vīra Śaiva teachers, Viśvārādhya, who was a successor. We identify Śrīpati Paṇḍita with Paṇḍitārādhya for two very important reasons. (I) His own reference to Ekorāma as his own teacher. This is important; because all the three teachers, whom he represents to have come in succession and to have been related to one another as teacher and taught in the descending order, are the earlier of the recognised five teachers of Vīra Śaivaism. (II) Paṇḍita is the last part of his name, as it is clear from its repeated occurrence in the colophon at the end of each chapter. And it seems to have been the practice during the period, to which he belonged, to refer to the authorities by stating the last part of their names, as he himself does in the case of Ekorāma, as Rāma.[1] Further, the word "Ārādhya" was a recognised reverential title added to the names of the persons, held in high esteem for their learning and devotion to the cause of the Vīra Śaivaism, as in the case of Viśvārādhya etc.

ŚRĪPATI PAṆḌITA'S DATE

Confining ourselves to the evidence, available in the Śrīkara Bhāṣya itself, we can definitely say that he belonged to the 14th century A. D. For, among the systems referred to and criticised by him is that of Madhva. There are two fundamental principles of it, which he refutes: (I) the all-pervasive nature of the soul[2]: and (II) dualism[3]. And the recognised date of Madhva[4] is 1238—1317 A. D. Madhva was founder of a School of philosophy and a religious sect. He may, therefore, be supposed to have been recognised as an authority in his own life time.

1 Sri. Bh., Vol. II, 269
2 Sri. Bh., Vol. II, 263.
3 Sri. Bh., Vol. II, 273.
4 H. S. L., 479.

We, therefore, need not suppose the lapse of any time between Madhva and Śrīpati Paṇḍita to justify reference to the former by the latter. This agrees with the reference to him in an inscription belonging to the reign of Rudrāmbā, the Kākatīya Empress, who ruled from 1295 to 1323 A. D. He seems to have been a younger contemporary of Rudrāmbā and to have continued to live long after her reign. He may, therefore, be assigned to the first half of the 14th century A. D.

If we accept the conclusion, arrived at in regard to the date of Śrīpati Paṇḍita, that he belonged to the first half of the 14th century A. D., there remains no difficulty in fixing the dates of his teacher, Ekorāma, grand-teacher, Marula, and great-grand-teacher Revaṇa. They may be said to belong to the period from the close of the 12th to the close of the 13th century A. D.

He had embraced asceticism[1], had become a Sanyāsin, at the time when he wrote the Śrīkara Bhāṣya on the Vedānta Sūtra. He had a number of followers of the same order. He was a Vīra Śaiva and wrote the commentary from the point of view of the Vīra Śaivaism. He called his system Viśeṣādvaita in order to distinguish it from the Nirviśeṣādvaita of Śaṅkara and the Viśiṣṭādvaita of Rāmānuja. He asserts[2] that while other systems can present only a part of the Vedic text as an authority, the Vīra Śaivaism can claim the whole of it as such, i.e. every section of the Veda admits of consistent interpretation in the light of the Vīra Śaivaism only. He holds that the Veda is of equal authority with the Śaivāgama.

In the Basaveśa Vijaya by Śaṅkarārādhya, a miracle[3] is attributed to him. It is said that he collected burning embers in a piece of cloth and suspended it at the end of a branch of Śamī tree. This miracle is referred to by a Kannaḍa poet also.

He holds that all the Śrutis propound the dualism-cum-non-dulism, Dvaitādvaita, and that it is also a fact of the common experience. For,[4] we experience duality in the states of wakefulness and sleep, but non-duality in the deep sleep and hold both the experiences to be equally real. In the field of philosophy also, therefore, dualism cannot be maintained to be antagonistic to and inconsistent with non-dualism. We can refer dualism to the em-

1 Sri, Bh., Vol, II, 2.
2 Sri. Bh., Vol. II, 2.
3 Sri. Bh., Vol. I, 9.
4 Sri. Bh., Vol. II, 189.

pirical level and monism to the transcendental level, at which the individual gets united with Śiva and becomes one with Him, as the water of a river does with that of the ocean, wherein it falls.

This analogy to convey the idea of union of the individual with the universal, in final emancipation, is found in the Kulārṇava Tantra also (MS. P. 123).

HIS COMMENTARY

Śrīpati Paṇḍita follows the brief commentary, the Vṛtti, on the Vedānta Sūtra by Agastya[1]. He mentions Agastya, as Kumbhodbhava, in the line of teachers[2] (Pāramparya). It is a very learned commentary, as is clear from references to and quotations from the Veda, Upaniṣads, Āgamas, Purāṇas and philosophical texts and commentaries on them, which were written from the earliest time down to that of his immediate predecessor, Madhva. It takes into consideration not only the systems, with which we are familiar, on account of references to them by Śaṅkara and Rāmānuja, but also those about which we can have no idea whatsoever from them.

The Viśiṣṭādvaita of Rāmānuja and Niṣprapañca-Brahmādvaita of Śaṅkara are the main targets, at which Śrīpati Paṇḍita's criticism is aimed. He criticises the former, for instance, in the course of his commentary on :—

(I) "Asminnasya ca tadyogam Śāsti" I, i, 6, 20.

(II) "Muktopasṛpyavyapadeśāt" .. I, iii, 1, 4.

(III) "Utpatterasambhavāt" .. II, ii, 9, 42.

In the course of his commentary on the last of the above quoted Sūtras, he enters into an interesting discussion about the caste of Viṣṇu and tries to show that Viṣṇu is recognised to be a Kṣatriya in all texts from the Vedas down to the Purāṇas, and that Viṣṇu is to be worshipped by Kṣatriyas only. In contrast to the above, he attempts to prove that Śiva is recognised to be Brāhmaṇa in all texts and as such is an object of worship to Brāhmaṇas. He asserts on the basis of the names of famous images of Viṣṇu, during his time, that the names of the images of Viṣṇu have the word "Rāja" at the end, for instance, (I) Govindarāja, (II) Varadarāja and (III) Raṅgarāja. This clearly means that

1 Sri. Bh., Vol. II, 2.

2 Sri. Bh., Vol. II, 1.

not only the scripture but the persistent religious tradition also recognises that Viṣṇu is Kṣatriya. He also points out that in the religious festivals of the Vaiṣṇava, which are celebrated according to the Pāñcarātrāgama, the word "Varma" is used for Viṣṇu. In contrast to this he points out that the word "Īśvara" is used at the end of the names of the images of Śiva, symbolic or representative.

AGGRESSIVENESS OF RĀMĀNUJA

In the above context, in the course of his commentary, Śrīpati Paṇḍita refers to the aggressive Vaiṣṇavaism of Rāmānuja. An objection is raised "How can it be asserted that the names of the images of Śiva alone have the word "Īśvara" at the end ?" For, the image of Viṣṇu (which still exists at Tirupati and is visited by thousands of pilgrims daily even now) is called Veṅkaṭeśvara.

In reply to this Śrīpati[1] asserts that the image of Veṅkaṭeśvara simply appears to be of Viṣṇu. In reality it is the image of Śiva "Veṅkaṭeśvarasya ābhāsa-viṣṇutvam". For, the image is decorated with snakes, and in the original image ("Mūlavigraha") there are no characteristic marks of Viṣṇu, such as Śaṅkha and Cakra. It may be pointed out here that Śaṅkha and Cakra, which we find in the image of Veṅkaṭeśvara, are not of stone, of which the whole body is made, but of metal. It was the image of Vīreśvara (Vīrabhadra) which was changed into Veṅkaṭeśvara by Rāmānuja. This is proved by an additional existing fact that just below the hand of the image, there is a Śiva Liṅga.

Similarly in regard to the use of the word "Īśvara" at the end of the name 'Viṭhaleśvara', he asserts that the image has Śiva Liṅga on the head and, therefore, has been called "Viṭhaleśvara". For, it has been accepted that the name is to be dissolved as the genetive determinative compound "Viṭhalasya īśvaraḥ".

He declares that the Vaiṣṇava Viśiṣṭādvaita of Rāmānuja, the characteristic philosophical technique of which consists of (I) Cit, (II) Acit and (III) Īśvara, is not based upon the authority of the Veda and, therefore, has to be rejected[2]. He says that the Brāhmaṇa Vaiṣṇavas, who are antagonistic to Śiva, should be treated as outcaste[3].

1 Sri. Bh., Vol. II, 241.
2 Sri. Bh., Vol. II, 247.
3 Sri. Bh., Vol. II, 242.

He is equally opposed to the Śaiva Viśiṣṭādvaita, propounded by Śrīkaṇṭha in his Brahmamīmāṁsā Bhāṣya, and says that it is to be ignored[1].

He seems to refer to Śaṅkara, when he talks of "a Bauddha in disguise" (Pracchanna Bauddha)[2] and gives the name "Nirviśeṣādvaita" to his philosophy. He holds that the section "Abhāvādhikaraṇa" in the Brahma Sūtra, II, ii, refutes the system that presents the world, the soul and the Īśvara to be nothing more than illusion. He attributes "Nirviśeṣādvaita" to Vaśiṣṭha and seems to point out that Śaṅkara, in his presentation of the triad of God, soul and world as an illusion, follows Vaśiṣṭha, who propounded this view for the first time[3]. Similarly another aspect of Śaṅkara's philosophy he seems to call Śūnyādvaita, and attributes it to Sāndīpa. He holds that the section "Sarvathānupapatti" of the Vedānta Sūtra refutes it. He asserts that "Niṣprapañca Brahmādvaitavāda", which holds that the phenomenal world is due to 'ignorance' (Avidyā) lacks the support of the Veda[4].

Other systems refuted by Śrīpati are (I) Raudra[5], the followers of which are branded with red-hot Śiva Liṅga, (II) Tantra Pāśupata, the followers of which bear the marks of Śūla and Ḍamaru, (III) Gāṇapatya, (IV) Saura, (V) Śākta, (VI) Kāpālika, (VII) Madhva, (VIII) Sāṅkhya, (IX) Yoga, (X) Nyāya, (XI) Vaiśeṣika, (XII) Bauddha and (XIII) Jaina etc.

SOME UNFAMILIAR AUTHORITIES REFERRED TO IN THE COMMENTARY

(I) Paramaśivārādhya. Two works are attributed to him : (1) Kaivalya Prakāśa and (2) Śivajñāna Candrodaya.[6] (II) Jyotirnātha (III) Ghanṭānātha (IV) Bhīmanātha and (V) Bhaṭṭa Bhāskara. These[7] are spoken of as masters of all the Vedas, opponents of the systems of Bauddha, Pāñcarātra and Advaita, and as expounders of the view that Śiva is Para Brahman. (VI) Durvāsā. There is a work, referred to as "Durvāsīya", wherein he is said to have discussed the implication of the affix "Śatṛ" in "Pivantau"[8] in the Vedic passage "Ṛtaṁ pivantau". He is also said to have refuted the views of those who hold that God, soul

1 Sri. Bh., Vol. II, 200.
2 Sri. Bh., Vol. II, 225.
3 Sri. Bh., Vol. II, 228.
4 Sri. Bh., Vol. II, 134.
5 Sri. Bh., Vol. II, 232-3
6 Sri. Bh., Vol. II, 24.
7 Sri. Bh., Vol. II, 28,74.
8 Sri Bh., Vol. II, 25.

and world are illusory. (VII) Upamanyu. He also, along with Durvāsā, Revaṇa Siddha and Marula Siddha, is said to have criticised the views, stated just above[1]. Is he identical with the author of the commentary on the Nandikeśvara Kāśikā by Nandikeśvara ? (VIII) Udbhaṭārādhya and (IX) Vemanārādhya. They, along with Revaṇa Siddha etc. are said to have held that the Vedic passages, such as "Īśānaḥ sarvavidyānām" speak of Śiva only as the Lord of all[2].

SRĪPATI'S VIŚEṢĀDVAITA.

The system, propounded by Śrīpati, was known by various names, such as (I) Dvaitādvaita, (II) Viśeṣādvaita, (III) Seśvarādvaita, (IV) Śivādvaita, (V) Sarvaśrutisāramata and (VI) Bhedābheda[3]. The word 'Viśeṣa' which differentiates his monism from those of others, is interpreted in various ways in different contexts[4]. We shall revert to this topic in the proper context. He admits thirty-six categories[5], common to the monistic school of Kashmir. Among the various exponents of the Vedānta, referred to by Bādarāyaṇa in his Vedānta Sūtra; such as Jaimini, Āśmarathya, Auḍulomi, Bādari and Kāśakṛtsna, he follows the last, Kāśakṛtsna, because he is an exponent of the Bhedābhedavāda, takes all the Śruti texts into account and represents the central view of the Vedānta[6]. He admits the powers of will[7], knowledge and action, which were earlier recognised by the monistic school of Kashmir. He also admits three impurities (mala) Āṇava, Kārma and Māyīya[8]: and refers to six ways[9] to final emancipation (Ṣaḍadhva) on which Abhinavagupta in his Tantrāloka has written at length.

1 Sri. Bh., Vol. II, 193.
2 Sri. Bh., Vol. II, 234,269.
3 Sri. Bh., Vol. II, 195.
4 Sri. Bh., Vol. II, 136,189.
5 Sri. Bh., Vol. II, 105,168.
6 Sri. Bh., Vol. II, 177, 333.
7 Sri. Bh., Vol. II, 494.
8 Sri. Bh., Vol. II, 176.
*9 Sri. Bh., Vol. I, 69.

(VI) NANDIKEŚVARA SAIVAISM

The school of Śaiva Philosophy, which is to be considered now, is monistic and has been called "Nandikeśvara Śaivaism", because it was propounded by Nandikeśvara, the author of the Nandikeśvara Kāśikā.

TRADITION ABOUT NANDIKEŚVARA

Upamanyu, the commentator on the Nandikeśvara Kāśikā, in the course of his commentary, Tattva Vimarśinī, records the following tradition, which persists even now among the students of Pāṇini's system of grammer:—

The sages, Nandikeśa, Patañjali, Vyāghrapāt and Vaśiṣṭha, etc. contemplated on Śiva for inspiration. As an act of grace to them, Śiva appeared and struck his hand-drum (Ḍamaru). The sounds, produced by it, symbolically presented the fourteen Sūtras. The Sūtras, found at the commencement of Pāṇini's Aṣṭādhyāyī, are articulate representations of the inarticulate sounds of Śiva's hand-drum. The sages, unable to understand the meaning of the Sūtras, approached Nandikeśvara for clarification. He (Nandikeśvara) expounded the meaning in Twenty-six verses, which constitute the text of the Nandikeśvara Kāśikā.

In the Nandikeśvara Kāśikā there is only one verse, number two, which is for the guidance of Pāṇini etc. This is referred to by Nāgeśa Bhaṭṭa in the Udyota[1]. It says that the last letter, at the end of each of the fourteen Sūtras, is for the sake of Pāṇini to enable him to build up the system of grammar. The rest of the verses present a monistic system of Śaiva philosophy.

THE DATE OF THE NANDIKEŚVARA KĀŚIKĀ

The literary tradition, referred to in the preceding section recognises Nandikeśvara to be a contemporary of Pāṇini. There seems to be some truth in this tradition. For, Patañjali, in his Mahābhāṣya[2], seems to refer to the interpretation of the system of sounds, represented in the fourteen Sūtras, by Nandikeśvara. For, he talks of it as "Brahmarāśiḥ". This view seems to find support in the interpretation of "Brahmarāśiḥ" as

1. M. Bh. 89. 2. M. Bh. 132.

"Brahmatattvam" by Kaiyaṭa. But in the opinion of Nāgeśa Bhaṭṭa, as expressed in the course of his commentary on the above, Patañjali had Nandikeśvara's view in his mind. For, Nāgeśa definitely quotes the fourth verse of the Nandikeśvara Kāśikā.

UPAMANYU, THE COMMENTATOR.

Upamanyu is the only known commentator on the Nandikeśvara Kāśikā. The commentary is called Tattva Vimarśinī. He seems to have come very long after Nandikeśvara. For, by his time variants of the text had become current. For instance, he refers to two readings of the verse number two, besides the one that he adopts. He seems to refer to the founder of another system of grammar "Indra"[1]. He quotes from (I) the Upaniṣads, (II) the Gītā, (III) Sanaka-Dakṣiṇāmūrti-Saṁvāda-Vivaraṇa, (IV) Mahāmantratattva Prakāśikā, (V) Svara Vimarśinī, (VI) Jñānottama and (VII) Tantrarāja. He declares that his commentary is in the light of the information on the subject, gathered from the Tantras.

It may be pointed out here that two recensions of this work are at present available. One was edited by Balakrishna Shastri and was published from Banaras. The other is included in the Mahā Bhāṣya. (Navāhnika), edited by Mahamahopadhyaya Pandit Shiva Dutta and published from Nirnaya Sagar. They truly represent two different recensions. The most important difference between them is that while in the former there is no commentary on the verse no. 18, in the latter there is commentary and therein the declaration given at the end of the preceding paragraph appears[2]. Besides this there are many other differences, such as difference in the names of the works referred to, e.g. in place of Svara Vimarśinī in the former, there is Īśvara Vimarśinī in the latter.

From the references, found in Upamanyu's commentary, he seems to belong to a period when the Śaiva-Āgamas or Tantras had assumed definite form and commentaries on some of them had already been written. And we know that the commentaries on the Śaivāgamas were begun to be written in the 9th century A. D. We cannot, therefore, assign him to a date earlier than this. Upamanyu is referred to as an ancient authority along with Revaṇa Siddha and Marula Siddha in the Śrīkara Bhāṣya by Śrīpati Paṇḍita[3]. Here he is spoken of as one who had refuted

1. N. K. 2.
2. M. Bh. 134.
3. Sri. Bh. Vol. II, 193.

false monism (Mithyādvaita), nihilistic monism (Śūnyādvaita) Jainism and Buddhism. And we know that Śrīpati Paṇḍita belonged to the middle of the 14th century A. D. As Upamanyu is referred to as an ancient authority, probably earlier than even Revaṇa Siddha, we shall, therefore, be not very wrong if we assign him to the close of the 11th and the beginning of the 12th century A. D. This conclusion seems to find some support in the fact that about this time various attempts were made to study and to systematise those sections of the Śaivāgamas, in which the Devanāgarī alphabetical system was presented as representing the Śaiva metaphysics. For, during this period Abhinavagupta wrote his famous Tantrāloka, in the third Āhnika of which this view is presented ; and Śrīkaṇṭha in his Ratna Traya and Rāmakaṇṭha in his Nāda Kārikā, attempted allied problems.

Nandikeśvara, according to Upamanyu, admitted thirty-six categories, though some of them are different from those of the monistic Śaiva School of Kashmir. He also held that Parama Śiva is beyond categories, exactly as did Abhinavagupta. There is close similarity between the Voluntaristic metaphysics of Nandikeśvara and that of the monistic Kashmir Śaivaism; compare, for instance,

"Svecchayā Svasya Cicchaktau
Viśvamunmīlayatyasau"

N. K. 12

and

"Svecchayā svabhittau Viśvamunmilayati"

P. Hr. Sūtra 2.

(VII) RASEŚVARA ŚAIVAISM

The Rasesvara system is so called, because its followers, though they admit the essential identity of soul with Maheśvara, assert that the liberation in life (Jīvanmukti) depends upon the stability of the bodily frame and that it is possible to have a perdurable body through the use of the processed and purified (Siddha) mercury (Raseśvara). They say that mercury is called "Pārada" because it is a means to get beyond the series of transmigratory states[1]; and that it is called Raseśvara, because it is the most powerful of all medicines, which are prepared by subjecting a metal to a medical process: it is the king of chemicals.

THE CAUSE OF THE RISE OF THE RASEŚVARA SYSTEM

It appears that seakers after liberation felt frustrated in their efforts, because of short life and diseases. The only means to liberation, known to people, before the rise of the Raseśvara system, was that which was pointed by the Yoga system, and which consisted in the control of vital air and the concentration on the Self. The practice of Yoga seems to have come to an abrupt and futile end in the majority of cases, because of disease or untimely death. Hence there seems to have grown a tendency to look upon the efforts at liberation as futile. Raseśvara Darśana, therefore, sprang up to fight this tendency. It emphasized the importance of healthy and durable body for the successful practice of Yoga. It gave the processed and refined mercury and mica as the means to the attainment of a perdurable and healthy body and thus revived the dying faith in the highest goal of human life, the liberation.

RASEŚVARA AS A ŚAIVA SYSTEM

The Rasesvara system is admittedly a Saiva system. Mādhavācārya, in the very beginning of his summary statement, attributes it to some Māheśvaras, the followers of the school of Philosophy that held the Maheśvara, the Highest Lord, to be the Ultimate metaphysical principle. There is no doubt about it that the Buddhists, such as Nāgārjuna, who is referred to as an authority on the system, made substantial contributions to it. The majority of the writers on it, however, have been the Śaivas, and the origin of Raseśvara, mercury, has been mythically attributed to Śiva. For,

1. S. D. S., 202.

mercury is held to be nothing but the semen, dropped from the body of Śiva.

Thus, in Rasasaṅketa Kalikā, Cāmuṇḍā says that the semen, that dropped from Śiva, was taken by Agni in his mouth and was scattered all round. On three sides there was water, wherein it got merged. On the fourth side there was earth whereon it fell and became mercury. This explains mythically the existence of mercury-wells in the west only. It is also said that it got deep down into the earth and was taken out by gods and Nāgas, who sank wells, thousand Yojanas deep. And this seems to refer to the fact that mercury is found at the depth of about 25 thousand feet.

The literary evidence seems to support the view that mercury came to India from the West, particularly Misra (Egypt). For, one of the names of mercury is Misraka, which may well be said, to convey the idea of the place wherefrom it came first to India, though the commentators interpret it differently. And Bhagavad Govinda Pāda, the teacher of Ṣaṅkara, in his Rasa Hṛdaya says that Rasendra (Pārada) should be worshipped in the west, probably because he knew that it came from that direction.

Another tradition says that Ṣiva, the founder of Chemistry, imparted instructions to Pārvatī about the method of subjecting mercury to some scientific process, so as to make it capable of converting iron into gold and of giving immortality to human body. These two effects of mercury on iron and on human body are known as (I) Lohasiddhi and (II) Dehasiddhi respectively.

It also says that at first mercury was processed and refined for converting iron into gold and that after its effect on iron had been tested, it was further processed to give immortality to human body. In fact, Bhagavat Govinda pāda[1], according to Mādhava, insisted on testing the efficacy of the processed mercury on iron to convert it into gold, before subjecting it to further process for using it on human body to give it immortality. The view that mercury, after subjection to certain processes, becomes capable of converting iron into gold is common to Misra.

That success had been attained in this field is testified by the literary tradition about Rasasiddhas. It asserts that there were persons, who actually attained immortality by the use of the processed mercury. The Vāgbhaṭa Saṁhitā by

1. S. D. S., 206.

Vāgbhaṭācārya, for instance, gives a list of twenty-seven Rasasiddhas, including Nāgārjuna and Bhagavad Govinda Pāda. They are as follows :—

1. Ādinātha (Śiva)	2. Candrasena.
3. Laṅkeśa	4. Viśārada
5. Kapāli	6. Matta.
7. Magaḍavya	8. Bhāskara.
9. Śūrasena	10. Ratnaghoṣa.
11. Śambhu	12. Sāttvika.
13. Naravāhana	14. Indrada.
15. Gomukha	16. Kambali.
17. Vyāḍi	18. Nāgārjuna.
19. Surānanda	20. Nāgabodhi.
21. Yaśodhana	22. Khaṇḍa.
23. Kāpālika	24. Brahmā.
25. Govinda	26. Lampaka
27. Hari.	

The Ānanda Kanda also gives a list of Rasasiddhas. It also includes Nāgārjuna and Govinda, though the latter is referred to as Bālagovinda. A similar list[1] is given by Mādhava also.

The tradition about the efficacy of the processed mercury to give immortality to human body, is common to Buddhism also. Rāhula Sāṅkṛtāyana in an article published in the Gaṅgā in Saṁ. 1993 (1936 A. D.) mentions 84 Rasasiddhas. Among these also Nāgārjuna is mentioned.

It seems that many scholars and sages wrote on the efficacy of mercury and on the ways of processing it for various purposes. The Vāgbhaṭa Saṁhitā gives a list of eighteen writers on Rasa Tantra.

Two works on Rasa by Nāgārjuna, are referred to by Chinese traveller Hiuen Tsang. They are Rasa Ratnākara and Rasendra Maṅgala. There is another work on Rasa, called Kakṣāpuṭa, attributed to Nāgārjuna.

Rasārṇava, which has been edited by Profulla Chandra Ray, eulogises mercury and says that the liberation, promised by the six Schools of thought, is got only after death : but such is the efficacy of mercury that it brings liberation right in the life time. It brings the liberation objectively before the user, like an

1. S. D. S., 204.

Āmalaka on the palm. There is a list of twenty-five works on Rasa, given in S. D. S. (P.520-1). Besides these MSS. of about 70 books on Rasa have so far been discovered.

PROBABLE TIME OF RASEŞVARA DARŞANA

There is no reference to mercury in the Vedas. In the Ṛgveda only three metals are referred to, i.e. gold, silver and copper. In the Yajurveda "Kṛṣṇa Āyasa" (Iron) also is mentioned. And in the Atharva Veda compound metals such as brass etc. are referred to in addition to the above. It is unknown in the Brāhmaṇic literature also.

There is evidence to show that nickel was used for coinage by Indian tribes, Kṣudrakas and Mālavas[1] in the time of Alexander (4th century B. C.). Kṣudrakas are said to have presented to Alexander the Great hundred pieces of nickel coins along with so many other things[2]. Nickel was, therefore, known in India long before the Indo-Grecian dynasties, though in Europe it was first shown to be a metal by the researches of Cronstedt in 1751. But there is no evidence to show that mercury was known in India in the 4th century B. C.

We find reference to mercury in Suśruta for the first time as an ingredient in some plasters. There it is not recognised as capable of giving immortality. In Caraka also there is no such talk. It seems, therefore, that the Raseśvara system arose about the commencement of the Christian era, particularly because Nāgārjuna is a recognised authority on it and he was a contemporary of King Kanishka and is credited with the authorship of a commentary on Suśruta. It seems to have lived up to the time of Şaṅkara ; because Śaṅkara's teacher Bhagavad Govinda Pāda also is a recognised authority on it.

*1. A. I. N. 143—4 | *2. I. I. A. 252.

(VIII) MONISTIC ṢAIVAISM OF KASHMIR

The historical survey of the seven systems of the Śaiva Philosophy, dealt with so far, has shown :—

(i) that in the Veda, though different names of Śiva occur, yet there is no reference to any of the distinctive features of the Śaiva Philosophy ;

(ii) that it is in the Taittirīya Āraṇyaka that we find the Vedic basis of the Lakulīśa Pāśupata, which arose in the second century A. D ;

(iii) that if we believe in the tradition about the origin of the fourteen Sūtras, which we find at the beginning of Pāṇini's grammar, and admit that Patañjali refers to the view of Nandikeśvara, the Nandikeśvara Śaivaism, a voluntaristic monistic system, belongs to the 4th century B. C ;

(iv) that if we accept the view that the Nyāya and the Vaiśeṣika follow an earlier Pāśupata system, which is referred to by Bādarāyaṇa in his Vedānta Sūtra, the dualistic Pāśupata School also may be said to belong to about the 4th century B. C. ;

(v) that the Dualistic Siddhānta Śaivaism was reoriented and revitalised by the great writers, who flourished in different parts of India, such as Chola and Kashmir, from the 8th to the 12th century A. D. ;

(vi) that Śrīkaṇṭha propounded the Viśiṣṭādvaita Śaivaism in the 11th century A. D. ;

(vii) that the Vīra Ṣaivaism, as we find it in the available literature was reoriented and revitalised by Basava in 1167 A. D. and was subsequently propounded by the five well recognised teachers, Revaṇa etc. ; and

(viii) that the Raseśvara system is more a science than a school of philosophy and as such it follows dualistic Śaivaism and grew from the second to the 8th century A. D.

Thus, as far as we can trace back the history of the Saiva Philosophy , we discover the two currents, monistic and dualistic, running parallel. In the pre-Christian era we find the voluntaristic monism of Nandikesvara side by side with the realistic dualism of the Pāśupata school. And similarly from the 9th to the 13th century we find the monistic Śaivaism of Kashmir developing along with the Siddhānta Śaiva Dualism. The Monistic Śaivaism of Kashmir thus historically and fundamentally owes its origin to Nandikeśvara Śaivaism exactly as the Siddhānta Śaiva Dualism does to the Pāśupata Dualism.

The two systems occupy the central position in the history of the Śaiva Philosophy, systematising logically what had been thought and said on the two systems by their respective authorities. But the Monistic Śaiva Philosophy of Kashmir attained predominance ;

(1) because the writers on it evolved out a system in terms of which every field of experience could be explained ;

(2) because they approached the problem of metaphysics from the psycho-epistemic point of view, in contrast to the traditional, which was stuck to by others ;

(3) because it was taken up for exposition by such an encyclopaedic thinker as Abhinavagupta, who applied its technique to explain not only the empirical and the transcendental experiences, but also the Aesthetic.

There is no room for any controversy about the dates of the authors of the works on the Monistic Śaivaism of Kashmir, because Abhinavagupta, in contrast to the writers in Sanskrit in general, mentions the dates of composition of three of his works. In relation to him, therefore, the dates of his predecessors and successors can definitely be fixed. The history of this school has been written at some length in Abhinavagupta : An Historical and Philosophical Study; and it has been summarised in the History of Philosophy, Eastern and Western, Vol. I, pages 382 ff. The reader may refer to them. We, therefore, need not present the historical approach to this system here.

PART II

PHILOSOPHICAL APPROACH

PRELIMINARY

The Veda, by common consent, is the earliest literary monument that humanity possesses. It is the presupposition of all currents of thought, religious, cultural and philosophical, which we find to-day. In tracing the historical development of any aspect of Indian life, therefore, beginning has to be made with early references to it in the Veda. Therein we find the foundations, on which almost all the systems of thought, with which we are familiar to-day, have been built. And if we use the word "Veda" for the entire literature from the Saṁhitā, collection of hymns, to the Upaniṣads, we find in it a fairly complete picture of the evolution of the earliest human thought from mythology to complex philosophical systems.

The Veda, as representing "Brahmanism", is prior to the Jainism and the Buddhism, which developed in antagonism to the Vedic ritualism. It is prior to the materialistic school of the Cārvāka or Lokāyatika, which denies all spiritual values and, therefore, ridicules the Veda, presenting it to be nothing more than the creation of buffoons, knaves and demons. It is the authority on which the six well known Vedic systems of Indian Philosophy are based. Vaiṣṇavaism, though it acknowledges the Pañcarātra Āgama as the authoritative basis of the system, holds that there is no antagonism between the teaching of the Veda and that of the Pañcarātra Āgama and interprets the Vedic texts so as to show that they maintain the Vaiṣṇava doctrines. All the eight systems of the Śaiva Philosophy, dealt with earlier here from the historical point of view, though they are based primarily on the Śaivāgama, trace their fundamentals to the Vedas, Brāhmaṇas and Upaniṣads. And the authoritative works on them very often quote from the Veda to show that the particular doctrine, under discussion, is in consonance with the Vedic teaching.

Art, religion and philosophy are closely connected. They constitute the final triad of the Hegelian system. Art is the thesis, religion the antithesis and philosophy the synthesis.

Opinions may differ about the exact nature of the relation of one of this triad, with the other, as Croce differs from Hegel on the relation of art and religion as thesis and antithesis. But religion seems to be an artistic conception of the phenomena of nature. This can very definitely be said with regard to religions that have grown on Indian soil. In the Vedas we find phenomena of nature artistically conceived as gods, which are recognised as the objects of religious worship. The earlier hymns of the Ṛgveda are addressed to the shining sun, the gleaming moon in the nocturnal sky, the fire, blazing on the hearth or on the altar or even the lightning, shooting forth from the cloud, the bright sky of day, or the starry sky of night, the roaring storms, the flowing waters of rivers , the glowing dawn and the spread-out fruitful earth. All these natural phenomena are, as such, glorified, worshipped and invoked. Only gradually is accomplished, in the songs of the Ṛgveda itself, the transformation of these natural phenomena into mythological figures, into gods and goddesses such as Sūrya (Sun), Soma (Moon), Agni (Fire), Dyaus (Sky), Maruts (Storms), Vāyu (Wind), Āpas (Waters), Uṣas (Dawn), and Pṛthivī (Earth), whose names still indubitably indicate what they originally were. So the songs of the Ṛgveda prove indisputably that the most prominent figures of mythology have proceeded from personifications of the most striking natural phenomena.

In the context of the Śaiva Philosophy the question would, therefore, arise: which phenomenon of nature is the basis of this philosophy? And we get a clear reply to it from the Ṛgveda. Śaivaism, as a religion, has sprung from the poetic conception of the terrific aspect of nature. For, if we try to trace the origin of the conception of Rudra, the earliest of the names of Śiva, we find that Rudra is the storm-god, because he is the father of storm-gods (the Maruts)[1].

This conception of Rudra is subsequently developed in mythology. The Vaiśeṣika system recognises four types of beings, belonging to the four elements, earth, water, fire and air, and holds that airy beings are Bhūta, Preta and Piśāca. And mythology represents Rudra as the Lord of Bhūtas, "Bhūtanātha". The science of control of vital air is attributed to Rudra, because it is concerned with air. Bhāsa in his Pratimā Nāṭaka refers to this tradition, when he talks of Māheśvaram yoga śāstram. Aestheticians have called the "terrific" basic emotion after Rudra. They have given it the name 'Raudra' and recognise Rudra to be its god.

---

[1] Wint., Vol. I, 77.

But closer observation of the terrific aspect of nature revealed that the apparently destructive and, therefore, terrific aspect of nature, the storm, is ultimately beneficial. It brings rains, on which the agricultural life and, therefore, the very existence of men and animals mostly depends. Therefore, the storm-god was soon conceived as "Śiva" (auspicious or propitious) and "Paśupati" (the lord of cattle). And in the Yajurveda, Rudra is spoken of as the Lord of all the three worlds (Jagatām pati, Yaju. XVI, 18).

This Vedic conception of Rudra as Paśupati is the basis of the two Pāśupata systems :—

(*i*) Dualistic, which was followed by Gautama and Kaṇāda; and

(*ii*) Dualistic-cum-monistic, which was presented by Lakulīśa and is known as Lakulīśa Pāśupata. And the two words which constitute one of names of Śiva "Paśupati", in the Vedic period, become the names of the two highest categories, (I) Pati, and (II) Paśu in the two Pāśupata systems and are admitted as such in the three Siddhanta Saiva systems of philosophy : (i) the Śaiva, which is a dualistic system, as we know from Mādhava's presentation of it in his Sarva Darśana Saṅgraha; (ii) the Śaiva Viśiṣṭādvaita of Śrīkaṇṭha ; and (iii) the Śaiva Viśeṣādvaita of Śrīpati Paṇḍita.

THE BASIS OF THE ARRANGEMENT OF THE SYSTEMS

A history of Saiva Philosophy, presenting the various known systems in a chronological order, such as may be beyond all controversies, and showing the logical evolution of a later school from an earlier one, is well nigh impossible. For, very few of the Śaivāgamas, on which many of the Śaiva systems are based, are available either in print or in MSS. Those which have been printed are mere copies of the MSS. They have not been critically edited. And those which are yet in MSS. are in so many different scripts that it is extremely difficult to make full use of them. Many of them have not so far been even traced. The same is true of most of the commentaries on them, which were actually written, as we know from references to them in many of the available works on Śaivaism . It is no less true of many of the philosophical works, which were written on the basis of the Śaivāgamas, and references to which we very often come across in the available works. Out of the several systems of Śaiva Philosophy, at least one is such as we know from references only ; that is the dualistic Pāśupata, which we know from Śaṅkara's criticism, and indirect references to it by Haribhadra Sūri and Rājaśekhara. The dates of many of the important writers cannot be fixed beyond doubt.

It was probably because of the reasons, stated above, that no History of Philosophy was attempted by thinkers in India before the British period. Thinkers, like Mādhava, Haribhadra Sūri and Rājaśekhara etc. put together various systems of Indian Philosophy, but on a basis other than the historical. Mādhava seems to have arranged the systems in a logical order. His presentation of a following system is prefaced with a criticism of the preceding. Haribhadra Sūri, according to his own statement, has recognised six systems only as the basic. The difference of one system from another, he holds, is due either to the deity, by whom it was revealed, or the conception of the categories[1].

All the eight systems, with which we are concerned here, have been revealed by Śiva. They, therefore, constitute one group. And if we are to speak on them in a logical order, we should begin with the dualism and pass on to the monism, through the Dualism-cum-monism. Out of the eight Śaiva systems, that we know, two are Dualistic. One of these had its adherents all over India from the 9th to the 12th century A. D. and was propounded by great thinkers, such as Sadyojyoti, Bṛhaspati and King Bhoja etc. We call this system Siddhānta Śaiva Dualism, for reasons to be stated in the course of the presentation of it. The tradition of this was unbroken from the time of Ruru, the founder of an Āgamic school, incorporated in the Rauravāgama, to the time of Sadyojyoti, whose works are available. And the other, the Pāśupata, belongs to the pre-Christian era, because it is presupposed by Lakulīśa Pāśupata, which arose in the first half of the Second century A. D.

In our arrangement of the Saiva systems in a logical order we give the first place to the Pāśupata Dualism, not because of the historial priority of the Pāsupata to the Siddhānta Saiva, but because we have no independent work presenting this system. We know it from references only. And logically Pāśupata Dualism seems to be prior to Siddhānta Saiva Dualism, because while the former admits five independent

1 S. D. Sam., 4.

categories, the latter admits only three, eliminating the two, Yoga and Vidhi, which are not philosophical categories but only the means to the attainment of the final emancipation.

After the two Dualistic Śaiva Schools, we come to the Lakulīśa Pāśupata, which is a Dualistic-cum-monistic (Bhedābheda) School. There is sufficient literature available on it. Then we come to the Viśistādvaita Śaivaism of Śrīkaṇṭha, which both historically and logically comes after the Dvaita and the Dvaitādvaita Schools. Next we deal with the Viśeṣādvaita of Śrīpati Paṇḍita for the same reason. Then we come to a monistic system, the Nandikeśvara Śaivaism. The Raseśvara Śaivaism has been put thereafter, because it is more a science than philosophy. And finally we deal with the Monistic Śaivaism of Kashmir, because it presents the crowning phases of the Śaiva Philosophy.

ŚAIVA DUALISM.

The Śaiva Dualism originally was propounded in the following ten Śaivāgamas :—

(1) Kāmaja; (2) Yogaja; (3) Cintya; (4) Kāraṇa; (5) Ajita; (6) Dīpta; (7) Sūkṣma; (8) Sahasra; (9) Aṁśumān; and (10) Suprabheda.

Though the system, presented in these Āgamas, admits three primary categories : (1) Pati, (2) Paśu, (3) Pāśa; and, therefore strictly speaking, it should be called "Pluralism", yet we have stuck to the word "Dualism", because Abhinavagupta, in his division of the Śaivāgamas into three groups, as the bases of three primary systems of the Śaiva Philosophy, puts the above stated ten Āgamas under the head "Dvaita". This school is different from the Siddhānta School of Śaiva Dualism. For, the Siddhānta School is based on the Twenty-eight Śaivāgamas, ten of the Dualistic School, and Eighteen of the Dualistic-cum-monistic school, which are the following :—

1. Vijaya,	7. Santāna,	13. Visara,
2. Niśvāsa,	8. Nārasiṁhaka,	14. Raurava,
3. Madgīta,	9. Candrāṁśu,	15. Vimala,
4. Pārameśvara,	10. Vīrabhadra,	16. Kiraṇa,
5. Mukhabimba,	11. Āgneya,	17. Lalita,
6. Siddha,	12. Svāyambhuva,	18. Saurabheya.

But the Śaiva Dualism is based on the ten Āgamas only.

It is very disappointing to find that no work, which is exclusively based on the ten Dualistic Śaivāgamas, is traceable.

The summary of the Dualistic Śaivaism, that we find in the Sarvadarśana Saṅgraha, under the title "Śaiva Darśana" is a presentation of Śaiva Dualism, based upon the authority of the Twenty-eight Śaivāgamas, including the Ten of the Dualistic and Eighteen of the Dualistic-cum-monistic group, which constitute the basis of the Siddhānta School. For, Mādhava refers not only to the Mṛgendrāgama, which is a part of the Kāmika, referred to above in the list of the Dualistic Śaivāgamas, but also to the Kiraṇa and the Saurabheya, which belong to the Dualistic-cum-monistic group, given above. He also refers to the Tattva Saṅgraha of Sadyojyoti, Tattva Prakāśikā of Bhoja, and the commentary on the Tattva Prakāśikā by Aghora Śiva, which are recognised authorities on the dualistic branch of the Siddhānta School.

That the Eighteen Śaivāgamas have a non-dualistic trend mixed up with the Dualistic, is clear from the fact that the twenty-eight Śaivāgamas, on which the Siddhānta School is based, have been interpreted by Śrīkaṇṭha to propound the Viśiṣṭādvaita Śaivaism in his commentary on the Brahma Sūtra; and Śrīpati Paṇḍita has similarly interpreted them to propound the Viśeṣādvaita in his Śrīkara Bhāṣya on the Vedānta Sūtra. It is interesting to find out how the Śaiva Dualism, as presented on the basis of the Twenty-eight Śaivāgamas differs from that, found in the admittedly dualistic Śaivāgamas. We have fortunately most of the Dualistic Śaivāgamas before us; some in print, such as Mṛgendra etc.; others in MSS., such as Sūkṣma and Ajita etc.; and still others in scripts other than the Devanāgarī, such as Kāraṇa, Suprabheda and Yogaja etc. But it is too big a topic to attempt in the introduction. We shall present the Śaiva Dualism on the basis of these Āgamas in the projected History of Śaiva Philosophy.

(I) PĀŚUPATA DUALISM

SALIENT FEATURES OF THE PĀŚUPATA DUALISM

The Pāśupata Dualism is the philosophic interpretation of the Vedic conception of God Rudra as Paśupati. In fact, two out of the five primary categories, admitted by this system, are elaborations of the two ideas, represented by the two words, constituting the name "Paśupati" ; and the first two categories are called "Pati" and "Paśu" or Kāraṇa and Kārya [1]. The individual souls are conceived to be under the control of and dependent on the Lord (Pati), exactly as are animals, dogs for instance, under the control of their master, hunter for instance, who holds them by chains.

The Pāśupata metaphysics seems to be the earliest. Its metaphysical theory, which is based upon the conception of the uncaused cause, was adopted by both, the Nyāya and the Vaiśeṣika. For, according to Haribhadra Sūri, Kaṇāda was a Pāśupata and Akṣapāda was a Śaiva. The former was earlier than the latter, who follows the metaphysical view of the former. It is presupposed by the Vedānta, because Bādarāyaṇa in his Vedānta Sūtra criticises it. It admits the material cause to be distinct from and independent of the efficient. It asserts the relation between the efficient cause and the material to be the same as exists between a potter and clay. It seems to be prior to the Buddhism and the Jainism. For, it is a presupposition of the Vaiśeṣika; and the Buddhist theory of Nirvāṇa is traced to the Asatkāryavāda of the Vaiśeṣika and the Astikāyas of the Jains, as well as their atomic theory are traced to the Vaiśeṣika, which is mentioned in many jain works and in the Lalitavistara[2].

We have no literature, presenting the Dualistic Pāśupata school, which, on the basis of references to it, we are speaking of as prior to the Vaiśeṣika. We, therefore, do not know the details of its metaphysical theory.

But if we put together what we find in the references to it by Śaṅkara, in the course of his commentary on the Vedānta Sūtra, and by his commentators such as Vācaspati and Ānandagiri,

1 P. Su. 6.

*2 I. Ph. Vol. II, 177.

we get a fairly clear idea of the fundamentals of the Pāśupata Dualism, which may be stated as follows :—

1—It admitted the Lord (Pati) to be the efficient cause only. It asserted the independent existence of the material cause, as we have already stated above.

2—It admitted the five primary categories : (1) Cause (Kāraṇa);(2) Effect (Kārya); (3) Union (Yoga); (4)Ritual (Vidhi); (5) Liberation as the end of all pains (Duḥkhānta).

These categories are common to the Lakulīśa Pāśupata, which is distinct from the Pāśupata. For, the former is Dualistic-cum-monistic and the latter is Dualistic. This view is supported by the two Śaiva commentators on the Vedānta Sūtra, Śrīkaṇṭha and Śrīpati Paṇḍita, both of whom refute pure Dualism, and assert that the system criticised by Bādarāyaṇa is a Dualistic Śaiva system.

3—It seems to have put under the Kārya the categories from Mahān to Earth, which are admitted by the Sāṅkhya, as dependent categories. These categories are admitted by the Lakulīśa Pāśupata also, but as the sub-divisions of 'Kalā', one of the three dependent categories, Vidyā, Kalā and Paśu.

4—It seems to have admitted Pradhāna as the material cause, separate from the Lord (Pati) the efficient cause.

5—It accepted the individual souls to be co-eternal with both the causes, the material and the efficient, a view which has been retained by the Vaiśeṣika.

6—It seems to have admitted that the Lord, in the creation of the diversity of the empirical world, is influenced by Karma.

7—It recognised the liberation (Mokṣa) to be nothing more than the end of all pains. The last two points also have been retained by the Vaiśeṣika.

(II) SIDDHĀNTA ŚAIVA DUALISM

The Siddhānta Śaiva Dualism, that is presented here, is an aspect of the Siddhānta school of Śaivaism, which admitted the authority of the Twenty-eight Śaivāgamas, as has already been stated. If we compare its fundamentals with those of the other systems of Indian Philosophy, we find that it has fundamental differences from the Vaiśeṣika, the Nyāya, the Sāṅkhya and the Vedānta.

SIDDHĀNTA ŚAIVA DUALISM AND THE VAIŚEṢIKA

(1) The metaphysical theory of the Siddhānta Śaiva Dualism is different from that of the Vaiśeṣika. It accepts the theory of evolution which is similar to that of the Sāṅkhya. It holds that the Māyā evolves, abandons a former state to assume a later ; just as milk does to assume the state of curd.

It is Satkāryavāda. It holds that the existing curd becomes manifest (Abhivyajyate). Accordingly it asserts that the Māyā evolves into Kalā etc. as milk does into curd. But the Māyā does not exhaust itself in its evolute as does milk in curd. The evolution is partial, just as change in Ghee, because of the fall of an insect into it, is only in a small quantity of it[1] (Ghṛtakīṭa-nyāya). Thus, it is Satkāryavāda, as opposed to the Asatkāryavāda of the Vaiśeṣika.

(2) Karma, according to the Dualistic Siddhānta Śaivaism, is a quality of Buddhi[2] and not of the Ātman as the Vaiśeṣika holds. For, to admit Karma to be a quality of Ātman is to admit it as transient, because of the changes, due to the changing Karma.

(3) Similarly Kāla, according to the Dualist Siddhānta Śaiva is non-eternal, because it is insentient and many, such as present, past and future[3]. For, whatever has insentiency and multiplicity is transient. But the Vaiśeṣika admits "Time" to be eternal.

(4) It differs from the Vaiśeṣika (I) in holding the Ākāśa to be 'space' wherein all material things exist, and (II) in asserting that the sound (Śabda) is not the quality of Ākāśa only, as the

1 R. T. 17-18.
2 T. P. 36.
3 T. P. 37.

Vaiśeṣika holds, but of earth, air, water and fire also, because the peculiar sounds are actually found in them[1].

It may be pointed out here, by the way, that because of the aforesaid conception of Ākāśa, the Siddhānta Śaiva Dualism differs (*a*) from the Cārvāka, who denies the existence of Ākāśa ; (*b*) from the Mīmāṁsaka, who holds that it is perceptible, and (*c*) from the Naiyāyika, who maintains that it is eternal in so far as it has an eternal being and does not owe its being to the Tanmātras.

(5) It does not admit eternal atoms[2], as do the Vaiśeṣika and the Nyāya. For, according to the Dualistic Siddhānta Śaivaism, all that has insentiency and multiplicity is transient.

(6) It holds that the individual soul is essentially sentient (Cit) or sentiency itself (Jñānasvarūpa). The Jñāna, therefore, is not a quality of the self as the Vaiśeṣika maintains.

THE SIDDHĀNTA ŚAIVA DUALISM AND THE SĀṄKHYA

The Siddhānta Śaiva Dualism differs from the Sāṅkhya on the following important points:—

(1) It does not admit that Puruṣa or individual self is originally pure, (Puṣkarapalāśavannirlepaḥ) as the Sāṅkhya maintains. It asserts that the self has beginningless impurities. For, otherwise the empirical experience, due to the tendency to enjoy, cannot be explained. But if it (the tendency to enjoy) be said to be inherent in the self, it would be difficult to explain why the liberated do not have it[3]. The Sāṅkhya cannot say that the tendency to enjoy is due to Rāga or attachment. For, the attachment (Rāga) can function in relation to that self only which is impure.

(2) Its conception of Bhoga is different from that of the Sāṅkhya, which may be stated as follows :—

Bhoga[4] involves the following four :—

(I) Puruṣa, identified with its reflection, falling on the Buddhi.

---

1 T. San., 4-5.
2 T. San., 5.
3 Bh. Ka., 3.
4 I. P. V. V. Vol. I, 153.

(II) Buddhi, which receives the reflection of Puruṣa from within and that of the object from without.

(III) The reflection of object on the Buddhi.

(IV) Ahaṅkāra[1] which is responsible;

(*a*) for the unification of the two reflections of the subject and the object;

(*b*) for identification of the reflection of the subject with the subject itself;

(*c*) for the use of this union of the subject and the object for practical purposes;

(*d*) for the rise of consciousness "I know this".

THE PROCESS

1. The Buddhi receives the reflection of the object from without.

2. The reflection of the subject comes from within.

3. Ahaṅkāra unites them.

4. The two reflections merge into each other.

5. The object shines. This shining of the object, because of union with the reflection of the subject, is the culminating point of the process, described so far. Hence it is spoken of as the fruit of the cognitive activity. It is called Jñāna.

Union of the reflections of the subject and the object, when used for practical purposes by Ahaṅkāra through giving rise to the consciousness "I know this", which refers the object to the subject without recognising the difference between the subject and its reflection, is called *Bhoga*, because it involves union of the two reflections in the common ground of the Buddhi and also because the consciousness, that has been aroused by Ahaṅkāra, has the common substratum with the reflection of the Puruṣa.

But the Siddhānta Śaiva Dualism holds that *Bhoga* is the awareness of the modifications of the Buddhi, involved in the judgements about external pleasure or pain, by the sentient self. It is a mere awareness of the affected Buddhi by the self. It does not involve real affection of the self by the modifications of the Buddhi. In *Bhoga*, the self is in contact with the affected Buddhi exactly as the moon is with the water wherein her

1. I. P. V. V., Vol. I, 155.

reflection falls. Accordingly it maintains that the sentient self is the enjoyer and, therefore, doer, and that the Buddhi is not the doer, because it is objective and insentient[1].

THE SIDDHĀNTA ŚAIVA DUALISM AND THE VEDĀNTA

The Siddhānta Śaiva Dualism differs from the Vedānta on the following points :—

(1) It denies the identity of the individual souls with the Universal Self, and asserts that they are innumerable and are distinct from the Brahman, though they are dependent on the Lord[2] for both, the enjoyment of the fruits of action (Karma) and the liberation. Accordingly it holds that all the Vedic texts, which are interpreted by the Vedāntin as propounding the identity of the individual and the Universal, admit of dualistic interpretation.

(2) It admits the material cause of the universe to be distinct from the efficient, and criticises the Vedāntin, who asserts that the Brahman is both. For, the effect can have those characteristic attributes only which belong to the cause and, therefore, if the Brahman be held to be the cause of both the sentient and the insentient, it (Brahman) will have to be admitted to be both[3].

(3) It criticises the monism of the Vedānta. For, the monism is inconsistent with the Vedāntin's assertion that the knowledge of the Brahman is the means to Liberation. It asks : where is the room for talk about the means and the end in extreme monism ?

(4) It asks : how can the Vedānta assert that the Brahman is characterised by pure being, sentiency and bliss ? For, the characteristics shine in relation to that which is distinct and separate from that which possesses them. For instance, the heat of fire becomes manifest in relation to wood only. Therefore, if in reality there be nothing external to the Brahman its characteristics cannot shine[4].

---

1 Bh. Ka. 39.
2 R. T. 8.
3 M. Ka. 12.
4 S. P. 25.

In the same way the Siddhānta Śaiva Dualism differs from and criticises every other system, because it flourished at a time when almost every system of Indian philosophy had taken a definite shape. Some of the important works on it definitely, openly and purposively take up the refutation of other systems: for instance, the Para Mokṣa Nirāsa Kārikā by Sadyojyoti, which has no other end in view than the refutation of the conception of Mokṣa of every known system.

THE PĀŚUPATA DUALISM AND THE SIDDHĀNTA ŚAIVA DUALISM

The Siddhānta Śaiva Dualism is distinct from the Pāśupata Dualism. The latter admits the five primary categories: (1) Kāraṇa, (2) Kārya; (3) Yoga; (4) Vidhi; and (5) Duḥkhānta. But the former admits three only: (1) Pati, (2) Paśu, and (3) Pāśa. It seems that the Siddhānta Śaiva Dualism and the earlier Śaiva Dualism which it represents, both were influenced by the Pāśupata system, which seems to be earlier. For, the Siddhānta Śaiva Dualism seems to have borrowed the conception of Kāraṇa, the uncaused cause, from the Pāśupata and to have called it 'Pati', because there is no conceptual difference between Kāraṇa and Pati. The difference is verbal only. For, in the Pāśupata Sūtra by Lakulīśa, we find the word "Pati" used for Kāraṇa[1].

At the present state of our information about the Pāśupata system, which is based upon Śaṅkara's reference to it, we do not know exactly what was the conception of the material cause, admitted by the Pāśupata. But if we follow the Ratna Prabhā, we are led to think that it was 'Pradhāna' (Kāraṇam Pradhānam Īśvaraśca). It also talked of Paśu and Pāśa. For, Śaṅkara in stating the purpose of propounding the five categories definitely says that it was to bring about the freedom of the individual self (Paśu) from bondage (Pāśa) (Paśupāśa-vimokṣaṇāya). It seems, therefore, that the Siddhānta Śaiva Dualism was influenced by the Pāśupata Dualism in the conception of the two categories: (1) Paśu and (2) Pāśa.

The Siddhānta Śaiva Dualism accepted the metaphysical theory of the Pāśupata, namely, that the material cause is different from the efficient. But it improved upon the conception of the liberation. For, while the liberation, according to the Pāśupata, consisted in the end of all pains, the Siddhānta Śaiva Dualism held that it was the attainment of similarity, in respect of powers of knowledge and action, with Śiva. Thus, it seems to have reoriented the earlier Pāśupata Philosophy.

1 P. Su. 6.

THE SIDDHANTA SAIVA DUALISM AND THE PHILOSOPHY OF GRAMMAR

The Philosophy of Grammar, which deals with the various aspects of speech, such as Parā, Paśyantī, Madhyamā and Vaikharī, and allied problems, is traced to the Vedic passages, such as:

(1) "Catvāri vākparimitā Padāni"; and

(2) "Catvāri śṛṅgāstrayo asya pādā"

which are quoted by Patañjali in his Mahābhāṣya. It may be pointed out here that there is difference of opinion between Kaiyaṭa and Nāgeśa Bhaṭṭa in the interpretation of these Vedic texts. For, while the former interprets the word "Catvāri" as referring to four kinds of words : (1) noun, (2) verb, (3) preposition (upasarga) and (4) particle (Nipāta) ; the latter holds that it refers to the four aspects of speech, stated above.

The well recognised work on it, is the Vākyapadīyam of Bhartṛhari. But Bhartṛhari himself declares that what he presents is based on an ancient tradition. He traces the tradition back to Pāṇini. He refers to a work, covering one lakh of Granthas, written by Vyāḍi, to expound the system of Pāṇini[1]. This work, however, was lost due to the neglect of it by the students of Grammar, because of its big size. Patañjali, therefore, in order that the tradition of 'Vyākaraṇa Smṛti' may not be broken, wrote his Mahābhāṣya, which closely followed the work of Vyāḍi. The followers of Patañjali, however, lost touch with it. The Mahābhāṣya, therefore, remained only in a book in South India. Thus again the tradition of the system of Grammar was lost.

Some time later a Brahmarākṣasa brought the original Vyākaraṇāgama, written by Rāvaṇa, from a place in Triliṅga in the mountain Trikūṭa, to Candrācārya and Vasurāta, who after properly understanding it expounded it in many ways to their pupils. Vasurāta, the teacher of Bhartṛhari, wrote a digest of the said Vyākaraṇāgama. Bhartṛhari's Vākyapadīyam is based on the same. It consists of three chapters : (1) Brahmakāṇḍa; (2) Vākyakāṇḍa and (3) Padakāṇḍa.

Bhartṛhari and his critic, Somānanda, the founder of the Recognitive (Pratyabhijñā) School of Śaivaism in Kashmir, both present the monistic tradition of the Philosophy of Grammar. But the Siddhānta Śaiva Dualism presents the Dualistic tradition of the same. According to the Siddhānta Śaiva

1 V. P. 283.

Dualism, the first category is the Śiva, which is also called Para Bindu. And the problem of the Philosophy of Grammar, concerning the four aspects of speech, is discussed in the context of this category. We shall revert to this topic in the course of our discussion on the Bindu. Rāma Kaṇṭha II in his Nāda Kārikā and Śrīkaṇṭha in his Ratna Traya deal with this problem from the Dualistic point of view.

THE CATEGORIES OF THE SIDDHĀNTA ŚAIVA DUALISM

The Siddhānta Śaiva Dualist's conception of the category is very closely connected with his conception of the universal annihilation (Mahārtha Saṁhāra). He holds that a category[1] (Tattva) is that which persists even when there is the universal annihilation, and is a condition, directly or indirectly, of all the experiences, empirical or transcendental. And the universal annihilation is that in which all that is the product of Māyā[2] or Mahāmāyā merges back into its material cause and has its being therein in the state of non-difference, of unity, which is a mere potentiality for diversity. He admits that the creation is of two types: (1) Pure (Śuddha); and (2) Impure (Aśuddha), and that the Māyā also is of two types; one, the products of which are the necessary conditions of the empirical experiences: this is called Māyā; and the other, the products of which are the equally necessary conditions of the transcendental experiences, which the transcendental subjects, like Mantra, Mantreśa and Mantra Maheśa, have. This is called Mahāmāyā. Accordingly he holds that at the universal annihilation all that constitutes the material condition of any experience, merges back into the Śakti, one of the dependent categories, on which we shall write in the proper context: and the Śakti merges back into the Mahāmāyā.

Thus, the Siddhānta Śaiva Dualist holds that there are only three Primary categories: (1) Māyā or, to state more accurately, Mahāmāyā, (2) Puruṣa and (3) Śiva[3].

It may be pointed out here that the conception of these categories is based upon metaphysical view: and that when the metaphysical thought does not dominate in the mind of an exponent of the system, these categories are called by different names: (1) Pati (2) Paśu and (3) Pāśa. And though there is no difference in the ideas when the word Pati is substituted for Śiva, and Paśu

1. T. P. 56.
2. T. P. 53.
3. T. P. 54.

for Puruṣa: yet the conception underlying the word 'Mahāmāyā' is different from that, for which the word Pāśa stands. For, the Pāśa as a primary category, in the original conception of the triad of categories, is more comprehensive than Mahāmāyā. The Pāśa as an original primary category has five dependent categories (1) Mala, (2) Rodhaśakti, (3) Karma, (4) Māyā and (5) Bindu, which is also called Mahāmāyā. When, therefore, a writer on the Siddhānta Śaiva Dualistic School, substitutes the word Māyā or Mahāmāyā, by either of which he means all that is implied by both, Māyā and Bindu, as the dependent categories of Pāśa, he presents a very much narrower conception than that for which the word Pāśa stands.

Further, though the Dualistic Siddhānta School admits three primary categories[1], (1) Pati, (2) Paśu and (3) Pāśa : yet it also talks of Thirty-six categories. But they are dependent categories of the above three. That is as follows :—

The first category is sub-divided into five : (1) Śiva, (2) Śakti (3) Mantra-maheśa (4) Mantreśa and (5) Mantra.

The second category, Paśu, though sub-divided into three:-- (1) Vijñānākala, (2) Pralayākala and (3) Sakala—is yet counted as only one category. Its sub-divisions are not included in the *thirty-six categories*.

The third category, Pāśa, is sub-divided into five : (1) Mala, (2) Rodhaśakti, (3) Karma, (4) Māyā and (5) Bindu. But none of these, excepting the Māyā, is counted in the thirty-six categories. The number Thirty-six is made up by adding the twenty nine sub-divisions of Māyā. From the Māyā in the descending order the succeeding evolves out of the preceding. The order may be stated as follows :—

(1) Kalā, (2) Kāla, (3) Niyati, (4) Rāga, (5) Vidyā and the twenty-four categories of the Sāṅkhya.

Thus, it tries to talk of the thirty-six categories of the monistic Kashmir Śaivaism. Probably, this is done to justify the interpretation of the passages in the non-dualistic Āgamas in the dualistic light. It may, however, be pointed out here that the authorities on the Siddhānta Śaiva Dualism differ in the conception of the dependent categories.

THE PRIMARY AND THE DEPENDENT CATEGORIES

The Siddhānta Śaiva Dualism maintains two sets of categories: (1) Primary and (2) Dependent. The primary categories are three:

---

1 T. P. 6.

(1) Pati, (2) Paśu and (3) Pāśa. These seem to have been borrowed from the earlier Pāśupata Dualism, which admitted five categories: (1) Kāraṇa, (2) Kārya, (3) Yoga, (4) Vidhi and (5) Duḥkhānta. For, even according to the scanty information, that we can collect about the Pāśupata Dualism from the references, it is clear that it admitted the existence of Paśu and Pāśa ; because the categories are said to have been expounded to bring about the freedom of Paśus, the limited individual selves, from the Pāśa, the bondage (Paśu-Pāśa-Vimokṣaṇāya) : and the first category, the cause, (Kāraṇa), seems to have been inclusive of both the causes, the efficient and the material.

(Kāraṇam Pradhānam Īśvaraśca)

The Siddhānta Ṣaiva Dualism , therefore, seems to have adopted the first category, perhaps with the modification, that it excluded the conception of the material cause from the first category and maintained it to be nothing more than the Īśvara or Pati, the efficient cause. It brought the material cause under Pāśa, which it admitted to be an independent category, subsuming under it the five dependent categories, including Māyā, the material cause of the limited objective world. Thus, the five dependent categories of Pāśa, are admitted to be: (1) Mala, (2) Māyā, (3) Karma, (4) Nirodhaśakti and (5) Bindu. Similarly Paśu is admitted to be an independent category ; and three types of the limited subject, (1) Vijñānākala, (2) Pralayākala and (3) Sakala, are subsumed under it.

Thus, in the early stages in its development, the Siddhānta Ṣaiva Dualism, discarded the two religious categories: (1) Yoga; and (2) Vidhi, amalgamated the last, Duḥkhānta, with the first, the Pati ; adopted Paśu and Pāśa as independent categories; widened the conception of Pradhāna as Māyā and subsumed it under the Pāśa. Thus, it propounded the three primary categories.

The Siddhānta Ṣaiva Dualism seems to be the outcome of a tendency to separate philosophy from religion. For, this seems to be the possible reason for discarding the two religious categories of the Pāśupata Dualism. This tendency seems to have continued to develop. For, King Bhoja, in his Tattva Prakāśikā towards the end, talks of three categories, (1) Ṣiva or Pati, (2) Puruṣa or Paśu and (3) Māyā[1]; eliminating Pāśa, under which are included the five impurities, which are of importance from the ritualistic point of view ; and assuming Māyā, which is one of the impurities, as a separate category, which constitutes the material cause of the limited objective world.

1 T. P. 54.

The Pāśupata Dualism thus seems to have been the origin, not only of the Nyāya and the Vaiśeṣika, but also of the Siddhānta Śaiva Dualism. It seems to have been the source of the Yoga and the Sāṅkhya also. For, the Yoga also talks of the three fundamentals, (I) Iśvara, (II) Pradhāna and (III) Puruṣa: and the difference of the Yoga from the Sāṅkhya lies in the acceptance of the Īśvara besides Pradhāna and Puruṣa, which are common to both and seem to have been borrowed from the Pāśupata Dualism.

(I) PATI, THE TRANSCENDENTAL ŚIVA.

The Siddhānta Śaiva Dualism sticks to the cosmological and teleological arguments, according to the Kantian terminology, to prove the existence of God, who is called "Pati" in this system. If we consider "Pati" in relation to the Bindu, the metaphysical matter of this system, we find Him to be very much like "Prime Mover" as Aristotle has presented God. And if we consider God in relation to the meaningful multiplicity of the objective world, we find Him to be very similar to the Efficient Cause, (the Agent, the Kartā) as Anslem, Acquinas, Descartes, Leibniz and Wolff have conceived God. Similarly, if we consider God in relation to Karma, we find Him to be nothing more than a presupposition of Ethics, as Kant presented God.

Pati, as the first independent category of the Siddhānta Śaiva Dualism is the magnification of the idea of Paśupati as found in the Vedas. In the Veda, Pati was the Lord of cattle. In the Dualistic philosophy, He is magnified into the Lord of every thing. In the Veda He had the power of protecting cattle. In the Dualistic philosophy He is omnipotent.

He is one. He is all-pervasive, eternal, without beginning or end. He[1] is eternally free or liberated (Mukta). He is free from all impurities, such as natural likes and dislikes etc. He is 'graceful' to all. He is sentient. He is the prompter of all. His freedom is uncaused. He is the uncaused cause. He remains unchanged in spite of His creating the worlds; just as the Sun does in spite of his causing the opening of the lotuses[2]. He is the efficient cause. He creates the objective limited world out of the material cause, the Māyā, by means of His power, Śakti, the instrumental cause.

1 T. P. 2. | 2 R. T. 104.

Śakti[1], the power, is the means wherewith the Śiva effects or creates the world, where the bound souls suffer or enjoy the fruits of their past deeds, and finally brings about the liberation of the bound. It is one, though because of the varying conditions, constituted by what is to be effected, it appears to be many. It is essentially sentient and, therefore, does not undergo modifications like Māyā. It is the principal power and is inherent in Śiva.

In the Ratna Traya it is said to be related to Śiva as the rays are to the Sun[2]. It knows no obstruction. It is always operative in some form or another. It is limitless and, therefore, indeterminate. It does not owe its being to anything. It is self-shining. It is all-transcending. It is extremely subtle. It is also said to be non-different from Śiva, (Svaśaktyānanyabhūtayā R. T. 42) and yet the difference between Śiva and Śakti[3] is recognised to be similar to that of substance and attribute. The fact is that the dualistic tendency in the Siddhānta School is mixed up with the monistic; because it recognises the authority of the 18 Śaivāgamas, which present Bhedābheda, in addition to those which present Bhedavāda.

In the Ratna Traya the dualistic-cum-monistic tendencies of the Siddhānta are clear. It is asserted that the Śiva and the Śakti are essentially identical inasmuch as both are essentially Cit. But there is relational, functional or logical difference in so far as the Cit, resting on itself, is Śiva (Svaniṣṭha), but resting on the object in order to know it, Cit is Śakti : and as such they are conceived as substance and attribute (Dharmin and Dharma). The one is unrelated to anything external to itself (Parānapekṣa), but the other is related to the external objective world (Parāpekṣa). Just as the capacity of fire to burn becomes manifest in relation to fuel, so the Śakti of Śiva shows itself in relation to the objective world.

The Siddhāntin rejects the view of the Śaktyadvayavādin, who asserts that Śakti alone is the cause of the world and that Śiva is an unnecessary assumption. He justifies the admission of Śiva on the basis that Śakti is an attribute (Dharma) and as such it can have no existence without a substratum (Dharmin)[4].

Accordingly, Pati is very often spoken of as possessing two powers. For, the word 'Cit', according to this system, means

1 T. P. 5.
2 R.T. 68.
3 R. T. 100
4 R.T., 103.

the powers of knowledge and action: (Jñāna-kriyā-Śakti). Therefore, when it asserts that the transcendental Śiva is 'Cidghana'[1], it means that the powers of knowledge and action are to Him, what body is to the soul. The idea intended to be conveyed by this analogy is that just as the soul effects its purpose by means of the body, so God does by means of the powers.

Equally often His powers are said to be three: Will (Icchā) knowledge (Jñāna) and action (Kriyā)[2]; and also five: creation, maintenance, destruction, obscuration (Nirodha) and grace (Anugraha) on the basis of His characteristic five functions. These five powers, under the five names, Īśa, Tatpuruṣa, Sadyojāta, Vāma and Aghora, referred to in the Taittirīya Āraṇyaka, are spoken of as the five faces of the Lord (Pañcavaktra) and the Śaivāgamas are said to have proceeded from the five mouths of Śiva exactly as the Vedas are admitted to have proceeded from the four mouths of Brahmā. It is, however, asserted that all this is merely figurative and the object of this figurative presentation of powers is only to make contemplation on Him possible[3].

THE DIFFERENCE IN THE CONCEPTION OF POWERS EXPLAINED.

Pati is a substance with an attribute; and both substance and attribute are essentially sentiency (Cit). The Śakti is conceived in two ways : (I) that which persists in its operation even when there is no objective world, created or in the process of creation : and (II) that which is operative in relation to the objective world. The two powers, the power of knowledge and that of action, the omniscience and the omnipotence, are admitted to be in Pati even when there is not even the idea of the objective world.

This becomes clear if we remember that, according to this system, the three independent categories, Pati, Paśu and Pāśa, persist even in Mahāpralaya : and that Pāśa includes the Mahāmāyā or Bindu, the material cause. Thus, the two powers, the omniscience and the omnipotence, are the powers attributed to Pati as He is conceived to be in Mahāpralaya. The power of knowledge is operative in relation to Mahāmāyā, which exists even in Mahāpralaya : and the power of action is the presupposition to account for the creative activity at the time of fresh creation after Mahāpralaya.

1 T. P. 2.
2 T. P. 27.
3 T. P. 8.

The power of will is attributed to Pati, due to the monistic trend in the Eighteen out of the twenty-eight Śaivāgamas, the authority of which is accepted by even the Dualist Siddhānta Śaivas. The Will is attributed to Him, when the evolutionistic metaphysics is substituted by the voluntaristic : when the Pati is represented to create the objective world not as a potter creates a jar, but by means of his will (Saṅkalpa mātreṇa : Icchāmātreṇa) as we shall soon show.

And He is spoken of as possessing five powers, when He is conceived in relation to the objective world, as its creator, maintainer, destroyer, as one that affords opportunities to the impurities of the individual selves to attain maturity and as one that does grace to the bound souls.

POWERS OF THE LORD (PATI)

(1) THE POWER OF KNOWLEDGE—

The power of knowledge of the Lord works independently of the Buddhi[1]. It is unlike the cognitive power of the indivi dual subject. This power of Śiva[2] has always objective reference. For, it is related to the eternal Bindu, even when there is no objective world. Hence it is not transitory but eternal.

(2) THE POWER OF ACTION—

The power of action or omnipotence is the presupposition of the powers of creation etc., which are attributed to Him, when He is presented in relation to the objective world, as its creator etc. It is the potentiality which expresses itself in the five functions of Pati, which are spoken of as His powers.

(3) THE POWER OF WILL—

The power of Will is talked of, as stated earlier, under voluntaristic influence. It is said that Śiva pervades the Bindu[3] with His power and, therefore, all that is below. He is not pervaded by anything higher. He, therefore, knows and does everything.

He pervades everything inasmuch as he is related to everything in the manner in which the Ākāśa is to the material things. It is because of this pervasion that the objects have their origin and continuance. The creation takes place because of the mere

1 R.T., 98.
2 R.T., 99.
3 R. T., 42—3.

presence of this power in a determinate form (Saṅkalpa mātreṇa), exactly as the opening of a lotus takes place because of the mere 'presence' of the rays of the sun.

Here the Siddhāntin seems to deviate from the Sāṅkhya in talking of the creation as due to determinate[1] presence of this power "Saṅkalpamātreṇa", which ordinarily means "Icchāmātreṇa".

(4) THE POWER OF CREATION—

Power of creation consists in creating the bodies, the senses, the worlds and the objects out of Bindu and Māyā[2] and in uniting the souls, according as their impurities are mature or immature, with suitable bodies in order that they may have the experiences befitting their impurities. For a clear understanding of this power, it is necessary to remember that the creation is of two kinds : (1) the pure and (2) the impure.

THE PURE CREATION

(1) The pure creation (Śūddhādhva)[3] is the direct creation of Śiva. The material cause of this is Bindu. It consists of the pure categories and the pure worlds wherein the liberated live. Here some of the liberated, such as Vidyeśvaras are united with bodies. which are made up of Bindu. Here Vidyā evolves out of Bindu, through the successive stages of modification such as Nāda etc. Śiva or Pati has all-transcending, pure and eternal powers of knowledge and action in relation to everything. He, therefore, creates the pure world without having a body exactly as an individual self, independently of a body, produces stir (Spanda)[4] in his body. Further, the efficient cause must necessarily possess a body if his creative activity is related to an object, which is to be grasped by determinate knowledge. As the pure creation is not the object of determinate knowledge, therefore, a body for Śiva, to create the pure world, is unnecessary. The pure creation is characterised by indeterminacy ; because it belongs to a higher level than that at which language evolves. And because determinacy consists in the affection of "Citi" by the words i.e. so long as the affection of consciousness is not associated with the words, there is no determinacy. Therefore, the pure creation is said to belong to the level of indeterminacy,

1 R. T. 43.
2 S. P, 20-1.
3 T. P. 9..
4 R. T. 20.

because here the affection of consciousness by language is not possible.

THE IMPURE CREATION

(II) *The impure creation*[1] is the product of the creative activity, not of the Lord but that of Ananta etc. i.e. the Vidyeśvaras, who have been given the bodies, made up of Bindu, and to whom the power to create has been delegated by the Lord. It is called the impure world, because its material cause is the Māyā and also because herein the bound live. It is characterised by determinacy ; because it evolves after the evolution of language. We shall discuss this point under Bindu.

The omnipotence of the Lord, however, does not become limited because of the creative activity of Ananta etc.[2], because He is the prompter of Ananta etc.; and the creative power, which the creators of the impure creation have, is the one that is delegated to them by the Lord.

This conception of Pati and Ananta etc. as the Supreme Lord and the dependent ones, seems to have been the basis of the form of government, which we call monarchy : or, it may have been the other way. For, just as the power of a monarch does not get limited, because of the exercise of the governmental power by the territorial lords, so the creative power of the Lord does not get limited because it is exercised by dependent lords, Ananta etc. For, power in both the cases is delegated.

(5) THE POWER OF MAINTENANCE (STHITI ṢAKTI)

The created objects, according to this system, are not momentary. They persist as means of enjoying or suffering the fruits of past deeds (Karma). The power, which is responsible for the short continuous existence of the created, is called the power of maintenance. It is responsible not only for the continuity of the created, but also for the relation of the souls[3] in bondage with the objects to make the various types of experience possible, so that the innate impurities of the souls may attain maturity and make the operation of the power of Grace possible to bring about the liberation of the bound. The relation of the souls with the objective world is due, not to the power of maintenance alone but to the co-operation with it of the power of obscuration.

1 T. P. 9.
2 R. T. 19.
3 M. Ka. 18.

(6) THE POWER OF ANNIHILATION (SAṀHĀRA ŚAKTI)

The view of the universal annihilation, maintained by this system, differs from that of the Sāṅkhya, inasmuch as it holds that not only the triad of Guṇas merge into Prakṛti but that the latter also merges into Māyā and that too in Mahāmāyā or Bindu. In Mahāpralaya the three primary categories, Pati, Paśu and Bindu, only persist[1]. The power, which is responsible for such a universal annihilation, is called Saṁhāra śakti.

The creation, according to this system, is of two kinds, pure and impure. In the dissolution of the pure creation Vidyā etc. merge back into Śakti and the latter into the Bindu[2]. The Bindu even then has separate existence from the Parama Śiva or Pati. It does not get related to Him by the relation of Samavāya.

Similarly in the dissolution of the impure creation all the evolutes from the earth to Prakṛti merge into Māyā and that too merges into Mahāmāyā, as stated earlier.

The universal annihilation is brought about to give rest to tired souls and the material cause of the objective world, in order that they may gain vigour and start vigorous fresh life when the world is created again[3].

(7) THE POWER OF OBSCURATION (TIROBHĀVA)

Modification or change in everything necessarily depends upon contact with something that is external. The Prakṛti evolves, because of contact with the Puruṣa. Milk changes into curd because of contact with heat. The impurity that obscures the perfect powers of knowledge and action, which are innate in the individual, can, therefore, change and attain maturity due to some contact only i. e. the contact with the products of the Māyā. To bring about this contact in co-operation with the power of maintenance is the function of the power of obscuration[4]. The individual is thus put in the field, where he can reap the fruits of his action and, with His grace, sow the seed that produces the fruit, called liberation. The Kashmir Śaiva conception of the power of obscuration is very different from the above. This power of obscuration is referred to as Rodhaśakti, Nirodhaśakti, Tiro dhānaśakti or Tirobhāvaśakti. It is also spoken of as the power,

1 T. P. 54.
2 T. P. 53.
3 M. Ka. 18.—19.
4 S. P. 2.

which is responsible for obscuring the knowledge that the objective world is to be shunned[1].

(8) THE POWER OF GRACE (ANUGRAHA ŚAKTI)

It is the power of Grace[2], to which the liberation is ultimately due. It removes the impurity which hides the omnipotence and the omniscience, which are inherent in the individual. It requires the maturity of the Mala or impurity in order that it may be able to remove it. It is like a surgical instrument, which can remove the film from over the eye only when it has matured. It is a prompter as it were of the creative power; because the motive of the operation of the creative power is nothing but grace.

II PĀŚA, THE BONDAGE.

Pāśa, the bondage, which binds the souls and is responsible for the distinction of Paśu from Pati, is the second of the three primary categories of the system. It has five sub-categories: (1) Mala, (2) Māyā, (3) Karma, (4) Nirodhaśakti and (5) Bindu. The dependent categories of Pāśa are very closely connected with the conception of liberation. Karma and Māyā are the two bondages, admitted by the Vedāntin also, who asserts that liberation is freedom from the two aforesaid bondages. But this system holds that such a liberation is of the lower type, inasmuch as it is partial liberation. For, another bondage, Mala, which is also called Paśutva Mala, is still there.

It may be pointed out here that this system admits that there are at least three stages, through which the souls, free from the bondages of Māyā and Karma, have to pass before they can attain final emancipation. The souls, which are free from the said two impurities but still have the third, inclined towards disappearance, are called Vijñānākalas. And when these are given the subtle bodies, made up of Bindu, and are put at higher levels of Vidyā, Īśvara and Sadāśiva, they are known as Mantra, Mantreśa and Mantramaheśa respectively.

But there is lack of definiteness, precision and uniformity in the statements about Pāśa. The number of the dependent categories of Pāśa, ordinarily stated, is five. But very often Bindu is not included and the number is stated to be four[3]. And the reason for its non-inclusion is that of the two types of liberation, (I) Para (Higher) and (II) Apara (Lower), the latter is attained, even

1. S. P. 21.
2. T. P. 10.
3. T. P. 18.

when there is the bondage of Bindu. And the liberated souls with this bondage are the Mantra and the Mantreśa etc., who belong to the "pure creation".

Similarly Nirodha or Tirodhāna Śakti is spoken of as a bondage, but in a secondary sense only[1]. Of these four bondages Karma and Mala are beginningless. But Māyīya and Tirodhāyaka, which are often used for Māyā and Nirodhaśakti respectively, are the products of the Lord's power.

(1) MALA

Mala is beginningless[2]. It conceals the powers of knowledge and action of the self. It is one but has innumerable powers. It conceals the powers of knowledge and action of each individual by means of a separate power. Hence the removal of Mala from one individual does not mean the liberation of all.

It covers the individual much as husk covers the rice seed or as the black substance covers the copper. The Siddhānta Śaivas admit three impurities in common with Kashmir Śaivaism. One of these they often refer to by the simple name Mala. But it is clear from other texts that by this they mean the same thing as Āṇavamala. It is very often called Paśutva Mala. It can be removed by His grace only. The impurity, according to them, is of the nature of a substance, similar to the film over the eye (cakṣuḥ paṭala)[3]. (This view has been very adversely criticised by Abhinava in the Tantrāloka.)

The maturity (paripāka) of the impurity, which comes through undergoing the discipline, prescribed for the purpose in the sacred texts, is the necessary condition of the operation of the power of grace, exactly as the maturity of the film over the eye is the necessary condition of the surgical operation of the eye.

Mala or Paśutvamala is spoken of as Adhikārimala, when it is related to the beings, who are free from the two impurities, Karma and Māyā. It is called Ādhikārikamala, because it is on account of the presence of this in a state of advanced maturity that the powers of creation etc. in regard to the impure creation (Aśuddhādhva) are delegated to the beings, belonging to the level of Īśvara. They are eight in number and are called (1) Ananta (2) Sūkṣma, (3) Śivottama, (4) Ekanetra, (5) Ekarudra, (6) Trimūrti, (7) Śrīkaṇṭha and (8) Śikhaṇḍin. The Lord

1 T. P. 19.
2 T. P. 19.
3 S. P. 2.

removes their Mala with His grace, reveals their perfect powers of knowledge and action and puts them in charge of the impure creation[1].

(2) MĀYĀ

Māyā[2] is essentially of the nature of being. It is real and not unreal as the Vedānta maintains. It is the material cause of everything gross or subtle at the empirical level. Māyā, as a bondage means the effects of the Māyā[3] and as such it is very often called Māyīyamala.

The superimposition of the self on body and intellect etc. is due to Māyāmala[4], which is responsible for mistaking "not-this" as "this".

The mere absence of the consciousness of distinction between the two, as admitted by the Sāṅkhya, cannot account for identi fication of the self with Buddhi. For, that which is uncaused, does not admit of destruction. Therefore, if the absence of cons ciousness of distinction between self and not-self, be admitted to be without a cause, it would be indestructible and, therefore, it would be difficult to explain why it does not persist in the so called liberated. Hence Māyā as an impurity, which is the cause of mistaking 'not-this' as 'this' has to be admitted[5], so that the destruction of the mistake may be accounted for in terms of the destruction of its cause and the non-rise of the mistake in the liberated may logically be explained. We shall deal with Māyā, as a metaphysical category, in the proper context.

(3) KARMA

Karma, the individual destiny, the accumulated effect of the past deeds of each individual soul, is cyclically beginningless[6]. It determines the kind of body and senses, which the soul gets at rebirth, as also the determinate experiences and their objects, which each individual has. In short, it determines all associations of each soul[7]. It determines the creative activity of the Lord also, because He creates the world, consisting of bodies, means and objects of experiences, according to the sum total of Karma or destiny of each of the individual souls, who are to be born into it to enjoy or suffer the consequences of their past actions.

---

1 T. P. 12.
2 T. P. 20.
3 T. P. 18
4 R. T. 85
5 R. T. 85.
6 T. P. 20.
7 R. T. 85.

Karma is a recognition of the fact that human being cannot always correctly foresee the consequences of his action. It is a force that leads a Caesar or Hitler to the tragic end. It accounts for the lack of proportion between act and its fruit. It is an ethical principle: and the belief that there is no ultimate escape from the deed done, if used as the determining principle of individual action, surely improves the individual morally.

(4) NIRODHAŚAKTI OR TIROBHĀVA

Rodhaśakti or Nirodhaśakti is counted not only among the five Malas but also among the five powers of the Lord. And it is admitted that really speaking it is a power of the Lord and that it is spoken of as a dependent category of Pāśa, in a secondary sense[1], because it is a means by which the Lord, in co-operation with other impurities, brings the individual souls, by means of a chain as it were, to the experiences[2], which are their deserts.

(5) BINDU

Bindu is conceived not only as an impurity but also as the material cause of the pure creation. It is spoken of as an impurity from the point of view of religious mysticism, and as the material cause of the pure creation from the metaphysical point of view. It is the first of the thirty-six dependent metaphysical categories of this system, as we shall soon show. It is very often talked of as Mahāmāyā.

BINDU AS AN IMPURITY OR MALA

The conception of Bindu as an impurity is very closely connected with the view that 'Liberation' (Mukti) is of two types, Para and Apara; and that even after a soul has got freedom from the bondages of Karma and Māyā, it is not perfectly free; it has freedom of the lower type only. For, the impurity of Mala, which is also called Paśutvamala, is still there.

The Siddhānta Saiva Dualism admits that there are worlds beyond the one in which we, the bound, live, and which is a creation of Māyā. It admits that there are five categories beyond Māyā; that there are three worlds, corresponding to the three categories, (1) Sadāśiva, (2) Īśvara and (3) Vidyā; and that the souls, who have got freedom from the bondages of Māyā and Karma and are called Vijñānakevalas, live in them.

1 T. P. 7. | 2 T. P. 10.

Such souls are of three types[1], according to the higher and higher stages of maturity of their Paśutvamala. They are accordingly called (1) Mantramaheśa, (2) Mantreśa and (3) Mantra, and live in the worlds belonging to the three categories, (1) Sadāśiva, (2) Īśvara and (3) Vidyā, respectively. They are partly liberated because they have still the Paśutvamala. In such a context of religious mysticism, Bindu or Mahāmāyā, as a dependent category of Pāśa, is spoken of as the material cause of the worlds beyond Māyā and of the bodies of the partly liberated beings, who live in them.

MYSTICISM OF THE ŚAIVA DUALISM AND PLOTINUS

The idea of the worlds beyond Māyā, will become clearer to the students of the Western philosophy, if we compare it with the 'world of Nous', according to Plotinus.

(1) Siddhānta Śaiva Dualism agrees with Plotinus in holding that the 'world of Nous' or 'spiritual world' is midway between the empirical world and the 'One'. For, it holds that the lower liberation (Apara mukti) is the intermediate stage between the bondage of Māyā and Karma, and the final emancipation (Paramukti or Śivasāmya); just as Plotinus holds that soul has to reach the level of spirit before the One can appear to her.

(2) It admits that in the pure creation there is the distinction of subject, object and means of knowledge at least logically, just as Plotinus admits the distinction of "Nous, Noeta and Noesis" or "Spirit, Spiritual world and Spiritual perception"[2].

(3) It differs from the monists in holding the individuality to be real, exactly as Plotinus differs from Plato and Aristotle. For, according to both, Plato and Aristotle, the individuality, both subjective and objective, is not ideal and, therefore, not real. It has no place in the world of ideas. It is due only to the peculiar nature of the matter, which splits up the universal into numerous individuals or particulars, just as prism splits up the light of the sun into rays of different colours. According to Plotinus, however, individuality is real and independent of the material condition. There are individual spirits in the real world.

(4) It asserts, like Plotinus, that the individuality of spirits at the spiritual level does not imply any limitation in their know-

1. R. T. 12.

*2. Inge. Vol. II, 38-9.

ledge and that the individuality of spirit is no bar to its knowing all the contents of the spiritual world. For, spirits are not separated from one another by physical barriers as souls are. They penetrate one another. The spiritual world is like a transparent sphere[1], placed outside the spirit, in which it can see all the contents of the spiritual world.

(5) It also agrees with Plotinus that the object of the Nous or spirit is the spiritual world, which is made up of ideas and that the ideas have their material constitution, but it is of supersensible nature[2]. For, it admits Bindu or Mahāmāyā as the material cause of the pure world and holds it to be distinct from Māyā, which is the material cause of the empirical world.

(6) But there is a fundamental difference between the philosophy of Plotinus and Siddhānta Śaiva Dualism. For, the former propounds the theory of emanation and holds that both, spirit and soul, emanate from the One : but the latter adheres to the theory of evolution and maintains that the individual souls in both the worlds, pure and impure, have eternal separate existence from the Lord (Pati).

BINDU AS THE FIRST DEPENDENT CATEGORY

Siddhānta Śaiva Dualism admits thirty-six dependent categories, as has already been stated. Bindu as the first dependent category is called Śiva. The word "Śiva", however, is very often used for the first primary category, Pati, also. The reader, therefore, has to take the context into account in determining the meaning of this word. In the available text, occasionally we find the word "Parama Śiva"[3], instead of Śiva, used for the first primary category and it is asserted that He is beyond the thirty-six categories.

Bindu or Śiva, the first dependent category, is the material cause of the pure creation and as such it is also called Mahāmāyā, as has been stated already. It is eternal, like Māyā. The other four categories (Tattvas) Śakti, Sadāśiva, Īśvara and Vidyā[4], are the effects or evolutes of it. It pervades the entire creation. It is one. For, if it had been many, being insentient, it would have been transient like jar etc. It reveals[5] the powers of knowledge and action to those who enter into the pure world by subjecting

*1. Inge. Vol. II, 194.
*2. Ueb. Vol. I, 248.
3. T. P. 26.
4. T. P. 22.
5. T. P. 25.

themselves to spiritual discipline. The powers revealed by it are different from those revealed by Māyā. For, the sphere of the former is the unlimited, while that of the latter is the limited. It reveals the wealth of knowledge and power to the souls, which really belongs to them. The powers of knowledge and action do not belong to it; because it is insentient.

This category is not to be confused with the transcendental Śiva. For, if it be supposed to be identical with the Parama Śiva, it being evolutionary, the insentiency of Parama Śiva will follow. It is not inherent in the transcendental Śiva, like the Śakti. Being the material cause, it is related to Him as clay is to a potter. It is also spoken of as Kuṇḍalinī. It is an external power (Śakti) of the Lord (Parigraha śakti). It is not free, because it is insentient. It works under the control of the powers of Parama Śiva[1], such as Icchā etc.

THE REASONS FOR ADMITTING THE BINDU

(1) *Bindu as the material cause of the Pure Creation—*

Siva and Sakti both are sentient. They do not undergo any modification or change, whether it be evolutionary as in the case of milk changing into curd, or formal as in the case of a piece of cloth changed into the shape of a house. Neither, therefore, can serve as the material cause of the pure world. Hence Bindu is necessary[2].

(2) *Bindu And The Impure World*

This system admits that the creation is of two types; pure and impure. The impure world is created by Ananta etc., to whom the power to create is delegated by Pati. Its material cause is Māyā. But the creation of an object of determinate knowledge presupposes determinate thought in the creator. The determinacy in thought, however, is due to words. But words, as sounds, are admitted by the logicians to be products or manifestations of gross ether (Ākāśa), which is a distant evolute of Māyā and, therefore, is non-existent at the commencement of impure creation. The question, therefore, arises: how is the determinacy in the thought of Ananta, the creator of the impure world, is to be accounted for? For, unless there be determinacy in the thought of the creator the created cannot be such as can be the object of determinate knowledge. Siddhānta Śaiva Dualism, therefore, maintains that there is a subtle sound

1. T. P. 27. | 2. R. T. 22.

(Śabda), which evolves out of Bindu, in consequence of its stirring by the Lord[1]. This subtle sound is called Vidyā or Nāda. It constitutes the body as it were of Ananta and gives determinacy as it were to his thought to enable him to proceed with impure creation.

(3) *Bindu and Individual Self—*

The problem is : what is the relation between the individual self and the empirical knowledge ? The relation cannot be admitted to be that of inherence. For, we find that the knowledge of the same individual grows and decays. The admission of the relation of inherence between knowledge and soul, as admitted by the Vaiśeṣika, therefore, would mean that soul changes and, therefore, is transient. This, however, is against the fundamental assumption of the eternality of the soul. Siddhānta Śaiva Dualism, therefore, maintains that the growing and decaying empirical knowledge of the individual subject belongs to him, not directly or inherently, but to a condition of his: and that this condition is constituted by Nāda[2].

This Nāda, as a condition of the individual subject, is an evolute of Bindu. It is as innumerable as are the souls, a limiting condition of each of which it forms separately. It is like a seed of the entire 'knowledge' which is signified by words at the empirical level (Abhidheyabuddhibīja)[3]. The power of knowledge of each individual self is related to a Nāda, and as such it grasps the objects determinately at the level of Māyā. The variety of forms of knowledge, are the forms of Nāda and the soul shines variously, not because of any change in itself, but because of the formal changes in its limiting condition, the Nāda[4]. The growth and decay in knowledge, therefore, do not imply any change in the soul and so do not mean that it is transient. Bindu, therefore, is admitted to account for eternality and changelessness of soul in spite of its changing knowledge.

Siddhānta Śaiva Dualism asserts that determinate knowledge cannot be explained in terms of Buddhi, because determinacy is found in those levels also, which are beyond Māyā. Ananta, for instance, belongs to the level of Īśvara, but he also has a kind of determinate knowledge. For, otherwise the creation of the empirical world would not be possible. Further, the function of

1 R. T. 21.
2 R. T. 23.
3 R. T. 23-4.
4 R. T., 24.

Buddhi is to judge (Adhyavasāya). Buddhi, therefore, employs[1] words and presupposes their existence. Bindu, therefore, as the cause of words, through Nāda and lower Bindu is necessary. We shall deal with Nāda etc. in detail in a subsequent section.

ANOTHER VIEW OF THE BINDU

Some hold that the Bindu is inherently present in the Śiva[2] like the power of knowledge. They assert that it is the power of action (Kriyāśakti). It does not have separate existence from Him, like the Māyā. It is the Parā Kuṇḍalinī. They hold that the two powers are inherent in Śiva, (I) the power of knowledge, Saṁvid or Vijñāna and (II) the power of action or the Parā Kuṇḍalinī. Through the former He knows and through the latter He creates.

The two are inseparable. Śiva has no being, isolated from the powers, nor do the powers exist independently of Śiva. Thus, Śiva is represented to be the creator of the pure world, the world of indeterminacy, as also of Nāda etc. Accordingly it is asserted that everything is within Bindu and, therefore, within Śiva, wherein Bindu inheres.

ITS REFUTATION BY THE DUALISTS

Dualists assert that whatever evolves is insentient like milk. The admission, therefore, that the insentient is inherently related to Śiva will mean bringing the Śiva[3], who is pure sentiency, down to the level of the insentient.

Further, this admission is against the texts[4], which present the Śiva to be the creator on the basis of inference, based on the analogy of the potter. Furthermore, if Śiva be admitted to be insentient, the selves also which belong to the category of Śiva, will have to be admitted to be insentient.

Similarly there are many other views of Bindu, which Siddhānta Śaiva Dualism refutes: for instance, the following:—

Māyā is of three types, gross, subtle and transcendental. The first is made up of qualities. The second is the undifferentiated state of all the categories from Kalā to earth. And the third is the Bindu or Mahāmāyā[5].

1 R.T. 27.
2 R.T. 44-5.
3 R.T. 47.
4 R.T. 48.
5 R.T. 55-6.

NĀDA AS A SUBSTITUTE FOR SPHOṬA OF THE PHILOSOPHY OF GRAMMAR

The problem, "How do the words and sentences of a language give rise to the consciousness of meaning in the hearer?" is the central problem in the philosophy of Grammar. And the Grammarians assert (I) that the last letter of a word, together with the revived residual traces of the preceding letters, manifests Sphoṭa, which is a unity of all letters, exactly as the yolk of peacock's egg is a unity of various colours and (II) that this Sphoṭa[1] is of three types, relating to (I) letter, (II) word and (III) sentence. It is this which is the cause of the rise of the consciousness of the meaning. It is eternal and all-pervasive.

The aforesaid view seems to have evolved as follows:— The letters of a word, which are the objects of the sense of hearing, come in succession one after another, are lost no sooner than they are uttered and do not affect one another. They, therefore, cannot be spoken of as the cause of the rise of the consciousness of meaning. Nor can a word or a sentence be said to be the cause. For, the words and sentences have no being apart from the letters, such as may be the object of perception. For, a word is said to be a collection of letters. But the letters being successive and momentary, there can never be a collection of them. And because word and sentence are never perceived, they cannot, therefore, be known through inference either[2]. Nor can the rise of the consciousness of meaning be said to be due to the last letter of a word[3]; for instance, the aspirate (Visarjanīya) at the end of the word "Gauḥ". For, in that case there will remain no reason why consciousness of a horned animal should not arise on hearing the word "Naraḥ", because the aspirate sound is at the end of both the words, cited above.

The Grammarians, therefore, asserted that the last letter together with the revived residual traces of the previous ones, is responsible for the manifestation of Sphoṭa, the eternal word and so for the rise of the consciousness of the meaning.

THE CRITICISM OF THE GRAMMARIANS' VIEW

The view that the last letter of a word, together with the revived residual traces of the previous ones, is responsible for the arousal of the meaning in the hearer, through bringing about the manifestation of Sphoṭa, cannot stand. For, the residual traces arouse the memory of that only, by which they are caused :

1 N. Ka 4.
2 N. Ka., 2.
3 N. Ka., 3.

for instance, the revived residual trace of a jar, arouses the memory of that jar alone, by which it was caused. But it cannot give rise to the consciousness of the new one which was never experienced before. The revival of the memory of the letters, preceding the last one, may, therefore, give rise to the consciousness of each letter separately, but it cannot give rise to the consciousness of the meaning. Nor can it be said that the word, which is made up of the letters, remembered and directly perceived, is the indicator of, or brings to light, the meaning (Abhidhāyaka). For, the remembered lamps can bring nothing to light[1].

And the assumption of Sphoṭa, as the universal and eternal word, which is supposed to be manifested by the last letter together with the revived residual traces of the previous ones, cannot help in explaining the rise of the meaning. For, the so called Sphoṭa is not experienced as distinct from letters. And it cannot be represented to be either different from or identical with the letters[2]. The former position is untenable; because Sphoṭa is not experienced as distinct from letters; hence it cannot be known through inference either. It cannot be said that it is unnecessary that the Sphoṭa should be experienced. For, the Sphoṭa is admitted to make the meaning known (Jñāpaka) and as such it must be perceived. For, only a perceived light makes the object known, just as a compression of the eye conveys the meaning of the person who compresses his eye, but only when it is perceived. Therefore, if Sphoṭa be admitted to make the meaning known, it must be perceived.

And the latter position, namely, that Sphoṭa is identical with letters, is no better. For, if it be admitted to be identical with letters and not distinct from them, it would mean that Sphoṭa is a synonym of Varṇa. It is, therefore, illogical to attribute to Sphoṭa a function, which the letters cannot discharge.

Further, the admission that Sphoṭa is eternal and all-pervasive is faulty: because if it be such, how is it that all people do not become conscious of meaning when the eternal and all-pervasive Sphoṭa is manifested ?

VIJÑĀNA AS THE AROUSER OF THE MEANING

Some account for the arousal of the meaning in the consciousness of the hearer as follows:—

The speaker determinately apprehends an object by means of the Buddhi[3], recollects the word that stands for it, and then utters

1 N. Ka., 4.
2 N. Ka., 5.
3 N. Ka., 6.

the gross word. Thus, a form of Buddhi,—which is due to its affection by an object, is associated with the remembered word that stands for it and is the cause of the utterance of the gross word,—is the arouser of the meaning in the consciousness of that hearer, in whose mind the heard word is associated with the particular meaning.

ITS CRITICISM AND A REPLY TO IT

The Siddhāntin criticises this view by pointing out that this would mean that the word and its meaning are essentially identical, because both are essentially of the nature of consciousness; both are mere affections of Buddhi and, therefore, there is no essential distinction between the signifying word and the signified meaning. But the exponent of the Vijñāna as the cause of the rise of meaning in the consciousness of the hearer, asserts in reply that the form of Buddhi[1], which represents the word, is distinct from that of its meaning, in so far as it (the word) is a form of consciousness that signifies what is outside it, namely, the external object, which is the meaning. It can, therefore, be maintained logically that what arouses the meaning is the significant form of consciousness (Buddhi), wherewith the external objects such as cow etc. are grasped.

THE THEORY OF NĀDA

The exponent of the theory of Nāda admits what has been asserted above, namely, that that which arouses the consciousness of meaning (Vācaka) is really a significant form of consciousness (Vimarśātmaka). But he points out that the significant form of consciousness is not without a cause, because it is occasional.

The point may be elaborated as follows:—

The object, to which the determinative judgement of the Buddhi is related, is not the product of the Buddhi itself. On the contrary, it has external existence and as such is perceived through one of the senses. The internal object, the reflection of an external object on Buddhi, which is determinately judged by the Buddhi, must, therefore, be something that has already been indeterminately grasped by some sense. For, such an assumption alone can explain why only a certain object is determinately grasped at a certain time. Hence he asserts that that which gives to Buddhi the subtle inner word (Antaḥ sañjalpa), by means of which it determinately grasps the object,

1. N. Ka., 7.

reflected in it, is the Nāda[1], which is nothing but the cause of the inner speech (Antaḥ sañjalpātmā), which is nothing more than Akṣarabindu. Hence he asserts that it is the Nāda, which really arouses the consciousness of meaning, because it is the cause of the inner speech, in terms of which the determinative judgement is formed. The external articulate sounds are only external forms of it and, therefore, are not the real causes of the rise of the consciousness of meaning in the hearer.

The process of the arousal of meaning in the hearer may be explained as follows:—

After the affection of a sense by an external object, the Nāda in the speaker presents to his Buddhi, an object in the form of inner speech, which is undifferentiated unity of the word and its meaning, for the determinative judgement of the Buddhi. The Buddhi judges. This judgement is expressed in articulate audible sounds. They manifest the Nāda in the hearer. It presents to Buddhi an object which is an undifferentiated unity of subtle word and the indeterminate object. Buddhi judges in so far as it differentiates between the two and relates them as signifier and signified. This arouses the consciousness of meaning.

The exponent of the theory of Nāda asserts that the statement in the Āgama that the last letter of a word, together with the revived residual traces of the preceding, is responsible for the arousal of the meaning, is to be interpreted in the secondary sense that it manifests Nāda.

Thus, Nāda is the undifferentiated cause of the subtle inner speech. It is nothing but an embodiment of all words and their meanings, all of which exist in a state of undifferentiated unity, exactly as the different colours exist in the yolk of peacock's egg. At the time of stimulation of an external sense by an object, this Nāda manifests a particular word and its meaning in an undifferentiated form. This constitutes the indeterminate object of the determinative judgement by Buddhi, which differentiates the two from each other and relates them as the signifier and the signified. This judgement is expressed in articulate sounds. Similarly at the time of stimulation of the sense of hearing by an uttered word, the corresponding word and its meaning as an undifferentiated unity is given rise to by Nāda. This forms the object of judgment by Buddhi and the consciousness of definite meaning as distinct from the word arises.

1. N. Ka., 8.

This conception of Nāda is very much like that of the 'Monad' of Leibniz, in so far as it is a microcosm, in which all expressions and their meanings exist in undifferentiated unity in a rudimentary form; and the representative activity in one monad gives rise to a corresponding activity in others, who become conscious of such an activity through sense of hearing. But the dualist Ṣaiva holds the soul (Paśu) to be different from Nāda. It is a condition of soul but not soul itself. It is because of this Nāda, the cause of Akṣara Bindu, that there is no confusion in the meaning. It is separate in the case of each individual. It is not identical with the self or its powers: because they are unchanging, but the Nāda changes. It is, therefore, different from both. It is a distinct associate of each limited self. It is the product of Mahāmāyā as a material cause. It is beyond Māyā, because it is an associate of pure beings also.

Ṣaiva Dualism asserts that the statement in the Āgama that one who thoroughly grasps the Ṣabda-Brahman realises the Highest Brahman (Ṣabdabrahmaṇi niṣṇātaḥ parambrahmādhigacchati), means that the grasp of the former is a means to the realisation of the latter. It recognises the distinction between the former and the latter. Ṣabda-Brahma, according to it, is nothing more than Nāda, an embodiment of all words and their meanings in an undifferentiated unity: and there are innumerable Nādas, as innumerable as are the souls. For, a Nāda is a necessary condition of each soul.

NĀDA AND THE PHILOSOPHY OF MUSIC

Nāda-Brahma-Vāda, the Philosophy of Music, propounded by the Siddhāntin, holds this Nāda to be the reality, which is to be grasped through the medium of music. It is the original motion. It is the first motion. It is the unity of all thoughts and expressions. It is the root or the seed, from which all words and meanings spring, or to put it in terms of music, it is the original vibration from which all musical vibrations and their meanings arise. It is this Nāda, the Original Vibration, that the Art of Music represents and suggests.

BINDU AND NĀDA

Bindu, as has been stated earlier, is the material cause of the pure world. It is also the cause of Nāda, which we have discussed above. In relation to Nāda, therefore, Bindu is called Para Nāda[1]. The set of subtle sound-images,---of which the articulate sounds, constituting a word, are mere gross forms, and

1 R. T., 11.

which in itself is the undifferentiated unity of a particular word and its meaning,—gets manifested from Nāda in the hearer when the sense of hearing is stimulated by its object, the articulate sounds. This manifestation of Nāda is technically called Akṣara-Bindu. And Akṣara-Bindu naturally consists of the letter-images and the meaning which is associated with them, because it is a unity of thought and expression. Thus, Bindu is very often spoken of as the cause of Nāda, Akṣara-Bindu and Varṇa.

BINDU AND THE THEORY OF PAṢYANTĪ ETC. IN THE PHILOSOPHY OF GRAMMAR

Bindu is called by various names, according as it stands for different conceptions, on the basis of which various problems are attempted. It is thus called (1) Ṣabda Tattva, (2) Amoghā-Vāk, (3) Brahma, (4) Kuṇḍalinī, (5) Vidyā, (6) Ṣakti, (7) Para-nāda, (8) Mahāmāyā and (9) Anāhatavyoma.

The last name, "Anāhata-vyoma"[1], represents the conception of Bindu as ether (Ākāśa), which is a mere ground or pos sibility of all sounds, but is without sound, because it is without any collision (Anāhata), which is the immediate cause of mani festation of sound from it (Ākāśa). This conception of Bindu is the basis of the Saiva Dualist's explanation of the various aspects of speech; (1) Parā, (2) Pasyantī, (3) Madhyama and (4) Vaikharī, which are important problems in the Philosophy of Grammar and have been dealt with by important authorities, such as Bhartṛhari and Nāgeśa Bhaṭṭa, in the Vākya Padīyam and the Mañjūṣā respectively.

Bhartṛhari has dealt with these topics from the monistic point of view and has asserted that there are only three aspects of speech: (1) Pasyantī (2) Madhyamā and (3) Vaikharī. He has not admitted Parā as higher than and distinct from Pasyantī[2]. He has been criticized for this non-admission by Somānanda in his Ṣivadṛṣṭi from the point of view of the monistic Ṣaiva Philosophy of Kashmir.

Ṣrīkaṇṭha in his Ratna Traya, as interpreted by Aghora Ṣiva in his commentary, Ratna Trayollekhinī, writes on these topics from the point of view of the Saiva Dualism. He splits up the problem, which is dealt with by Bhartṛhari under the heads of Paśyantī etc. into two. Bhartṛhari attempts together the problem of the different stages in the gradual separation of meaning and expression from the stage of their unity; and that of the different stages in the growth of gross expression from the subtle. No doubt, he talks of Paśyantī etc. in the context of the

1 R. T., 30. | 2 V. P., ch. I, V. 144.

former and of Sphoṭa in that of the latter. But, as pointed out by Somānanda, the admission of two Ultimate Realities is illogical[1]. And accordingly it is admitted that the distinction between the meaning and the expression is imaginary.

Śrīkaṇṭha deals with the different stages of separation of meaning and expression from the stage of their undifferentiated unity in Nāda, under the heads, Nāda, Akṣara-Bindu, and Varṇa, as we have discussed in an earlier section. And similarly he deals with the problem of the rise of gross audible word from the most subtle, through different stages of grossification, under the heads of Sūkṣmā, Paśyantī, Madhyamā and Vaikharī. He identifies Parā, which he calls Sūkṣmā, with Nāda[2], and Paśyantī with Akṣara-Bindu[3]. And Madhyamā is nothing but a clear mental picture of the successive letters, which constitute the word. It is prior to the activity of the vital air (Prāṇa) which is the cause of the gross audible sound. Similarly Vaikharī, the gross audible word, is due to vital air, which being checked at different places of articulation and then let off, produces the word, which is audible.

THE DIFFERENCE BETWEEN BHARTṚHARI AND ŚRĪKAṆṬHA

We have already spoken on the common text, on which both, Bhartṛhari and Śrīkaṇṭha base their views. There is not much difference between them in regard to the last two i.e. Madhyamā and Vaikharī. But in regard to the first two there is fundamental difference.

(1) Bhartṛhari identifies Sūkṣmā with Paśyantī, holding that the word Sūkṣmā does not stand for an aspect of speech, higher than Paśyantī, but it is simply an adjunct, qualifying Paśyantī. But Śrīkaṇṭha holds that Sūkṣmā stands for the highest aspect of speech; that it is distinct from and higher than Paśyantī; that it is identical with Nāda, that it is the first evolute of Bindu or Mahāmāyā and that it is insentient because the principle of sentiency, Paśu, is a distinct and separate entity from it.

(2) Paśyantī is the highest aspect of speech, according to Bhartṛhari. It is an undifferentiated unity of all words and meanings. It is exactly what Nāda is, according to Śrīkaṇṭha; but with this difference that, according to Bhartṛhari, it is sentiency itself (Saṁvidrūpā)[4]. But, according to Śrīkaṇṭha, it is insentient, because it is an evolute of Mahā māyā. Further, Śrīkaṇṭha identifies Paśyantī, according to Aghora Śiva's inter-

1. S. Dr., 73.
2. R. T., 32.33
3. R. T., 31
4. V. P., 117. (Ben.)

pretation, with Akṣara-Bindu. His conception of Paśyantī, therefore, is fundamentally different. It is an undifferentiated unity, not of all words and meanings but of a particular word and its meaning; and the word also at this stage is not split up into letters. It is, therefore, marked by the absence of all duality and succession. It is what is manifested by Nāda, in consequence of affection of a sense by an object. It is responsible for the sound-picture of a particular word, detailed into distinct letters, which controls the movement of vital air to definite places of articulation, the speech-organs. It is the cause of Madhyamā.

(3) Bhartṛhari holds that the realisation of Paśyantī is the realisation of the Ultimate; because, according to him, Paśyantī is the Brahman. But Śrīkaṇṭha, in consonance with his dualistic philosophy, holds that the realisation of distinction of Sūkṣmā from Puruṣa frees a man from subjection to limited experiences (Bhogādhikāra)[1]. Sūkṣmā or, in the context of Bhartṛhari, Paśyantī is not Brahman but distinct from it.

(4) The Śabdabrahmavādin, who differs from Bhartṛhari, maintains that Parā or Sūkṣmā Vāk is one of the sixteen aspects of Puruṣa[2], and that it is inherent in Him. But the Śaiva Dualism holds that it is separate from Puruṣa and that it is a creation of Mahāmāyā[3].

NĀDA AND THE SECOND DEPENDENT CATEGORY, ŚAKTI TATTVA

The transcendental Śiva or Pati operates on the Mahāmāyā by means of his powers, Icchā, Jñāna and Kriyā. The first evolute of the Mahāmāyā under the direction of the power of will (Icchāśakti) is in the form of Nāda[4] and that of the world of peace etc. (Śāntyādi bhuvanātmaka). It is called Śakti Tattva. It is without parts (Niravayava). It is the effect of the Bindu or Mahāmāyā. This category arises when the desire arises in the Parama Śiva to create the world with a view to doing grace (I) to the limited selves by providing opportunities to them to reap the fruits of the past deeds and to get liberation and (II) to the bondages by giving them the power to function as such.

SADĀŚIVA TATTVA, THE THIRD DEPENDENT CATEGORY

The Sadāśiva category is the second evolute of the Bindu under the control of the powers of knowledge and action in perfect equilibrium[5]. It is the third dependent category.

1. R. T., 32.
2. R. T., 32.
3. R. T., 33.
4. T. P., 28.
5. T. P., 29.

ĪŚVARA TATTVA, THE FOURTH DEPENDENT CATEGORY

The Īśvara Tattva[1] is the third evolute of the Bindu, when it is under the control of the power of action with the power of knowledge, occupying a subordinate position to it. Ananta etc. belong to this category. They are called Vidyeśas. It is the fourth dependent category.

VIDYĀ TATTVA, THE FIFTH DEPENDENT CATEGORY.

Vidyā Tattva[2] is the fourth evolute when the Bindu evolves under the direction of the power of knowledge with the power of action as its subordinate. The beings, belonging to this category, are omniscient. It is called the Vidyā, because here it is that the omniscience of the souls is revealed for the first time.

These five categories belong to the pure creation, wherein there is no limitation to the knowledge of the pure beings which belong to it. They are very much like the five categories, Śiva, Śakti, Sadāśiva, Īśvara and Vidyā, admitted by the monistic Śaivaism of Kashmir. The difference being confined to the fundamental assumptions of monism and dualism, namely, the identity or difference of the efficient and the material causes. All these five categories[3] are beyond time and, therefore, without any order of succession. They are conceived separately, because of their functional difference.

BINDU, SUBTLE AND GROSS

The Bindu and the Nāda are frequently represented to be of two types, gross and subtle. The subtle Bindu and Nāda are identified with Śiva and Śakti Tattvas respectively. But the gross Bindu, which is the material cause of the articulate sounds and the gross Nāda[4], which is the material cause of the inarticulate sounds, according to this view, are included in the Sadāśiva Tattva. Ananta etc. belong to Īśvara Tattva. The Mantras, seven crores in number, the words, the Vidyās, Vyomavyāpi etc. and the 28 Āgamas, Kāmika etc. belong to the Vidyā Tattva.

MĀYĀ, THE SIXTH DEPENDENT CATEGORY

Pāśa is one of the three primary categories of the Dualistic Śaivaism, Pati, Paśu and Pāśa. And under Pāśa five dependent categories are subsumed; Mala, Māyā, Karma, Nirodhaśakti and Bindu. Māyā, therefore, is one of the dependent categories of Pāśa. It is distinct from Mahāmāyā or Bindu. For, it is

1 T. P., 29.
2 T. P., 30.
3 T. P., 31.
4 T. P., 30-1.

the material cause of the impure, the empirical world; while Mahāmāyā is the material cause of pure creation. It is one[1], eternal, all-pervasive in the gross world, subtle and related to Parama Śiva or Pati, exactly as clay is related to a potter. It is common material cause of all bodies of all individual selves, as also of all the gross worlds, wherein they live[2]. It is painted over or affected (Khacita) by the sum total of the effects of deeds (Karma) of all the individual souls. For, according to the Dualist Śaiva, Karma is not related to soul as its quality but to Buddhi only: because Karma grows and is destroyed; and, therefore, its admission as a quality of soul, would mean that soul changes, and, therefore, is transient. It is the cause of the ignorance of the true nature of the objects of experience, because of which individual souls take the objects, which are really transient, polluting, painful and not-self, to be eternal, holy, pleasant and self. All the thirty dependent categories from Kāla to earth, excepting Puruṣa, exist potentially in Māyā, at the time of the universal annihilation. Thus, it is from Māyā that all the lower categories, mentioned above, evolve and the variety of the gross world comes into being, when it is stirred to action by the Lord in accordance with the sum total of Karmas of all souls.

KĀLA, THE SEVENTH DEPENDENT CATEGORY

The categories of the impure creation, which evolve out of Māyā, are stated in two different orders ; the order of creation and that of function. Kāla, time, is the first category in the order of evolution from Māyā, though it functions only after the Kāla, Vidyā and Rāga have functioned. It is the cause (Nimitta)[3] of the idea of priority and posteriority; quickness and slowness; second and minute etc. Śaiva Dualist's conception of time, thus, seems to be the same as that of the Nyāya and the Vaiśeṣika. The following, however, are the points of difference:—

It is not an independent eternal substance as the Nyāya holds. It is only a limiting condition of Jīva or Paśu. It is not one; but there are as many times as are individual subjects. It is not eternal but non-eternal, because it is insentient and many: and all that is such is not eternal[4].

NIYATI, THE EIGHTH DEPENDENT CATEGORY

Niyati, order, is the second evolute of Māyā. It also is a limiting condition of each individual self. It is because of Niyati that each individual reaps the fruits of what he sows; but no

1. T. P., 35.
2. T. P., 35-6.
3. Mr. T., 264.
4. T. P., 37.

other can enjoy or suffer the consequences of what one does. It is like an order of the King, in the absence of which the bad characters (Dasyavaḥ) enjoy the food, produced by the cultivators[1].

KALĀ, THE NINTH DEPENDENT CATEGORY.

Kalā is a very important dependent category of the Śaiva Dualism. It is the category from which the subsequent three dependent categories, Vidyā, Rāga and Pradhāna evolve. It brings about partly the manifestation of the essential nature of the individual subject. We know that, according to this system, the powers of knowledge and action, without any limitation, are inherent in each individual self. The individual self is omnipotent and omniscient in reality. But its powers are shrouded by the impurities (Mala) ; and consequently it cannot experience the fruits of its Karma, so as to exhaust it and attain 'liberation'. Kalā, therefore, removes the shroud partly and partly manifests the inherent powers of the individual. It is an inner and the chief limiting condition of each soul ; because it helps to give rise to the individual as a limited experiencer (Bhoktṛsvarūpopakārakatvena)[2].

VIDYĀ, THE TENTH DEPENDENT CATEGORY.

Vidyā is the first evolute of Kalā. It is self-luminous (Prakāśasvarūpā)[3]. It is a means of knowledge of what is objective. But it may be asked here:—

Kalā is assumed to remove the shroud partly and to manifest partly the inherent powers of the individual subject. The objective knowledge will, therefore, arise in consequence of the operation of the power of knowledge. What is then the use of admitting an additional dependent category, called Vidyā, to account for the awareness of the object?

To this the Śaiva Dualist replies:—
The power of knowledge, though partly manifested, because of the operation of Kalā, which partly removes the shroud of Malas, cannot grasp the object without a means ; exactly as a person, though capable of going, cannot reach the destination without the help of a path and light. (Pathā dīpikayā vā yāti)[4]. And in reply to the objection that Buddhi and senses being there as the means of knowledge, the assumption of another means, the Vidyā, is unnecessary; the Dualist Śaiva points

1. T. P., 38.
2. T. P., 38-9.
3. T. P., 39.
4. T. P., 40.

out that Buddhi and senses are the external means: but Vidyā is the internal means. This point may be elaborated as follows:—

The Buddhi determines the object, which is presented to it by the senses, under the control of Manas. Such an object, the individual self grasps[1]. Buddhi cannot be an instrument of grasping the object by Puruṣa ; because her function is only to determine. Hence the admission of Vidyā, as an internal means to get at the object, determined by Buddhi, is necessary. Further, just as the knowledge of an external object is not possible without senses, Manas and Buddhi, so the knowledge of inner feelings, like pleasure and pain, is not possible without the instrumentality of Vidyā.

It may be pointed out here that the word "Vidyā" is used as the name of two dependent categories, the fifth and the tenth. It has, therefore, to be remembered that the former belongs to the pure but the latter to the impure creation.

RĀGA, THE ELEVENTH DEPENDENT CATEGORY.

Rāga is the innate tendency of the subject towards the external objects. It is the cause of desire, which necessarily has an objective reference. It cannot be said that to draw the subject to itself and so to arouse desire in him is a quality of the object ; and, therefore, assumption of Rāga, as a separate dependent category, is useless. For, such an assumption would make freedom from desire for object (Vairāgya) impossible. It is distinct from "Avairāgya"[2], admitted by the Sāṅkhya. For, the Avairāgya as a quality of Budhhi is simply a set of residual traces of unfulfilled desires. Therefore, it cannot account for the rise of desire itself.

III PAŚU, THE THIRD PRIMARY CATEGORY AND PURUṢA, THE TWELFTH DEPENDENT CATEGORY.

The Paśu is the individual self, called by such words as Kṣetrajña etc. It is not identical with body, as according to the Materialists: nor is it an object of knowledge, as acc... to the Naiyāyikas. For, such an admission leads ...gress. Nor is it of the size of the body, as admitted ... nor is it momentary, as according to the Bauddha; ...se unification of facts of experience would be im- ... not limited by time and space. It is not one ... the Brahman, as the Vedāntin holds; for,

... 2. T. P., 41.

the distinct experiences of different individuals clearly establish the plurality of individual selves. It is not without the power of action, as the Sāṅkhya says; for, after the removal of the impurities, the eternal Caitanya, consisting in the unsurpassed powers of knowledge and action, is admitted to become manifest through His grace.

Paśu is of three types; (1) Vijñānākala, (2) Pralayākala and (3) Sakala. Vijñānākala is free from the impurities of Karma and Māyā. He is, therefore, free from Kalā etc., which are the means of reaping the fruits of Karma. He has (Āṇava) Mala only[1].

TWO TYPES OF VIJÑĀNĀKALA

(1) The Vijñānākalas are of two types: (1) Those whose Mala has fully matured and consequently in whose cases the power of obscuration is inoperative. They are made Vidyeśvaras, Ananta etc. (2) Those whose Mala has not fully matured. Such are made Mantras, which are seven crores in number. They are limited selves, their limitation is nothing more than Mala.

(2) *Pralayākala* is the second type of Paśu. It is different from Vijñānākala in so far as it has not only Paśutvamala, but also Kārma Mala[2]. It is the individual self as it exists at the time of universal annihilation (Pralaya), when all the dependent categories from Kalā to earth merge back into Māyā and, therefore, Māyā-mala does not itself exist. It is given the appropriate bodies etc., according to its Karma at the creation and made to transmigrate.

(3) *Sakala* is the third type of Paśu. It has all the three Malas[3]: Paśutva, Karma and Māyā. It is associated with all the thirty categories from Kalā to earth in so far as it has a gross body, made up of the five gross elements, five senses of perception; five organs of action; five subtle elements (Tanmātra); Pradhāna and Guṇas; three internal senses; Manas; Buddhi and Ahaṅkāra; five inner limitations, in terms of which all experiences and actions at the empirical level are finally explained, i.e. Kalā, Niyati, Vidyā, Rāga and Kāla. These thirty dependent categories are very often divided into eight groups and are referred to as Puryaṣṭaka[4]. It may be pointed out here that the Kashmir Śaiva conception of Puryaṣṭaka is very different from the above.

1 S. D. S. 182.
2. T. P., 11,
3. T. P., 11.
4. T. P., 14.

Puruṣa, the twelfth dependent category of this system is Paśu, the Sentient Subject, possessing perfect powers of knowledge and action, but limited or covered by the shroud of the last thirty dependent categories. As such he is an experiencer of the fruits of the accumulated effect of all the past deeds (Bhoktā)[1].

AVYAKTA, THE THIRTEENTH DEPENDENT CATEGORY.

Avyakta, Pradhāna or Prakṛti, is the third evolute of Kalā, the first two being Vidyā and Rāga. It is subtle, because the three Guṇas, Sattva, Rajas and Tamas, are in it in a subtle state. It is the cause of the Guṇas, the forms of experience, the pleasure, the pain and the senselessness. Hence the Dualist Śaiva conception of Pradhāna is different from that of the Sāṅkhya. The Śaiva Dualist holds that all that is insentient and many must have a cause. For, that is our common experience. Guṇas, therefore, being insentient and many must have a cause. And that cause is Pradhāna.

It is transient and not eternal. There is a separate Prakṛti for each Puruṣa. It is, therefore, many. It is insentient. And all that is insentient and many is transient. Therefore, Prakṛti is transient. This is another point of difference from the Sāṅkhya[2].

GUṆA TATTVA, THE FOURTEENTH DEPENDENT CATEGORY.

Guṇa Tattva implies all the three Guṇas, Sattva, Rajas and Tamas. It is said to be the product of Pradhāna[3]. The Dualist Śaiva conception of Guṇas agrees with that of the Sāṅkhya in other respects. There is difference of opinion among the authorities on Śaiva Dualism on Guṇa as a separate dependent category. Many do not accept it as such. In any case, if Guṇa be accepted as a separate dependent category, the number of dependent categories cannot be asserted to be thirty-six[4]; it would come up to thirty-seven. For, Śaiva Dualism accepts the twenty-three categories from Buddhi to earth in common with the Sāṅkhya. Thus, the Dualist Śaiva holds that there are thirty-six dependent categories from Bindu or Śiva to earth. They may be stated as follows:—

(1) Śiva, (2) Śakti, (3) Sadāśiva, (4) Īśvara, (5) Vidyā, (6) Māyā, (7) Kāla, (8) Niyati, (9) Kalā, (10) Vidyā,

1. T. P., 42.
2. T. P., 43.
3. T. P., 43.
4. T. P., 24.

(11) Rāga, (12) Puruṣa, (13) Pradhāna and (14-36) Buddhi to Earth, which are in common with those admitted by the Sāṅkhya.

No doubt, there are differences between the Sāṅkhya and the Śaiva Dualism in the conceptions of these categories and we have referred to the difference in regard to Buddhi in an earlier section. But to point them out in detail is more than what can be done in a summary.

LIBERATION OR MOKṢA

The Liberation is admitted to be of two types : (I) Higher (Para) and (II) Lower (Apara)[1]. The first consists in freedom from all the five types of impurity (Mala) and in the revelation of the perfect powers of knowledge and action and consequent similarity with Śiva (Śivasāmya). This is attainable through the grace of Śiva. Thus, Mantra Maheśvara etc. are said to have attained higher liberation.

The lower liberation, however, consists in the partial maturity of Mala, technically called Paśutva; in freedom from Māyā and Karma; and in the possession of a body made up of Bindu. For, according to this system, the souls, whose Paśutva Mala has partly matured, may still be empowered by Śiva to carry on the creative activity in a limited sphere. This type of liberation is called Apara, simply because of the association of the freed souls with the "Baindava Śarīra".

It is not something that can be brought about by the individual subject[2], as is implied by the Upaniṣadic passages like "Ātmā Jñātavyaḥ". For, the limited subject is to be freed from impurities by the Lord and, therefore, he is objective in his nature. It is a peculiarity which is made to manifest itself in the limited self by the Lord.

Thus, Mokṣa consists in the attainment of similarity with Parama Śiva in respect of powers of knowledge and action. The powers are not a new acquisition. They do not come from outside; they are in the individual, but are obscured by impurities. Therefore, Mokṣa is nothing but coming to light of what was obscured by the impurities: it is the emergence of the powers of omniscience and omnipotence, which were merged in the impurities ; it is the becoming manifest of the essential nature of the individual.

---

1. T. P., 8 | 2. M. Ka., 25.

THE EXPERIENCE OF THE LIBERATED

The experience of the liberated is characterised by indeterminacy when the limited Saṁvid, which is essentially identical with Parasaṁvid, is free from bondage. To the liberated the objectivity shines only as such, without limitation or determination: it does not shine as an object of enjoyment or aversion. Hence the experience of the liberated is characterised by omniscience[1]. It is not a mere self-consciousness, free from limitations. For, not to know what really exists, means ignorance and is due to Moha. Thus, if the liberated were not to know the objective world, he would be ignorant and, therefore, not liberated. The liberated is above Akṣara Bindu. He, therefore, does not have determinate knowledge. Though possessed of omniscience and omnipotence, he does not actively employ the creative power[2]. For, there is no reason to admit many creators.

THE DUALIST ŚAIVA CONCEPTION OF MOKṢA AND THAT OF THE VEDĀNTIN.

The Dualist Śaiva conception of Liberation is distinct from that of the Vedāntin, which is technically called Kaivalya[3]. For, Kaivalya means freedom from the impurities of Māyā and Karma only, but not from that of Āṇavamala also. This is clear from the fact that no Vedāntic text talks of omniscience as the characteristic of liberation. The implication of this silence is that they do not admit the liberated to be omniscient. For, had the impurities been thoroughly removed, there would have certainly been omniscience.

The Dualist Śaiva criticises the Vedāntin in the context of Mokṣa, on the following points:—

(1) The Vedāntin does not admit anything apart and distinct from the Self, which is characterised by pure being, sentiency and bliss[4]. He denies the existence of all that is objective. The question, therefore, arises: how can he maintain that the Brahman or Ātman is characterised by pure being etc., as stated above? For, the characteristics of everything, that has them, shine only in relation to what is external to it; for instance, the heat of fire becomes manifest only in relation to wood. Therefore, if in reality there be no object external to the Brahman, its characteristics will have no objective relation and, therefore, they cannot shine. Their admission, therefore, would be a mere matter of belief, without any rational foundation. If, however, he were to say that the objective world is, but only imaginary

1. R. T. 86.
2. R. T., 88.
3. S. P., 24.
4. S. P., 25.

or illusory, it would follow that the characteristics, which shine in relation to it, are also equally illusory and if so, it would follow that the Brahman, that has them, is also illusory and so is Mokṣa.

(2) The Vedāntin denies the duality of the subject and the object. He maintains monistic idealism. But if his position be taken to be right, it would follow that all the texts, which talk of contemplation (Upāsanā) are useless. For, every relation depends on two. And contemplation is a relation and would be impossible in the absence of a real contemplator, distinct from the object of contemplation. If it be said that the one shines as many, because of the limiting condition, the question will arise: "Is the condition real?" If so, monism fails. If not, the contemplation, which is practised only with the object of getting freedom from the limiting condition, becomes useless.

The Siddhāntin, therefore, asserts that the distinction between the Lord, the Īśvara, and the soul, the Jīva, has to be admitted to be real. These would become the objects of knowledge to each other. For, only such an admission can justify the admission that the Brahman is omniscient and establish the utility of the texts dealing with contemplation, which leads to Mokṣa.

(3) The Dualist Siddhāntin criticizes the Vedāntin, who maintains that Mala is nothing but ignorance, which disappears at the dawn of knowledge, exactly as ignorance in the form of mistake, such as the one which consists in mistaking a piece of mother-of-pearl for silver, disappears when the mother-of-pearl is known as such. For, ignorance must be admitted to be either an attribute of the self or 'nothing'. In the former case, if it be admitted to disappear, that will mean that the self changes. In the latter case, it being nothing and, therefore, being without causal efficiency, the knowledge, as a means of driving it away, would be a useless assumption[1].

Accordingly the Dualist Siddhāntin asserts that it is not an attribute of the self, but something material, similar to the film over the eye[2]. He replies to the objection that if the Mala be admitted to be a substance, the jñāna will not be able to drive it away, as follows:—

The Ajñāna, ignorance, is of two types:—

(I) That which is due to non-recognition of similarity and consists in mistaking one thing for another, e. g. mother-of-pearl for silver.

---

1. M. Ka., 28.

2. M. Ka., 28.

(II) That which is due to jaundice etc., because of which white things also look to be yellow. The first goes because of the dawn of knowledge. But the second can be removed by God only, like a physician or surgeon[1].

(4) The Vedāntin holds the Brahman to be both the final and the material cause. Hence just as the Brahman is insentient, at least partly, in so far as He is the material cause also, so will become the liberated, who attain oneness with Him. Further, the Vedāntin maintains monism and denies reality to everything besides Brahman. How can then he talk of the knowledge of Brahman as a means to the realisation of Him (It)? For, the same thing cannot logically be spoken of as both the means and the end[2].

LAKULĪŚA PĀŚUPATA CONCEPTION OF MOKṢA CRITICIZED

The Śaiva Dualist criticizes the Lakulīśa Pāśupata system also, which holds that the union with or acquisition of the perfect powers of knowledge and action is Mokṣa and that the powers of the Lord pass on to the liberated. He points out that if the powers of the Lord pass on to the Mukta, the Lord will become powerless and that it is against the fact of experience that the qualities leave the substance in which they inhere, and pass on to another.

OTHER CONCEPTIONS OF MOKṢA, CRITICIZED BY THE ŚAIVA DUALIST

(1) *Utpattisamatāpakṣa*—

Some maintain that the omniscience and the omnipotence do not originally belong to the limited subject: but they arise at liberation and consequently Mokṣa consists in the attainment of similarity with Śiva[3].

(2) *Samatāsaṅkrānti Pakṣa*—

Others maintain that just as the fragrance of musk passes on to other things, so the omniscience and the omnipotence of Śiva pass on to the limited subject at liberation This is the position of the Lakulīśa Pāśupatas.

(3) *Āveśa Pakṣa*—

Still others maintain that just as a Graha, while at its own place, enters into or possesses a man (Grahairiva puruṣaḥ), so do the powers of Śiva.

---

1. M. Ka., 28—9.
2. M. Ka., 67.
3. P. K., 12.

The three views of Mokṣa are refuted as follows:—

(1) If the powers arise at Mokṣa, it is transient. For, everything, that has a beginning, has an end also[1].

(2) If the powers were said to pass on to the liberated, the position is untenable; because the powers being imperceptible, their passing into the person, to be liberated, cannot be perceived: nor is the inference possible; because there is no analogy[2]. Further, it would mean that that from which the powers pass becomes powerless.

(3) If at liberation, powers enter into or possess the liberated like a Graha; the liberation is without freedom, because the liberated is possessed by an evil spirit or Graha as it were.

Similarly the Śaiva Dualist criticizes the conception of Mokṣa of almost every system. In fact, Sadyojyoti has written the Para Mokṣa Nirāsa Kārikā, which aims at nothing else than the refutation of the rival theories of Mokṣa.

THE TEACHER AND THE LOWER LIBERATION

The liberation, according to the Siddhānta School is of two types : (I) Higher (Para) and (II) Lower (Apara). Only that person can be a teacher, who has attained lower liberation[3]; that is, one who is free from the impurities of Karma and Māyā and, therefore, is omniscient, but who has still a little of the impurity of Āṇavamala and, therefore, has a body made up of Bindu, which enables him to know everything; who is free from the body that is a creation of Māyā, the cause of ignorance. He is an external body of the Lord himself. He, therefore, possesses the qualities similar to those of the Lord. He is the instrument, through which the Lord bestows grace[4] on the deserving. He is, accordingly spoken of as the Lord himself. He is also prompted to action like an ordinary mortal by the Lord. But the action, to which he is prompted, is of a different nature. It is not the action, which leads to the enjoyment of the fruits of the past Karmas, but the action which is purely for the sake of others[5], the action which brings no merit or demerit to the performer.

FUNDAMENTAL IDENTITY OF THE TAMIL ŚAIVA SIDDHĀNTA AND THE SIDDHĀNTA ŚAIVA DUALISM

If we compare the fundamentals of the Dualistic Śaiva Siddhānta with those of what is known as Tamil Śaiva Siddhānta,

1. P. K., 19.
2. P. K., 19-20.
3. S. P., 37.
4. S. P., 39.
5. S. P., 38.

we find that the two are fundamentally identical. The difference is confined to the language only. Both admit the same three primary categories, Pati, Paśu and Pāśa[1]; the same thirty-six dependent categories; three impurities, Mala, Māyā and Karma; two types of creation, pure and impure; four aspects of speech, Parā, Paśyantī, Madhyamā and Vaikharī; and the authority of the same twenty-eight Śaivāgamas, Kāmika etc. In fact Meykaṇḍadeva, the author of the Śivajñānabodha, the basic philosophical work on Tamil Siddhānta Śaivaism, belonged to the 13th century A. D., when most of the works on the Siddhānta Śaiva Dualism had already been written in Sanskrit by great writers from Sadyojyoti to Aghora Śiva, on whom we have spoken earlier in this section. There are, no doubt, minor differences here and there between the presentation of the Siddhānta School in Tamil and that in Sanskrit. But, as we have already pointed out, such differences are found in the works of the exponents of this system in Sanskrit also.

---

*1. H. Ph. E. W. Vol. I. 369—79.

(III) DUALISM-CUM-MONISM OF LAKULĪŚA PĀŚUPATA

The Lakulīśa Pāśupata system is different from the Pāśupata, which is a dualistic system, though both admit the same five primary categories; (1) Kāraṇa, (2) Kārya, (3) Yoga, (4) Vidhi and (5) Duḥkhānta. Pāśupata system is, therefore, a presupposition of Lakulīśa Pāśupata. The distinction of this system from the pāśupata, seems to be referred to in the commentary, called Ratna Ṭīkā, on the Gaṇa Kārikā[1] of Bhāsarvajña, when it points out the distinction of the Lakulīśa Pāśupata from another system (Śāstrāntare). The statement of the distinctive features looks to be authoritative, because it is quoted by Mādhava in his Sarva Darśana Saṅgraha. This may be stated as follows:—

(1) In another system the liberation is nothing more than the end of all miseries. But, according to this system, it is the attainment of Supremacy or the divine perfection.

Here the distinction of the Lakulīśa Pāśupata from the Pāśupata seems to be pointed out. For, Lakulīśa seems to begin his Pāśupata Ṣūtra with the object of pointing out the distinction of his system from the earlier Pāśupata system: because the aim of the work, as stated in the very first aphorism, is to present the spiritual discipline, necessary for union with the Lord, as propounded by the Lord Himself (Athātaḥ Paśupateḥ pāśupatam yogavidhiṁ vyākhyāsyāmaḥ). We know that the Pāśupata conception of liberation was adopted by both the Nyāya and the Vaiśeṣika. For, the Nyāya Sūtra of Gautam clearly refers to it in the course of the second aphorism; and Vātsyāyana, in his commentary, makes it clearer still when he says:—

"How can a wise man not like this liberation (Apavarga), which is characterised by the total cessation of all miseries and is nothing more than the absence of consciousness of all miseries" (Katham buddhimān sarva—duhkhocchedaṁ sarvaduḥkhā—saṁvidamapavargam na rocayet.)

(2) Another system admits that the effect (Kārya), has no being before coming into being. But, according to this system, the effect (Kārya), under which are subsumed three dependent categories, (1) Kalā, (2) Vidyā and (3) Paśu, is eternal. At the present state of our knowledge of the Pāśupata system, which we

---

1. G. K., 14-5.

get from references to it by Śaṅkara and his commentators, we cannot say definitely how far this point refers to the Pāśupata system. But if we admit that the view of the Vaiśeṣika that the effect has no being before coming into being (Asatkāryavāda) is adopted from the Pāśupata, like the conception of the liberation as the end of all miseries, we may say that this is another point of distinction of the Lakulīśa Pāśupata from the Pāśupata. For, the former holds that all effects exist as identical with the Lord's power (Śakti) from which He manifests them at will.

(3) According to another system, Īśvara and Pradhāna, the two causes, the efficient and the material, are not free; because the creation cannot begin in the absence of either. But, according to the Lakulīśa Pāśupata, the Lord is free, because, as we shall show, metaphysically this system is rationalistic voluntarism. This point of difference definitely refers to the Pāśupata system. For, as we pointed out earlier on the authority of the Ratna Prabhā, the Pāśupata admits the two distinct causes, Īśvara and Pradhāna[1]. Other two points of distinction, stated there, seem to refer to the systems of the Yoga and the Mīmāṁsā respectively.

LAKULĪŚA PĀŚUPATA AND THE VEDA

The tradition of the Lakulīśa Pāśupata system is found, not only in the miscellaneous portion of the Taittirīya Āraṇyaka in the five Anuvākas from the 17th to the 21st, but also in the main body of the book, in the five Anuvākas from the 43rd to the 47th. The Mantras, which constitute the text of these Anuvākas, have been adopted by Lakulīśa in his Pāśupata Sūtra with very few modifications to represent the Brahman or Śiva, as He is to be contemplated upon at the various stages of the path to final emancipation. These five Mantras are at the basis of his division of the book into five chapters. They also seem to have directed the thinkers of this school to think mostly in number five. Thus, in the Gaṇa Kārikā, which summarily gives the fundamentals of this system, we find eight groups, each consisting of five constituents.

Sāyaṇa, in the course of his commentary on the Taittirīya Āraṇyaka refers to the following points, which are important features of Lakulīśa Pāśupata system:—

THE CONCEPTION OF BRAHMAN OR PATI

It appears that at the time of the rise of the Lakulīśa Pāśupata system, the word Brahman did not stand exclusively for the Vedāntin's conception of the Ultimate Reality. For, in the

1. S. Bh., 488.

Pāśupata Sūtra of Lakulīśa, we find the word "Brahman" used for the Reality as an object of contemplation at different levels. Keeping this fact in mind, if we read Sāyaṇa's commentary, we find that what he says about the Brahman is very much like what the authorities on the Lakulīśa Pāśupata system say about Pati, the first category.

Thus, the Taittirīya Āraṇyaka, according to Sāyaṇa, admits:

(*a*) That the Brahman is the cause of the objective world. It is the material cause in so far as the Māyā is its power and, therefore, has no being independently of the Brahman. It is, therefore, Māyin[1] and hence Saguṇa and Māyāviśiṣṭa[2].

(*b*) That just as it is the very nature of the Nirguṇa Brahman to be the unity of Saccidānanda, so it is that of Saguṇa Brahman to create, to maintain and to destroy the world (Svabhāva)[3].

(*c*) That the Īśvara gives the fruits of the action and not Karma by itself[4].

(*d*) That the objective world and the limited selves are the effects of the Brahman, qualified by Māyā.

(*e*) That the effect can have no being outside the cause, therefore, the Brahman is all pervasive and Ananta.

(*f*) That the Brahman is Sat[5] : it creates the world and then enters into it, just as a man builds up a house and then enters into it and sits there. The Brahman, after creating all, from Ākāśa to Puruṣa, enters into it as if it were. For, it is found as the perceiver and knower in the Buddhi in the 'Lotus of the heart'. (To this there is reference in the Pāśupata Sūtra.)

(*g*) That the Brahman becomes everything perceptible and imperceptible, determinate and indeterminate, sentient and insentient, truth and untruth[6].

(*h*) That Brahman is Sukṛta[7]; because it creates everything independently. This idea is expressed through the word "Svatantra" in the Pāśupata Sūtra.

1. Tai. A., 564.
2. Tai. A., 566.
3. Tai. A., 571.
4. Tai. A., 571.
5. Tai. A., 622.
6. Tai. A., 641.
7. Tai. A., 642.

(*i*) That Rudra is everything[1]: He is the self of all living beings : He is "being" : He is all-transcending: He is all that had, has or will have being: He is Umāpati i.e. the Lord of learning[2].

(*j*) That the Brahman is the cause of the origin, persistence and destruction of the objective world[3].

(*k*) That the Brahman is distinct from the five Kośas[4] ; Anna, Prāṇa, Manas, Vijñāna and Ānanda.

(*l*) That the Brahman has various forms Jyeṣṭha[5] etc They are nine in number. They are the lords of the nine powers, Vāmā etc.

(*m*) That the Brahman has three forms corresponding to three qualities, Sattva, Rajas and Tamas : (1) that which is predominantly Sattva and, therefore, is calm, (Śānta), is called Aghora; (2) that which is predominantly Rajas and, therefore, is terrific, is called Ghora; (3) that which is extremely terrible, because of predominance of Tamas, is called Ghoratara.

THE CONCEPTION OF MOKṢA

According to Sāyaṇa, the Taittirīya Āraṇyaka admits

(*a*) That Mokṣa[6] consists in the Jīva's having Pratiṣṭhā in the Brahman who is imperceptible.

(*b*) That Pratiṣṭhā means the firmness of the thought of identity of the individual and the universal or the realisation that the Brahman is the very self of one's own self.

(*c*) That the person who knows the identity of the Ānanda that is the individual with that which is the Brahman, slowly gets union with the Brahman, the Ānanda, (Upasaṅkrāmati). The word "Saṅkramaṅa"[7] implies strong union, similar to that which a leech has with a living organism from which the blood passes into it. (Saṅkramaṇaṁ nāma dṛḍhasaṁyoga-rūpaprāptiḥ Jalūkā tṛṇe saṁkrāmatītyādau tathā dṛṣṭatvāt). Here Sāyaṇa seems to use the word "Tṛṇa" in a special sense. Another implication of this analogy is that, just as leech gets on a piece of grass without leaving the

1. Tai. A., 736.
2. Tai. A., 737.
3. Tai. A., 662.
4. Tai. A., 590.
5. Tai. A., 754.
6. Tai. A., 644.
7. Tai. A., 652.

place from which it gets on, so the individual gets related to the Universal, but does not give up the individuality. The liberated belongs to the highest category. The liberation, therefore, consists in the penetration into Brahman by Jīva so that the powers of Brahman pass into it, exactly as the blood of a living organism passes into a leech, which penetrates it. This text seems to have been the basis of the conception of Sāyujya Mokṣa in the Lakulīśa Pāśupata system. But some earlier authorities, under the influence of the monistic Vedānta, as pointed out by Sāyaṇa, held that the word "Saṅkrāmati" in the text, under discussion, is used in the secondary sense of the fruit of knowledge, which destroys illusion[1].

(*d*) That the liberated (Mukta) goes to the world of the Brahman.

(*e*) That the object of contemplation may be the Brahman or an aspect of it: that the contemplation may be strong or weak. Accordingly if the contemplation be strong and its object be the Brahman, the contemplator gets union (Sāyujya) with the Brahman. But if it be weak, he gets to the world of the Brahman (Salokatā). Similarly if the object of contemplation be an aspect of the Brahman and the contemplation be strong, middling or weak, the contemplator gets union with, similar powers (Sārṣṭikatā-Samānaiśvaryatā) or the world of the divinity (Samānalokatā)[2].

(*f*) That the final emancipation is attained through various stages and that in the final stage the liberated attains the greatness (mahimā) of the Brahman[3].

OTHER POINTS COMMON OR SIMILAR TO THE LAKULĪŚA PĀŚUPATA

According to the interpretation of Sāyaṇa, Taittirīya Āraṇyaka admits :

(*a*) That the self in the Guhā, made up of the five kośas, is essentially identical with Brahman[4] and the person, who realises this, experiences the entire objectivity simultaneously.

Tai. A., 652.
Tai. A., 781.
2. Tai. A., 734-5.
4. Tai. A., 562.

(*b*) That the Puruṣa is an effect (Annāt Puruṣaḥ)[1].

(*c*) That Ākāśa[2] is both (1) space and (2) the substance wherein the sound inheres.

(*d*) That the creation is to enable the limited subjects to enjoy and suffer the fruits of Karma.

(*e*) That there is no fundamental contradiction between identity and difference[3]. The identity refers to the essence, the Brahman, and the difference to the form (Ākāra). (Brahmākāreṇa Advaitam, Bhoktṛbhogyākāreṇa Dvaitam).

Thus, the Taittirīya Āraṇyaka presents the Dualism-cum-monism (Bhedābhedavāda).

SĀYAṆA'S INTERPRETATION OF THE TEXT, THE VEDIC BASIS OF THE LAKULĪŚA PĀŚUPATA.

We have referred to the five Anuvākas in the Taittirīya Āraṇyaka, which are the basis of the Lakulīśa Pāśupata system. Sāyaṇa in his interpretation of this text agrees that they refer to Śaivaism in general, both as a religion and as a philosophy. Thus, he asserts that the five Mantras, (1) Sadyojātam (2) Vamadevāya (3) Aghorebhyaḥ (4) Tatpuruṣāya (5) Īśānaḥ, present the five faces[4] (Vaktra) of Mahādeva or Śiva. Of these faces the first four, face four directions, one each, and the fifth is at the top (ūrdhva) and is turned upward.

His interpretation may be put as follows:—

1. "I approach Sadyojāta, the Western face, the Lord in that form. I bow to (namaḥ) Sadyojāta. O Lord ! prompt me, not to transmigratory existence, but to get beyond it. I bow to him who frees from the cycle of births and deaths.

2. I bow to Vāmadeva, the Northern face, which has nine aspects, represented by nine powers, (1) Jyeṣṭha, (2) Śreṣṭha, (3) Rudra, (4) Kāla, (5) Kalavikaraṇa, (6) Balavikaraṇa, (7) Balapramathana, (8) Sarvabhūtadamana and (9) Manonmana.

3. I bow to Aghora, the Southern face, which has three types of forms: (I) those which are calm and quiet, because of the predominance of Sattva, (II) those which are terrific, because of the predominance of Rajas and (III) those which are surpassingly terrible, because of the predominance of Tamas. O All-inclusive Lord! I bow to all the terrific forms, which work destruction at the time of universal annihilation.

1. Tai. A., 563.
2. Tai. A., 566.
3. Tai. A., 576.
4. Tai. A., 753—55.

4. I know Tatpuruṣa, the Eastern face. I contemplate on the Great Lord (Mahādeva). May Rudra prompt me to knowledge and contemplation.

5. Īśāna, the top-face (Ūrdhva-Vaktra), is the master of all knowledge, the controller of all beings, the protector of the Vedas. The all-transcending Self is higher than even Hiraṇyagarbha Brahman. May He be graceful to manifest His peaceful aspect to me. I am Sadā Śiva.

We shall point out the difference (1) of Sāyaṇa's interpretation of these Mantras from the one, given by Lakulīśa in his Pāśupata Sūtra, and (2) of the text of these Mantras, as found in the Taittirīya Āraṇyaka, from that as adapted by Lakulīśa.

THE DISTINCTIVE FEATURES OF THE LAKULĪŚA PĀŚUPATA SYSTEM

(1) It is distinct from the Nyāya in the conception of Mokṣa. According to this, Mokṣa does not consist in the cessation of all miseries (Duḥkhānta) only, as according to the Nyāya, but also in the attainment of the powers of knowledge and action.

(2) The effect, according to some other systems, the Vaiśeṣika, for instance, is that which has no being before coming into being (Asatkāryavāda) : but, according to this system, it is eternal. Thus, Kalā, Vidyā and Paśu are eternal.

(3) According to some other systems, the efficient cause depends upon something external in the creation of the effect. The Īśvara of the Nyāya and the Vaiśeṣika, for instance, depends on the atoms and Karma. But, according to this system, the cause is thoroughly independent.

(4) The rituals, prescribed by some other systems, lead to heaven etc., from which there is sure fall. But the Pāśupata rituals lead to *Sāmīpya*[1] etc., from which there is no return to transmigratory existence.

(5) The Lakulīśa Pāśupata rejects the conception of Mokṣa, as propounded or represented by Rāmānuja and Ānanda Tīrtha, which is technically called "Servitude" (Dāsatva)[2]. For, servitude, does not matter to whom it is, is painful and, therefore, cannot be the end of all miseries. Accordingly it asserts that the liberation is the attainment of the attributes of the Supreme.

1. S. D. S., 171.
2. S. D. S., 161.

THE POINTS OF DIFFERENCE BETWEEN THE DUALIST ŚAIVA AND THE LAKULĪŚA PĀŚUPATA

(1) According to the Lakulīśa Pāśupata, the Lord is independent of Karma in His creative activity. But according to the Dualist Śaiva, He depends on Karma.

(2) According to the Lakulīśa Pāśupata the powers of knowledge and action pass into the liberated (Saṅkrānti) : but, according to the Dualist Śaiva, they become manifest (Abhivyakti). The one holds that the powers do not belong to Paśu: but the other asserts that they do, but are obscured.

(3) The Dualist Śaiva admits the Śiva to be the creator on the basis of inference. His argument is cosmological. He holds that the dependence on the means, such as Karma, is not inconsistent with the freedom of the creator. For, freedom of a king, in making gifts, is not affected though he makes them through the treasurer. The freedom of the creator consists in having none to prompt Him to action and in making use of the instruments and not in being independent of them[1]. But the Lakulīśa Pāśupata holds that the Lord is independent of Karma in His creative activity; and that the object of creation has its being in Him as His power. He, therefore, is independent of everything, that is external, in the act of creation. He is free (Svatantra). He manifests the effect at His Will.

LAKULĪŚA PĀŚUPATA AS RATIONALISTIC VOLUNTARISM

According to the Lakulīśa Pāśupata, the Lord (Pati) is free. He does not depend upon anything that is external to Him in His creative activity. The so called matter is not independent of and external to Him but within Him as His power. He is not controlled in his creative activity by Karma also. Fruition of action depends upon Him : therefore, the limited subjects depend upon Him for fruition of action. But He is independent of both. (This idea is common to the Nyāya, which holds : "Īśvaraḥ Kāraṇam puruṣa Karmāphalya darśanāt".) His creative activity, however, is always in accordance with the causal laws. He does not change the essential nature and order of the effect (Kārya). He does not unite the liberated again with pain and suffering : nor does He subject them to transmigratory existence[2]. Thus, rationalism is implied in the very conception of the ultimate category as the cause (Kāraṇa).

1. S. D. S., 177.
2. P. Su., 60.

Thus, this system is **rationalistic voluntarism**. It is distinct from pure voluntarism; because of its rationalism, its recognition of causal law as inviolable, as absolute. This is responsible for admission by this system that what is subsumed under the category of Kārya, i.e. Vidyā, Kalā and Paśu, exists in Him as His power. He is, therefore, not dependent on what is external to Him, as is the Īśvara, as conceived by the Nyāya and the Vaiśeṣika. For, the matter, according to them, is external to the Īśvara, as the clay is to the potter. Matter, on the contrary, according to the Lakulīśa Pāśupata, is within the Lord as the stars are in the sky or as the seed is within the earth or as colour is in water.

The Lakulīśa Pāśupata is not idealism. It does not admit matter to be essentially mind, to be of the nature of idea, but non-idea, which is yet within that which is essentially of the nature of mind (Cit). The matter has its being in the potentiality (Śakti)[1] of the Lord, which is non-different from Him and is just an aspect of Him exactly as the heat is that of the fire. It is thus monism-cum-dualism (Bhedābhedavāda). For, though it admits the essential difference between mind and matter and the individual and the universal, yet it holds the matter to be not outside the Cit, the Lord, but within Him. It is Saguṇa Brahmavāda [2]. It admits that the Gods and celestial beings also have their being in the power of Rudra[3] as the objects of His creative and destructive activities.

THE CATEGORIES OF THE LAKULĪŚA PĀŚUPATA.

The commentary on the Pāśupata Sūtra of Lakulīśa by Kauṇḍinya is called Pañcārtha Bhāṣya, because it deals with the five primary categories of the system. The word, therefore, for which "Category" is used in this presentation, is "Artha". The word "Artha" seems to stand for more than what "Padārtha", (for which the word, in English, is "category"), signifies. "Padārthas" and "Categories," stand for metaphysical concepts, in terms of which the entire field of experience is explained. By the words "Categories" and "Padārthas" we understand the metaphysical and, therefore, philosophical categories. But the five principal categories of this system include three religious categories. Only the first two, Pati and Paśu, are purely philosophical categories. This system, therefore, does not seem to recognise the bifurcation between philosophy and religion. Thus the five categories are (1) Kāraṇa (Pati) (2) Kārya (Paśu) (3)

1. P. Su., 58.
2. P. Su., 63.
3. P. Su., 63.

Yoga (4) Vidhi and (5) Duḥkhānta, or (1) Cause (Lord), (2) Effect, (3) Union, (4) Ritual and (5) Liberation.

THE CAUSE (PATI), THE FIRST PRIMARY CATEGORY.

It appears that at the time when the Lakulīśa Pāśupata system arose, there was not much antagonism between the Vedānta and the Lakulīśa Pāśupata. In the Pāśupata Sūtra, the word Brahman is used for the object of contemplation. The words, Pati, Kāraṇa, and Brahman are synonymous. For, the Sūtra "Atredam Brahma Japet" is repeated five times at the commencement of the presentation of Brahman or Pati on the basis of each of the five Mantras, "Sadyojātam" etc.

Pati or Brahman is "being" (Sat), as distinct from "not-being" (Asat). He is eternal (Ādya). But His eternality is distinct from that of the liberation. For, the Lakulīśa Pāśupata holds that eternality is of two kinds, (I) that which has no beginning and no end and (II) that which has beginning but no end. To the first type belongs the cause, the Pati : and to the second type belongs liberation, mokṣa[1]; because it has beginning but no end. Pati is the uncaused eternal cause. His beginninglessness is distinct from that of Puruṣa, as conceived by the Sāṅkhya and the Yoga. The puruṣa is subjected to birth and death but Pati is free from them.

The above is the interpretation of the word "Sadyojātam" by Kauṇḍinya. But this word, according to Sāyaṇa, is a mere name of the Western face of Śiva, who is artistically conceived by the religious minds as five-faced (Pañcavaktra).

This Sadyojāta has to be grasped mentally to the exclusion of everything else and the contemplator has to dedicate his whole being to it[2]. The object of this dedication is to get beyond the created, the effect, i.e. all that which is subsumed under the category, technically called 'Kārya' and to deserve "Grace"[3].

(Bhave bhave nāti bhave, Bhajasva mām)

Here it may be pointed out that not only this interpretation is different from that of Sāyaṇa, but the text also is slightly different from that, found in the Taittirīya Āraṇyaka. Here we have "Bhajasva" instead of "Bhavasva". Pati is the cause of all that is of the nature of effect (Kārya) i.e. Vidyā, Kalā and Paśu[4]. He is the material as well as the efficient cause of the universe. From Him the universe springs up (Bhavodbhavaḥ),

1. P. Su., 52
2. P. Su., 53,
3. P. Su.,54.
4. P. Su., 55.

exactly as does a sprout from a seed. He is the cause of both the coming into being and the dissolution of the world. He bestows grace. He transcends all. He is playful[1] and creation, dissolution and grace are mere manifestations of the playfulness. He is higher than the liberated (Siddha)[2], those who are striving for liberation and those who are in bondage. He has the perfect powers of knowledge and action (Dṛk kriyāśakti). They constitute His essential nature exactly as heat does that of fire. He inspires fear of the immoral deeds in the bound souls and unites them with the merit and demerit of the deeds[3]. Compare :

"Bhavodbhavāya namaḥ. Vāmadevāya namo jyeṣṭhāya namaḥ. Śreṣṭhāya namo Rudrāya namaḥ." (Tai. A)

and

"Bhavodbhavaḥ"..........Rudrasya (P. Su., 55-7.)

Pati pervades the individual selves through the power of knowledge (Jñāna śakti) and it is because of His Will that the individual is connected with individuality. The relation of the individual with body, action and inaction etc. depends upon His Will[4].

Pati is responsible for disintegrating as well as reintegrating the world[5], consisting of the fourteen kinds of beings, their objects and their abodes.

He controls all the powers. He is responsible for inspiring attachment to body, senses, their objects and homes in all the limited beings, excepting the Siddhas[6]. He is not limited by Manas, i.e. all that is subsumed under Kalā i.e. thirteen Indriyas, five Tanmātras and five elements. He is the controller, the director, of all effects and means (Kārya and Karaṇa in the sense of the Sāṅkhya). He is, therefore, spoken of as Sakala[7], only by transference of epithet. But in reality He is above and beyond them. He is, therefore, spoken of as Akala or Amanas[8]. Compare:

Kālāya namaḥ Kalavikaraṇāya namaḥ Balāya namo Balapramathanāya namaḥ Sarvabhūtadamanāya namo Manonmanāya namaḥ. (Tai. A.)

and

Kālāya namaḥ. ....Mano manāya namaḥ.

(P. Su., 72-6)

1. P. Su., 56.
2. P. Su., 57.
3. P. Su., 57.
4. P. Su., 5
5. P. Su., 73.
6. P. Su. 75.
7. P. Su., 74.
8. P. Su., 76.

He is the cause[1] of diverse objects of opposing nature. He is, therefore, conceived to be of diverse forms. He has terrific as well as peaceful forms. He has bewildering forms also[2]. He is the abode of all that is subsumed under the category "Kārya", that is, Vidyā, Kalā and Paśu.

Compare:

Aghorebhyothaghorebhyo Ghora ghoratarebhyaḥ
Sarvebhyaḥ Śarva sarvebhyo namaste astu Rudrarūpebhyaḥ

(Tai. A.)

and

Aghorebhyaḥ............Rudrarūpebhyaḥ.

(P. Su., 89-91).

Pati is also referred to as Mahādeva[3]. He is the God of gods. Playfulness is His essential nature. He is higher and more powerful than any being. He is different from the individual selves. He creates all that is of the nature of effect i.e. Vidyā, Kalā and Paśu, because of His playfulness. He is the cause of creation, maintenance, destruction, obscuration and grace[4]. He is one, though spoken of differently as Pati and Ādya, because of the various attributes and functions. He is called Pati, because He possesses all-transcending powers of knowledge and action. (Niratiśaya dṛkkriyāśaktimattvam). His powers are beginningless and endless.

Compare:

Tatpuruṣāya vidmahe Mahādevāya dhīmahi.
Tanno Rudraḥ Pracodayāt. (Tai. A) and
Tatpuruṣāya..............Pracodayāt (P. Su., 107-8)

His power is manifest in all that is limited, unlimited, or limited in one aspect and unlimited in another, beautiful or ugly[5]. He is the god Rudra, the ocean, the sun, the ether, the Self, the Brahman. Nothing can be looked upon as different from Him. (Na śakyam bhedadarśanam).

The Lord is spoken of as the beginningless and causeless cause, which is essentially of the nature of "being" in the first Chapter,Sūtra 38, 40, 44. He is also spoken of as many, because of His being presented as possessing many attributes and discharging

1. P. Su., 89.
2. P. Su., 90.
3. P. Su., 108.
4. S. D. S., 168.
5. P. Su., 93.

diverse functions in Chapter two, Sūtra 1,4,5,20, 23—27. He is also admitted to have forms of the opposing natures, such as Ghora, Aghora and Ghoratara. The question, therefore, arises : "Is the Ultimate Reality, according to this system, a multiplicity"? And the reply is : He is one in many forms : the Ultimate Reality is unity in multiplicity (Tatpuruṣa)[1]. He is spoken of Ṛṣi[2] because He controls all that is of the nature of effect (Kārya). He is called Vipra, because He is omniscient. His power of knowledge extends over the entire field of knowledge. He is great (Mahān), because His powers of knowledge and action, are natural and not acquired and far surpass those belonging to any other being. They belong to Him as His qualities. In fact He is called Īśvara, because these qualities are in Him (Aiśvaryam Tadguṇasadbhāvaḥ)[3]. He is beyond the sensible. He is higher than Puruṣa. He is to be meditated upon, leaving the speech and Manas. For, He is beyond the reach of words and Manas. He is Niṣkala and yet He is different from Pralayākala. Even as Niṣkala[4], He has his qualities of omniscience and omnipotence.

He is the master, the Lord, of all learnings, which lead to the attainment of the four recognised goals of humanity[5]. He is the lord of all sentient beings, excepting Siddhas and Īśvaras. He is called Brahman[6], because He is responsible for the grossification of Vidyā, Kalā and Bhūtas, and yet is beyond them. He is the Lord of Brahmā, the sentient being, who is distinct from all limited subjects and is spoken of as Viriñci. He is called Śiva[7] because He is free from all miseries and as such represents the eternal (Nitya) final experience of the liberated.

Compare:

Īśānaḥ sarvavidyānām Īśvaraḥ sarvabhūtānām.

Brahmādhipatiḥ Brahmaṇodhipatirbrahmā.

Śivo me astu Sadāśivom. (Tai. A.)

and

Īśānaḥ.............Śivaḥ (P. Su., 144-6)

---

1. P. Su., 107.
2. P. Su., 126.
3. P. Su.. 127.
4. P. Su., 128.
5. P. Su., 144.
6. P. Su., 145.
7. P. Su., 146.

THE EFFECT (KĀRYA) OR PAŚU, THE SECOND PRIMARY CATEGORY.

The conception of the effect or Kārya, according to the Lakulīśa Pāśupata, is very different from that according to the other systems. It is not what Vikṛti, as opposed to Prakṛti is, according to the Sāṅkhya. For, it includes not only all that is called "Vikṛti" by the Sāṅkhya, but also the Puruṣa, the subject, which is neither Prakṛti, the cause, nor Vikṛti, the evolute. Further, it does not admit the theory of evolution that Mahān evolves from Prakṛti and so on. On the contrary, it holds that everything exists in the power (Śakti) of the Lord and that creation is nothing more than grossification of what so exists and organisation of what exists separately, into wholes, according to His free will.

Nor is the effect of the nature of mere "idea" in the Universal Mind, as the Idealistic voluntarism of Kashmir holds. For, the Lakulīśa Pāśupata recognises the distinction between the sentient and the insentient (Cit and Acit) even as they exist in the power of the Lord. Nor is the effect mere illusion, as the Vedāntin asserts. For, the Lakulīśa Pāśupata is not Monism, but Dualism-cum-non-dualism. It admits that the Reality is not pure unity but unity in multiplicity and, therefore, the multiplicity, according to it, exists in the unity just as do the stars in heaven. Nor is the effect not-being before coming into being, as the Asatkāryavādins, the Nyāya and the Vaiśeṣika, hold. For, the effect, according to them, is non-eternal; but the effect, as a category, according to the Lakulīśa Pāśupata, is eternal.

It seems that the Lakulīśa Pāśupata was influenced in the conception of the second primary category, the effect, by its conception of the first primary category, the Pati, which, perhaps only at a later stage in the development of the system, was called the cause (Kāraṇa). For, "Pati" is the only word that is used for the first category in the Pāśupata Sūtra in the first aphorism: and similarly the word "Paśu" is used for the second category. The original conception of the second category, therefore, seems to have been that which is controlled by the Lord (Pāśanāt Paśuḥ)[1]. And subsequently the first two, which are the only metaphysical categories, were given the more philosophical names, the Cause (Kāraṇa) and the Effect (Kārya). The word Kārya, as the name of the second category, therefore, in this philosophy, does not mean "that which is effected or produced and which has no being before the production"; but that which is the object the Lord's Free Will i.e. that which is "not free"

1. P. Su., 5.

(Asvatantra) as opposed to the Lord (Pati) who is Free. For, this system points out that "Pati" the Lord, has no meaning without Paśu, the lorded over. Accordingly this system subsumes under the second primary category, Kārya or Paśu, three dependent categories: (1) Vidyā, the attribute of the limited subject (Paśuguṇo Vidyā), (2) Kalā, the matter and (3) Paśu, the individual subject.

THE RELATION BETWEEN THE CAUSE (PATI OR KĀRAṆA) AND THE EFFECT (KĀRYA).

Many systems of Indian thought admit the cause of the world. They, however, differ from one another in holding the cause to be dependent or independent. Some hold that God is the cause of the world but depends upon the external matter for creation. To this class belong the Nyāya and the Vaiśeṣika etc. According to them, God is the efficient cause only and the matter that is external to Him, is the material cause. The Vedāntin admits the cause, the Brahman, to be both the material and the efficient cause. The Lakulīśa Pāśupata holds that the effect, the Kārya, the triad of Vidyā, Kalā and Paśu, springs up from Pati (Bhavodbhavāya)[1]. The so called effect has its eternal being in the Lord. And creation is nothing more than the arrangement of what exists, in a certain form (Vṛttilābha)[2]. He is the origin, the abode, the Āsana of the triad. The triad lies in His Śakti[3], which constitutes His very being, the most essential nature, the principal attribute, the chief characteristic, Dharma or Guṇa. The objective world is in Him as the starry heaven is in the Ākāśa or the ether. The cause and the effect have no confused being (Vṛttisaṅkara)[4] like water in milk. They have, on the other hand, distinct being, like the light of the eyes and that of the sun or of lamp, which illumines the object at the time of perception. He is all-pervasive. But the pervasiveness of the different dependent categories of the 'effect' (kārya), is of limited nature. Each higher category pervades the lower. Thus the Puruṣa, the self, pervades the twenty-four categories, as conceived by the Sāṅkhya. And similarly Pradhāna, for which Kalā seems to be substituted here, pervades all the lower categories beginning with Mahat or Buddhi and so on[5].

Different effects do not have their being in isolation from each other, like cells in a honey-comb. But the higher pervades the

1. P. Su., 55.
2. P. Su., 60.
3. P. Su., 58.
4. P. Su., 59
5. P. Su., 58.

lower, as stated just above. The pervaded and the pervading are grasped distinctly as water is grasped distinctly from the colour that colours it. In water that is coloured with the root of turmeric (Haridrā) for instance, we perceive water in so far as we see liquidity and feel cold touch: and we perceive turmeric in so far as we experience colour, smell and a certain taste[1].

Thus, the cause (Kāraṇa) and the effect (Kārya) exist together, but maintain their respective entities, because they have distinctive beings: though both of them are pervasive. The effect is as eternal as the cause. For, the cause cannot be logically represented to be the cause without the effect : nor can Pati (Lord) be spoken of as Pati without something to lord over. The effect has its being in the cause as does a seed in the earth. Kāraṇa and Kārya are synonymous with Free (Svatantra) and 'Not-Free' (Asvatantra)[2]. The former is the Lord (Pati) and the latter is the 'Lorded over' (Paśu). The one stands for the Cit and the other for both Cit and Acit. The one is the cause of the world, the other is the effect, the world.

(1) VIDYĀ OR SENTIENCY

Vidyā is the first of the three dependent categories of the Effect (Kārya). It is an attribute of the individual subject. It is the basis of the Lakulīśa Pāśupata theory of knowledge and Ethics. It is the sentiency, which, as an attribute of the limited subject, distinguishes him from the insentient Kalā, the matter, the second dependent category of the Effect (Kārya). As the basis of the theory of knowledge, it is self-luminous and illumines what is external to it, the object, like a lamp[3]. It reveals the hidden meaning of the sacred texts and leads to the knowledge of the essential nature of the impurities (Mala), the means (Upāya) to get rid of them and the acquisition (Lābha) consequent on freedom from the impurities[4]. It is the light of learning, that is manifested by the Lord and leads to the attainment of the four goals of humanity, Dharma, Artha, Kāma and Mokṣa. It is the first acquisition, consequent on the disciplined life, according to the Lakulīśa Pāśupata[5], and as such it is called knowledge (Jñāna). It is the right knowledge and as such is opposed to wrong knowledge (Mithyājñāna), which is due to the defective means of knowledge (Pramāṇābhāsajam jñānam)[6]

1. P. Su., 59.
2. S. D. S., 167.
3. P. Su., 92.
4. P. Su., 88.
5. G. K., 9.
6. G. K., 22.

and includes doubt, error, attachment, aversion and anger together with their root cause Thus, the word "Vidyā", in different contexts, stands for (1) the attribute of the individual subject; (2) the knowledge that is got through it; and (3) the lore that is manifested by the Lord and therefore, is the object of knowledge. It is subdivided as follows :—

- Vidyā[1]
  - Bodhasvabhāvā
    - Vivekapravrtti
    - Sāmānyavṛtti or Avivekapravṛtti
      - Dharma
      - Adharma
  - Abodhasvabhāvā
    - Saṁskāra

Vidyā, as a dependent category, is conceived in relation to the individual subject, as his limiting condition, attribute or quality. Its sub-divisions present this attribute as it appears and functions in different situations, in which the individual is put or finds himself. In a religious situation, in which a devotee is listening with devout attention to a lecture on the Ultimate Reality, Vidyā, the sentiency, appears as mere awareness of the Ultimate Reality, as presented by the teacher. To such an awareness, the spiritual instruction (Upadeśa) is the only means. This is called "Vivekavṛtti"[2].

It is interesting to find in this context, slight difference in the terminology, used by Mādhava in his Sarva Darśana Saṅgraha, and that which we find in the commentary on the Gaṇa Kārikā by an unknown author, from which Mādhava mostly quotes in his presentation of the Lakulīśa Pāśupata. Mādhava uses "Pravṛtti" instead of "Vṛtti" as found in the commentary on the Gaṇa Kārikā. The word "Pravṛtti" ordinarily means the movement. But "Vṛtti" ordinarily means an affected state of mind. It means that state of mind, in which the affections of the external objects appear, very much like the reflection of an object in a mirror. The question, therefore, arises: what is the meaning of "Pravṛtti" in the present context? It seems to stand for both (1) the affected state of mind and (2) the cognitive activity of the mind.

1. S. D. S., 167 and G. K., 10.
2. G. K., 10.

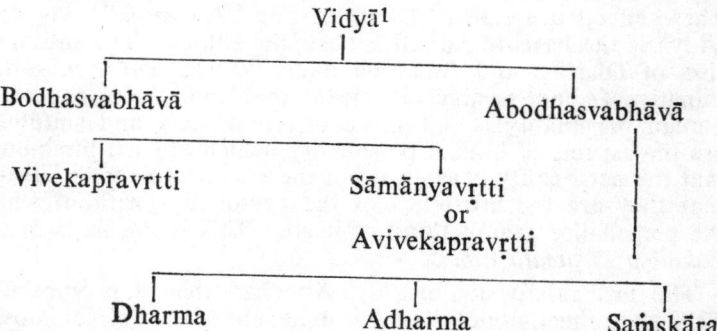

Vidyā, sentiency, is self-luminous. But it may or may not be illumining. When it illumines an object it is called "Bodhasvabhāvā" illuminative. But when it does not illumine an object but is self-luminous only ; it is called "Abodhasvabhāvā", non-illuminative. To this class belong the effects of the deeds done, pious or sinful, on the central aspect of human personality. These effects are called "Dharma" and "Adharma". As such Vidyā is the basis of Lakulīśa Pāśupata Ethics. The subsumption of Dharma and Adharma under Vidyā, that is non-illuminative (Abodhasvabhāvā) means that the ethical aspect of human personality is self-luminous : that piety and sinfulness are the aspects of human personality, which are self-luminous : that the personality is as aware of these as it is aware of itself : that they are the attributes of the personality, without which the personality cannot think of itself. This is the basis of the *Lakulīśa Pāśupata Ethics.*

The third subdivision of Vidyā Abodhasvabhāvā, is *Saṁskāra.* This is the effect, not of the deeds done, but of the objects known. It is related, not to the theory of Ethics, but to the theory of knowledge. This accounts for memory, a very important factor in the rise of determinate knowledge. For, the determinacy of knowledge consists in the relation of the object, known, with a word, remembered.

Let us now consider the other sub-division of Vidyā, which is illuminative (Bhodhasvabhāvā). This subdivision, as shown in the table, is further subdivided into Vivekavṛtti or Vivekapravṛtti, and Sādhāraṇavṛtti or Avivekapravṛtti. It is to be noted here that there is a difference of opinion between the commentator on the Gaṇa Kārikā and Mādhava on this point. For, while the former calls the second sub-division of Vidyā-Bodhasvabhāvā "Sāmānyavṛtti", the latter names it as "Avivekapravṛtti". We have dealt with the Vivekavṛtti, an affected state of the sentiency, in which the Ultimate Reality appears in the consciousness of a devotee in consequence of his listening to a lecture on the ultimate Reality, with devout attention.

The second sub-division "Sāmānyavṛtti" or Avivekapravṛtti is the basis of the Lakulīśa Pāśupata theory of Empirical knowledge, as pointed out earlier.

LAKULĪŚA PĀŚUPATA THEORY OF PERCEPTION

The Lakulīśa Pāśupata accounts for perception in terms of "Citta". It is a means of perception. But it is not one of the inner senses (Antaḥ karaṇa), as according to the Vedāntin. It is the activity of the self-luminous and illuminating sentiency

(Vidyā-Bodhasvabhāvā-Sāmānyavṛtti), which is an attribute of the individual subject. This activity consists in the movement of the light, which proceeds from the illuminating aspect (Bhodhasvabhāvā) of the sentiency (Vidyā). It illumines the object of knowledge like the light of a lamp[1]. Consequently internal and external senses work and an affection of the sentiency by the object follows. This is called perception. It is of two kinds : determinate and indeterminate. When the memory, which is nothing but revived re idual trace (Saṁskāra), co-operates in presenting to consciousness the word, which stands for the object, known, as related to the affection, the perception is determinate. But when the memory does not co-operate, the perception is indeterminate. In the former case, we have determinate knowledge and in the latter, indeterminate.

THE THEORY OF KNOWLEDGE

The Lakulīśa Pāśupata admits three means of knowledge: (I) Perception (II) Inference (III) Verbal testimony. It holds that all other means, admitted by other systems, such as Arthāpatti, Sambhava, Abhāva, Aitihya and Pratibhā, are included in them.

PERCEPTION

It is of two types: (I) Sensuous perception (Indriya Pratyakṣa (II) Spiritual perception (Ātma Pratyakṣa).

(I) The valid sensuous perception is due to the contact of a sense with its object. It depends upon the set of illuminating causes and the co-operation of merit and demerit, light, time, place and His will.

(II) the spiritual perception is due to the contact of Citta and the inner sense (Antaḥkaraṇa).

INFERENCE

Inference is due to the contact of Citta and inner sense (Antaḥ Karaṇa). Its main cause is the memory, aroused by merit, demerit, time, place and His will. It is of two types: (I) Relating to what was perceived before in particular (Dṛṣṭa) and (II) to what was perceived before in general (Sāmānyatodṛṣṭa). The former is further subdivided into (I) Pūrvavat and (II) Śeṣavat.

This is very similar to the division of the inference by the Sāṅkhya, who calls the main divisions Vīta and Avīta. And the similarity with the Nyāya on this point is the same as bet-

1. S. D. S., 167. and commentary.

ween the Sāṅkhya and the Nyāya. For, the latter primarily divides inference into three. The instances, with the exception of that of dṛṣṭa-Pūrvavat, are the same as those given by Vātsyāyana. The instance of Dṛṣṭa-Pūrvavat is "This six-fingured man was seen before. He is the same"[1].

ĀGAMA

Āgama, the verbal testimony, as a means of knowledge, is the scripture, which emanates from the Lord and comes to the follower of religion or philosophy through an unbroken line of teachers.

(2) KALĀ

Kalā, the second dependent category of Effect, is insentient (Jaḍa). It is very much like Pradhāna in the Sāṅkhya system, in so far as the twenty-three categories, subsumed under it, are common to the Sāṅkhya. It constitutes the psychophysical limitation or condition of the individual subject. But it depends upon the sentient[2]. It is under the control of the sentient very much as a chariot with horses is under that of a charioteer. Its subdivisions may be presented in the form of a table as follows:—

1. P. Su., 6.—7.
2. G. K. 10—11.

- Kalā
  - Empirical Effect (Kārya)
    - Five Elements (Pañca bhūta)
    - Qualities of Elements (Bhūtaguṇa)
  - Empirical Means (Karaṇ)
    - Five senses of perception (Pañca Jñānendriya)
    - Five Organs of action (Pañca Karmendriya)
    - Three internal senses (Antaḥ Karaṇa)

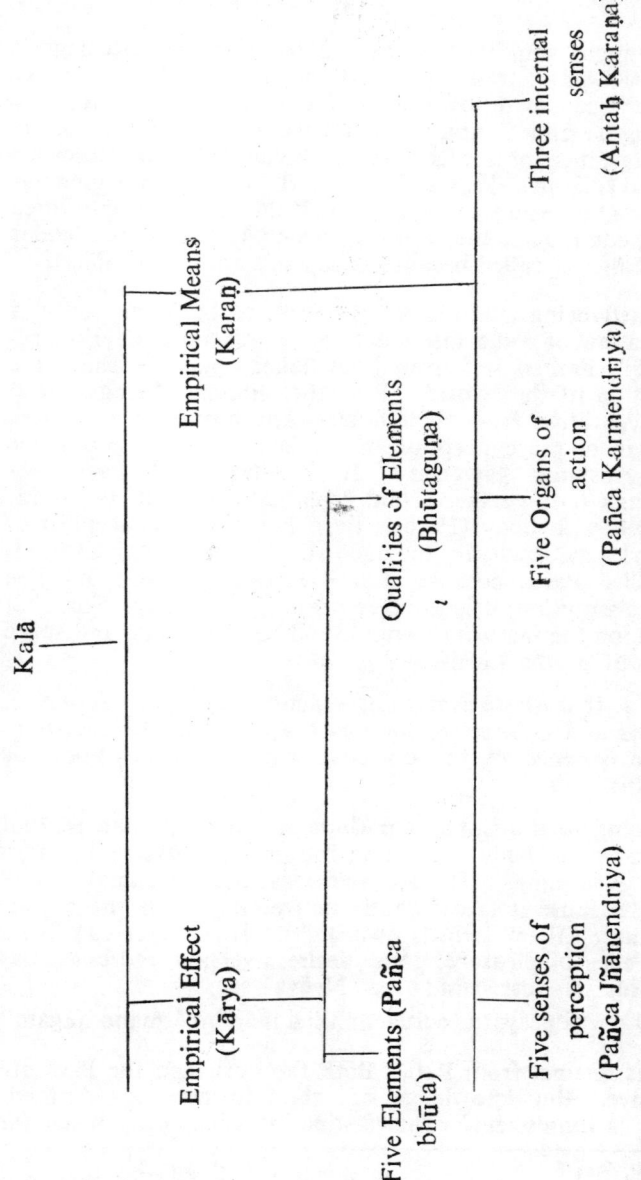

(3) PAŚU.

The sentient subject, Paśu, is the third dependent category of Effect (Kārya). It is subsumed under effect, because it is what it has been made by Lord. Eve y sentient being, excepting Siddha and Īśvara, is Paśu. Paśu is so called because it is in bondage, it is not free (Svatantra); because its power to cause is restrained (Kāraṇaśakti sannirodha)[1]. Its bondage is beginningless: it has a limitation, constituted by Kalā and the twenty-three categories, common to the Sāṅkhya, which are subsumed under it. Paśu is also so called because it depends on what is objective.

A limited being (Paśu) does not cease to be limited even if the limitation of the insentient Kalā disappears. For, separation of limited self from body takes place at the time of dissolution of the world. But the limited beings, who thus get separation from their bodies, are born again. (Here is the origin of the conception of Pralayākala, as found in the monistic Kashmir Śaivaism). It is also called Paśu, because though it is pervasive and essentially sentient, yet it identifies itself with body. (Here is the origin of the conception of Dehapramātā as found in the monistic Kashmir Śaivaism). It is also called Paśu; because after it is separated from body in universal dissolution, it is not free to assume a body. For, that depends upon the maturity of merit and demeri , time and space and the will of the Lord[2].

Paśu is that whose everything,—action, inaction, existence, attainments and failures, relation with a body and its cessation, and the experience of the objective world,—depends upon the Lord (Pati).

According to the Lakulīśa Pāśupata, self or Ātman is that which knows the body, including internal and external senses. It is the Kṣetrajña[3]. It is self-conscious (Cetana). It is so called, because it is constantly active: it knows the objects by illuminating them with its own light. It is inferred[4] from the experience of pleasure, pain, desire, aversion and conscious effort. This is just what the Nyāya says:—

"Icchā dveṣa prayatna sukha duḥkha jñānāni ātmano liṅgam"

Paśu is distinct from Pati. Both the Paśu and the Pati are all-pervasive. But knowledge of the former is limited: the latter is omniscient. This distinction exists only when the

---

1. P. Su., 5.
2. P. Su., 5.
3. P. Su., 111.
4. P. Su., 112

Paśu is at the empirical level. But when he ascends the higher spiritual level[1], he gets united with the powers of knowledge and action, becomes omniscient and capable of creating and destroying things at his own will.

IMPURITIES (MALA) OF THE INDIVIDUAL SUBJECT (PAŚU).

The Lakulīśa Pāśupata admits five impurities (Mala) : (1) wrong knowledge (Mithyājñāna) (2) Demerit (Adharma) (3) Attachment and its cause (Saktihetu) (4) Fall of mind (Cyuti) and (5) Subjective-individuality (Paśutva). This conception of five impurities is slightly different from that, accepted by the Dualist Śaiva, with which we have already dealt.

(1) Wrong knowledge [2](Mithyājñāna) is the knowledge that is due to the defective means of knowledge, such as doubt and error etc. It is also all that is of the nature of filth to the mind (Kaluṣa), which makes the mind dirty, the base emotions, such as love of earthly objects, anger, avarice, pride and enmity etc.

(2) Demerit (Adharma) is the accumulated effect of the sinful deeds on the individual subject.

(3) The cause of attachment together with the attachment to the wordly objects (Saktihetu) is the tendency, because of which the individual subject identifies himself with body, vital air and intellect, and feels attached to their respective objects. It is due to the accumulated effect of the performance of the rituals, prescribed by other systems than the Lakulīśa Pāśupata.

(4) The fall (Cyuti) is that because of which the mind of the devotee gets away from the object of devotion and inclines towards the empirical objects, though it does not get into touch with them.

(5) The subjective-individuality is that impurity, because of which the individual subject (Paśu) is the opposite of the Lord (Pati). It has fourteen characteristics. These characteristics distinguish Paśu, the soul in bondage, from a Siddha, the liberated soul. They are the opposite of those which belong to Siddha[3]. They may be stated as follows:—

(1) Absence of omniscience and (2) omnipotence. These distinguish the Lakulīśa Pāśupata conception of the individual self from that of the Sāṅkhya. For, the Sāṅkhya holds that the

1. P. Su., 41--51
2. G. K., 22
3. G. K. 23

self is free or liberated as soon as it gets freedom from the Prakṛti and its twenty-three evolutes. This is called "Isolation" (Kaivalya) and is got through the dawn of knowledge of distinction between the sentient principle, the Puruṣa, and the insentient, the Prakṛti. But the Lakulīśa Pāśupata asserts that the attainment of Kaivalya does not mean liberation. For, the impurity, called Paśutva, which is characterised by the absence of omniscience and omnipotence is still there; that such souls as attain Kaivalya only, are reborn[1]; and that there is no true freedom so long as there is no Union (Sāyujya) with the Lord, which is characterised by passing of the powers of the Lord, such as omniscience and omnipotence, into Paśu.

(3) Absence of the power of Will. (4) Relation with the limited means of Knowledge. (5) Absence of the capacity to know and to do all, even without any relation with the "means" and the "effects". (6) Absence of the capacity to control all. (7) Absence of the capacity to enter into all. (8) Absence of the capacity to separate body from the principle of life. (9) Subjection to fear; (10) to decay; (11) to old age; and (12) to transmigratory existence. (13) Restricted motion. (14) Absence of the power to lord over[2].

The subdivisions of Paśu may be presented in a table as follows :—

PAŚU

- Sāñjana (with the limitation of body and senses)
  - Saṁhṛta (The individual self as it exists at the time of dissolution)
  - Kaivalyagata (The individual self as it is when it gets isolated from the Kalā or Prakṛti)
  - Niṣṭhāyogayukta. (Paśu as he is when in Union with the Lord)
- Nirañjana (Free from the limitation of body and senses)

EIGHT PENTADS (PAÑCAKAS) OF THE LAKULĪŚA PĀŚUPATA

The conception of the five impurities, discussed above, seems to have lead the Lakulīśa Pāśupata to think in terms of the

1. G.K. 23.

2. P. Su., 43—51.

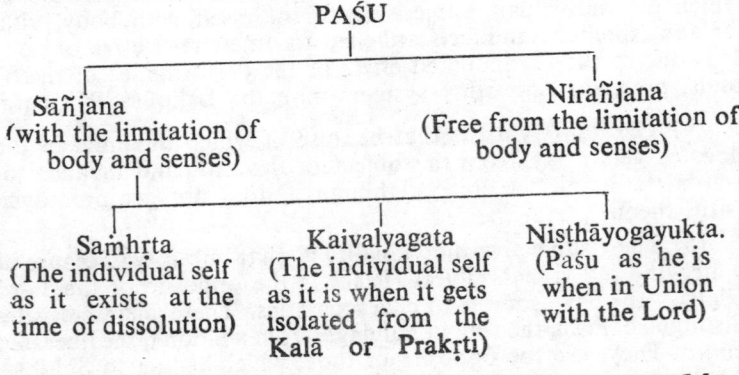

"Pentads" (Pañcaka). There are eight "pentads", including the one, constituted by the five impurities. The remaining seven are as follows: —

(I) The five means to freedom from five impurities:—

(1) *Bāsa*: It is the intellectual capacity to grasp and assimilate the real meaning of the lectures, delivered by the teacher (Bāsa)[1].

(2) *Caryā*[2]: It is the means of acquiring religious merit, Dharma, according to this system. It includes the mode of life and the mode of worship. It is presented in the Pāśupata Sūtra from the 2nd Sūtra Chapter I to the 8th Sūtra Chapter IV. Of course, there are other topics, dealt with in between. It may be pointed out here that Caryā, the means of acquiring religious merit, is often taken in a very much wider sense than the one, indicated above. The commentary on the Gaṇa Kārikā, for instance, subsumes under it the entire discipline, physical, mental and spiritual and, therefore, includes within Caryā the principal means of union with the Lord, such as japa-dhyāna (including within it Pratyāhāra, Dhāraṇā and Samādhi). The Caryā may be presented in the form of a table as follows:—

1. G. K., 17.
2. G. K., 17.

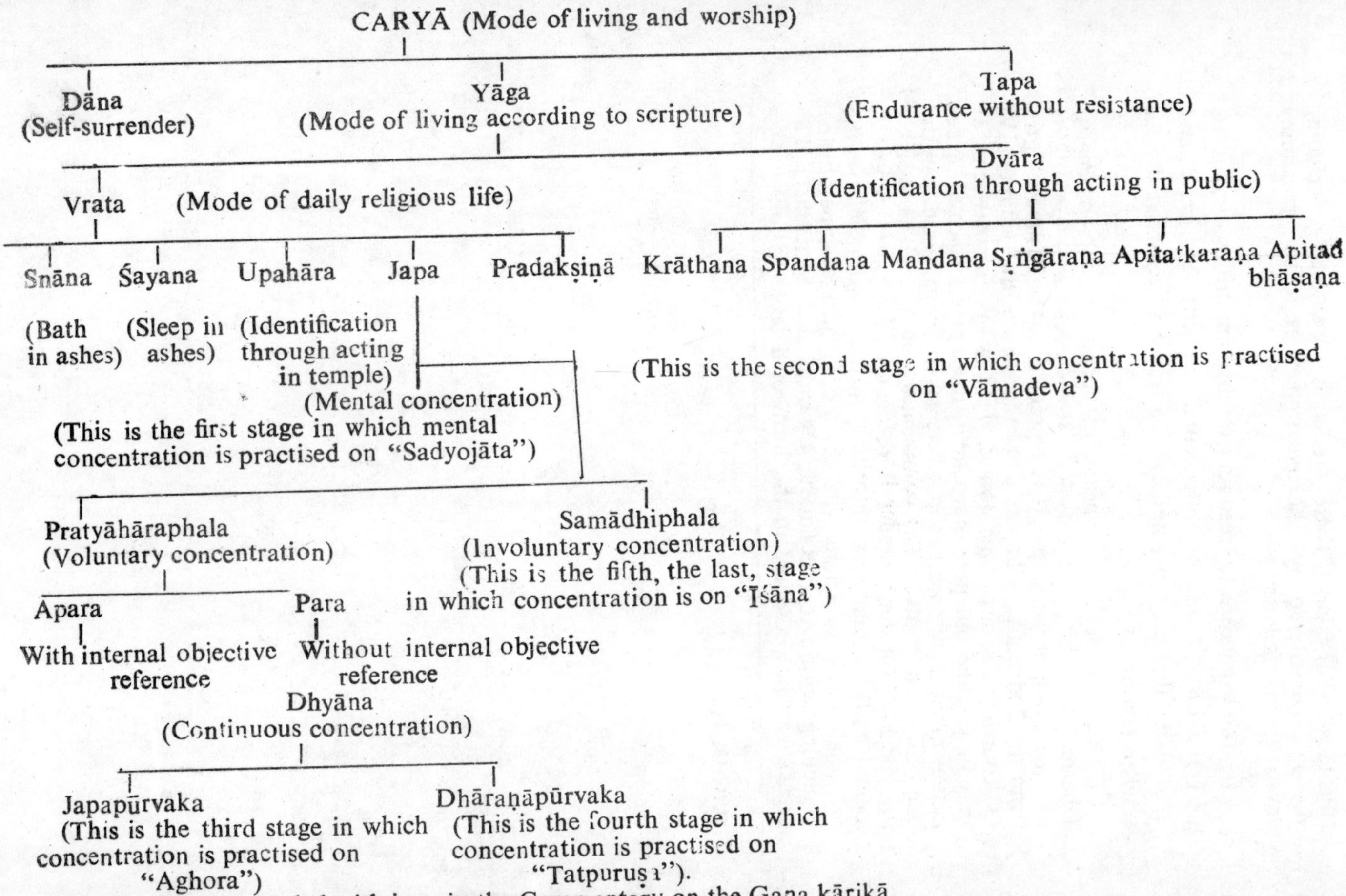

Dhyāna is compounded with japa in the Commentary on the Gaṇa kārikā.

(3) Japa-Dhyāna

In the table, presented above, on the basis of the commentary on the Gaṇa Kārikā, we find that 'Japa-Dhyāna' are closely connected with Caryā. The only distinction between Caryā and Japa-Dhyāna, is that the former is physical discipline, while the latter are mental.

Japa necessarly involves the withdrawal of the mind from the external objects (Pratyāhāra). It may be due to the voluntary effort of the internal senses (Antaḥkaraṇa pūrvakaḥ). As such it is called lower (Apara)[1]. But when, because of the continuous effort at withdrawal of the mind from the external objects and its concentration on the object of meditation, the mind gets automatically withdrawn and is uninterruptedly related to the object of meditation i.e. when there is no gap in the mental activity in relation to the object of meditation, in so far as it does not get related to any external object, just as there is none in the circle of light, when a fire-brand is moved circularly with great velocity (Ālātacakravat), the Pratyāhāra is higher (Para). The higher concentration destroys the accumulated effect of Karma and fixes the mind on the object of meditation like a nail on wood.

Dhyāna is the continuous flow of mental activity towards the object of concentration. It is of two kinds. (1) Japapūrvaka : this has been discussed just above. (2) Dhāraṇāpūrvaka : Dhāraṇā consists in the freedom of the mind of the individual subject, who is neither in the state of the universal annihilation nor in a fainting fit, from the objective reference. In Dhāraṇā the object of contemplation does not figure objectively, as distinct from the subject and as external to it. In it the object of concentration is not something that is outside the mind, towards which the mental activity is to be directed. It is simply an affection of mind, as one with it.

(4) *Sadārudrasmṛti :* The uninterrupted recollection of Rudra (Sadārudrasmṛti) is the principal means to the fixity of mind on the object of meditation. It prevents the mind from running away from the object of concentration.

(5) *Prasāda* (*Grace*) *:* It is the means to freedom from the impurity, technically called "Paśutva", which has already been discussed earlier.

(II) Deśa : It is the second pentad. The places (Deśa), where the person, striving for final emancipation, should live during the five stages, are also five :—

(1) Temple (2) Place, where the devotees assemble (3) Cave (4) Cremation ground and (5) Rudra.

---

1 G. K., 20.

(III) Avasthā : It is the third Pentad. The states (Avasthā), in which an aspirant for 'freedom' is enjoined to live in the aforesaid places, are also five:—

(1) Vyakta[1] is the state in which the aspirant is enjoined to have all the characteristic marks of a follower of the Pāśupata path to final emancipation.

(2) Avyakta is the state in which the external marks are discarded.

(3) Jaya is the state in which the aspirant has acquired control over his senses. (Indriyajaya).

(4) Cheda is the state of complete detachment from the world. It is also called Dāna[2], because it means giving up all possessions (Sarvasvatyāga).

(5) Niṣṭhā is complete cessation of all activities.

(IV) Śuddhi : It is the fourth pentad. The purification (śuddhi) that is attained through the five means, stated above, is also of five kinds:—

(1) Disappearance of ignorance; (2) of Adharma; (3) of attachment; (4) of getting of the mind away from the object of concentration; and (5) of the impurity, called Paśutva.

(V) Bala : It is the fifth pentad. The powers of the individual subject, which enable him to use the means, stated above, are also five:—

(1) Devotion to the teacher[3], (2) Freedom of mind from the disturbing passions (Prasāda), (3) Equanimity of mind in the midst of pains and sufferings of all types, (4) Religious merit, (5) True knowledge.

(VI) Dīkṣākāri : It is the sixth pentad. The means of spiritual initiation (Dīkṣākāri) are also five:—

(1) The 'Material' (Dravya)[4] is a technical term; which means (a) Vidyā, the learning, which the disciple and the teacher possess, (*b*) Kuśa etc. and (c) the Brāhmaṇa disciple, who is to be initiated. (2) Time (Kāla), prescribed for initiation in the scripture. (3) Ceremony, as described in the Saṁskāra Kārikā. (4) The image of the deity. (5) Teacher.

---

1 G. K., 8
2 S. D. S., 164.
3 G. K., 5.
4 G. K., 8.

(VII) Lābha : It is the seventh pentad. The attainable (Lābha) is that which is attained through initiation (Dīkṣā). This is also of five types:—

(1) The mastery over the Lakulīśa Pāśupata system(Jñāna)[1]. (2) The religious merit, accruing from the performance of the daily ritual (Tapas)[2]. (3) Capacity to concentrate on the object of meditation, without break or interruption (Nityatva)[3]. (4) The fixity of mind on Rudra, because of the disappearance of distracting factors (Sthiti). (5) The powers of the liberated (Siddhi), because of which a person is called "Siddha".

SIDDHA

The Pāśupata system is primarily concerned with pointing out the spiritual discipline which gradually leads to the union with the Lord. But in order to induce the pupils to undergo the discipline, the powers of a Siddha, the man who has attained the union, are stated.

A Siddha gets the powers of knowledge and action. The power of knowledge is really one but is called by different names, such as the power of seeing far distant object (Dūradarśana), because of its relation with different kinds of objects[4]. The power of action consists in having the speed of mind in the productive activity, so that there is no gap between the thought of production and the production itself[5], as there is in the case of Prajāpati etc., who are said to practise austerity after the rise of the thought of production, before they can actually produce. He produces all 'forms' at will. He has at his command the matter, which produces 'forms' (Earth etc.). His mind is pervasive. Therefore, he can think in all sentient beings, who can think. He is one with, non-different from, Maheśvara, because he is all-pervasive. This is one of the implications of "Rudra-sāyujya".

In all these cases there is a clear consciousness of the triad (Trika) ; the subject, the object and the means. *This idea Nāgārjuna seems to be refuting in his Mādhyamika kārikā.* He is also capable of annihilating all that he produces[6]. He is not like Viśvāmitra, who can create but cannot destroy. The dissolution is brought out by his mere rising above the level of means (Vikaraṇa). That is, the dissolution of the creation is

---

1 G. K., 9.
2 G. K., 15.
3 G. K., 16.
4 P. Su., 43.
5 P. Su., 44.
6 P. Su., 45.

nothing but the dissolution of the idea of creation, which coincides with his rising to the level of pure consciousness(Kaivalya).

A Yogin is Siddha, when he gets the capacity to see the remotest etc. Such a person is not affected by Karma[1], done in consequence of his relation with body, senses and their objects.

(III) YOGA, THE THIRD PRIMARY CATEGORY OF THE LAKULĪŚA PĀŚUPATA.

The word "Yoga" in this system is used, not in the sense, in which Patañjali uses it in his Yoga Sūtra, namely, "Checking the rise of mental affection" (Yogaścittavṛtti nirodhaḥ) but in the sense of "Union with the Lord". Thus, according to Patañjali, Yoga is simply the means to Kaivalya, but it is the end, according to this system. It may, however, be noted that in some contexts it is used for the means also.

The system aims at giving the discipline, which brings about union with the Lord, a union which is of a distinct type from others, as presented in other systems. This union takes place in successive stages[2]. It is consequent on the withdrawal of senses from their objects. The practice of austerities is a means to it. It is the union of an individual subject, who strives for it, with the Lord and in the Lord. It consists in the realisation of the Maheśvara as the very self of himself by the aspirant. It is the cessation of the idea of identity of the individual self with body. It presupposes the freedom of the mind from all tendencies such as attachment and enmity etc. The occupation of mind with the Śaiva thought, because of close application to the study of scripture or because of concentration on Śiva (Adhyayana dhyānādilakṣaṇaḥ Kriyāyogaḥ)[3] is the first stage of union with the Lord.

Yoga, the union with Śiva or Īśvara, is not due to the activity of the limited subject only, as in the case of the contact of a bird with a rock. But it is due to the activity of both, the limited self and the Īśvara, as in the case of the two fighting rams. This means that howsoever hard an individual may try for the union, it cannot be achieved without His grace.

The individual soul is admitted by the Lakulīśa Pāśupata, just like the Nyāya and the Vaiśeṣika, to be all-pervasive (Vibhu).

1 P. Su., 121.
2 P. Su., 41.
3 P. Su., 41.

Therefore, in reality, the soul is always in union with the Īśvara. Its separation consists in the inoperation of the powers of knowledge and action, due to the beginningless bondage. The union presupposes freedom from the bondage, the limiting condition that separates the individual from the Lord. It can be achieved through the spiritual discipline, including Samādhi[1], as enjoined by the Pāśupata Śāstra.

The Lakulīśa Pāśupata system admits eight means to union with the Lord, which are known as the eight parts of yoga (Aṣṭāṅgayoga) i. e. (1) Daily observances (Niyama) (2) Abstention (Yama). (3) Posture (Āsana). (4) Breath-control (Prāṇāyāma). (5) Withdrawal of mind from external things (Pratyāhāra).(6) Concentration with objective reference (Dhyāna). (7) Concentration without objective reference (Dhāraṇā). (8) Involuntary concentration (Samādhi).

The ideas, signified by these technical expressions, are different from those, for which these expressions stand in the Yoga system of Patañjali. We shall show this in the future work on this system.

This system admits super-normal powers of a Yogin and asserts that within six months, in quick succession, arise the powers of distant vision etc. in a Yogin, who lives in a cave and has his mind firmly fixed on the Lord[2].

According to the Lakulīśa Pāśupata, Yoga is primarily of two types : (1) Kriyālakṣaṇa, that which is characterised by physical activities. The Lakulīśa Pāśupata system recognises acting of four types, dance and vocal music, as the means to spiritual union with the Lord. It also admits that there are five stages of union, similar to the five stages of action in a drama. The first stage of Yoga is the beginning, in which the aspirant has to embrace asceticism, bathe in ashes[3], sleep in ashes, bathe in ashes as many times as he gets polluted, because of the contact or even the sight of polluting things ; put on the garland etc., which are offered to the deity in temple ; bear the characteristic external signs of a follower of the Lakulīśa Pāśupata sect ; wear only one piece of cloth or none; live in the vicinity of a Śaiva temple; stick to the vow[4] of non-violence in thought, word and deed ; of celebacy, truth, detachment, abstention from theft, freedom from anger, devotion to teacher, piety of life, light food and assiduity in the observance of the rules of asceticism. Thus, when the aspirant gets freedom from all passions, he should

1 P. Su., 6.
2 P. Su., 116—18.
3 P. Su., 8—13.
4 P. Su., 16.

practise breath-control (Prāṇāyāma) and concentrate his mind on the meaning of the first of the five Mantras of the Taittirīya Āraṇyaka, "Sadyojātam Prapadyāmi" etc., sitting to the south of the deity in temple. At the end of contemplation, he should attempt to merge in, surrender to, or identify himself with the Lord through acting Śiva, in respect of his loud laughter (Aṭṭahāsa) or his Bull, in respect of bellow (Duṇḍukāra). He should also attempt to do the same by means of dance and vocal music[1].

When, as a result of the discipline in the first stage, as stated above, the true knowledge dawns in him and he is perfectly free from passions, he should enter into the second stage to test that he has no trace of passion left in him. In this stage, in public, he should act deep sleep (Krāthana), trembling (Spandana), irregular and slow movement like that of one whose legs are paralysed (Mandaṇa), acting a lover at the sight of young beautiful woman (Śṛṅgāraṇa) ; doing the condemnable things, like one who does not distinguish the right act from the wrong (Apitatkaraṇa) ; and speaking incoherently and irreleventlv (Apitadbhāṣaṇa). All these he has to do in order that he may become the object of condemnation and hatred, and satisfy himself that no passion arises in him in the face of insult and injuries[2].

Lakulīśa, in his Pāśupata Sūtra, records a tradition, which says that Indra followed this Pāśupata method of acquiring accumulated merit of the demons (Indro vā agre asureṣu Pāśupatamācarat)[3]. This constitutes the second stage, at which the aspirant has to concentrate his mind on the second of the five mantras "Vāmadevāya namaḥ". At this stage the aspirant attains to a higher spiritual level than the one, attained by the followers of the Sāṅkhya and the Yoga. Here the mind of the aspirant gets the union with the Lord (Yoga), which is technically called "proximity" (Samīpa)[4]. This seems to have given rise to the conception of Sāmīpya Mokṣa.

Thus, the union, which is characterised by action, i. e. attained through living the life as presented above, is the first type of union technically called Kriyālakṣana Yoga. (2) Kriyoparama Lakṣaṇa, is the second type of union (Yoga), which needs no physical action of the above type. It needs nothing but pure mental concentration. The remaining three stages of Yoga come under this.

---

1 P. Su., 13.
2 G. K., 19.
3 P. Su., 101.
4 P. Su., 106.

The third stage begins with the retirement of the aspirant to a cave and the practice of concentration, with his mind completely withdrawn from all that is empirical. Here the mind of the aspirant moves towards, reaches and touches the object of contemplation presented by the third Mantra "Aghorebhyaḥ". But soon after the touch, the mind gets away from the object, because of the weakness of concentration. Here the mind moves forward and backward, so much so that its touch with the object seems to be unbroken and uninterrupted, very much as a circle of light seems to appear when a fire-brand is moved with great velocity, in a circle, (Brahmaṇyeva ālātacakravat avatiṣṭhate G. K. 20). This is attained through concentration (Dhyāna), which is accompanied by withdrawal of the mind from all that is empirical and its voluntary movement towards the Lord.

The fourth stage begins with the stay in the cremation ground. At this stage the mind gets fixed on the object of contemplation, the Lord, as presented by the fourth mantra "Tatpuruṣāya vidmahe" as a nail does on a piece of wood, (Stambhanikṣipta ayaḥ kīlavat niścalīkaroti. G. K. 20). This is attained through "Dhāraṇā", as discussed above. This kind of union with the Lord is technically called "Niṣṭhāyoga" or "Devanityatā". At this stage the ascetic eats anything that is put in his bowl, even meat[1].

The last stage is that of such a penetration into the Lord that the powers of the Lord pass into the individual. This is got through "Samādhi" on the Lord as presented in the fifth Mantra "Īśānaḥ sarvavidyānām". This is technically called "Sāyujya" (Labhate Rudra Sāyujyam P. Su., 139). The individual becomes Śiva for ever (Sadāśiva P. Su., 146). This idea seems to have been the basis of the Sadāśiva category in the monistic Śaivaism of Kashmir.

(IV) VIDHI

Vidhi is the fourth primary category of this system. It includes ascetic life, devotional rites and control of senses. Lakulīśa very much emphasises the conquest of the senses for the spiritual insight and the union with the Lord or Maheśvara. He holds that mere intellectual knowledge of the distinction between the Prakṛti and the Puruṣa is not sufficient for the attainment of Kaivalya and that the discipline, as prescribed in the Lakulīśa Pāśupata system, has to be undergone for its realisation. We have already spoken on the various aspects of the discipline, under Caryā. For the convenience of the reader it may be presented in the form of a table as follows:—

1 P. Su., 119.

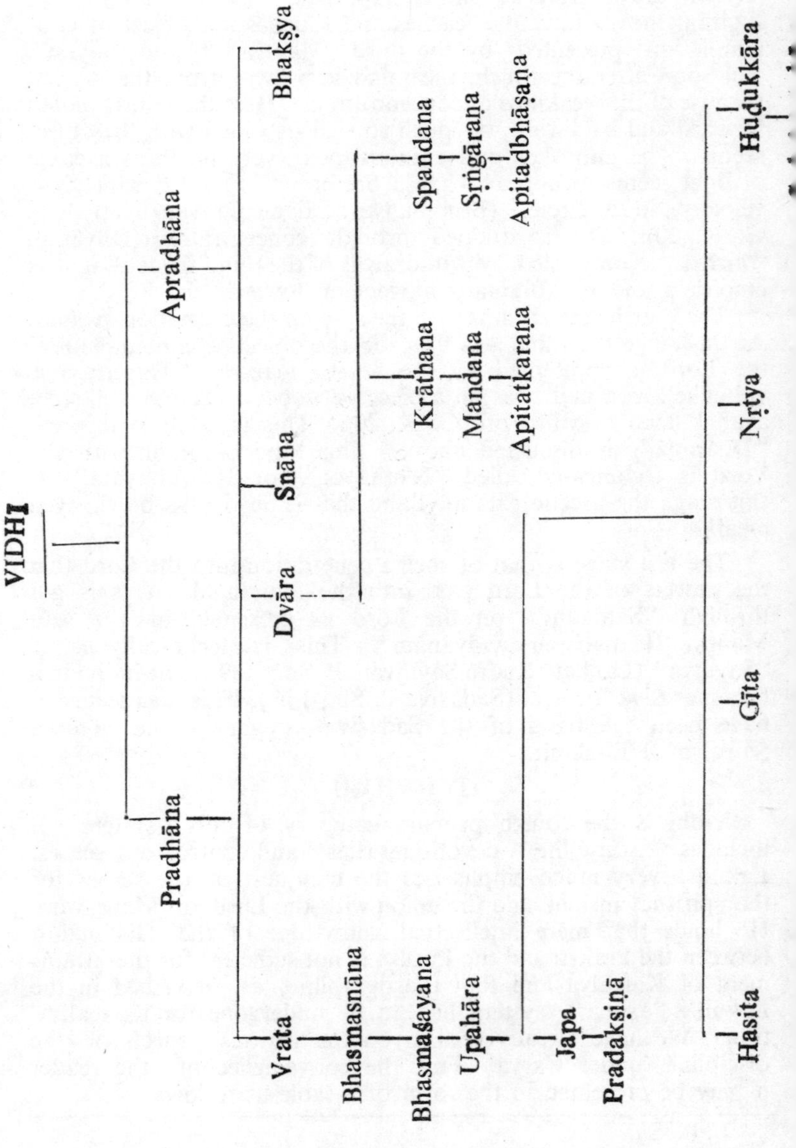
VIDHI
Pradhāna
Apradhāna
Vrata
Bhasmasnāna
Bhasmaśayana
Upahāra
Japa
Pradakṣiṇā
Dvāra
Snāna
Bhakṣya
Krāthana
Spandana
Mandana
Sṛṅgāraṇa
Apitatkaraṇa
Apitadbhāṣaṇa
Hasita
Gīta
Nṛtya
Huḍukkāra

(V) DUḤKHĀNTA (END OF ALL MISERIES)

Duḥkhānta, the end of all miseries, is the fifth and the last primary category of this system. Lakulīśa asserts that it is ultimately due to His grace and that it cannot be got through knowledge and detachment (Jñāna-Vairāgya) independently. It is of two types (1) Anātmaka and (2) Sātmaka[1].

The Anātmaka consists in mere cessation of all miseries. This seems to represent the conception of Mokṣa as presented by Gautama in his Nyāya Sūtra. This lends some support to the view that Gautama was a Pāśupata. For, his conception of Mokṣa as given in "Duḥkhajanmapravṛtti" (N. S. ch. I, S. 2) is just what is presented here as Nirātmaka. The same may be said about the Vaiśeṣika.

The Sātmaka consists not only in the freedom from all miseries, but also in the attainment of the powers of knowledge and action, which characterise a Siddha, a clear picture of whom has already been given earlier. It is attained when the individual penetrates into the Lord so that the powers pass into him ; when he attains the Yoga, which is technically called Sāyujya, as discussed above.

YUKTA AND MUKTA

The liberation, according to the Lakulīśa Pāśupata, is not only freedom from bondage but also union (Yoga). In fact, union is very much emphasised in this system to bring out its distinction from the Yoga, the Sāṅkhya, the Bauddha and the Vedānta, according to which the liberation consists in mere freedom from the limiting conditions ; in losing the individuality ; in the disappearance of the separate existence, similar to that of ether in a jar (Ghaṭākāśa) when the jar is broken. It declares that the spiritual insight (Darśana)[2] of the Sāṅkhya and the Yoga is defective, just as is the perception of the moon by the man with dim vision.

THE CHARACTERISTICS OF THE UNITED (YUKTA)

The Lakulīśa Pāśupata admits the limited self-consciousness, selfhood, or personality to be simply a limited form of the 'mind' (Vṛtyākārasya)[3]. Accompanied by the Manas, it flies to the objects and rests on them like a bird on a tree. When this limited form, the affected 'Mind' (Citta) that constitutes

---

1. G. K., 9. 2. P. Su., 115. 3. P. Su. 111.

personality, disappears and the mind does no longer run towards the object to rest there ; on the contrary, it rests on Maheśvara, it is said to be Yukta or united.

THE CONDITIONS OF THE UNION

The limited self gets united with the Lord, when it gets freedom from the limiting conditions ; when it is purified from the impurities (Doṣa) ; when it is no longer drawn by the objective world; when it gives up the thought of the sensuous objects[1] ; when its activity is constantly and exclusively directed towards the Lord; when it rises above all that is grasped by the internal or external senses (Aja) ; and when it is free from all desires and aversions[2] and has the Citta irremovably fixed on the Lord (Maitra). These conditions arise as soon as the Citta gets fixed on the Lord, though it is still connected with body and senses.

1. P. Su., 110. 2. P. Su., 112.

TABLE OF THE CATEGORIES OF THE LAKULĪŚA PĀŚUPATA SYSTEM

(*PRIMARY CATEGORIES*)

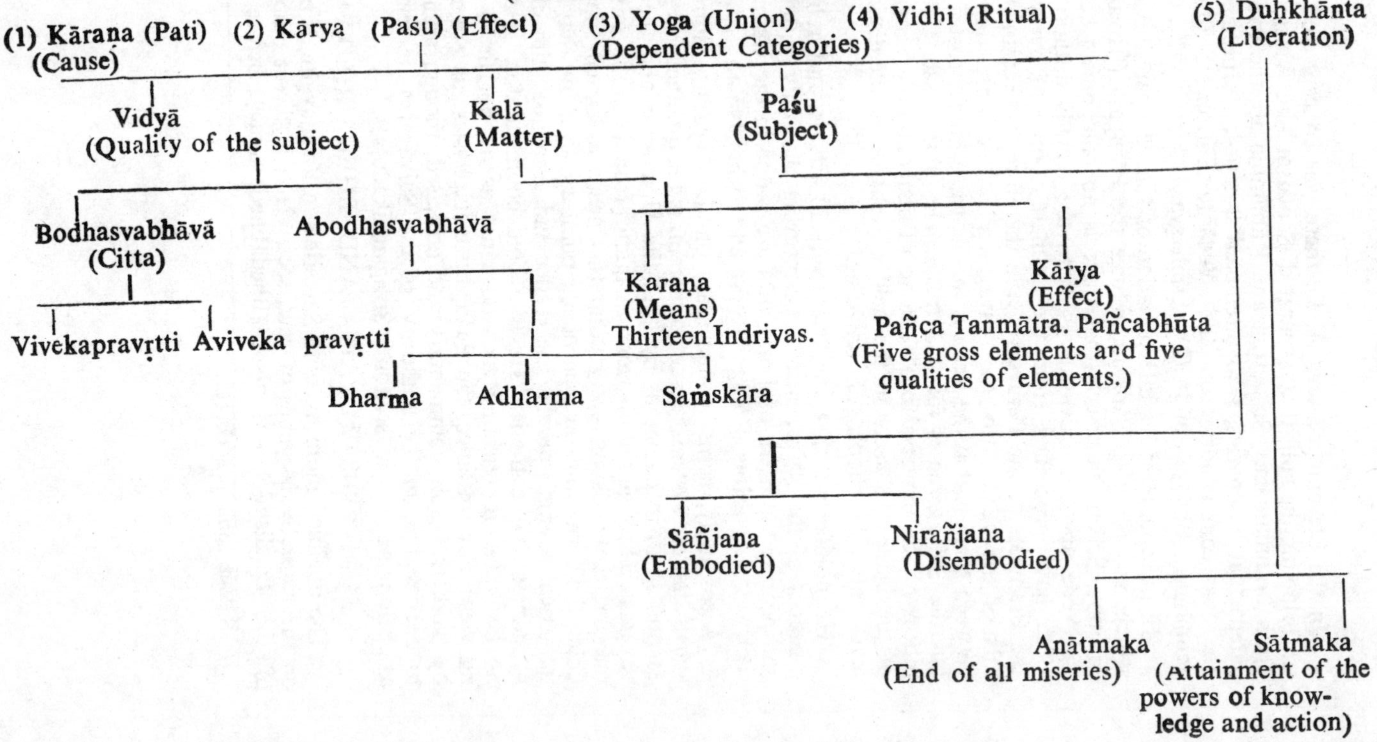

(IV) VIŚIṢṬĀDVAITA OR QUALIFIED MONISTIC ŚAIVAISM

In the Eleventh century A. D. there was concentrated effort at bridging the gulf that separated Śaivaism and Vaiṣṇavaism from Brahmanism. Śrīkaṇṭha and Rāmānuja are the two great intellectual luminaries, who attempted this task, as presented in the two commentaries on the Vedānta Sūtra, (1) Brahmamīmāṁsā Bhāṣya and (2) Śrībhāṣya.

In the course of his interpretation of the Pāśupatādhikaraṇa, which, according to Śaṅkara, refutes the Pāśupata (Śaiva) Philosophy, Śrīkaṇṭha asserts that there is no antagonism between the Veda and the Śaivāgama. Both are equally authoritative. Both have proceeded from the ultimate source of everything, the Brahman or the Para Śiva, and therefore, it is reasonable to talk of the Veda also as "Śivāgama". The only difference between them is that the Veda is for the three higher castes only; but the Śaivāgama is for all, irrespective of the caste. Recognition of the universal brotherhood of man and non-recognition of the barrier of caste in the field of religion is the distinctive mark of all schools of Śaivaism.

He points out that the characteristic rituals and religious practices of the Śaiva, such as besmearing the body with ashes and bearing the mark of Tripuṇḍra, are stated in the Upaniṣads such as Atharvaśiras, Kālāgni Rudra and Bṛhajjāvāla.

Accordingly in his commentary on the Vedānta Sūtra, he shows that the system, presented therein, is the qualified Monism, as presented, in common, by both the Upaniṣads and the Śaivāgamas. Through out his work, he quotes from both the Śaivāgama and the Veda on every point that needs a textual support. Often the quotations on a particular point are so many that mere numerical strength dazzles the reader and convinces him of the soundness of the thesis. He is a bold commentator. He has no hesitation in rejecting such doctrines as do not fit in with his view. For instance, the Pāśupata metaphysics as presented by Śaṅkara in his commentary and criticised, though admitted to be based upon the authority of the Śaivāgama, is rejected as belonging to a section (Śivāgamaikadeśa)[1].

VIŚIṢṬĀDVAITA AND BHEDĀBHEDA

The qualified monism, both Śaivaite and Vaiṣṇavaite, is based on the respective Āgamas of each sect. It is a direct outcome of the Dualism-*cum*-Monism (Bhedābhedavāda). Before the

1 Srikam. Bh., Vol. II, 111.

rise of the Vaiṣṇava Qualified Monism, two great authorities had spoken on Bhedābheda. One, Yādava Prakāśa, was the teacher of Rāmānuja himself. And the other, Bhāskara, was a non-sectarion authority belonging to the 9th century A. D. Similarly the Ṣaivāgama literature, openly propounding Bhedābheda, and the Lakuliśa Pāśupata system, presenting the same, were already there before the rise of the Viśiṣṭādvaita Ṣaivaism of Ṣrīkaṇṭha.

THE INFLUENCES

The Viśiṣṭādvaita Ṣaivaism, as presented by Śrīkaṇṭha, arose in the 11th century A. D. There is definite evidence in support of this view. For, he quotes from Utpalācārya's Īśvara Pratyabhijñā Kārikā the oft quoted verse:—

"Cidātmaiva hi devontaḥ".

Śrīkaṇṭha differes from Abhinavagupta in his interpretation of the above quoted verse and holds that "independently of the material cause" (Nirupādānam) does not mean without any material cause[1], but only without any material cause that is external to the Lord.

He is a follower of the Śiddhānta School of Ṣaivaism which, as pointed out earlier, accepts the authority of the 28 Ṣaivāgamas, out of which eighteen present Dualistic-cum-Monistic (Bhedābheda) philosophy. He adopts the basic philosophical ideas of the Dualistic Siddhānta Ṣaivaism, as presented in an earlier section. Thus, he admits (1) that there are three primary categories ; Pati, Paśu and Pāśa[2] : (2) that from another point of view there are thirty-six categories : this seems to be due to the influence of the Monistic Ṣaivaism of Kashmir, as we know from the statement of his commentator, Appayya Dīkṣita[3] : (3) that there are three impurities ; Paśutva, Kārma and Māyīya[4] : they are material like blackness in copper : (4) that Mokṣa (Liberation) is the attainment of similarity (Sāmya) with Ṣiva : (5) that the individual subject possesses omniscience and omnipotence, but these powers are obscured by the impurities, so that when he gets freedom from them his hidden powers become manifest and he becomes similar to the Lord : (6) that Para Ṣiva transcends all categories and possesses the power (Ṣakti) which is inherent in Him and constitutes His essential quality (Guṇa).

1. Srikam. Bh., Vol. II, 29.
2. Srikam. Bh., Vol. II, 111.
3. Srikam. Bh., Vol. II, 109-10
4. Srikam. Bh., Vol. II, 142-3.,

The Lakulīśa Pāśupata system flourished in the 2nd century A. D. And its tradition continued to live during the time when independent works on Dualistic Siddhānta Śaivaism and the commentaries on them were written down to the 12th century A. D. It is clear from the criticism of the Lakulīśa Pāśupata view that at liberation the powers of knowledge and action pass into the individual from the Lord (Saṅkrānti) by Sadyojyoti in his Paramokṣa Nirāsa Kārikā and Rāmakaṇṭha II in his commentary on the above. A careful comparison of the conception of the Lord, His power (Śakti) and the relation between the two, as presented in the Lakulīśa Pāśupata system, with the one as found in the commentary of Śrīkaṇṭha on the Vedānta Sūtra, as interpreted by Appayya Dīkṣita, leaves very little doubt about the fact that Śrīkaṇṭha has adopted the Dualistic-cum-Monistic view of the Lakulīśa Pāśupata.

BHEDĀBHEDA AND VIŚIṢṬĀDVAITA DISTINGUISHED

Śrīkaṇṭha openly declares that he is opposed to the Bhedābheda[1]. He admits that there are Vedic texts, which talk of the identity of the objective world and the Ultimate Reality, such as are referred to by "Tadananyatvamārambhaṇaśabdādibhyaḥ" and that there are also such texts as speak of the difference of the two ; for instance, those to which "Adhikantu bhedanirdeśāt" refers. But he asserts that this does not mean that both the assertions in regard to the relation of the Śiva with world have equal validity and, therefore, Bhedābheda is the only sound philosophy. For, such a view is illogical, because it makes contrary assertions in regard to one and the same.

According to him, the objective world does not exist independently of and separately from the Brahman, as one worldly object does from another, e.g. a jar from a piece of cloth. For, such a view is against the texts which speak of the identity of the two (Tadananyatva). Nor are they so thoroughly identical that one is merely an illusion and the other is the basis from which it arises, just as are the illusory silver and the mother-of-pearl, from which the illusion of silver arises. For, such a view militates against other texts which talk of the difference of the Brahman or Śiva from the objective world ; because of the difference of the inherent qualities of the two. And Duality-cum-non-duality is illogical, as has already been stated.

It has to be carefully noted that here Śrīkaṇṭha is denouncing Bhedābheda of a particular type. The view that he rejects

1. Srikam. Bh., Vol. II, 31.

is the one, according to which Bhedābheda means that identity and difference are on the same level and that they co-exist and have the same importance, much as the two objects, which are related by a conjunctive particle. The rejected view is the one, according to which the compound word "Bhedābheda" is to be split up as "Bhedaśca abhedaśca", as a co-ordinative compound (Dvandva samāsa). It seems to be similar to the one, propounded by Nimbārka[1].

In contrast to the Bhedābheda, as presented above, he propounds Viśiṣṭādvaita. He asserts that the relation between the objective world and the Brahman or Śiva is similar to that which we find between a body and a soul; or between a quality and a substance, in which it inheres ; the one is subordinate to the other. They are identical much as are a jar and the clay, of which it is made ; or a substance and a quality ; because of the material causal relation or the relation of inherence. Identity means the non-existence of one without the other. For, jar does not exist without clay ; nor does lotus exist without a perceptible colour.

He rejects extreme Monism, extreme Dualism, Dualism cum-Monism and also the view that holds it difficult to assert definitely either Monism or Dualism. He asserts that the two,—the true knowledge of one of which is not possible without that of the other; or one of which cannot exist without the other,—are related as substance and attribute. And such is the case with the Brahman and the empirical multiplicity. Therefore, the latter is related to the former as an attribute. For, according to him, the multiplicity has its being potentially in the power (Śakti) of the Brahman ; the empirical multiplicity is nothing but a gross form of what exists in a subtle form in the power of the Brahman, much as does a tree in a seed. Hence because the power that gives rise to the multiplicity, cannot exist without Brahman and because the knowledge of Brahman is not possible without the power, much as is not that of fire without heat ; therefore, the power is an attribute of the Brahman, and accordingly the empirical multiplicity also, which is potentially in His power and does not exist independently of Him even when it assumes gross form, is His attribute. Hence Śrīkaṇṭha asserts that his theory of qualified Monism is in perfect accord with the scriptural texts, which speak of both identity and difference. The texts, which speak of the identity, refer to the fact that empirical multiplicity has no being independently of Him; and those which talk of the difference refer to the

1. I. I. Ph, 430.

fundamental difference between the Lord on the one hand and the multiplicity of limited subjects and objects on the other. For, the Lord is free, but subjects and objects are not free (Asvatantra) : and the latter two are different from each other also : one is the experiencer but the other is only the object of experience[1].

It may, however, be pointed out here that the word "Bhedābheda" as it occurs in the Śaivāgamas, implies all that is intended to be signified by the word "Viśiṣṭādvaita". But to get this implication, the compound word has to be split up, not as a coördinative compound (Dvandva samāsa), but as a determinative compound (Tatpuruṣa samāsa) as "Bhedaviśiṣṭaḥ abhedaḥ". In fact , if we cast a glance at the analogies, by means of which Śrīkaṇṭha attempts to bring out the exact nature of relation between the Brahman or Śiva and the empirical multiplicity, and compare them with those which are found in the Taittirīya Āraṇyaka, the Pāśupata Sūtra and the commentaries on them from the Bhedābheda point of view, we find them to be almost the same. The reader can satisfy himself on this point by referring to the preceding section on the Lakulīśa Pāśupata system.

BRAHMAN OR ŚIVA

The Ultimate Reality, the Brahman or Śiva, is free from temporal, spatial and formal limitations and, therefore, is incomparably "Great". He possesses the highest power (Parama Śakti) which is responsible for the rise of the entire empirical multiplicity, including both the sentient and the insentient. The objective world is nothing but the gross form of what lies in a subtle state in His power. The multiplicity is real and not a mere illusion: it is related to Him as a quality is to a substance, through His power. The multiplicity is within Him ; He is, therefore, not limited by anything that is external to Him and yet is real as He is. He is different from the multiplicity and the constituents of the multiplicity have differences from one another ; but all this is within the Śiva himself. He has difference within Himself[2]: but He is not different from anything that is different from Him and yet has reality similar to His, just as a jar is from a piece of cloth. Nor is He different from anything that differs from Him as one cow does from another. For, there is nothing that is different from Him in either of the two ways. He is called "Brahman" because He is what the word signifies. He is Brahman, because He is Great, as stated just

1. Srikam. Bh., Vol. II, 32-4.
2. Srikam. Bh., Vol. I, 68-70.

above (Bṛhattvāt). He is also Brahman, because He is responsible for the grossification of what lies in Him in subtle state, at the time of creation ; and also because the Greatness, which the individual self attains at liberation, is due to Him (Braṁhaṇatvāt)[1].

It is only to indicate that all that is necessary to use the word Brahman for Śiva, is in Śiva, that so great a personality as Puṣpadanta, the King of Gandharvas, in his Mahimna Stotra refers to Him in eight words, which stand for His essential attributes ; (1) Bhava, (2) Śarva, (3) Śiva, (4) Paśupati, (5) Parameśvara, (6) Mahādeva, (7)Rudra, (8) Śambhu. He is called : (1) "Bhava" because He is the origin of the universe : this idea is found in Taittirīya Āraṇyaka "Bhavodbhavāya" (2) Śaṅkara, because He always does good ; the creation and dissolution are only for the good of the souls in bondage : (3) Śiva, because He has all the good attributes : (4) Śarva, because He annihilates the universe at the time of dissolution : (5) Paśupati, because He controls the souls in bondage much as a hunter does the dogs, whom he holds by chains: (6) Parameśvara, because He lords over the universe : (7) Mahādeva, because He rests in His own transcendental Bliss : (8) Rudra, because He frees the bound from the chain of the transmigratory existence. Thus, these attributes define the ultimate Reality both subjectively and objectively. Subjectively He is good and Blissful ; and objectively He is the cause of creation, maintenance, annihilation, obscuration and grace (Pañcakṛtya) and is all—pervasive. He is the object of contemplation etc., as presented unanimously by all the sacred texts, including both, the Vedic and the Āgamic[2].

Though the determinate knowledge of the Brahman or Śiva, such as can completely grasp Him exactly like an object on the palm, is not possible : yet He admits of definition. Though He cannot be defined exhaustively as "this and of such and such definite nature" ; yet definition of Him in terms of differentiation from known things is possible. In fact, no definition exhaustively presents all the attributes of the object defined. It simply presents the main attributes so as to enable us to know the object under definition as distinct from other known things. Thus, through the grasp of His attributes as presented by the scripture, He is known as distinct from other objects of knowledge[3].

The unity of Brahman or Śiva is the unity similar to that of the aesthetic experience. Just as the aesthetic experience is a unitary experience, because of the harmonious unification

---

1. Srikam Bh., Vol. I, 69.
2. Srikam. Bh., Vol. I, 70.
3. Srikam. Bh., Vol. I, 96.

of all the contents ; so Śiva is a unity because all that is within Him forms a unity similar to that which is formed by the various ingredients of "Pānaka Rasa"[1]. He is, therefore, not pure unity, but unity in multiplicity. He is not without attribute (Nirviśeṣa)[2]. For, the power to produce gross multiplicity is as natural to Him as heat is to fire. He is the material as well as the efficient cause: because of the possession of the Power, in which the entire multiplicity has its being in a subtle form; and because He directs this power in the production of the gross multiplicity.

The objective world with all its multiplicity is not different from Śiva; exactly as foam, waves and bubbles etc. are not different from the ocean. This, however, does not mean that Śiva changes or evolves. For, the evolution is not in Śiva but in the power (Śakti)[3] that is stirred to action by His will. But how can Śiva be maintained to be changeless when His power, which is identical with and non-different from Him, is admitted to evolve ? In reply to this question, the Viśiṣṭādvaita Śaivaism asserts that identity and non-difference can be talked of only when there is the duality of that which is identified and that with which it is identified; and similarly non-difference can be only when there is that which differs and that from which it differs. Therefore, in this context, non-difference does not mean absolute unity ; nor does difference mean absolute diversity. But non-difference means the inseparable existence, similar to that of a jar and its perceptible colour: and similarly difference means separate existence as an object of a separate cognitive activity. Thus, the power of Śiva is different from Him; though it is identical also with Him at the same time. Hence the change in the power does not mean that Śiva changes. The power is related to Śiva exactly as are the rays to the Moon[4].

Even in the state of universal annihilation, in which Sun and Moon, time and space as limiting conditions, and name and form completely disappear; the individual selves and the material cause (Paśu and Pāśa) do not cease to exist as such. They simply get beyond name and form, and as such have their being in the power of the Lord[5]. At the time of creation, therefore, He has not to depend upon anything that is external to Him, as clay is to potter. He is, therefore, both the material and the efficient cause of the universe. He paints the picture of the universe on the wall of His power of will[6].

1. Srikam. Bh. Vol. I, 115.
2. Srikam. Bh. Vol. I, 124-5.
3. Srikam. Bh. Vol. I, 300.
4. Srikam. Bh. Vol. I, (Comm) 300.
5. Srikam. Bh Vol. I, 340.
6. Srikam. Bh. Vol. I, 345

He is merciful. His creative activity is prompted by mercy that He has for the souls in bondage. The diversity that we find in the objective world is not due to His caprice merely. He is guided in the production of the diversity by the purpose of giving diverse opportunities to the souls in bondage to enable them to experience the fruits of their accumulated effects of pious and sinful deeds and thus to get freedom from the bondage of Karma. He, therefore, cannot be said to be cruel because of the creation of deformed, ugly and painful, because in so doing He is prompted by the Karmas of the individuals[1].

THE INDIVIDUAL SUBJECT OR PAŚU

Paśu is the second of the three primary categories. He is essentially sentient but has three beginningless impurities. (1) Paśutva (2) Karma and (3) Māyā. On account of the first he identifies himself with body, vital air and intellect etc., and, therefore, is subjected to varying experiences, befitting his action, in different bodies, which he gets and has to leave, according to his Karma[2]. He is capable of bearing boundless hardship and suffering. He is not free (Asvatantra). He is eternal and not a product of Śiva. All the texts, which talk of his origin from Śiva or present him to be related to Śiva[3] as sparks to fire, refer only to the rise of name and form as related to him.

He is a knower (Jñātā) in himself i.e. independently of any external condition. The quality "to know" is inherent in him[4]. In fact, his powers of knowledge and action are unlimited, but appear to be limited because of the beginningless impurities and, therefore, when the impurities are removed, his inherent powers of knowledge and action become manifest and he attains similarity with Śiva (Śivasāmya). But in the state of bondage he is an experiencer of pleasure and pain, because of relation with empirical "Manas" (Prākṛtamanaḥ sambandhāt).

He is atomic and not pervasive, because he exits from and enters into the body and even goes to the higher worlds. Though atomic, he pervades the whole body with his quality "to know" and, therefore, experiences all affections, wheresoever they may be in the whole body, much as the light of a lamp spreads over, "pervades" an object and illumines it. The quality of knowing is different from him, much as smell

---

1. Srikam. Bh Vol. II, 46-7.
2. Srikam. Bh. Vol. I, 89-90.
3. Srikam. Bh. Vol. II, 140.
4. Srikam. Bh. Vol. II, 142.

is different from earth[1]. Therefore, when a text talks of the individual self as knowledge (Jñāna), it means to point it out as the chief quality of him.

He is also doer (Kartā)[2]. For, only such an admission can justify the existence of the injunctive and prohibitive texts. His being a doer is also implied by such texts as talk of his adopting the means. In fact, the conception of the internal senses as means of knowledge implies the existence of a doer, who makes use of them, and denies that Prakṛti (Buddhi) is the doer.

The relation between Pati or Śiva and the individual subjects is conceived on the analogy of relation between a king and his dependents. The individual souls act according to the maturity of the effect of the deeds, done in the past, (Karmaparipākavaśena)[3], but not without the consent of the Lord. He (the Lord) is the prompter of the individuals to action in accordance with the Karma of each. This, however, does not mean that the textual injunctions and prohibitions do not relate to the individual. For, just as a child, lifting a heavy piece of wood with the help of powerful persons, can be commanded to act or not to act in a certain way, so also can be the individual, though he is not independent in his action.

The individual subject is not identical with the universal Self, as the Vedāntin holds that the Universal Self appears as individual because of the limitations, exactly as the universal ether (Ākāśa) appears as limited because of the limitation of an object such as a jar, wherein it is. Both the sentients and the insentients, in their totality constitute as if it were the body of Śiva. Therefore, they are His parts (Aṁśa). And the texts, such as "that thou art" (Tattvamasi)[4], do not mean absolute identity, but identity in difference. They talk of identity because of the relation of the pervading and the pervaded between them; exactly as we talk of a piece of wood, that is pervaded by fire, as fire. The individual, atomic in himself, is connected with a subtle body in transmigrating from one gross body to another[5].

IMPURITIES OR MALAS

The Śaiva Viśiṣṭādvaita generally follows the philosophical technique of the Śaiva Dualism. Accordingly it admits three impurities: (1) Mala (Paśutva) (2) Karma and (3) Māyā[6]. That

1. Srikam. Bh. Vol. II, 146-7
2. Srikam. Bh. Vol. II, 152-3.
3. Srikam. Bh. Vol. II, 156-7.
4. Srikam. Bh. Vol. II, 158-9.
5. Srikam. Bh. Vol. II, 196-7.
6. Srikam. Bh. Vol. II, 142.

he admits the first, which is variously called Mala, Āṇavamala or Paśutvamala, and the characteristic function of which is to conceal the powers of knowledge and action, which inherently belong to the individual subject, is abundantly clear from Śrīkaṇṭha's own statement :

"Malatirohita svajñāna karaṇatayā"
(Srikam. Bh. Vol. I, 340). Similarly the other two impurities are directly admitted in "Anādi karmanigaḍena baddhaḥ tatphala bhogānukūla māyāmaya" etc. (Srikam. Bh. Vol. I, 351). And if we follow his commentator, Appayya Dīkṣita, we come to the conclusion that Śrīkaṇṭha's conception of Mala is the same as that of the Śaiva Dualism. It is substantial in its nature : it is similar to blackness in copper and it is removed by His Grace. Not only this. He admits the fourth impurity (Mala) also, which is technically called "Tirodhāna"[1]. But he does not count it amongst the primary impurities, because, as Appayya Dīkṣita points out, it is really the power of the Lord and is spoken of as Pāśa in the secondary sense, because of its being responsible for the individuality of the individual[2].

LIBERATION OR MOKṢA

The Viśiṣṭādvaita Śaivaism recognises the importance of forty rituals, ceremonies and sacrifices, recognised by the Brahmanism, in the attainment of liberation, in so far as they free the individual from sins and so make him fit for following the path to liberation[3]. But it asserts that ultimately it is due to His Grace; and that study of the texts and attendance at the lectures on the essential nature of Śiva, the rational conviction that He is as the texts present, and the inner visualisation of Him through complete self-surrender to Him, win His Grace. He is the just Lord and graces the deserving only. The Grace removes the impurity, called simply "Mala" or Paśutvamala or Āṇavamala, and therefore, the inherent qualities of unsurpassed knowledge and bliss, which are similar to those of Him, become manifest[4].

The textual problem that arises in this context is : "If the object, to which self-surrender is to be made, is Śiva only, how can Indra talk of himself as an object, through self-surrender to which the liberation can be attained ?" And the reply is that Indra talks of himself as such an object, not as Indra, but as Śiva, with whom he is one, with whom he has attained identity, exactly

1. Srikam. Bh. Vol. II, 145.
2. Srikam. Bh. Vol. I, (Comm) 567-8.
3. Srikam. Bh. Vol. I, 40.
4. Srikam. Bh. Vol. I, 91-2.

as the various constituents of an aesthetic object do with the basic mental state which art primarily presents[1].

INFLUENCE OF AESTHETICS

It is important to keep the implication of the analogy of aesthetic object, or to be more specific, Rasa as it figures in the consciousness of an aesthete, to get at the implication of "Sāmyamokṣa", the similarity with the Ultimate, Śiva, which is realised at the liberation. This system arose at the time when the problem of aesthetics was being discussed in all its aspects. The two aspects, the influence of which is reflected on this system are : (1) the theory of suggestible meaning and (2) the view on the relation of the constituents of the aesthetic object as it figures in the consciousness of a deindividualised or universalised aesthete. According to the competent authorities, like Ānanda Vardhana and Abhinavagupta, the suggestible meaning is not objective but subjective : it is due, not to the objective cognition, but to the subjective realisation: it is due to the latent becoming patent ; it is due to becoming manifest of what lies hidden within. Both the Dualistic and Qualified Monistic schools of Śaivaism, accepted this view, and accordingly maintained that, at liberation, the powers of unlimited knowledge and action, which are inherent in the individual subject, but lie hidden by the impurities, become manifest (Abhivyakta) when the last impurity (Paśutvamala) is removed by His Grace.

This is one important point on which both, the Dualistic and the Qualified Monistic, schools of Śaivaism differ from the Lakulīśa Pāśupata, according to which the perfect powers of knowledge and action pass on to the individual from the Universal (Saṅkrānti).

Similarly in regard to the objective aspect of the aesthetic experience, it was asserted that it consists, not in the Sthāyin or basic emotion as such, as isolated from the situation, mimetic changes and transient emotion (Vibhāva, Anubhāva and Vyabhicāribhāva) ; but in the harmonious unification of all these so that there arises an objective unity, which is very different from that which can arise from a mere juxtaposition of them, unity which is responsible for a very different experience from that which each one separately or all of them taken together, but not harmoniously unified, can give rise to. It was also asserted that this unity is not pure and absolute unity, in which the constituents completely lose themselves ; and that they have their being with such a similarity with the basic or central fact that it

1. Srikam. Bh. Vol. I, 287-8.

needs a separate and concentrated mental activity to become aware of them as such. The objective aspect of aesthetic experience was thus recognised to be identity in difference or unity in multiplicity. Under the influence of such an idea, the qualified Ṣaiva Monism admits the identity of the deindividualised individual with the Universal in respect of the qualities of knowledge and action ; but at the same time it admits difference in the substance. Hence it talks of the Liberation as attainment or manifestation of similarity with Ṣiva (Ṣivasāmya). The freedom from impurity, called Paśutva mala, is the most necessary condition of such Liberation. (Nirañjanaḥ paramaṁ sāmyam upaiti" (Srikam. Bh. Vol. I, 409).

The Viśiṣṭādvaita Ṣaivaism asserts that even at liberation the deindividualised individual has a separate existence from Brahman or Ṣiva ; that the liberated does not have the consciousness of the empirical multiplicity and that he sees nothing but Brahman, with whom the entire multiplicity is unified[1].

THE NATURE OF IDENTIFICATION AT LIBERATION

The Viśiṣṭādvaita Ṣaivaism admits that Parama Ṣiva is beyond everything and is different from Paśu even when he is liberated[2]. The question, therefore, arises : "How can the identity of the individual and the Universal, implied by such texts as "That thou art" (Tattvamasi), is to be explained ?" And the reply is that the identity, referred to in the text, implies such identity as is found in the identification of the aesthete with the focus of the situation, the hero, at the emotive level. Just as the aesthete, identifying himself with the hero, does not completely lose himself in the object with which he identifies himself ; because in that case subsequent remembrance of the aesthetic experience would be impossible ; so the individual, contemplating on Ṣiva, gets identified with Him, without losing his own entity. Just as at the emotive level of the aesthetic experience, there is identity with the focus of the situation in respect of emotion ; because the latent emotion becomes patent : so at the mystic level there is the identity of the contemplator and the object of contemplation in respect of the attributes, the powers of knowledge and action and the Bliss ; because the powers, which are inherent in the individual but are hidden by the impurity, called Paśutva, become manifest[3] in consequence of its removal. Just as the deindividualisation of the individual is the necessary

1. Srikam. Bh. Vol. I, 416-7.
2. Srikam. Bh. Vol. II, 427-8.
3. Srikam. Bh. Vol. II, 481-2

condition of the aesthetic experience ; so is the freedom from impurities for the mystic.

Accordingly, Ṣrīkaṇṭha asserts that in such texts as "One who knows Brahman becomes Brahman" (Brahmaveda Brahmaiva bhavati) mean that one who knows Brahman becomes like Brahman ; and that the word "eva" therein is used in the sense of "iva"[1]. The text, therefore, he holds, does not mean the loss of the individual in the Universal, similar to the loss of the ether, confined within a jar, in the universal ether, when the jar gets broken. He maintains that similarity always implies difference : and the sacred texts taken together mean that the liberated becomes similar to and not completely one with Brahman or Ṣiva. For, this is the implication of the admission that the liberated is Brahman in every way, excepting the one, namely, that he cannot create or destroy the universe (Jagadvyāpāravarjam)[2]. Similarity of the liberated with the Brahman consists in having the same experience as that of the Brahman, but not doing what Brahman does (Bhogamātrasāmyaliṅgācca)[3].

The talk of identity of the individual with the Universal and consequent use of the word Brahman or Ṣiva in reference to the individual is figurative only, just as the use of the word "Lion" for a man. The word "Sāyujya", according to the Viśiṣṭādvaitin does not mean "penetrative union" but similarity (Sāmya)[4] only. He maintains that the atomicity of the individual remains in tact, but the light that spreads from the atomic individual, spreads and covers all so that he becomes omniscient, because of the disappearance of the impurity (Paśutva) ; exactly as the light of a lamp spreads and illumines all that is round about it, when the cover, which prevented the spread of the light, is removed[5]. The universal annihilation does not affect the liberated. The liberated is endless. He belongs to the first of the thirty-six categories, "Śiva". He is Ṣiva, because he is different from both Paśu and Pāśa (Paśupāśa Vilakṣaṇatvam hi śivatvam. Srikam. Bh. Vol. II, 504).

1. Srikam. Bh. Vol. II, 484.
2. Srikam. Bh. Vol. II, 484.
3. Srikam. Bh. Vol. II, 496.
4. Srikam. Bh. Vol II. (Comm) 501.
5. Srikam. Bh. Vol. II, 493.

(V) THE VIŚEṢĀDVAITA OF ŚRĪPATI

The Viśeṣādvaita system is referred to by various names, Pure Dvaitādvaita, Seśvarādvaita, Śivādvaita, Sarvaśrutisāramata and Bhedābheda, as we have stated earlier. They refer to the central philosophical doctrine from different points of view. It is called Dvaitādvaita ; because it holds that devotion (Bhakti) is the principal means to union (Sāyujya) with the Ultimate Reality, Śiva. Devotion presupposes the reality and separate being of both, the subject and the object ; the devotee and the object of devotion, the worshipper and the object of worship ; the self that surrenders itself and the one to whom it surrenders ; the contemplator and the contemplated. But the end, that is realised through it, is not the one, in which the subject and the object have separate existence ; but the one in which the former becomes one with the latter, exactly as does a river that falls into the ocean becomes one with it. Hence it is called Dvaitādvaita.

It is called "Seśvarādvaita" ; because the first category, according to this system, is "Pati" or "Lord" ; and the conception of the ultimate category is not that it is contentless, empty being, such as does not admit of any definition ; but that it is all-powerful ; that the entire multiplicity of the universe, both the subjective and the objective, has its being within His power, exactly as the multiplicity, that constitutes a tree, is within the seed, from which it springs ; that He is the Lord or Pati, because He has the power, though it is non-different from Him, as the warmth is from fire.

It is called Viśeṣādvaita or Saviśeṣādvaita ; because it is opposed to the Nirviśeṣādvaita of Śaṅkara : it is Saguṇa-Brahmavāda and is opposed to Nirguṇa-Brahmavāda; to the theory that the empirical world is a mere illusion; to the distinction between the practical reality (Vyāvahārika Satya) and the true reality (Paramārtha Satya) ; and to the view that the liberation is negative in its nature.

Śrīpati Paṇḍitārādhya points out the significance of the word "Viśeṣādvaita" as follows[1]:—

> The word "Viśeṣa", which is prefixed to "Advaita", denies that this school presents a kind of Monism: it denies that pure dualism or pure monism can be maintained from every point of view and at

1. Sri. Bh. Vol. II, 136.

all levels : it asserts that pure dualism and pure monism are against the fact of experience : it directs the attention to the fact that though the individual subject (Jīva) and the Universal (Śiva) are identical, inasmuch as both are essentially sentiency (Cit), yet they are different in so far as the one is atomic and the other is all-pervasive, the one has limited powers of knowledge and action, but the other is omniscient and omnipotent : though logically they are one as genus, yet they belong to different species: the identity and difference between them are of the same nature as we find between the insentient empirical objects, which are identical in respect of their insentiency, but are different in their causal efficiency. He splits up the compound"Viśeṣādvaita"as "Viśca śeṣaśca tayoḥ advaitam" and interprets it as the identity of "Vi", the individual subject, and "Śeṣa", the Universal. The word "Viśeṣādvaita" stands for the distinctive feature of this school, which admits that the beginningless and, therefore, natural difference of the individual from the Universal disappears, because of the force of constant contemplation ; that the Jīva becomes Brahman, exactly as a fly becomes a bee, (Bhramarakīṭavat).

It is called Śivādvaita ; because it holds that the Ultimate Reality is Śiva, the All-inclusive Universal Being, in whom the entire multiplicity of the objective world has its being potentially and springs up from Him effectually at His Will : and because the latent multiplicity, even when it becomes patent, or the subtle, even when it grossifies, is not outside Him.

It is called Sarvaśrutisāramata ; because it asserts that it presents the basic, the central, the essential point of view of all the sacred texts : because it maintains that the consistent and harmonious interpretation of all the apparently conflicting statements, found in the Śrutis, is possible in the light of Dualistic-cum-monistic view. It is called Dualism-cum-monism, (Dvaitādvaita); because it holds that Dualism and Monism, though opposed and antagonistic to each other, if they be asserted at the same level and from the same point of view; yet they are thoroughly reconcilable, if they be maintained to belong to different levels and be asserted from different points of view. It points out that everything is unity from one point of view but multiplicity from another : the individual is different from Śiva at the empirical level, but is one with Him, when he merges into Him at liberation, exactly as a river is different from the ocean, when it is flowing on the plain , but becomes one with it when it falls into the ocean. Monism refers to the causal state, and Dualism refers to the state of effect. The seed is one, but leaves, branches, flowers and fruits, which spring from it, are many. Hence it asserts that Dualism-cum-monism is the only sound philosophy.

It is called Şakti Viśiṣṭādvaita, because the Vīra Şaiva 'declines to accept the statement that in self-consciousness the distinction of matter and form is abolished. For, even in self-consciousness he distinguishes a material and a formal side, a potential and an actual moment. The potential and material moment of the Absolute he terms Şiva ; the actual and formal moment of the Absolute he terms Şakti. He does not visualize an incurable antinomy between Şiva and Şakti, between being and knowing, rather he effects a synthesis by saying that Şakti is the very soul of Şiva, that knowing is inherent in being. He envisages an integral association between Şiva and Şakti.'[1]

The Kriyā Sāra by Nīla Kaṇṭha presents the Şakti Viśiṣṭādvaita[2], accepted by the followers of Vīra Şaivaism. It interprets in verses the Brahma Sūtra of Bādarāyaṇa in the light of the Şakti Viśiṣṭādvaita. In doing so it follows the commentary on the Brahma Sūtra by Nīla Kaṇṭha Şivācārya[3], alias Şrīkaṇṭha[4], on the basis of which we have presented the Viśiṣṭādvaita Şaivaism in the preceding section.

VĪRA ŚAIVAISM

The word "Vīra Şaiva" seems to have a historical significance. It refers to the heroic attitude of the followers of Şaivaism, as has already been stated. The word "Vira" as a part of the name of the Liṅgāyat sect "Vira Şaiva" is interpreted in other ways also. The Siddhānta Şikhāmaṇi, which contains a dialogue between Reṇuka and Agastya, the two well recognised authorities on Vīra Şaivaism, states the meaning of Vīra as **follows:—**

(1) "Vi" means the knowledge (Vidyā) that the individual subject (Jīva) and Şiva are identical. Those followers of Şaivaism, who find satisfaction in such a knowledge, are "Vīra Şaivas."[5]

(2) "The knowledge that one gets from the study of the Vedānta, is referred to by the word "Vi". "Vīra" is one who finds peace of mind in it."

---

*1. H. Ph. E. W., 398.
2. K. S., 15.
3. K. S., 39.
*4. S. Sri., 18.
5. S. Si., 30.

The Kriyāsāra gives an additional meaning to the word "Vīra" as follows:—

(3) "Vi" means "doubt" (Vikalpa). "Ra" means "without "Vīra Ṣaiva" accordingly means "the Ṣaiva faith and philosophy which is free from all doubts"[1].

VĪRA ŚAIVAISM AND ŚĀṄKARA VEDĀNTA

Ṣrīpati Panditārādhya has attempted to distinguish his Viśeṣādvaita from various other types of monism, such as Ṣuddhādvaita, Buddhādvaita, Ṣuṣkādvaita and Ṣūnyādvaita. Mainly, however, he attempts to draw the attention of the reader to the points of difference between his system and that of the Vedānta, as presented by Ṣaṅkara. He criticises the distinctive features of the Ṣāṅkara Vedānta such as Adhyāsa or superimposition, illusory nature of the objective world (Māyā); and Vyāvahārika satya or the theory that the objective world is only practically real. In fact, according to him, the second section of the chapter III of the Vedānta Sūtra aims at refuting the view that the Ultimate Reality is absolutely beyond the empirical multiplicity; that it is without any quality or attribute; that it is absolute unity without any touch of multiplicity and, therefore, all the experiences which we have in the states of wakefulness, dream, deep-sleep and fainting fit, are illusory[2].

CRITICISM OF THE THEORY OF SUPERIMPOSITION (ADHYĀSA)

The Ṣāṅkara Vedānta admits that the Brahman is without any attribute or quality and that the entire phenomenal world, including both the sentient and the insentient, is nothing more than illusion (Māyā), which is due to superimposition (Adhyāsa) which also in itself is due to beginningless ignorance (Anādi Avidyā). Brahman alone is real. All else is a mere appearance. Brahman appears as the world because of the Avidyā, which superimposes the world on it, exactly as a rope appears as a snake, because of the superimposition of the latter on the former, on account of the defect in the sense of sight, through which it is seen. The world, therefore, is an illusion, much as snake is, as stated above: because both of them are due to superimposition of the attributes of one thing on another.

In criticising the above view Ṣrīpati Paṇḍitārādhya points out that superimposition presupposes the residual traces of the knowledge of what is superimposed. But, according to the Ṣāṅkara Vedānta there is nothing truly existing apart from the Brahman.

1. K. S., 3.

2. Sri. Bh., Vol. II, 313.

It also presupposes a spatial difference: the two, (I) that which is superimposed; and (II) that on which it is superimposed, must be at different points of space: the snake must exist truly at a particular point of space, different from that of rope, to make the superimposition possible. But there is no spatial point at which the Brahman is not. To say that the former superimpositions are the causes of the later ones, is to commit the fallacy of argumentum- ad-infinitum (Anavasthā). Moreover, such a statement is against the sacred texts, which talk of the causal relation between the Brahman and the world.

The Ṣāṅkara Vedānta holds that the Brahman is not an object of knowledge. But if so, asks Ṣrīpati, how can there be the possibility of superimposition of the world on Brahman. For, superimposition is always on what is objective. And to say that superimposition does not have objective reference, is to admit that illusion arises without any basis (Niradhiṣṭhāna bhrama Prasaṅgaḥ)[1].

CRITICISM OF THE PRACTICALLY REAL (VYĀVAHĀRIKA SATYA)

It has been shown in the preceding section that illusion is difficult to account for, in accordance with the strict monistic view. But even if all the objections against it, as stated before, were waived and its possibility be admitted ; the difficulty of accounting for the practical life remains unsurmountable, if we admit the entire world to be nothing more than illusion. For, illusion has no practical value ; the water of mirage cannot quench the thirst. The Ṣāṅkara Vedānta, therefore, admits 'real' (Satya) to be of three types; (1) Pāramārthika; (2) Vyāvahārika, and (3) Prātibhāsika. The first is the obsolutely real. And the Brahman alone is such. The second is practically real. The entire phenomenal world, including God or Īśvara, the creator, the individual souls and all that is objective, is such. And the third is illusively real. Mirage and the snake that appears, due to the defective sight etc. when only a rope is before the percipient, are such.

In regard to the practically real Śrīpati raises the following three questions :—

Does it mean (1) that the thing, which is only practically real, is such as does not persist through futurity. (Kālāntarānavasthāyitva) or

(2) that it is such as is different from both 'being' and 'not-being' ; or

(3) that it is such as cannot be spoken of either as 'being' or as 'not-being' ?

1, Sri. Bh,, Vol, II, 31,

The first position does not present any distinctive view of the Śāṅkara Vedānta. For many systems, including the Viśeṣādvaita of Śrīpati, admit the transitory nature of the world. But the admission by the Śāṅkara Vedānta that nothing else than the Brahman persists through all times and that even 'nature' (Prakṛti) is only practically real is against the sacred texts, which present Prakṛti to be eternal[1].

The second position is untenable[2]. For, the distinction can be drawn from that only, the existence of which is well defined and equally well recognised. But the Śāṅkara Vedānta does not recognise 'being' and 'not being' as distinct and different from what it presents as practically real. Similar argument can be advanced against the third position also. Śrīpati's arguments against the view of the 'Practically real' are very subtle, abstruse and difficult, and, therefore, need more space than we can give in this "Outline".

CRITICISM OF THE ILLUSORY NATURE OF THE WORLD

Śrīpati speaks of Śaṅkara, as a Bauddha in the guise of a Vedāntin, (Pracchanna Bauddha). He calls Śāṅkara Vedānta "Nirviśeṣādvaitamata" because it holds all the three, God, world and individual subjects, to be illusory. He holds that a system like that of Śaṅkara is refuted by Bādarāyaṇa in the "Abhāvādhikaraṇa" of the Vedānta Sūtra. He asks : "Does the negation (Abhāva) of God, world and individual subjects, mean that they have no being whatsoever, like the horns of a hare and the son of a barren woman ; or that they are illusory or unreal like the multiplicity that is experienced in a dream ? He asserts that the negation of the first type is against the fact of experience. For, we actually perceive the objective multiplicity at the empirical level and find it effective : but the horns of a hare are neither perceptible nor effective. The individual subject also is distinctly experienced at the time of the rise of the phenomenon of knowledge as distinct from the object and the means. To hold, therefore, that knowledge (Jñāna) alone is, without the distinction of the subject, the object and the means, is to make one's self an object of ridicule[3]. And God also is the object of religious or mystic experience. The absolute negation of the objective world and God, therefore, is untenable.

Nor can the objective world be represented to be illusory (*Mithyā*) like a dream. For, the objective world of the wakeful

1. Sri. Bh., Vol. II, 64.
2. Sri. Bh., Vol. II, 65.
3. Sri. Bh., Vol. II, 225-6.

state is very different from what we see in dream. The latter is contradicted by the wakeful experience, inasmuch as we do not find what we experience in dream, when we wake up. But the objects which we experience in the wakeful state are found even after dream. Further, the pious and sinful acts, performed in dream, do not result in merit or demerit to the dreaming individual. But those, done in the wakeful state, do. Hence the denial of reality to the empirical world, on the basis of the supposed similarity with the dream-world, is illogical. It is, therefore, wrong to assert that the experiences of the wakeful state are without real objective references, just like those in dream. Moreover, if all knowledge be admitted to be without objective reference (Jñānānām arthaśūnyatve)[1], the point that the Vedāntin desires to prove, cannot be proved. For, the Advaita Vedāntin attempts to prove the existence of the Brahman by inference. But inference also is a kind of knowledge and, therefore, cannot refer to what is truly existent.

But the Advaita Vedāntin may say that the true existence of the objective world is denied simply because it is contradicted by the mystic experience (Brahma jñāna bādhyatvam). To this, Śripati replies that non-experience of the objective world does not necessarily mean negation or contradiction of its existence : it does not mean that the objective world does not truly exist. For, non-experience of it is due to the rise of the subject beyond the level of objective affection. The non-experience of objectivity at the mystic level is similar to its non-experience at the level of deep dreamless sleep.

Nor can the Nirviśeṣādvaita Vedāntin prove the existence of the Nirviśeṣa Brahman on the basis of the sacred texts. For, they also are means of knowledge. And the Advaitin admits that the means of knowledge have no reference to true object. The Brahman, therefore, as proved with the help of Śruti, will also be nothing but an illusion. And everything excepting the Brahman, being illusory, the sacred texts themselves will have to be admitted to be as such and, therefore, cannot prove the Brahman to be non-illusory and real[2].

CRITICISM OF THE THEORY OF REFLECTION

There is a difference of opinion amongst the Advaita Vedāntins in regard to the conception of God and that of individual subject. According to one section, both God and individual soul are mere reflections of a single universal sentiency, which is the reflected (Caitanyamātram Bimbam)[3].

1. Sri. Bh., Vol. II, 227.
2. Sri Bh., Vol. II, 227.
3. V. Pari. 183.

The sentiency, reflected in the Māyā, the universal nescience, is God. But the same sentiency, reflected in the inner sense (Antaḥkaraṇa) is the individual soul. The difference between God and soul is quantitative, just like the difference between the reflection of the sun in a tank and that in a cup. The former is all-pervasive, because that in which the sentiency is reflected, namely, the universal nescience or Māyā is all-pervasive. But the soul is limited, because the inner sense, wherein the sentiency is reflected, is so.

This view Śrīpati criticises as follows :—

Any view, that is propounded, must be in consonance with the fact of experience, if it is to command general acceptance. The view, however, that God and soul are mere reflections of a single universal sentiency, is against the fact of experience and, therefore, cannot be accepted. For, that only which is perceptible casts reflection and that alone receives reflection which definitely exists. But neither the Brahman is perceptible nor does the Māyā definitely exist. The talk of reflection of ether (Ākāśa) in tank, has no other basis than illusion. Further, the reflection is necessarily at a spatial point where the reflected is not. But Brahman is all-pervasive. Therefore, its reflection is not possible. In "Guhām praviṣṭāvātmānau hi taddarśanāt" (Ch. I. Sec. 2 Sūtra II) Jīva and Brahman are spoken of as occupying the same space. Does it not contradict the theory of reflection ? How can the reflection and the reflected be at the same place ? The destruction of that where the reflection is, means the destruction of the reflection. Will not, therefore, the destruction of the Māyā at the liberation mean the destruction of Jīva ? The theory, therefore, that Jīva is a mere reflection of the Brahman, is untenable.

CRITICISM OF THE VIŚIṢṬĀDVAITA

Śrīpati Paṇḍitārādhya begins his criticism of the Viśiṣṭādvaita by pointing out that the position of those who propound qualified non-dualism is self-contradictory[1]. For, the word qualified implies duality of that which qualifies and that which is qualified, of the substance and the attribute, of the possessor of the qualification and the qualification itself. Further, the term "qualified" seems to be indefinable and, therefore, to signify what is illusory. Does the term signify the attribute, the substance and their relation, or something that is different from them all ? In the former case the question will arise : "Does it stand for a mere collection of substance, attribute and their relation, exactly as does "rod-man-relation" (Daṇḍa

1. Sri. Bh. Vol. II, 71.

puruṣasambandhāḥ) ?" If so, it means that it does not stand for the "qualified". For, the awareness of a mere collection, is not the awareness of the "qualified": nor is it the awareness of non-duality. In the latter case, that is, if the term "qualified" stands for something different from the triad of substance, attribute and their relation; it is difficult to establish that the Highest Self (Paramātman) is the Qualified Non-duality (Viśiṣṭādvaita)[1]. For, in the case of "Man with a rod" (Daṇḍin), we do not admit anything different from rod, man and their relation. And it is difficult to understand what is the "attribute". For, an attribute cannot be said to be that which arouses the idea of elimination (Vyāvṛttibuddhi janaka) : because such an idea is also aroused by what is known to be a substance.

But let us find out what is the substance, what is the attribute and what is the exact nature of relation between the two when the word "Viśiṣṭādvaita" is used for a system of Philosophy. We cannot say that the soul is the attribute, and the Highest Self is the substance. For, that means the admission that there is only one atomic soul. But if the souls, the attributes, are admitted to be many, it will be difficult to establish oneness of the Highest Self, that has them as its attributes : because difference of the attribute means the difference of the substance also. For instance, it is difficult to assert that a personality, which has many attributes, is one to the extent that reference to one of them implies reference to all of them. For, in that case, even when only one attribute is referred to, reference to all of them would be supposed to be implied. Therefore, reference to only one of them, because the personality has only one of them, would mean reference to all. Hence the personality, which has been known to possess many attributes, would be understood to have all of them even when it has only one and as such has been referred to.

Moreover, the relation between the Highest Self and the souls has to be defined, before we can talk of them as substance and attribute. It cannot be said to be inherence (Samavāya) ; because they exist in isolation from each other. Nor can it be said to be mere 'contact' (Saṁyoga) ; because, if it be said to be pervasive (Vyāpyavṛtti) it would mean the admission of identity of the two ; and the partial contact (Avyāpyavṛtti saṁyoga) is not possible between them, because both of them are without parts. As for the "Svarūpasambandha", it is not logical and, therefore, is not generally admitted. And even if it be admitted,

1. Sri. Bh. Vol. II, 72.

being a relation and, therefore, dependent on the two, which are related, it contradicts non-duality. Hence on the basis of this relation also "Viśiṣṭādvaita" is contradiction in terms[1].

Śrīpati refers to the great exponent of the Śaiva Viśiṣṭādvaita, Śrīkaṇṭha. He distinctly refutes the latter's conception of liberation (Mokṣa) as attainment of similarity with Śiva[2] and asserts in opposition to him that the liberation is the union with Śiva (Sāyujya).

BHEDĀBHEDAVĀDA OF ŚRĪPATI

Śripati follows the authority of the twenty-eight Śaivāgamas[3], which were collectively called "Siddhānta" by the Dualist Śaivas. He differs from Abhinavagupta, in maintaining that all of them present the Ultimate Reality to be unity in multiplicity and asserts that both, unity and multiplicity, are equally real. He does not twist the passages referring to unity so as to make them yield the dualistic meaning, as do the Siddhānta Dualists. He admits the three primary categories ; Pati, Paśu and Pāśa[4]. He also admits three types of bondage (Pāśa): Mala, Karma and Māyā[5]. But very often he seems to emphasise the importance of Māyā so much that he seems to think that all of them are essentially Māyā[6] (Malatrayātmakamāyā pāśa). He attempts to show that the conception of the primary Śaiva categories is not only in consonance with the teaching of the Vedas, but also is propounded therein[7].

And just like the Siddhānta Śaiva, he accepts the thirty-six categories also, from another point of view, as has already been stated. He refers to Bṛddhajāvālopaniṣad and quotes from it to show that thirty-six categories, admitted by him, are referred to there. It is interesting to note that the categories, referred to in the passage that he quotes, are slightly different from those admitted by the Siddhānta Dualists. It says that the first five, Śiva, Śakti, Sadāśiva, Īśvara and Śuddhavidyā, are pure category. The next seven, Māyā, Kāla, Niyati, Kalā, Vidyā, Rāga and Puruṣa, are pure-cum-impure (Śuddhāśuddha). The remaining twenty-four are impure (Aśuddha). Of these twenty-four, the first is Prakṛti, which is accepted in common with the Sāṅkhya.

1. Sri. Bh. Vol. II, 72.
2. Sri. Bh. Vol. II, 200.
3. Sri. Bh. Vol. II, 8.
4. Sri. Bh. Vol. II, 4.
5. Sri. Bh. Vol. II, 6.
6. Sri. Bh. Vol. II, 5.
7. Sri. Bh. Vol. II, 94.

The next three are different from those of every other system. The systems, which admit Prakṛti, generally accept Buddhi, Ahaṅkāra and Manas, as three of the twenty-four categories. But here the three Guṇas, Sattva, Rajas and Tamas (Prakṛterguṇatrayam)[1] are stated instead. The remaining are the four groups of subtle and gross elements and of senses (Indriya) of perception and of action.

He refutes the monistic theories of superimposition (Adhyāsa), illusion (Mithyā) and reflection, as discussed earlier. He is a Realist. He admits the reality of the objective world and definitely denies that it is a mere illusion. He believes in the theory of evolution and asserts that multiplicity is real and eternal, because it always exists. Though it may not always exist in a gross form, yet that does not mean its non-existence. For, even then it exists potentially in the power (Śakti) of the Lord, much as the various parts of a tree exist in a seed. He asserts that unity and multiplicity are the two states of the same reality. Unity is the unevolved state and the multiplicity is the evolved. Hence Bhedābheda or Dvaitādvaita is the only sound philosophy.

The unevolved state, which is the state of unity, is not pure unity but the unity of the two, the Lord and His power, Śiva and Śakti. The one is the efficient cause and the other is the material cause. But the former is one with the latter ; the relation between them is that of identity (Tādātmya), similar to the one that is between magnet and its power to draw iron or between fire and its power to burn.

BHEDĀBHEDA AND LIBERATION

Śrīpati admits the difference between soul (Jīva) and Brahman in so far as the former is the worshipper, has spatial limitation and possesses limited knowledge ; but the latter is the object of worship, all-pervasive and omniscient. He also admits that the aforesaid limitations of the soul are beginningless and natural (Svābhāvika). But he asserts that soul gets freedom from these natural differences and limitations and becomes one with the Brahman, exactly as does a river with the ocean into which it falls. He holds (1) that even the beginningless qualities and limitations disappear and (2) that what comes into being (Āgantuka) is not necessarily transient. For instance, we find that a fly of natural birth changes its inborn nature

1. Sri. Bh. Vol. II, 168.

and becomes a bee, and rain water, getting into a mother-of-pearl, becomes pearl. Thus, he concludes that there is beginningless difference between soul and Brahman: but at liberation there is the union of the two. Therefore, Bhedābheda is the only sound philosophy[1].

SACRED TEXTS AND BHEDĀBHEDA

Śrīpati admits that there are sacred texts, which totally deny all multiplicity; but he also asserts that that is no justification to hold that those texts, which talk of the difference between soul and Brahman, are to be taken to present the difference as merely due to the limiting conditions and, therefore, are to be interpreted as referring to the difference between them secondarily only (Aupacārika). According to him, the texts which deny multiplicity and present Brahman as free from all qualities and attributes, refer to Brahman as 'It' is before the creation of multiplicity; and similarly those texts which talk of multiplicity of the objective world and the difference between Jīva and Brahman refer to the created multiplicity. Of course, the multiplicity is present in the power (Śakti) of Brahman even before creation; but the power and the possesser of it are admitted to be identical[2].

It is, he points out, inconsistent with the admission of the authority of the Veda to stick to either pure monism or pure dualism. For, in the Veda, there are passages, propounding both. The acceptance of pure monism would mean the refusal of the authoritativeness of the passages which present dualistic view and vice versa[3]. To reject the Bhedābhedavāda on the ground that it involves contradiction, is illogical. For[4], the admission of the opposite attributes or qualities in one and the same thing is common to many systems of thought. Does not the Sāṅkhya admit the Sattva and the Tamas, which are opposed to each other like light and darkness, to be the constituents of Prakṛti ? Does not the Vaiśeṣika admit the first four elements, earth, air, water and fire, to be both eternal and transient ? Do not piety and sin coexist in humanity ? Is not glow-worm light and not-light at the same time ? Do not light and darkness coexist in the evening ? Does the Veda present only one means to liberation, namely knowledge (Jñāna): or does it present the additional two also, namely, action and devotion (Karma and

1. Sri. Bh. Vol. II, 71.
2. Sri. Bh. Vol. II, 135.
3. Sri. Bh. Vol. II, 174.
4. Sri. Bh. Vol. II, 175.

Upāsanā)[1] ? If the Veda presents the latter two also, where is the room for them in extreme monism ?

We find that the admission of the opposite attributes in one and the same thing in its different states, is common to most of the systems. Thus, subtlety and grossness are attributed to Prakṛti in its unevolved and evolved states respectively. The theory of Bhedābheda, therefore, cannot be represented to be illogical. For, Brahman is spoken of as one in its causal or unevolved state, and as many in its evolved state. Further, if we admit Brahman to be the material cause of the world, the relation between the two can be nothing but of the nature of identity in difference; because such is the relation between clay and jar. If we are to admit any relation between Brahman and its power, it can be nothing but of the nature of identity in difference : because such is the relation between fire and its power to burn. Thus, from every point of view Bhedābheda is the only sound philosophy.

BRAHMAN, PARA ŚIVA OR PATI

The words, Brahman, Para Śiva and Pati, are used by Śrīpati as synonyms. Brahman or Pati is the first primary category. It is beyond the thirty-six categories, admitted by this system. It is called Para Śiva to distinguish it from Śiva, the first of the thirty-six categories. It naturally possesses innumerable and inexhaustible powers. It is both the efficient and the material cause of the world. It controls the remaining two primary categories, Paśu and Pāśa. It is responsible for the being of the bound and the liberated, the subtle and the gross, and the sentient and the insentient. It is the substratum of the innumerable auspicious qualities such as reality, sentiency and eternality etc. It is definable (Saviśeṣa) but not indefinable (Nirviśeṣa). Definability does not necessarily mean limitedness. For, even the negative definition, such as is implied by the texts "It is not this" (Neti neti) is after all a definition, in so far as it marks out the Brahman, referred to therein, from every other thing, which belongs to the same or even different genus (Sajātīya Vijātīya) at the empirical level. But the positive definition is not lacking. In fact, Bādarāyaṇa, in his Brahma Sūtra, gives such a definition and by doing so he refutes the view that Brahman is indefinable.

Para Śiva is the creator, maintainer, annihilator and obscurer of and doer of grace to the entire world, consisting of both

1. Sri. Bh. Vol. II, 177.

the sentient and the insentient[1]. It is spoken of as free from all attributes (Nirguṇa)when its power is inoperative, but as possessed of attributes, when its power is operative[2]. It is the abode of everything, including heaven and earth etc. It is the ultimate goal that is reached by human soul when it gets freedom from the bondages. It is related to the individual soul at the empirical level exactly as soul is to body; but still it remains unaffected by pleasant or painful experiences, exactly as ether remains unaffected by the qualities of the things, to which it is related[3]. It is eternally free and is not subjected to any experience that is the effect of an action (Karma).

The entire objective world, including both, the sentient and the insentient, is within Para Śiva, exactly as all the leaves and fruits etc. are within the seed from which they spring. The Vedic texts, therefore, which talk of not-being of the world, refer only to the absence of the gross form before creation or evolution. Just as a Yogin withdraws vital air etc. at the time of concentration (Samādhi) and lets them off to function when he descends to the empirical level, so Para Śiva withdraws the world within at the time of annihilation and spreads it out at the time of creation. The world is not an illusion; it is real[4]; it has its potential being in the power (Śakti) of the Lord even at the time of the universal annihilation; it is non-different from Him much as the tree is from the seed from which it springs.

Para Śiva is free (Svatantra). He, therefore, can rise above all forms and also assume forms. Even when He assumes a body he remains unaffected by pleasure and pain, because the body is causal and not a product of action (Karma). He bestows grace much as Gods do favour on the devotee. He frees the souls from their natural impurities and unites them with Himself. The souls have beginningless difference from Him, but ultimately become one with Him as do the rivers with the ocean[5]. The variety of pleasant and painful situations, in which individual souls are put at the time of creation, is due, not to Him but to Karma, which constitutes a beginningless impurity of each soul. He, therefore, cannot be spoken of as cruel and partial, because of His creating the objects, to which the experiences of the individuals are related[6].

1. Sri. Bh. Vol. II, 29.
2. Sri. Bh. Vol. II, 59.
3. Sri. Bh. Vol. II, 194.
4. Sri. Bh. Vol. II, 198.
5. Sri. Bh. Vol. II, 202-3.
6. Sri. Bh. Vol. II, 208.

The aforesaid is the objective definition of Para Śiva or Brahman. This is how the sacred texts and logic make us understand Him. It is the Taṭastha lakṣaṇa. In Himself He is pure being, pure sentiency and pure bliss. This is what mysticism presents Him to be. This represents the ultimate experience of the liberated.

PAŚU, JĪVA OR INDIVIDUAL SOUL

Paśu is the second primary category. It is beginningless and has beginningless impurities, Mala, Karma and Māyā. It identifies itself with body, vital air and intellect etc. and there fore, is subjected to varying experiences in different bodies, which it gets according to its Karma or past action[1]. It is categorically different from Para Śiva[2]. It is not a mere reflection of Brahman. For, we find at the empirical level that the reflection lacks sentiency and the essential quality of that which casts it, For instance, the reflections of man, deer, Sun and Moon are neither sentient nor have the qualities of those which cast them. It is naturally sentient[3] and also naturally different from Brahman. The difference of Jīva from Brahman is not mere conditional. For, the sacred texts present the Brahman to be (1) the object of worship, knowledge and contemplation: and (2) the goal, which the individual soul has to reach and realise. Further, if we admit the difference of Jīva from Brahman to be due to the conditions only the question arises: "Does Brahman know the soul as nothing but itself, at the time when it is in great distress and suffering, because of the conditions or does not?" If not, Brahman ceases to be omniscient. But if it knows, it is inexplicable why does it allow the souls, which it knows to be nothing but itself, to remain in suffering and does not free them immediately. The difference between the two is, therefore, similar to that between genus and species. The soul is essentially sentiency just as is Brahman and,therefore, belongs to the same genus as Brahman, much as do iron, copper and gold to the same genus, metal. But it is different from Brahman, much as iron is from gold[4]. This difference alone can explain various types of Liberation (mukti), such as attainment (1) of the world of Brahman (Sālokya) (2) of the proximity to Brahman (Sāmīpya)[5], (3) of the attributes of Brahman (Sāmya) and (4) of union with Brahman (Sāyujya).

1. Sri. Bh. Vol. II, 4.
2. Sri. Bh. Vol. II, 114.
3. Sri. Bh. Vol. II, 190.
4. Sri. Bh. Vol. II, 199.
5. Sri. Bh. Vol. II, 201.

It is atomic[1] in size and not all-pervasive. For, the sacred texts talk of its flight from the body and its movement from one world to another. Though atomic yet it does the act of knowing the affections all over the body exactly as the sandal paste, though it is just on the forehead, yet it does the act of producing cooling sensation all over the body: or just as light, though it is just at a particular place in the room, yet illumines the whole of it[2]. And the knowledge (Jñāna) is a quality of soul, exactly as smell is that of the earth[3]. It is a part of Brahman, exactly as a spark is that of the fire[4]. It is, therefore, not absolutely identical nor is essentially different from Brahman.

LIBERATION OR MOKṢA

The individual soul has three beginningless impurities (Mala) or bondages (Pāśa), Mala, Karma and Māyā. The liberation consists in the everlasting freedom from these bondages and consequent union with Para Śiva[5]. It is a complete union similar to that of rivers with the ocean. It means complete transformation of personality similar to that of a fly into a 'bee' (Bhṛṅgī). It is the ultimate goal of humanity. It is realised through successive stages (Kramamukti). It is not a mere discovery of what already exists within, but is unknown because of ignorance. It is the attainment of what is outside. There are different ways of attaining it. They are meant for different types of soul, according to the difference in the capacity. Thus, the path of devotion leads the devotees to the attainment of similarity, in respect of the attributes, with the object of devotion through Sālokya and Sāmīpya[6]. Similarly the path of knowledge leads to union with Para Śiva[7], similar to that of a river with the ocean. Different paths have to be followed in succession.

The soul that attains the final union with Brahman, which is possible both in the life time and after the separation from body, is characterised by total absence of the consciousness of all objectivity. There is no doubt about it that the soul, that attains final union with Brahman, while it is connected with the body, has separate existence in so far as it is associated with internal sense (Antaḥkaraṇa). But this separateness is without any sepa-

1. Sri. Bh. Vol. II, 263.
2. Sri. Bh. Vol. II, 264-5.
3. Sri. Bh. Vol. II, 265.
4. Sri. Bh. Vol. II, 276.
5. Sri. Bh. Vol. II, 5.
6. Sri. Bh. Vol. II, 201.
7. Sri. Bh. Vol. II, 132.

rate knowledge. The inner sense of the liberated experiences nothing but Brahman in its varying affections. The soul that attains liberation during life time is like the flame of camphor in the bright light of the Sun. It is all light; it is nothing but consciousness of Brahman[1]. But after the fall of the body even this formal separateness disappears. It is attained through His Grace[2].

SIX WAYS TO UNION (ṢAḌADHVA) AND SIX FORMS OF GRACE (ṢAḌVIDHAŚAKTIPĀTA)

Vīra Śaivaism seems to think in terms of number six, exactly as Kashmir Śaivaism thinks in terms of number three. The latter is definitely called Trika. But the former has not been given any such name as Ṣaṭka. It recognises six paths to final union, one leading to the other. They are technically called (1) Varṇa, (2) Pada, (3) Mantra, (4) Kalā, (5) Bhuvana, (6)Tattva[3]. It recognises six forms of Grace also.

(1) Maheśvaratattvāvirbhāva, the intellectual awareness or grasp of the Lord as eternal and transcendental bliss. It is got through hearing the sacred texts, contemplation on them and visualisation of their meaning.

(2) Sadāśiva tattva sākṣātkāra, the realisation of the third category, technically called Sadāśiva. It is a spiritual level, at which the objectivity and subjectivity, "I" and "This", free from all individual elements, shine equally. It may be pointed out here that Śrīpati very often uses the word Sadāśiva for Para Śiva, who is beyond categories. For instance, in the course of his commentary on the Vedānta Sūtra, chapter I, Pāda I, Sūtra 21, he uses the word "Sadāśiva" for the "being" (Puruṣa), who is within the Sun and says that it is no other than Para Śiva[4]. It is due to the removal of the veil of ignorance and consequent coming to light of pure Sattva.

(3) Śivaśaktisaṁyoga, the contact with the power of the Lord. It is due to the practice of Yoga, as given in the Śaivāgama, and is technically called Śivayoga. This contact takes place in Brahma-randhra. It is consequent on breaking of six circles (ṣaṭcakra), because of the passage of Prāṇa through Suṣumṇā to Brahma-randhra.

1 Sri. Bh., Vol. II, 138.
2 Sri. Bh., Vol. II, 202.
3 Sri. Bh., Vol. II, 95.
4 Sri. Bh., Vol. II, 73.

(4) Sarva-bhuvana-gamana Parokṣadarśana, the capacity to go to all worlds and to see the imperceptible. It is got when the teacher, who has realised the Ultimate Reality, abandons his own body and enters into that of the pupil, because he wants to do great favour to the disciple; clears up all the Nāḍis and thus enables the Kuṇḍalinī to move through seven circles (Saptacakra).

(5) Aṇimādyaiśvarya, the attainment of the powers to become atomic or all-pervasive etc. It is due to the union of the two vital airs, Prāṇa and Apāna. It is consequent on the attainment of the auspicious power (Kalyāṇa vibhūti) which is nothing but a part of the Universal Consciousness (Citkalāmaya) and illumines the mid-passage, Suṣumṇā.

(6) Unmanyavasthāprāpti, the attainment of the transcendental state, which is the level of indeterminacy, because the Manas does not function, or rather is dissolved here. It is due to the realisation of Para Śiva, who is distinct from both knowledge and ignorance, who transcends all, is eternally free from all impurities, is changeless, has no parts and is the abode of all exactly as the ether is of the empirical things. It is beyond the state, in which the individual has his being in the Universal, as all-light and completely free from darkness of ignorance, like a steady flame of camphor in the bright sunshine. It is characterised by complete absence of knowledge of all that is internal or external, includiug body, senses, Manas and vital air etc.[1]

SIX SECTIONS OF THE SACRED TEXT (ṢAṬSTHALA)

Vīra Śaivaism follows the Twenty-eight Śaivāgamas, beginning with the Kāmika and ending with the Vātula. The characteristic doctrines of Vīra Śaivaism are found in the later Āgamas of this set[2]. This probably refers to the Eighteen Āgamas which, according to Abhinavagupta, present Bhedābheda. The followers of Vīra Śaivaism are divided into six sub-sects, according as they follow the authority of one or the other of these six sections (Sthala) of the sacred text and practise the discipline given therein, according to their qualifications. These six sections of the sacred text are known as (1) Bhaktasthala, (2) Māheśvarasthala, (3) Prasādisthala, (4) Prāṇaliṅgisthala, (5) Śaraṇasthala and (6) Aikyasthala[3].

Each of these sections has a number of sub-sections, which are called by different names. They are forty-four and are dealt

1. Sri. Bh., Vol. II, 316
2. S. Si, 29
3. Sri. Bh., Vol. II 316. and S. Si. 31.

with in the Siddhānta Śikhāmaṇi, a collection of dialogues between Reṇuka and Agastya. In the same text, the various kinds of Liṅgas, the modes of worship and contemplation also are given in detail: and Ṣrīpati also refers to such Liṅgas in Sri. Bh. Vol. II, 95, 96, 105, 106 etc.

(VI) ADVAITA ŚAIVAISM OF NANDIKEŚVARA

The available material on this system, is vary scanty. We have just one small work, consisting of twenty-six verses and a brief commentary on it, to which we have referred earlier. But it is a very important work inasmuch as it states the fundamentals of the monistic Śaiva Philosophy, as incorporated in the first fourteen aphorisms of Pāṇini's grammar, according to the interpretation of Nandikeśvara.

At the end of each of these fourteen aphorisms there is a consonant. Nandikeśvara holds that such a consonant stands for a predicate, exactly as Pāṇini holds that it is for the formation of a technical term such as "Aṇ" (Pratyāhāra).

THE IMPORTANCE OF NANDIKEŚVARA ŚAIVAISM

If we accept the view that Nandikeśvara was a contemporary of Pāṇini, because of the persisting tradition and indirect reference to his view by Patañjali, the system, presented by Nandikeśvara, is very important indeed. For, it is then the earliest voluntaristic Philosophy, which was subsequently developed by Lakulīśa in his Pāśupata Sūtra, in the light of Dualism-cum-non-dualism, and by the thinkers of Kashmir, such as Somānanda, Kallaṭa, Utpala, Abhinavagupta and Kṣemarāja etc., in the light of monism. In fact, the very brief statements about the philosophical principles in the Nandikeśvara Kāśikā, have meaning, only when they are studied in the light of what Kashmir thinkers have said on allied topics.

The fact that the system, presented by Nandikeśvara, is very similar to, if not identical with what is now known as Monistic Kashmir Śaivaism, becomes evident if we compare the benedictory verse at the beginning of the Spanda Kārikā with the one at the beginning of the commentary by Upamanyu on the Nandikeśvara Kāśikā. These two verses not only present the same philosophic thought but also present it in almost identical expressions.

Yasyonmeṣanimeṣābhyām Jagataḥ pralayodayau.

S. K. 3.

Yasyonmeṣanimeṣābhyām Vyaktāvyaktam idam jagat.

N. K, 1.

THE MAIN TENDENCIES OF THE SYSTEM

(1) Nandikeśvara Śaivaism has mystic tendency. This tendency may be said to be predominant. For, the circumstances, which were responsible for coming to light of this system, were mystic. The sages practised austerity for mystic light. As an act of grace to them, Śiva appeared mystically and taught them that the Reality is beyond all categories; that it is the self, the "I" or "Aham", the all-transcending; that it is all-graceful, the Grace being to it what body is to soul; and that it is the transcendental witness of everything[1].

Here we find three fundamentals of mysticism: (1) the Reality as it is finally realised; the final and everlasting experience that a mystic aims at attaining through mystic life and practices; (2) the Reality as it appears to a mystic in a mystic vision; and (3) the faith, with which and in which a mystic lives. The all-transcending nature of the mystic Reality, the appearance of this Reality in a mystic form in a mystic vision and faith in His Grace are the fundamental pre-suppositions of mysticism.

(2) We also find the voluntaristic tendency in Nandikeśvara Śaivaism in the context of its metaphysics. Every mystic system has its metaphysical theory also. But the Reality as it is presented in the context of mysticism is generally slightly different from the Reality as it is postulated in the metaphysical context. The former is beyond all categories and, therefore, is indefinable unless we take the indefinability itself to be a definition. The latter, however, is spoken of as cause, source or manifester of everything. But the mystic Reality is not essentially different from the metaphysical. For, the Ultimate is admitted to be both transcendental and immanent.

Plotinus, for instance, on the one hand, speaks of the One as so transcendent that it is beyond the reach of mind and speech; it cannot be presented even in terms of the highest category; it is realisable only in mystic ecstacy. On the other hand, he represents the One as the source and goal of everything, from whom all oppositions and diversities emanate.

Similarly Nandikeśvara also, in the course of his interpretation of the first aphorism of the Māheśvara Sūtras, speaks of the metaphysical Reality, which is identified with the first letter "A", as Brahman[2], which is free from all Guṇas, is present in

1. N. K. 15. | 2. N. K. 3—6.

everything and in all forms of speech, Paśyantī etc. and is the source or origin, not only of all letters, but also of the entire universe, including many different worlds. This Brahman becomes or manifests itself as the Universe through its power, technically called "Citkalā" or "Cit-śakti", and, therefore, is called "Īśvara". The letters "I" and "U" in the aphorism signify the "Power" (Citkalā) and the "Lord" respectively.

There is an interesting point, worth noting in the commentary on the verse No. 3, on which the statement, made in the preceding paragraph, is based.

The word "Citkalā" is interpreted as "Māyā". It has, therefore, to be made clear here that the word "Māyā" in this context does not have the meaning that it has in the Vedānta Philosophy, i.e. the principle of ignorance and illusion, which cannot be presented as either "being" or "not-being". For, in the system of Nandikeśvara, there is no such category as Māyā, distinct from Śakti, as in other Śaiva systems. No doubt it admits thirty-six categories, but they are slightly different from those of other Śaiva systems, as we shall show. The question, therefore, arises. what does "Māyā" mean ? And the answer is that it means what Vimarśa means in the monistic Śaivaism of Kashmir. It means "Free Will" (Svātantrya). For, this system admits that the universe owes its being to His Will[1].

That the word "Citkalā", which is interpreted as "Māyā" by the commentator, means what is stated above is borne out by another fact. That is, Nandikeśvara talks of "A" the Brahman, as "Prakāśa"[2], as distinct from "I", the Citkalā, and also of the inseparable relation between the two. The principle, represented by "I", is said to be the cause, in so far as it is 'the potentiality' 'the power' the Śakti, to which everything owes its being. But 'Śakti' is so only in relation to Śiva, Brahman, Prakāśa or "A"[3]. And we know that the monistic Śaivaism of Kashmir, which talks of the first category as "Prakāśa" and of the second as "Vimarśa", uses the words "Citi" and "svātantrya" as synonymous with Vimarśa[4]. The word 'Citkalā', therefore, seems to mean Vimarśa or free Will.

Nandikeśvara himself uses the word "Māyā", in the sense of "Manovṛtti", the activity of the mind, manifested by the

1. N. K. 7.
2. N. K. 4.
3. N. K. 6.
4. Bh., Vol. I, 250.

Lord, and the relation of this with the Lord is spoken of as the same (Samāśritya)[1] as that which He has with Citkalā in bringing the universe into being. It may be pointed out here that in this context the commentator uses the words "Māyā", "I" and "Citkalā" as synonymous; and that Nandikeśvara himself propounds the voluntaristic world-view and presents it in almost the same words as those used by Kṣemarāja in his Pratyabhijñā Hṛdaya, as has been stated in the Historical section. Therefore, there is little doubt about the synonymity of Citkalā with Svātantrya and about the voluntaristic tendency of the system of Nandikeśvara.

MONISM OF NANDIKEŚVARA

We have talked of the relation between Brahman and Śakti or Citkalā. Does not the admission of the two ultimate metaphysical principles mean Dualism ? The reply to this question is given in the course of the interpretation of the second aphorism "Ṛ L K." The Brahman is the Mind. And the Māyā is the activity, which it manifests. The Brahman, being active, being in relation with its activity, which is its own outflow, brings the world into being. The active has no being in isolation from the activity. The two are inseparable, much as are the Moon and her rays, or a word and its meaning[2].

Nandikeśvara seems to advocate the type of monism which is the characteristic of the Philosophy of Grammar. He identifies the Brahman, the "A", with Parā, as presented by Nāgeśa Bhaṭṭa, under the influence of the Śaivāgama. He talks of Parā as pure Jñapti, or sentiency (Jñaptimātra)[3]. The word Jñapti seems to be used as a synonym of "Citi". For, Patañjali, a near successor of Nandikeśvara, in his Yogasūtra, in presenting the self[4], uses the words "Citi" and "Dṛsi", in stating its essential nature. And Utpala and Abhinavagupta have interpreted it to show that Patañjali's conception of the Self is the same as that of monistic Kashmir Śaivaism and that it implies voluntarism.

If we accept this view, namely, that 'Jñapti' stands for "Citi" and presents the essential nature of the Self, the word "Citkalā", the meaning of which we tried to settle earlier, gets a significance, which explains the use of the analogy of the Moon and her

1. N. K. 7.
2. N. K. 7.
3. N. K. 6.
4. Bh. Vol. I, 245.

rays to bring out non-difference between Brahman and Citkalā. If Brahman or Self is 'Citi', the power of Brahman, which is responsible for the being of the whole universe, is spoken of as 'Citkalā', because it is an aspect of Brahman and, therefore, non-different from it, exactly as the ray of the Moon is an aspect of her and is non-different from her.

The monistic view, presented on the basis of aphorism "Ṛ Ḷ K", implies that the relation between Brahman and its power is the same as between Ṛ and L. We know that, according to the grammarian, there is the relation of identity between the two, Ṛ and L, similar to that between one "A" and another (Ṛ Ḷ varṇayormithaḥ sāvarṇyam vācyam)[1]. Nandikeśvara Śaivaism, therefore, is a monistic system, because it admits the identity of the mind and its potentiality and activity, of Śiva and Śakti, or Brahman and Citkalā.

THE THEORY OF MANIFESTATION

The relation between the Brahman and the universe is not that of the creator and the created. The world does not exist apart from the Brahman as does a jar from a potter, who makes it. It is, on the contrary, like that of thought and the thinking subject. The world is nothing but the thought of Brahman. It is external manifestation of what is potentially within. It is essentially identical with Brahman, much as thought is with the thinking subject. Similarly the transcendental Reality (Nirguṇa) and the immanent (Saguṇa)[2] are identical. For, the latter is a manifestation of the former. All the categories are the manifestations of the Brahman.[3]

THE CATEGORIES

Nandikeśvara admits thirty-six categories and holds that Para Śiva is beyond the categories. They may be stated as follows:—

1. Śiva 2. Śakti 3. Īśvara: 4—28. twenty-five categories of the Sāṅkhya system[4]: 29—33. five vital airs, Prāṇa etc. : 34—36. three Guṇas, Sattva etc.

It is interesting to note that Kashmir Śaivaism also admits thirty-six categories with some modifications, which may be stated as follows:—

---

1 S. K., 6.
2 N. K., (Comm.), 9.
3 N. K., 9.
4 N. K., 14-15.

(1) The first three categories are common to both the Nandikeśvara Ṣaivaism and the Kashmir Ṣaivaism, excepting that in between Ṣakti and Īśvara Kashmir Ṣaivaism recognises another category, called Sadāśiva.

(2) Twenty-five categories, accepted by the Sāṅkhya, are accepted by both. In this case Abhinavagupta points out the difference in the conception of these categories from those of the Sāṅkhya, though the same names are retained.

(3) Kashmir Śaivaism does not recognise five vital airs as separate categories. Instead it admits the five limiting conditions of individual self, technically called Kalā, Niyati, Rāga, Vidyā and Kāla, as distinct categories.

(4) Kashmir Śaivaism does not recognise Sattva, Rajas and Tamas as distinct categories. Instead, it accepts Sadāśiva, Vidyā and Māyā.

(5) Both hold that Paramaśiva is beyond the categories. This view has fully been stated by Abhinavagupta in the very first verse of prayer in the I. P. V.

(VII.) RASEŚVARA ŚAIVAISM

Raseśvara system is more a science than a School of Philosophy. It does not propound any new metaphysical, ethical or epistemic theory. But still it is included amongst the systems of philosophy, even by such a great authority as Mādhava in his Sarva Darśana Saṅgraha, because it is concerned with a way to final emancipation (Mukti). In fact, Mādhava[1] himself begins with referring to the acceptance by this system of the essential identity of the individual self with the Lord, in common with some other Śaiva systems.

CONTRIBUTORS TO THE RASEŚVARA SYSTEM

Although Mādhava represents this to be a Śaiva system, yet it would be a mistake to think that the discovery of different methods of processing and purifying mercury so as to make it efficacious in giving perdurable body to the user of it, was exclusively made by the followers of Śaivaism only. No doubt the Śaivas made the largest number of discoveries, but others also made substantial contributions to the mercurial science. In some of the available works, which are collections of researches on mercury, we find references to the contributors to this science, other than the Śaivas. Thus, Rasopaniṣad, which aims at giving the essence of the practices, prevalent in different schools, mentions, besides Vātula, which is one of the recognised Śaivāgamas, such schools as Prābhrata, Brāhma, Vaiṣṇava, Aindra, Śāṅkara, Śaukra and Bṛhaspati Mata[2]. And Mādhava himself refers to the admission of the perdurable body by the followers of Vaiṣṇavaism, such as Garbhaśrīkānta Miśra[3], who admits that the body of Narasiṁha is perdurable and that it was actually seen as such by Sanaka etc.

The Bauddhas also made substantial contributions to it. Nāgārjuna, as we have stated earlier, is said to have gone abroad, brought mercury from there, processed and purified it so as to make it capable of converting iron into gold. He is also mentioned in the list of the persons, who became Siddhas in consequence of the use of the purified mercury. He is also referred

---

1 S. D. S., 202.
2 R. U., 2.
3 S. D. S., 208.

to as an original contributor to the mercurial science among twenty-seven such persons by Vāgbhaṭa in his Rasa Ratna Samuccaya[1].

THE PERSISTING TRADITION

The tradition of the mercurial science seems to have persisted for centuries. In the list of the authoritative contributors, in addition to the names, unknown to the history of Sanskrit literature, there are names of the well known persons also. And there is sufficient evidence to justify the identification of the persons, referred to therein, with the historical. Such two names are (1) Nāgārjuna (Circa 120 A. D.) and (2) Bhagavad Govindapāda (780 A. D.). The research on mercury, therefore, seems to have been carried on for about six hundred years. The results of these researches are contained in the large number of books, available even now on the subject.

Some of these works admit of arrangement in an historical order. The original material on the subject is found mainly in the Śaiva Āgamas or Tantras; and subsequent works are mostly based on them. In some of the Tantras, there is a mere reference to the processing and purifying of mercury. For instance, in the Rudra Yāmala Tantra, which is primarily concerned with the Yogic practices, as related to different Cakras, there is nothing more than a mere reference to the mercurial science (Pārada Sādhana)[2]. Such references seem to be referred to in the Rasārṇava[3], which is a very authoritative work on the Raseśvara system, because Mādhava quotes from it mostly.

It may be pointed out here that the Rasārṇava, as we have it in the printed edition, is fairly authoritative and seems to be a faithful copy of the text, as Mādhava had it before him. All the five quotations from the Rasārṇava, occurring on pages 202, 203, 204, 205-6 and 208, in the Sarva Darśana Saṅgraha, are found in the Rasārṇava (Chowkhamba Edition) on pages 4, 2, 3, 161-2 and 4 respectively.

Similarly Rasopaniṣad, a work on Rasa, consisting of Eighteen Chapters, is simply a digest of a bigger work, called Rasa Mahodadhi, consisting of thirty Chapters. It refers to Nāgārjuna[4] as a great authority. And Vāgbhaṭa in his Rasa Ratna Samuccaya[5] distinctly refers to it as the first of those works, on

---

1 R. R.S., 2.
2 R. Y., 7.
3 R. A., 1-2
4 R. U., 76.
5 R. R. S. 291.

which his digest on Rasa is based. He quotes from the Rasahṛdaya also. The verses, quoted from this work in the Sarva Darśana Saṅgraha "Iti Dhana" (203) and "Bhrūyuga" (209), are found in the Rasa Ratna Samuccaya on pages 7 and 10 respectively.

THE VALUE OF THE RASA TRADITION

The persistence of the tradition of processing and purifying mercury in various ways for different purposes, and its association with great names in the history of Sanskrit literature, such as Nāgārjuna and Bhagavad Govinda Pāda, should compel us to think seriously of the subject. Not only is there vast literature on the subject, but also there are references to Siddhas, which the mercurial science aimed at producing and actually produced, in the standard works in Sanskrit Literature. The Ratnāvali of Harṣa (600 A. D.) and the Mṛcchakaṭika of Śūdraka, who probably belonged to the beginning of Christian era, refer to Siddha and his powers. Kallaṭa and Somānanda are well known Siddhas amongst Kashmir Śaiva philosophers, Bhagavad Govinda Pāda, the teacher of Śaṅkarācārya, was a recognised Siddha.

But there is a prejudice against the authenticity and correctness of the statements, which are found in the books in Sanskrit, particularly when they deal with the scientific subjects; and more so if they belong to the Tāntric literature. No doubt the Tāntric literature, even when dealing with a scientific subject, such as Chemistry, is not free from the influence of religion and mixes up religion with science and talks of things, which to a person familiar with the modern Chemistry, sound ridiculous: for instance, acquisition of a body, that is free from death and aging and conversion of iron into gold. But assuming, for the sake of argument, that the Tāntric literature lacks the spirit of the science of today and contains extremely exaggerated statements about the powers of the chemical processes and preparations, of which it talks; are we justified in ignoring and neglecting it ?

India had a culture, long before the period, to which cultural history of any of the advanced western nations, which have developed various sciences to the modern extent, could be traced. She knew of the chemicals. She had her Chemistry, Metallography, Metallurgy, Mineralogy and Medical system, etc. If, therefore, we want to know, what Indian genius did on these subjects in the distant past, the only source, that we can refer to is the Tāntric. And approaching the Tāntric literature from the point of view of the modern sciences, we find enough material therein, as has been testified by the researches of Prof. P. C. Ray, recorded in his Hindu Chemistry.

The religious element that we find mixed up with the treatment of a scientific subject, is nothing but the reflection of the main tendency of the period, during which Tantras were written. And the exaggerated statements about the powers of chemical processes and preparations, even if they be accepted to be such, can well point to the ideals of Chemistry and other sciences. And it is interesting to learn that Russian scientists, like O. B. Lepeshinskaya, are carrying on researches with a view to discover something for "prolonging man's life span". It would, therefore, be of great historical value and may be of some practical also, to know what writers in India have said on such a problem.

THE SCIENTIFIC ASPECT OF THE RASEŚVARA SYSTEM

The Raseśvara system presents the crowning phases of the Indian system of medicine, called Āyurveda. Among the eight well recognised branches of Āyurveda, medicine, surgery and midwifery etc., Rasāyana is well known. The Raseśvara system presents an advance on the earlier conception of Rasāyana. According to Caraka[1], Rasāyana was efficacious in prolonging life, strengthening memory etc. and restoring youth. But the Raseśvara system holds that mercury (Rasendra) processed and purified, in accordance with the ways and means, stated in the authoritative texts on the system, is capable of giving immortality (Amaratva) to the user[2].

The Raseśvara system maintains that alchemy is an effective science. It asserts that mercury, processed and purified in the manner, given in the literature on the system, if mixed with an other metal, such as iron, copper, silver and tin etc. in proportion of one thousandth of the total weight of the other metal, converts it into gold[3]. It gives information about everything that is necessary for such a processing and purification of mercury. It states the medicines, metals and mechanical contrivences, necessary for the said purpose. It gives colour, taste and smell and other details to identify the herbs. It states the characteristics of the places, where they can be found.

It holds that metals can be given any colour, that the original natural colour of any metal can be changed, and states the ways

1 Car. 376
2 R. A. 6.
3 R. U. 14, (36, 39, 47.)

and means of doing so[1]. It classifies vegetables, plants and trees on the basis of their metallic content[2]. It states the characteristics of the regions where mines of different metals exist[3] and the ways and means of purifying metals.

It claims to give very correct ways and means of processing and purifying mercury, which if and when used, makes the body of the user such as can walk on water, can go thousands of miles without feeling fatigued, as cannot be bound and restrained by iron chains, cannot be cut or pierced by any weapon and cannot be burnt by fire ; as can fly in the air, can talk to gods in heaven and can come back to earth[4].

RELIGIOUS ASPECT OF THE RASEŚVARA SYSTEM

According to this system, there is no antagonism or opposition between science and religion : they go hand in hand. There are certain religious practices to be maintained and certain religious rites to be performed in order to attain success in processing and purifying mercury so as to get freedom from death, diseases and old age through its use. The internal repetition of a certain set of symbolic sounds (Mantrajapa)[5], the spiritual initiation[6] and worship of the phallic form of Śiva, made up of mercury (Rasaliṅga)[7] are all necessary. And finally success in the undertaking depends upon His Grace[8]. It recognises caste system and admits that birth in a higher caste, which means life in a certain atmosphere, makes a man better fitted to follow this system; but it holds that birth in a lower caste is no barrier; that a Śūdra can follow this system as well as can a Brāhmaṇa[9]. It asserts the importance of the teacher, emphasises the necessity of devotion to him and warns against the dangers of doing the practical side without the supervision of the teacher[10].

---

1 R. U. 32.
2 R. U. 192.
3 R, U. 188.
4 R. U. 106.
5 R. A. 116.
6 R. A. 10.
7 R. A. 11.
8 R. A. 3.
9 R. A 8.
10 R. A. 6.

PHILOSOPHICAL ASPECT OF THE RASEṢVARA SYSTEM

The system of philosophy, on which the mercurial science is based, is different from that which serves as the basis of the medical science as presented by Caraka. The origin of Āyurveda, as a science, which aims at preserving the health of the healthy and curing the diseases of the suffering, is traced to the Atharva Veda[1]. But the philosophy, on which the science was based in the early stages, as we find in Caraka Saṁhitā, was a mixture of the principles of the Vaiśeṣika, the Sāṅkhya and the Vedānta, with slight modifications. Thus, we find the acceptance of the Vaiśeṣika categories, universal, particular, substance, quality, action and inherence by Caraka in the very first Chapter[2]. The three means of right knowledge, perception, inference and verbal testimony are admitted, though apart from them, reason (Yukti) also is acknowledged as a valid means[3]. The theory of perception is identical with that of the Vaiśeṣika. Three types of inference, as found in the Nyāya, are admitted[4].

Caraka follows the Sāṅkhya in presenting the twenty-four constituents of Puruṣa. But here he identifies Puruṣa with Prakṛti, for the simple reason that both are Avyakta[5]. In presenting Puruṣa in the light of the Vaiśeṣika, however, he talks of Puruṣa as a configuration of six, i.e. five elements, ether etc., with the principle of sentiency (Cetanā) as the sixth.[6] He talks of the principle of sentiency (Cetanā) also as a 'Dhātu'. He holds that Puruṣa is of two types: (1) the one that is a mere configuration, as stated above; and (2) the other, which is a mere principle of sentiency (Jñaḥ) and as such is beginningless, causeless and eternal; it has objective knowledge, only when it is associated with the means of knowledge[7]. It is pervasive (Vibhu)[8].

He asserts that knowledge and action and fruition of the latter, as well as pleasure, pain, ignorance, birth and death are related to Puruṣa, which is of the nature of a configuration, as has been stated above. The relation of Puruṣa, as pure sentiency, with other Tattvas, is due to predominance of Rajas and Tamas. When, therefore, because of the predominance of pure Sattva,

1 Car. 186.
2 Car. 9—13.
3 Car. 70.
4 Car. 71.
5 Car. 288.
6 Car. 287.
7 Car. 292.
8 Car. 293.

they are cast aside (Nirākṛta)[1], the man is on the sure way to liberation. He states the means to purify Sattva, which, when purified, shines like the sun, free from dust, cloud and mist, or like a lamp in a breezeless place[2]. Consequently true knowledge (Satya Buddhi)[3] arises, the veil of ignorance is torn, the mind withdraws from the external objects and rests on the Self or Ātman, the Reality is grasped and the liberation, the eternal peace, is attained[4]. The liberated sees no difference between himself and the objective world.

ŚAIVA DUALISM AS THE BASIS OF RASEŚVARA SYSTEM

The Raseśvara system does not follow the technique of the Nyāya, the Vaiśeṣika or the Vedānta. It adopts the technique of the dualistic Śaivaism. We have not so far been able to trace a text, in which the philosophy of the system as such has been dealt with; nor do we find in the available literature any section that can give a clear idea of the fundamentals of the Raseśvara as a system of philosophy. We can, however, get a glimpse of the system from stray philosophical references and they clearly demonstrate that it is a Śaiva system.

Thus, in the Rasārṇava, we find references to 'Śaktipāta' and "Pāśa[5]". Īśa and Sadāśiva also are mentioned[6]. Rasa Bhairava, as an object of contemplation, is presented in the same terms, as those in which Śiva is presented; that is, an embodiment of Sadyojāta, Vāmadeva, Aghora, Īśāna and Tatpuruṣa[7]. It also talks of Bindu, Nāda, Śakti, Unmana and Paramavyoma, and presents the following as higher than the preceding in the order, stated above. It speaks of the liberation as attainment of similarity with Śiva[8].

In the context of metaphysics, it presents Maheśvara, the Highest Lord, as omniscient and omnipotent; essentially subtle (Sūkṣmarūpa) and free from all impurities (Nirañjana). Here we find the Dualistic tendency mixed up with the Voluntaristic. The Highest Lord is represented to create and annihilate

1 Car. 290.
2 Car. 327.
3 Car. 328.
4 Car. 328.
5 R. A. 3.
6 R. A. 133.
7 R. A. 16-7.
8 R. A. 169.

everything by His will[1]. The entire universe springs from Him, has its being in Him and is essentially identical with Him[2].

The individual self, as has been stated earlier, is admitted to be essentially identical with the supreme[3]. It has innate impurities[4] and can get freedom from them through His Grace. It can acquire an immortal and unaging body, made up of mercury and mica, through the use of the said metals, processed and purified in accordance with the directions, given in the texts. It can attain liberation in the very life time on the earth and have the supernatural powers, referred to earlier.

LIBERATION IN LIFE (JĪVANMUKTI)

This system holds, as has been shown earlier, that through the use of the processed and refined mercury an unaging, non-decaying or immortal and divine body can be acquired: that this body is made up of pure mercury and mica and as such is different from that which is made up of flesh, blood and bones: that the acquisition of the former does not mean the loss and destruction of the latter: on the contrary, when the mercurial divine body is got, the physical body itself, which is the abode of the divine, becomes so strong that there is no fear of accidental death[5].

Accordingly it holds that the liberation in life (Jīvanmukti) is the consciousness or awareness of identity of the soul, which is within the unaging and immortal body, with Ṣiva (Ajarāmara dehasya Ṣiva tādātmya Vedanam)[6].

It is very sceptic about the liberation after death, which is promised by some schools of thought. It says that there is no direct evidence to convince us that the liberation after death does certainly take place, so that we can follow the path, pointed out by these systems, without any doubt in our minds about the attainment of the objective. It condemns 'Vāmamārga' as a way to liberation. It is antagonistic to "Aghorapantha"[7].

Accordingly it shows a way to acquiring an unaging and immortal body, the presence of which within the physical body frees it from aging, diseases and accidental death, and enables

1 R. A. 117.
2 R. A. 1.
3 S. D. S. 202.
4 R A. 3.
5 S. D. S. (Comm) 203.
6 R. A. 2.
7 R. A. 2.

the soul to realise similarity with the Brahman in the life time. The liberation of such a soul is directly perceptible, because the body, wherein it is, is entirely free from accidental death, diseases and old age, cannot be cut by weapons, knows no obstruction of any kind, can freely go to other worlds and come back.

If we take different texts together we find that it admits gradual liberation (Kramamukti). Thus, the first stage seems to be the liberation in life (Jīvanmukti). Here there is awareness of qualitative identity of the individual in the perdurable body with the Brahman. Here the duality of the individual and the Universal persists, much as does the distinction between the actor on the stage and the imaginary hero, with which he identifies himself. A soul that has a mercurial body is free to realise perfect identity with Śiva in respect of all attributes[1], at its own will[2].

It also says that the soul that has a mercurial body goes to the world of Śiva at the end of universal annihilation (Pralayānte)[3]. Thus, it seems to talk of the type of liberation, which is technically called "Sālokya". It admits three stages of liberation or three types of liberation ; (1) Jīvanmukti, (2) Sālokya and (3) Śivatā(gamana). It holds that the mercurial body of the Siddha dissolves just where the divine bodies of the gods do[4]. The final stage of liberation, according to this system, is the attainment of similarity with Śiva[5]. It is, therefore, a dualistic system.

THE MEANS TO LIBERATION IN LIFE (JĪVANMUKTI)

It admits that true knowledge is the means to final emancipation; but it asserts that such a knowledge is not possible without the practice of Yoga, the control over breath. The successful practice of Yoga, however, needs a healthy and perdurable body. Such a body can be got through the use of "Rasendra" only. Hence Rasendra is the basic means to liberation; because Yoga, without which true Knowledge is not possible, depends upon it.

1 R. A. 169.
2 R. A. 107.
3 R. A. 165.
4 R. A. 174.
5 R. A. 164.

(VIII) MONISTIC ŚAIVAISM OF KASHMIR AS PRESENTED IN THE ĪŚVARA PRATYABHIJÑĀ VIMARŚINĪ

THE monistic Śaivaism of Kashmir has already been presented in detail in the Second part of Abhinavagupta: An Historical and Philosophical Study, and summarily in the History of Philosophy Eastern and Western in Chapter XV (B) and in the introduction to the Bhāskarī vol. II. Here, therefore, an attempt is made to present this system on the lines of its presentation in the Īśvara Pratyabhijñā Vimarśinī so as to enable the reader to follow the Translation easily. The Translation covers the original work of Utpalācārya, the Īśvara Pratyabhijñā, and a commentary on it, the Vimarśinī, by Abhinavagupta.

AUTHOR'S MOTIVE AND POINT OF VIEW

According to the learned philosophical tradition, the essential qualification of a teacher or author was not the learning so much as the realisation within himself of the Reality which he propounded. Utpalācārya's Īśvara Pratyabhijñā, the view that the means to the realisation of the Highest Reality is the recognition, found a large following, because he had himself realised the Reality before he started to speak on it. He had come to the stage of the Self-realisation at which the motive is purely objective and not in the least subjective. He undertook the work, not for any gain or advantage to himself but simply for the good of mankind in general. All this is stated in the very first verse. And Abhinavagupta in the course of the commentary on it discusses the doctrines of devotion, Bhakti or Dāsya, and of Grace or Anugraha. He shows that the point of view of the author is logical. For, the book presents the theory of Recognition in the form of a syllogism, including five terms : (i) Proposition ; (ii) Reason ; (iii) Examples; (iv) Application ; and (v) Conclusion.

THE INTRODUCTION

Utpalācārya is very modern in his form of presentation. He puts in an *Introduction* in the beginning . And the purpose of it is nothing but to give a summary-view of the system so as to enable the reader to follow with greater ease what is presented in the body of the book. He holds (i) that the Ultimate Metaphysical Principle, the Maheśvara, is omniscient and omnipotent; He is free and, therefore, He does not depend upon anything external to Him to bring the entire universe into being; the universe is nothing but His idea or thought and, therefore, arises in Him, much as do the limited thoughts in the limited souls: it is simply a limited manifestation (Ābhāsa) of the Universal Mind: (ii) that He is the self-luminous and self-sufficient presupposition of all thoughts and acts, much as logically the universal is that of the individual : the means of right knowledge, therefore, do not apply to Him, because He is their presupposition, much as the flame is of the spreading rays: (iii) that He is not objective but purely subjective: all individual subjects are essentially identical with Him as self-luminocity and self-consciousness, and have no being separately from and independently of Him; therefore, in reality there is no independent subject to which He may be related as an object: (iv) that the means to the realisation of the Ultimate is not knowledge or cognition (Jñāna) but *Recognition* (Pratyabhijñā): it is related to, not the unknown but the known : it is a new way to the realisation of the Ultimate metaphysical Reality, the Maheśvara. The realisation consists, not in the actualisation of the potential; nor in the attainment of something new, nor in knowing what was unknown before; but in penetrating through the veil, that makes the Maheśvara appear as the individual, of which every one is immediately aware, and in recognising the Maheśvara in the individual. He holds that the individual is essentially free ; freedom is the inner being of the individual. But it is hidden by the veil of ignorance. The ignorance has to be removed to recognise it, to realise it as identical with the Reality.

BUDDHISM AND MONISTIC ŚAIVAISM OF KASHMIR

The relation between Buddhism and Monistic Śaivaism seems to be similar to that between Empiricism of Hume and Transcendental Philosophy of Kant to some extent. The Monistic Śaivaism of Kashmir is concerned with the Buddhistic view of the soul, not as it was propounded by Buddha himself. For, Buddha, according to Nāgārjuna, in his commentary on the Prajñāpāramitā Sūtra, sometimes taught that the Ātman exists, and at other times he taught that the Ātman does not exist. "When he preached that the Ātman exists and is to be the receiver of misery or happiness in the successive lives as the reward of its own Karma, his object was to save men from falling into the heresy of nihilism (Ucchedavāda). When he taught that there is no Ātman in the sense of a creator or a perceiver or an absolutely free agent, apart from the conventional name given to the aggregate of the five Skandhas, his object was to save men from falling into the opposite heresy of eternalism (Ṣāśvatavāda)".

The Monistic Ṣaivaism of Kashmir takes into account the Bauddha view of the soul as presented by Nāgasena etc., who dismiss the immortal soul as an illegitimate abstraction ; who affirm the negative position of non-existence of soul ; who hold that self is nothing but a stream of ideas ; who in the manner of Hume argue that we do not find anywhere in our experience anything answering to the conception of permanent self; and that the so called self is nothing but a series of varying cognitions, determinate or indeterminate, which belong to no permanent subject, because such a subject is not a fact of experience. And it attempts to prove, like Kant, that the position of the Bauddha, who denies permanent subject, like Hume, is untenable, because synthesis, which is an essential feature of all determinate cognitions, cannot be explained without a permanent subject.

Omniscient and omnipotent God is admitted by all theistic systems. But such a conception of God is generally based on Dualism, the recognition of the matter as comparatively independent of and separate from the Mind or God. The Nyāya and the Vaiśeṣika are theistic systems and, as has already been stated, they represent earlier Śaiva theism: because Kaṇāda was a Pāśupata and Gautama was a Ṣaiva. The Bauddha, who denied the existence of permanent individual subject naturally criticised the conception of omniscient and omnipotent God. And the monistic Ṣaivaism replies to this criticism, not on the dualistic hypothesis, but on the monistic. It interprets 'omnipotent' and 'omniscient' in a way different from that in which these words were interpreted earlier.

Utpalācārya and Abhinavagupta present the Bauddha objections against permanent subject and omniscient and omnipotent God in the Īśvara Pratyabhijñā and the Vimarśinī, Adhi. I, Āh. 2. And in the rest of the Adhikāra I, and in the whole of the Adhikāra II, they reply to the Bauddha objections in detail. The first two Adhikāras form the major portion of the book. The remaining two Adhikāras, the Āgamādhikāra and the Tattva Saṅgrahādhikāra, discuss the categories of the system and give a summary of it respectively.

BAUDDHA OBJECTIONS AGAINST ŚAIVAISM

The Bauddha does not admit permanent subject, individual or universal; nor knower as distinct from knowledge; nor action as something different from the series of momentary beings, which can be perceived directly or inferred ; nor any relation other than the causal. Accordingly he criticises the Śaiva conception of the omniscient and omnipotent God. For, omniscience presupposes knowledge as something distinct from the one to whom it is related and who, because of this relation, is called knower (Jñātā) : similarly omnipotence presupposes action as something different from the one to whom it is related and who, in consequence of this relation, is called doer (Kartā). He, like Hume, points out that however closely we observe and analyse our experiences, we do not discover the experiencer as distinct from the experiences. Nor is the knowing subject a necessary assumption to account for the phenomenon of remembrance. For, it can be accounted for in terms of the residual traces of the past experiences. As regards the I-consciousness, the Bauddha asserts that it refers to different constituents of the ever changing personality, such as body, feeling and intellect, according as the I-consciousness is related to various experiences such as "I am fat"; "I am happy" or "I understand this". He, therefore, holds that permanent subject or knower is an illogical abstraction.

And permanent doer or Kartā also is an equally illogical assumption. For, there is no action apart from a series of momentary beings at different spatial points in a temporal order. For instance, if we analyse the action, to which we refer when we say "Devadatta goes", we find nothing more than the body of Devadatta at different spatial points in a temporal order. But the body of Devadatta is not the same through out the time during which it is seen at different spatial points. It is momentary, according to the Bauddha. Hence, the Bauddha talks of "series of momentary beings". Therefore, permanent doer or Kartā also is an illogical assumption. And if conception of individual knower and doer is illogical, the illogicality of the conception of the omniscient and omnipotent God automatically follows.

THE REPLY OF THE MONISTIC ṢAIVAISM OF KASHMIR

The Monistic Ṣaivaism of Kashmir agrees with the Buddhism in denying the distinction between the knower or subject and the knowledge, such as is admitted by the Vaiśeṣika, namely, that the subject is the substance wherein the knowledge inheres as a quality. But it asserts that permanent subject is necessary to account for remembrance and that remembrance cannot be explained in terms of mere residual traces as the Bauddha holds. Its approach to the problem of remembrance is psychological. It analyses remembrance and shows that the characteristic nature of remembrance, which is expressed by the word "that" cannot be explained in terms of the residual traces only of the past experience.

This assertion is based on the view of the monistic Śaivaism of Kashmir: (1) that knowledge (Jñāna) is self-luminous; (2) that one knowledge cannot be the object of another. In remembrance we are aware not only of the object of a past experience but also of the experience that we had in relation to that object. And remembrance is recognised to be similar to the past experience in respect of having the object of a past experience as its object. Now the residual traces can explain the relation of remembrance to the object of a past experience, but they cannot account for the relation of the remembrance to the past experience. For, the past experience cannot appear as an object of remembrance, because luminosity of every cognition is self-confined and, therefore, one cognition cannot become an object of another; and the Bauddha does not admit permanent subject, different from the cognition, which can synthetize various experiences. Further, even the awareness of similarity of remembrance with the past experience is not possible, because every cognition is momentary and there is no subject, according to the Bauddha, which can hold together the two experiences to make the consciousness of similarity possible.

But remembrance is an important factor in practical life. All our activities to acquire or to shun a particular object are determined by remembrance. We strive for an object, because we know it to be a source of pleasure through remembrance of the past experience, because of the synthetic activity of a permanent subject, which holds various experiences together and relates them in various ways. Even the determinate knowledge of an object, which is the presupposition of all practical moves, depends upon memory and synthesis of various percepts.

But because synthesis of experiences is not possible on the basis of the Bauddha philosophy of momentariness of subject, Utpalācārya, therefore, asserts :—

"Thus, all human transactions, originating from unification of various kinds of cognitions, which mutually differ and cannot become one another's object, will come to an end."

"If there be not one great Lord, who is essentially self-luminous, holds within all the innumerable forms of the universe and possesses the powers of cognition, remembrance and differentiation."

EPISTEMIC BASIS OF THE ŚAIVA METAPHYSICS

The approach of the Īśvara Pratyabhijñā Vimarśinī to the problem of metaphysics is very interesting inasmuch as it shows that the metaphysical principle, presented in it, is the presupposition of every phenomenon of knowledge and that the practical life is possible only on the basis of the monistic Śaiva metaphysics. It synthetizes Realism and Idealism and presents a metaphysical theory, which is technically called "Ābhāsavāda" (Realistic Idealism). It points out how the explanations of the phenomena of knowledge of different kinds, as given by other schools of thought, such as various schools of Buddhism, the Sāṅkhya, and the Mīmāṁsā etc. are unsatisfactory.

It denies the essential difference between mind and matter, thought and thing, or subject and object. It rejects the dualistic explanation of the phenomena of knowledge on similar grounds as those advanced by the subjectivists such as the Vijñānavādin in the East and Berkeley in the West. It rejects subjectivism also, because the subjectivist hypothesis completely shuts up every individual subject in his own world and thus fails to explain the common objective world, wherein the individuals can co-operate in a common undertaking. It also rejects pure Idealistic Monism which holds the world to be mere illusion.

It denies the essential difference between the individual mind or subject and the Universal. Its conception of the Universal Mind is based upon an acute analysis of the individual mind. Knowledge (Jñāna), remembrance and differentiation are the distinctive functions of individual mind. They, therefore, are attributed to the Universal Mind also; because the individual and the universal are identical not only in essence but in functions also ; and because without the admission of such functions of the Universal Mind the phenomenon of determinate knowledge cannot be explained. The reason may be stated as follows:—

The explanations of the phenomenon of knowledge, as given by the dualists and pluralists are unsatisfactory, because they present an insurmountable difficulty in bridging the gulf that divides the self from the not-self. If the subject and the object are completely cut off from each other, have exclusive and independent existence , and are of opposite nature, like light and darkness (Tamaḥprakāśavad viruddhadharmiṇoḥ. Ś. Bh.) how can there be any connection between the two, which is so very necessary for the production of the phenomenon of knowledge.

The meeting of the self and the not-self, in this case, seems to be as difficult as that of the two logs which are carried by two different currents, which separately lose themselves in the sands. The Īśvara Pratyabhijñā Vimarśinī, therefore, declares that the All-inclusive Universal Mind is the logical necessity to account for the phenomena of knowledge.

THE ALL-INCLUSIVE UNIVERSAL MIND AND ITS OMNISCIENCE

The Monistic Śaivaism of Kashmir is a synthesis of the realistic , idealistic, voluntaristic and mystic tendencies. Accordingly it admits that the Universal Mind has two aspects, transcendental (Viśvottīrṇa) and immanent (Viśvamaya). It presents the Universal Mind as transcendental in the context of mysticism, and as immanent in the context of metaphysics, which primarily aims at explaining the practical life. It admits the Universal Mind to be not conscious but consciousness itself, not free but freedom itself (Prakāśa vimarśamaya). (This point has been dealt with in Abhinavagupta pp. 199-207.) Its theory of emanation of the whole universe, including subject, object and means of knowledge, reminds us of the philosophy of Plotinus. The universe can be in the state of identity with or of difference from the Universal Mind. And emanation is nothing but the manifestation of what is identical with itself as separate from itself; but the manifested, even in the state of separateness from the Mind, is no less within the Mind than in the state of identity, exactly as our thoughts are within ourselves even when they are objectified. The universe has no existence independently of the Mind exactly as the dream has no being independently of the dreaming subject. The world-process is the process within the Mind. The phenomena of knowledge, related to the individual, are the phenomena in the Universal Mind, exactly as thoughts, feelings and cognitions of different types, which the individuals figuring in the dream have, are in the dreaming subject. Just as it is the dreaming subject that knows, remembers and differentiates in the figures which appear to do so in dream, so it is the Universal Mind that does so in all individual minds. Hence in the context of Metaphysics, which aims at explaining the phenomena of determinate knowledge, on which practical life depends, the Īśvara Pratyabhijñā Vimarśinī speaks of the Universal Mind as expressing its "freedom" (Svātantrya) in the forms of the powers of knowledge (Jñāna) remembrance (Smṛti) and differentiation (Apohana) which consist in uniting and separating the Ābhāsas so as to give rise to such subjects and objects etc. as are necessary for the rise of aforesaid phenomena. These topics are fully discussed in the Jñānādhikāra Āhnika IV, V and VI respectively. All-inclusiveness and Freedom are dealt with successively in Āhnikas VII and VIII.

Thus, omniscience of the Universal Mind consists not in objectively knowing everything that exists independently of and separately from it, but in freedom to manifest and to unite the Ābhāsas so as to give rise to all that is necessary for the rise of the phenomena of knowledge. The Universal Mind is omniscient, because all phenomena of knowledge emerge from and merge back into it exactly as dream does from and back into the dreaming individual.

OMNIPOTENCE (KRIYĀŚAKTI) OF THE LORD AND PHENOMENON OF ACTION

The distinction between body and mind is undeniable and so is that between thought or knowledge and action. Thus, the recognition of distinction between omniscience and omnipotence is natural. But omnipotence, if it is the power or capacity to do everything, includes the power to bring about all that is necessary for the phenomena of knowledge. This is admitted in the very beginning of the Īśvara Pratyabhijñā. In fact, the word "Kartari" with which the book begins is just to indicate this.

The phenomena of knowledge and action are similar in so far as both presuppose the existence of subject, object and means. But action can be viewed more objectively than knowledge. And the Bauddha, who is the chief opponent of the Monistic Śaivaism of Kashmir, viewed the action purely objectively and so criticised the conception of 'doer' (Kartā) and of the Omnipotent God.

THE BAUDDHA CONCEPTION OF ACTION

The Bauddha conception of action and its difference from that of the Monistic Śaivaism of Kashmir have been discussed in the two introductions to the two earlier volumes of the Bhāskarī. The Bauddha views the action objectively or empirically and asserts that it is only a definite mental construct, which is based upon the observed series of spatial points at which a particular body of man, animal or anything else is seen in a temporal succession ; and that no 'doer' apart from the body is seen and, therefore, the admission of a permanent 'doer' (Kartā) is baseless. The following are the points which he emphasises against the Śaiva:-

(I) Action is a series; it is characterised by succession and, therefore, is multiple. Hence it cannot be spoken of as one. For, unity is the opposite of multiplicity and, therefore, cannot co-exist with multiplicity. Accordingly it is illogical to say that action is one and serial or successive also at the same time . (II) Unity of action cannot be asserted on the ground that it resides in one, has one substratum; because there is no experience of a substratum, different from the momentary beings, which constitute the series. The momentary beings (Kṣaṇas) alone, coming in succession, are experienced. (III) Even if, for the sake of argument, a substratum be accepted, how can it, being affected by the various constituents of the series, characterised by temporal, spatial and formal differences, be spoken of as one? (IV) Recognition of the body, that is found at various places in a temporal order, as the same is not sufficient to establish its identity and unity. For, it is due to similarity of the body of the preceding moment with that of the following, just as in the case of the flame of a lamp; because though a layman thinks that the same flame persists through successive moments, yet really it does not: it is replaced in successive moments by other flames, into which the oil, that is drawn by the wick to the spatial point of the going out flame, is converted. (V) Action is not real (Satya) because it is made up of a series, the members of which are held up together in the order of priority and posteriority by the determinative activity of the mind. For, whatever is determinately grasped is not real: the real is momentary and indeterminate.

THE ŚAIVA CONCEPTION OF ACTION

The monistic Śaivaism of Kashmir, as has already been stated, is a synthesis of the realistic, idealistic, voluntaristic and mystic tendencies. The Śaiva conception of action is, therefore, based, not upon the observation of its external objective aspect only, but also on the subjective grasp and analysis of the internal subjective aspect. It approaches the problem of action not only from the point of view of empiricism but also from that of voluntarism. Accordingly while it accepts the serial and, therefore, multiple nature of the action as an observable external phenomenon, it points out the subjective and internal aspect as well. It asserts that the appearance of a particular body at successive points of space in temporal order, which we empirically observe and call action, is only an expression of the will of the individual. This assertion is based upon the fact of experience. We experience within some kind of internal stir (Āntara spandana) before the commencement of the series, which constitutes the external aspect of the action. The worldly action, therefore, is a unity, because of oneness of the will, of which it is an expression, and the will is one because of the oneness of the purpose that it aims at. Thus, action, taken in both of its aspects, is unity in multiplicity : the unity is internal and subjective and multiplicity is external and objective. The Śaiva disagrees with the Bauddha in holding that the action, as discussed just above, is real, because our experience of it, both subjective and objective, remains uncontradicted by any subsequent experience and because it has the causal efficiency of bringing about the realisation of the purpose, aimed at.

The word "Kriyā" (Action) is used in the texts on the Monistic Śaiva philosophy of Kashmir, not only in the sense of the empirical action, but also in that of the metaphysical power of action (Kriyā Śakti). And the latter is the basis of the Śaiva conception of the omnipotence of the Lord. The Bauddha criticism of the omnipotence was based upon the conception of action as serial, as seen from the empirical point of view. He denied the permanent subject, agent, doer or Kartā, to whom the action is related, simply for the reason that it is not an empirical fact. And the Śaiva reply to it is based upon the idealistic, voluntaristic and epistemic points of view, as is presented in the Īśvara Pratyabhijñā Vimarśinī. The establishment of the permanent subject, both individual and universal, is the central problem of the book, in opposition to the denial of it by the Bauddha from the empirical point of view. The Śaiva points out that the empirical point of view does not give us the whole truth, but only an aspect of it ; that it fails, particularly if it is mixed up with the theory of momentariness, to explain satisfactorily the phenomena of knowledge ; that it means the denial of all ethical values, because permanent subject that enjoys or suffers the fruits of action in future is the presupposition of ethics and that it means atheism.

The dualism of mind and matter or subject and object, without their essential identity and common substratum, cannot account for the relation between the subject and the object, nor can a momentary subject, whatever it be, account for the synthesis of percepts into a concept. The permanent subject, therefore, is an epistemic necessity and, therefore, a practical necessity also, because action presupposes knowledge of the thing towards which the activity is to be directed and also remembrance of the past experiences of it or of something similar to it, to determine the nature of the activity.

If, therefore, dualism and empiricism are to be rejected, and the abstract monism, that looks upon the whole universe as mere illusion, is unsatisfactory, because, according to extreme monism, there is nothing apart from the Mind on the basis of which illusion can arise, the Realistic Idealism or, to put it in Hegelian term, Concrete Monism as opposed to Abstract Monism appears to be a fair alternative to account for the phenomena of knowledge and practical life. But even concrete monism of the Hegelian type, which admits the Ultimate metaphysical principle to be purely rational, fails to explain the irrational, the existence of which cannot be denied. The ultimate metaphysical principle, therefore, has to be admitted to be 'Free' (Svatantra). Svātantryavāda, therefore, seems to be the only sound philosophy. This "Svātantrya" is the philosophic doctrine, which the Īśvara Pratyabhijñā Vimarśinī presents.

Therefore, when it talks of the omnipotence of the Lord (Sarvakriyā svatantra) it does not mean that the Lord has perfect freedom of action in regard to what exists separately from and more or less independently of Him and what would continue to exist even if He were not there, as the God of the dualists has in regard to the matter and the world that is created out of it. On the contrary, it means that the universe is the concretisation or manifestation of the free Universal Mind or Will ; that the universe has no existence separately from and independently of the Mind; that the relation between the Mind and the universe is similar to that between a mirror and the reflections which are cast on it; that the difference between the Mind and the mirror is that the affections of the latter are due to external objects, but those of the former are due to its own Freedom. Thus, the objection of the Bauddha: "How can the doer, in spite of his relation with action, which is serial in its nature, be spoken of as one ?" is answered in the very beginning of the Kriyādhikāra by asserting that just as the unity of mirror remains in tact in spite of affection by reflections of different kinds, so the unity of the Universal Mind or the Lord remains unaffected in spite of the appearance of the multiplicity of the universe in it.

Kriyāśakti is responsible for the manifestation of temporal and spatial orders and, therefore, it is free from the temporal and spatial limitation. The temporal and spatial orders shine in relation to the individual mind only. To the universal Mind the whole universe shines as identical with itself. In the context of Kriyāśakti some important philosophical problems such as that of the "Relation" including the relation of the subject and the object and of the cause and the effect, are discussed. Here the characteristic doctrine of the system, technically called "Ābhāsavāda", is presented in detail: the three means of knowledge, perception, inference and scriptural authority, are discussed and the distinctive feature of the Śaiva theory of inference is pointed out: the essential nature of 'being' (Sattva) and that of 'Not-being' are stated and the distinction of these conceptions from those of the other schools is drawn: and in conclusion it is said: "Icchaiva hetutā Kartṛtā Kriyā".

THE LAST TWO ADHIKĀRAS

In the Āgamādhikāra, besides the presentation of the thirty-six categories, admitted by this system, the characteristic features of different types of 'subject' (Pramātṛ) and different levels of experience, at which these characteristics become clear, are described. The last Adhikāra, called "Tattva Saṅgraha" gives an illuminating summary of the system, discusses the essential nature of the three qualities, Sattva, Rajas and Tamas and concludes with a clear presentation of 'Recognition' (Pratyabhijñā) which constitutes a part of the title of the book "Īśvara Pratyabhijñā."

APPENDIX

Textual authorities indicated by foot-notes.

Page 1

(४) न यातव इन्द्र जूजुवुर्नो न वन्दना शविष्ठ वेद्याभि : ।
स शर्धदर्यो विषुणस्य जन्तोर्मा शिश्नदेवा अपि गुर्ऋतं नः ।।

Page 2

(२) वेदेऽस्ति संहिता रौद्री वाच्या रुद्रश्च देवता ।
सान्निध्यकरणेऽप्यस्मिन् विहितः काल्पिको विधिः ।।

Page 6

(१) अतश्च भेद-भेदाभेदाभेदप्रतिपादकं शिव-रुद्र-भैरवाख्यं त्रिधैवेदं शास्त्रमुद्भूतम् इति सिद्धान्त : ।

Page 7

(१) एवमष्टाविंशतिभेदा दिव्यागमाः । परार्ध-शंख-पद्म-षट्पञ्चाशत्सहस्राधिकैः षडुत्तरषष्ठ्या लक्षन्यूनं पद्मं चेत्येतावत्संख्या ग्रन्थाः । तदुपभेदाः अष्टोत्तरद्विशतसङ्ख्याः ।

Page 8

(२) षट्त्रिंशत्तत्त्वानि द्वितीयश्लोकोल्लासे विवृतानि । पञ्चभूतानि पञ्चप्राणाः चतुर्दशेन्द्रियाणीति चतुर्विंशतिः, महान् कालः प्रधानं माया विद्या पुरुष इति षट्, बिन्दुनादौ शक्तिशिवौ शान्तातीताविति षट्, एवं षट्त्रिंशत्तत्त्वानि यानि शैवागमे प्रसिद्धानि ।

Page 9

(१) एवं सदुःखान्तः कार्यं कारणं योगो विधिरिति पञ्चैव पदार्थाः समासत उद्दिष्टाः ।

(२) माहेश्वरास्तु मन्यन्ते कार्य-कारण-योग-विधि-दुःखान्ताः पञ्च पदार्थाः ।

(३) अत्र 'भव' इति विद्याकलापशूनामेव ग्रहणम् । तस्योत्पत्तिकर्त्ता भगवानित्यतो भवोद्भव इति ।

(४) यदेतत् पत्युः पतित्वं शक्तिः सामर्थ्यमैश्वर्यं स्वगुणः सद्भावः सतत्त्वं तत्त्वधर्मः तद् आसनम् ।

Page 10

(१) अन्यत्र दुःखनिवृत्तिरेव दुःखान्तः । इह तु पारमैश्वर्यप्राप्तिश्च ।

(२) एतद्वृत्ति प्रणेतॄणां श्रीमदाचार्य गुणरत्न सूरीश्वराणां सत्तासमयो वैक्रमिक १४६६ प्रतीयते ।

(३) तत्पदपयोजभृङ्गो विद्यातिलको मुनिर्निजस्मृतये ।
षड्दर्शनीयसूत्रे चक्रे विवृतिं समासेन ।

Page 11

(१) दर्शनानि षडेवात्र, मूलभेदव्यपेक्षया ।
देवतातत्त्वभेदेन, ज्ञातव्यानि मनीषिभिः ।।
बौद्धं नैयायिकं साङ्ख्यं, जैनं वैशेषिकं तथा ।
जैमिनीयं च नामानि, दर्शनानाममून्यहो ।।

(२) 'एवं धरणिधरणीधरतरुपुरप्राकारादिकं बुद्धिमत्पूर्वकम्, कार्यत्वात्, यद्यत् कार्यं तत्तद्बुद्धिमत्पूर्वकं दृष्टम्, यथा घटः, कार्यं चेदं तस्माद्बुद्धिमत्पूर्वकमिति प्रयोगः ।

(३) शिवदैवतसाम्येऽपि तत्त्वादिविशेषविशिष्टत्वाद्वैशेषिकाः, तेषां वैशेषिकाणां काणादानां नैयायिकैरक्षपादैः समं सार्द्धं देवताविषये शिवदेवताभ्युपगमे भेदो विशेषो नास्ति ।

Page 13

(१) शैवाः पाशुपताश्चैव, महाव्रतधरास्तथा ।
तुर्याः कालमुखा मुख्या भेदा एते तपस्विनाम् ।।

Page 14

(१) कम्बलिकाप्रावरणा जटापटलशालिनः ।
भस्मोद्धूलनकर्त्तारो नीरसाहारसेविनः ।

Page 15

(१) शिवात्परंपरायातौ भोगमोक्षौ ससाधनौ ।
आत्रेयाय मुनीन्द्रेण रुरुणा संप्रकाशितौ ।।

Page 16

(१) सुवृत्तिः सद्वृत्तिरिति रौरववृत्तेर्नाम तत्कर्त्रेदं निर्मितमित्यर्थः ।

(२) तथोक्तमाचार्येण स्वायम्भुववृत्तौ 'यद्यशुद्धिर्न पुंसोऽस्ति'
इत्यत्रान्तरे, व्याख्यातं च तट्टिप्पकेऽस्मत्पित्रा तत्र भवता भट्टनारायणकण्ठेनेति तत एवावधार्यम् ।

(३) वरसिद्धान्तसंसिद्धौ भोगमोक्षौ ससाधनौ ।
वच्मि साधकबोधाय लेशतो युक्तिसंस्कृतौ ।।

(४) सिद्धान्तशब्दः पङ्कजादिशब्दवद्योगरूढ्या शिवप्रणीतेषु कामिकादिषु दशाष्टादशसु तन्त्रेषु प्रसिद्धः ।

(५) यं चानुशासयामास भगवानीशसंमतः ।
उग्रज्योतिर्गुरुः श्रीमान् सर्वविद्यासरित्पतिः ।।

(६) आश्रयान्तरसंक्रान्तिः पूर्वाश्रयविवर्जनम् ।
विना नैव प्रसिद्धा स्यात्त्यागे पूर्वस्तु निर्गुणः ।

(७) शङ्करनन्दन-सद्योज्योतिर्देवबल-कणभुगादिमतम् ।
प्रत्याख्यास्यन्नवमं व्याचख्यावाह्निकं जयरथाख्यः ।।

(८) याभ्यां प्रकाशितं वर्त्म सिद्धान्ते सिद्धभावतः ।
गुरूणामपि तौ वन्द्यौ सद्योज्योति-बृहस्पती ।।

Page 17

(१) शङ्करनन्दन-सद्योज्योतिर्देवदल-कणभुगादिमतम् ।

Page 18

(१) अद्वैतवासनाविष्टैः सिद्धान्तज्ञानवर्जितैः ।
व्याख्यातो ऽत्रान्यथाऽन्यैर्यत्सततोऽस्माकमुद्यमः ।।

(२) श्री मच्छ्रीकण्ठनाथाज्ञावशात्सिद्धा अवातरन् ।
त्र्यम्बकामर्दकाभिख्यश्रीनाथा अद्वये द्वये ।।

(३) साक्षाच्छ्रीकण्ठनाथादिव सुकृतिजनानुग्रहायावतीर्णाच्छ्रुत्वा
श्रीरामकण्ठाच्छिवमतकमलोन्मीलनप्रौढभास्वान् ।

(४) श्रीरामकण्ठसद्वृत्तिं मयैवमनुकुर्वता ।
रत्नत्रयपरीक्षार्थःसंक्षेपेण प्रकाशितः ।

Page 19

(१) साक्षाच्छ्रीकण्ठनाथादिव सुकृतिजनानुग्रहायावतीर्णा-
च्छ्रुत्वा श्रीरामकण्ठाच्छिवमतकमलोन्मीलनप्रौढभास्वान् ।
श्रीविद्याकण्ठभट्टस्तदिदमुपदिशन्नादिदेशैतदेनाम्
स्पष्टार्थामत्र लघ्वीं विरचय विवृतिं वत्स सर्वोपयोग्याम् ।।

(२) रामकण्ठमहाकण्ठकण्ठीरवपदानुगः ।
न कुतार्किकमातङ्गगर्जितेभ्यो विभेम्यहम् ।।

(३) एतच्च विस्तरेणोक्तं तत्र भवता रामकण्ठेन नादकारिकासु ।

Page 20

(१) स्वरूपज्योतिरेवान्तः सूक्ष्मावागनपायिनी ।

(२) मुक्तापीड इति प्रसिद्धिमगमत्कश्मीरदेशे नृपः ।
श्रीमान् ख्यातयशा बभूव नृपतेस्तस्य प्रभावानुगः ।
मन्त्री लक्ष्मण इत्युदारचरितस्तस्यान्ववाये भवो
हेलाराज इमं प्रकाशमकरोच्छ्रीभूतिराजात्मजः ।

(४) See textual authority Page 19 (१)

Page 21

(१) तत्त्वसङ्ग्रहचन्द्रस्य प्रकाशाय वितानिता ।
श्रीनारायणकण्ठेन वृहट्टीका शरन्निशा ।।

(२) केचित्स्वबोधविभवप्रथनाय ताव-
द्गर्जन्त्यलं न किल यत्प्रकृतोपयोगि ।
अन्ये पुनः पटुधियो न विवेचयन्ति,
स्पष्टार्थमेतदिति तत्तदुपेक्षमाणाः ।

(३) यदाह तत्र भवान् खेटकनन्दनः—

(४) तदिदमुक्तं तत्र भगवद्बृहस्पतिपादैः ।

(५) तदुक्तं तत्वत्रयनिर्णये ।

(६) तदुक्तं भोगकारिकासु ।

Page 24

(१) अन्यच्च सूतसंहिताव्याख्याने विद्यारण्ययतीन्द्रैः तत्र तत्र एतत्प्रकरण-गताःश्लोकाः प्रमाणीक्रियन्ते ।

(२) परं तु श्रीमदघोरशिवाचार्यकृतपद्धत्यामुत्सवविधौ गोत्रविधि-निर्णयपटले–"ततोऽ भूल्लाट उत्तुङ्गशिवो विन्ध्ये व्रतीश्वरः ।
कल्याणनगरीवासी गुरुः पद्धतिकृत्सुधीः ।।
सर्वविद्याधिपो यस्य कनीयानार्यदेशजः ।
सर्वागमार्थनिर्णेतुश्श्रीभोजनृपतेर्गुरुः ।।"

(३) श्रीमदघोरशिवाह्वयेन गुरुणा श्री जन्यया व्याख्यया ।
लोकेपि प्रथितेन कुण्डिनकुलं चोलेष्वलङ्कुर्वता ।।

(४) नादज्ञेये शकस्याब्दे वर्तने कलौ युगे ।
ग्रन्थतास्त्रसहस्रेश्च (?) संयुक्ता पञ्चभिः शतैः ।।
कलौ शालिवाहनशकाब्दे अशीत्युत्तरसहस्रे स्वेन कृतेयं पद्धतिरिति च स्पष्टं प्रकटीकृतम् ।

(५) इति लक्षद्वयाध्यापक–श्रीमदघोरशिवाचार्यविरचिता तत्त्वप्रकाशिकावृत्तिः समाप्ता ।

(६) श्री सर्वात्मशिवङ्घ्रिपद्मरजसामाराधकेनामलाढ्यी-तत्त्वत्रयनिर्णयस्य विवृतिर्लेशादियं निर्मिता ।

Page 25

(१) इत्यादि विस्तरेणास्माभिर्मृगेन्द्रवृत्तिदीपिकायां दर्शितं साधितञ्च रामकण्ठादिभिर्मतङ्ग वृत्यादाविति ततोऽवधार्यम् ।

(२) श्रीमत्स्वायंभुबकिरणमतङ्गादिवृत्तिष्विति ततोऽवधेयम् ।

(3) See above (१)

(४) यदुक्तं कालोत्तरवृत्तौ तत्र भवता रामकण्ठेन शिवभेदाष्टकप्रकरणे ।

Page 27

(१) सांहिती वारुणी याज्ञिकी चेति । तत्र प्रथमप्रपाठके संहिताध्याय-- स्योक्तत्वात्तद्रूपोपनिषत्सांहिती । द्वितीयतृतीययोः प्रपाठकयोर्या ब्रह्मविद्याऽभिहिता तस्याः संप्रदायप्रवर्तको वरुणस्तस्मात्तदुभय-- रूपोपनिषद्वारुणी । चतुर्थप्रपाठके यज्ञोपयुक्ता अपि मन्त्रास्तत्रतत्रा-- ऽऽम्नाता अतस्तद्रूपोपनिषद्याज्ञिकी ।

(२) तथेयं नारायणीयाख्या याज्ञिक्युपनिषदपि खिलकाण्डरूपा तल्लक्षणोपेतत्वात् ।

(३) तदीयपाठसम्प्रदायस्तु देशविशेषेषु बहुविध उपलभ्यते ।

(४) सदसस्पतिमद्भुतं प्रियमिन्द्रस्य काम्यम् ।
सनिं मेधामयासिषम् ।

(५) इत ऊर्ध्वं तेषु तेषु देशेषु श्रुतिपाठा अत्यन्तविलक्षणाः । तत्र विज्ञानात्म- प्रभृतिभिः पूर्वैर्निबन्धकारैर्द्राविडपाठस्याऽऽदृतत्वाद्वयमपि तमेवादृत्य व्याख्यास्यामः ।

Page 30

(१) कुशिकभगवानभ्यागत्याचार्ये,

(२) तेषां नामान्यथ ब्रूमो लकुलीशोऽथ कौशिकः ।

(३) नकुलीशः कौशिकः गार्ग्यः,

Page 34

(१) अतः शिवागमो द्विविधः, त्रैवर्णिकविषयस्सर्वविषयश्चेति । वेदः त्रैवर्णिक- विषयः । सर्वविषयश्चान्यः । उभयोरेक एव शिवः कर्ता ।

(२) शिवागमैकदेशे शिवस्य परब्रह्मणः केवलनिमित्तत्वमुपपादितम् । तत्परिहारार्थमिदमधिकरणमिति पूर्वाचार्याणां व्याख्या ।

(३) भेदाभेदकल्पनं विशिष्टाद्वैतं साधयामः ।

Page 35

(१) न शिवः शक्तिरहितो न शक्तिर्व्यतिरेकिणी ।
शिवः शक्तस्तथा भावानिच्छया कर्तुमीहते ।
शक्तिशक्तिमतोर्भेदः शैवे जातु न वर्ण्यते ।।

Page 38

(२) सुप्रभेदागमे :—

रेवणो मरुलश्चैकोरामः पण्डित एव च ।
विश्वाराध्य इति ख्याताः कलौ गुरुवरोत्तमाः ॥

(३) इति सामजंगीषीयशाखायां सदानन्दोपनिषदि जीवस्य प्राणलिङ्गमुख्यत्वं सूचितम् ।

Page 39

(१) वेदशास्त्रपुराणेषु कामिकाद्यागमेषु च ।
लिङ्गधारणमाख्यातं वीरशैवस्य निश्चयात् ।

Page 40

(१) श्रीमच्छिवाचारविचारदीक्षं स्वशिष्यसत्प्रीणनपूर्णपक्षम् ।
दुर्वारकामादिविदारदक्षं भजाम्यहं रेवणकल्पवृक्षम् ॥

(२) मिथ्याद्वैत शून्याद्वैत जैन बौद्ध लोकायतनाद्यवैदिकाश्चापि व्याख्याताः ।

(३) कामिकाद्यागमविरुद्ध पाशुपत पाञ्चरात्राद्यागम निराकरणमुपादेयम्, एवं रेवणसिद्ध मरुलसिद्ध रामसिद्ध उद्भटाराध्य वेमनाराध्यादिभिः श्रौतशैवाचार्यैर्व्यपदेशात् ।

(४) अतस्सर्ववेदान्तमुख्यार्थवेदिभिः रेवणसिद्ध मरुलसिद्धोद्भटाराध्य-वेमाराध्यादिभिः सगुणश्रुतीनां सर्वासाम् शक्तिविकासपरत्वं निर्गुणश्रुतीनां शक्तिसङ्कोचविषयत्वमिति व्यवस्था निर्णीता ।

(५) वीरशैवसिद्धान्तस्थापक.....सहस्रशीर्षानुवाकस्य शिवपरत्वेन राद्धान्तितम् ।

(६) शङ्करसंहिता सिद्धान्तशिखामण्यादौ कर्मकर्तव्यतादर्शनात् ।

Page 41

(१) रेणुकभगवद्·····इत्यन्तेन सिद्धान्तशिखामणौ तस्यैवोपदेशात् ।

(३) श्रीमत्सर्वकलासु कोविदतमः प्रालेयशैलात्मजा-
जानेः पूर्णकृपाविशेषनिचयप्रज्ञानधीर्यो बभौ ।
सम्यग्रेवण देशिकेन्द्रधृतषड्लिङ्गावधानोज्ज्वलं
सिद्धार्यं मरुलप्रभुं बुधनुतं तं मन्महे श्रेयसे ॥

Page 42

(१) दुर्वासोपमन्युरेवणसिद्ध मरुलसिद्धादिभिश्च निराकृताः ।

(२) तस्मान्निर्गुणश्रुतीनां सर्वासां तत्कालपरत्वमिति वेदितव्यमत एव ।

(३) एकोरामाख्यसिद्धं प्रथितगुणगणागण्यपुण्योदयश्री-
सम्यक्संसेव्यमानं बुधनुतचरितं द्वापराचार्यवर्यम् ।
उद्यद्वेदान्तशास्त्रोभयगतविलसच्छैवसंस्थापनाढ्यं
पूर्वाचार्यप्रशिष्यं शरणमहमिमं देशिकेन्द्रं प्रपद्ये ॥

(४) एकोरामसिद्धभगवत्पादाचार्यैः--

(५) एकोरामसिद्धाराध्यभगवत्पादाचार्यादिभिः स्वीकृतत्वादेतदेव सम्यगुपादेयम्।

Page 43

(१) रेवणसिद्ध-मरुलसिद्ध-रामसिद्ध।

(२) मध्वाद्वैत क्षपणक तार्किकादयो जीवानां विभुत्वाङ्गीकारात्तन्निरसनार्थमेतदधिकरणप्रारम्भः।

(३) तार्किक-मध्वादिकेवलभेदवादिनां बौद्धादिवत्सर्वश्रुतिसमन्वयाभावात्।

Page 44

(१) श्रीमच्छ्रीपति पण्डितेन्द्रयतिना व्याचक्षते भाषनम्।

(२) वीरशैवैकसिद्धान्ते सर्वश्रुतिसमन्वयः।

(४) यथा जाग्रत्स्वप्नयोर्द्वैतसिद्धिः।

Page 45

(१) अगस्त्यमुनिचन्द्रेण कृतवैयासिकां शुभाम्।
सूत्रवृत्तिम् समालोक्य कृतं भाष्यं शिवङ्करम्।

(२) सदाशिवं शक्तिधरं सुकेशं चण्डीश्वरं भृङ्गिरिटं शिलादम्।
कुम्भोद्भवं चिन्मयवामदेवं श्रीरेवणासिद्धगुरुं प्रपद्ये।।

Page 46

(१) वेङ्कटेश्वरस्याभासविष्णुत्वम्। तदङ्गे नागभूषणादि--
धर्माणां द्योतनात्। मूलविग्रहे शङ्खचक्रादिलाञ्छनानामदर्शनात्।

(२) चिदचिदीश्वरपरिभाषाप्रधानरामानुजशास्त्रं वेदमूलत्वाभावादवैदिकमिति घण्टाघोषः।

(३) रुद्रद्वेषिणां ब्राह्मणेभ्यो बहिष्कार इति घण्टाघोषः।

Page 47

(१) अत्र शैवाग्रगण्यश्रीकण्ठशिवाराध्यकृत ब्रह्ममीमांसाभाष्ये विशिष्टाद्वैतं स्वाभिप्रेतत्वेन प्रसाधितम्। .... अतस्तन्मतमुपेक्षणीयम्।

(२) एवं बुद्धमतं निरस्य प्रच्छन्नबौद्धाभिधानजीवेश्वरजगन्मिथ्यात्व--
प्रतिपादक श्रुत्याभासप्रधान निर्विशेषाद्वैतमतमधिकरणान्तरेण निराकरोति।

(३) एवं निःश्रेयसविरोधेन शुष्कवेदान्तनिर्विशेषाद्वैतवादकवासिष्ठमतं निराकृत्य स्वात्महननसिद्धान्तशून्याद्वैताख्यसान्दीपमतमधिकरणान्तरेण निराकरोति।

(४) तस्माद्रज्जुसर्पवदविद्याकल्पितवादप्रधाननिष्प्रपञ्चब्रह्माद्वैतवादस्त्ववैदिकः इति वेदितव्यः।

(५) तप्तलिङ्गमुद्राङ्कितरौद्रमतात्तप्तशूलडमरुकमुद्राङ्किततन्त्रपाशुपत— मताच्छ्रौतशिवलिङ्गधारणावच्छिन्नशैवमतस्य सर्वाधिकत्वमनिवार्यम्।

(६) दर्शितश्चतादृशान्वयो ज्ञानाय विचारः कर्त्तव्य इति परमशिवाराध्यस्वामिना शिवज्ञानचन्द्रोदये।

कैवल्यप्रकाशे व्याख्यातं च परमशिवाराध्यभट्टाचार्येण।

(७) तथा चतुर्वेदपारङ्गतैर्ज्योतिर्नाथ घण्टानाथ भीमनाथ भट्टभास्करादिभि- र्वैदिकैर्वेदमार्गप्रतिष्ठापनाचार्यैरपि पाषण्डपाञ्चरात्रबुद्धाद्वैतादिदुर्मत- निराकरणानन्तरम्। नीलकण्ठ भगवत्पाद भट्टभास्कर घण्टानाथ ज्योति- र्नाथादि पूर्वाचार्यैः छान्दोग्यभाष्ये।

(८) "ऋतं पिबन्तौ" इत्यत्र बुद्धिक्षेत्रज्ञसाधारणार्थशतृप्रत्ययस्य कर्तृत्व- शक्तस्य कारकत्वमात्रलक्षणाया दुर्वासीये प्रतिपादनाच्च।

Page 48

(१) वेदवेदान्तनिष्ठागरिष्ठमनुवामदेवागस्त्य दुर्वासोपमन्यु रेवणसिद्ध मरुल- सिद्धादिभिश्च निराकृता इति सूत्रावयवार्थः।

(२) (i) ईशानस्सर्वविद्यानामीश्वरस्सर्वभूतानाम्, इत्यादि श्रुतिशतेषु शिवस्यैव सर्वपतित्वोपदेशात्।

(ii) बहुश्रुतिसिद्ध रेवणसिद्ध मरुलसिद्ध रामसिद्ध वेमाराध्योद्भटाराध्यादि- ब्रह्मनिष्ठाचरितभक्तिवैराग्यश्रद्धाश्रवणमननाद्युपासना— फलकमोक्षवैफल्यप्रसङ्गः।

(३) एतद् द्वैताऽद्वैतमतमेव केचिद्विशेषाद्वैतमिति सेश्वराद्वैतमिति शिवाद्वैतमिति सर्वश्रुतिसारमतमिति भेदाऽभेदमिति पर्यायत्वेन प्रवदन्ति।

(४) विश्च शेषश्च विशेषौ। विशेषयोरद्वैतं विशेषाऽद्वैतमिति निरुक्ता।

(५) (i) षट्त्रिंशत्तत्त्वरूपत्वं तल्लिङ्गस्यैव सर्वदा।

(ii) षट्त्रिंशत्सङ्ख्योपपत्तेर्न पञ्चविंशतिसङ्ख्याप्रतिपत्तिरित्युपदिश्यते-

(६) (i) तदुत्तरसूत्रे सन्धिकालदृष्टान्तेन तदुभयसिद्धान्तस्थापनाद् भेदा- ऽभेदप्रधानकाशकृत्स्नमतमेव मुख्यसिद्धान्त इति घण्टाघोषः।

(ii) भेदाऽभेदमतस्यैव सर्वाधिकत्वम् "अनवस्थितेरिति काशकृत्स्नः" इति सूत्रेण राद्धान्तितम्।

(७) शरीराभिमानरहितेच्छाशक्ति-क्रियाशक्ति-ज्ञानशक्ति-व्यापाराणां नित्यवैभवपरमानन्दकन्दस्वप्रकाशविभूतिमय–शिवसामरस्य–सारूप्यरसैक- प्रपञ्चावगाहिनां परिपूर्णसर्वशिवात्मकभावप्रकटनं श्रुतिर्दर्शयति।

(८) सकामानुष्ठितकर्मणां फलस्वातन्त्र्येऽपि निष्कामानुष्ठितकर्मणामाणवादि-
मलत्रयनिर्मुक्तपरमपुरुषार्थोपपत्तेः ।

Page 49

(१) अन्त्यवर्णचतुर्दशं तु पाणिन्युद्देशेनैवोपदिष्टमित्यपि तत्रैव स्पष्टम् ।

(२) सोयमक्षरसमाम्नायो... ब्रह्मराशिः ।

Page 50

(१) तथा चोक्तमिन्द्रेण ।

(२) अत्र केषांचिद्ग्रन्थे अकारादिक्षकारान्ताः षट्त्रिंशत्तत्वमयाः कतिचित्तन्त्र-
राजादिग्रन्थे पञ्चभूतक्रमेण लिपिप्रकारेण ।

(3) See textual authority page 48 , (१)

Page 52

(१) संसारस्य परं पारं दत्तेऽसौ पारदः स्मृतः ।

Page 53

(१) तत्प्रपञ्चस्तु गोविन्द भगवत्पादाचार्य-सर्वज्ञ रामेश्वर भट्टारक प्रभृति-
भिः प्राचीनैराचार्यैर्निरूपित इति ग्रन्थभूयस्त्वभयादुदास्यते । ·····पूर्वं
लोहे परीक्षेत पश्चाद्देहे प्रयोजयेत् ।

Page 54

(१) गोविन्दभगवत्पादाचार्यो गोविन्दनायकः ।
चर्वटिः कपिलो व्याडिः कापालिः कन्दलायनः ॥

Page 61

(१) दर्शनानि षडेवात्र, मूलभेदव्यपेक्षया
देवता तत्त्वभेदेन, ज्ञातव्यानि मनीषिभिः ।

Page 64

(१) एवं पशुपतेरिति कार्यकारणयोः प्रसादस्य चोद्देशः ।

Page 66

(१) ततश्च घृतकीटन्यायेन एकदेशेनैव माया परिणमत इत्यदोषः ।

(२) कर्म हि कृष्यादिवत्प्रकृतिसंस्काररूपत्वाद् बुद्धिगुणत्वेनैवेष्यते ।

(३) तस्य भूतादिरूपेण त्रिविधत्वादचैतन्ये सत्यनेकत्वेनास्यानित्यत्वं सिद्ध-
मिति भावः ।

Page 67

(१) अतएवाश्रयादन्यत्रोपलब्धेराकाशैकगुणः शब्द इति यद्वैशेषिकादिभि-
रुक्तम्, तदयुक्तम् ।

(२) अनेनैतेषां परमाणुरूपतामभिदधाना नैयायिकादयः प्रतिक्षिप्ताः ।

(३) ननु निर्मल एवाऽऽत्मा सांख्यैरभ्युपगतः । तदयुक्तम् । निर्मलस्य भोगासक्त्यसम्भवात् । तत्संभवे वा मुक्तस्यापि प्रसङ्गात् ।

(४) तस्मात् तयोरात्मविषययोर्भोक्तृभोग्यतायोग्ययोर्बुद्धितत्त्वे संबन्धो यावद्गतिपरस्पररूपमेलनात्मा वासगृह इव यूनोः यः स एव भोक्तृभोग्यभावः ।

Page 68

(१) बुद्धिबोधं हि यदात्मनि अविशिष्टतया अहङ्कारो व्यवहरति, स एव अयं भोगः ।

Page 69

(१) अतो भोक्तृत्वाच्चेतनस्य पुरुषस्यैव कर्तृत्वं नाचेतनानां भोग्यानां बुद्ध्यादीनामिति मन्तव्यम् ।

(२) तथा ह्यात्मैकत्वं तावत्साधयितुमशक्यम् अनेकत्वप्रतिपादकानां श्रुतीनां सम्भवात् । एकत्वश्रुतीनामन्यपरत्वादनेकत्वज्ञापकस्य दृश्यमानस्य जननमरणादिप्रतिनियमस्यानपह्नवनीयत्वाच्च ।

(३) चिदचिद्विश्वसंभूतिः
आत्मनो यदि सोपि हि ।
चिदचिज्जायते यस्मात्
कार्यं कारणधर्मगम् ।।

(४) सर्वस्यापि हि धर्मिणो धर्मः सर्वत्र स्वेतरविषयेष्वेव प्रकाशते । यथा वह्नेरुष्णत्वादि काष्ठादौ ।

Page 70

(१) एवं पशुपतेरिति कार्यकारणयोः प्रसादस्य चोद्देशः ।

Page 71

(१) इह पुरा पाणिनीयेऽस्मिन् व्याकरणे व्याड्युपरचितं ग्रन्थलक्षपरिमाणं संग्रहाभिधानं निबन्धनमासीत् ।

Page 72

(१) आप्रलयं यत्तिष्ठति सर्वेषां भोगदायि भूतानाम् ।
तत्तत्त्वमिति प्रोक्तं न शरीरघटादि तत्त्वमतः ।।

(२) मायायाः परतोऽध्वा शुद्धः शक्तौ निलीयते सकलः ।
परमात्मनि सापि शिवे तिष्ठत्यविभागमापन्ना ।।

(३) माया पुरुषः शिव इत्येतत् त्रितयं महार्थसंहारे ।

Page 73

(१) शैवागमेषु मुख्यं पतिपशुपाशा इति क्रमात् त्रितयम्।

Page 74

(1) See textual authority Page 72 (३)

Page 75

(१) चिद्घन एको व्यापी नित्यः सततोदितः प्रभुश्शान्तः।

(२) विधाता कमलस्योष्णगभस्तिः स्यात्तथा शिवः।
कर्त्ता सर्गादिकार्याणामविकारोऽपि शक्तिमान्॥

Page 76

(१) शक्तो यया स शम्भुः भुक्तौ मुक्तौ च पशुगणस्यास्य।
तामेकां चिद्रूपामाद्यां सर्वात्मनाऽस्मि नतः।

(२) यथैका सवितुः शक्तिर्दानादानादिकर्मभिः।

(३) शिवशक्त्योरात्मभेदाभावेऽपि धर्मिधर्मभेदः।

(४) शक्तेर्धर्मत्वेनाश्रयं विनाऽवस्थानासम्भवात् तदाश्रयः स एव शक्तिमान् सङ्कल्पमात्रेण विश्वकर्ता।

Page 77

(१) चिच्छब्देनात्र ज्ञानक्रिये वक्ष्येते।

(२) अस्मिन्निलीय निखिला इच्छाद्याः शक्तयः स्वकं कार्यम्।

(३) ध्यानार्थमेवेश्वरस्य पञ्चवक्त्राद्याकारः श्रूयते, निराकारे ध्यानपूजाद्ययोगात्।

Page 78

(१) नित्यमुक्तत्वादीश्वरस्य ज्ञेयादिविषये शक्तिव्यतिरेकेण न बुद्ध्यादिकरणापेक्षा।

(२) शिवस्य सर्वदा विन्द्वादेर्नित्यस्य विषयस्य ग्राह्यत्वात्।
ग्रहणसामर्थ्यस्य गृहीतृसमवेतत्वेन सर्वदावस्थानाच्च।

(३) व्यापको भुवनादीनामभिव्याप्तः स बिन्दुना।
विन्दुश्शक्त्या शिवेनैषा नान्येन व्याप्यते शिवः॥

Page 79

(१) चितिः चैतन्यात्मिका शिवस्य समवायिनी शक्तिः।
सङ्कल्पमात्रेण सृष्ट्यादिकृत्यं विदधाति।

(२) वक्ष्यमाणलक्षणानां पशूनां पक्वापक्वयोरुभयोर्वर्गयोः क्रमेण शुद्धाशुद्धभोगनिष्पत्तये बिन्दुमायोत्पादितैस्तनुकरणभुवनभावैः संबन्धजननात्मिका सृष्टिः।

(३) शुद्धेऽध्वनि शिवः कर्ता प्रोक्तोऽनन्तोऽसिते प्रभुः।

(४) यद्येवं शिवस्यापि शुद्धविषये कर्तृत्वात् शरीरेन्द्रिययोगादिप्रसङ्गः । तन्न, तस्य नित्यनिर्मलनिरतिशयसर्वार्थज्ञानक्रियायुक्तत्वात् । अशरीरस्यापि आत्मनः स्वदेहस्पन्दादौ कर्तृत्वदर्शनाच्च ।

Page 80

(१) अशुद्धाध्वविषयेत्वनन्तादिद्वारेणेत्युक्तम् ।

(२) यद्येवं शिवस्यासर्वकर्तृत्वप्रसङ्गः । तन्न, साक्षात्कर्तृत्वम् अत्र निषिद्धम् न तु प्रयोजककर्तृत्वम् ।

(३) जगतानेन संयोज्य तान् पुंसो लोलिकावतः ।
भोगार्थं साधनाकारां करोति स्थितिमीश्वरः ।।

Page 81

(१) माया पुरुषः शिव इत्येतत्त्रितयं महार्थसंहारे ।
अवशिष्यते पुनस्तत्प्रवर्तते पूर्ववत् सृष्टौ ।।

(२) मायायाः परतोऽध्वा शुद्धः शक्तौ निलीयते सकलः ।
परमात्मनि सापि शिवे तिष्ठत्यविभागमापन्ना ।

(३) स्थित्यन्ते सोपि संसारे विश्रमार्थं प्रधावताम् ।
पशूनां प्रकृतीनां च क्षमत्वोत्पादनाय च
ततः सर्वोपसंहारं विधत्ते भगवानिति ।

(४) मायेयार्थसंबन्धनिमित्तम् अनादिकर्मभोजनात्मकं संसारमापादयति । तदापादनमेवास्य सृष्टिस्थितिसंहारानुगतं तिरोधानाख्यं कृत्यमुच्यते ।

Page 82

(१) तेषु हेयताज्ञानरोधात्मकं तिरोधानम् ।

(२) अनुग्रहोपि पाशतिरोधानेनात्मनां परापरमोक्षदानमिति ।

(३) ननु प्रागर्थपञ्चकं पाशा इत्युक्तम् अत्र चतुर्विधत्वोक्तिर्विरुद्धेति चेन्न । बिन्दोर्महामायात्मनः परमुक्त्यपेक्षया पाशत्वेपि तद्योगस्य विद्येश्वरादिपदप्राप्तिहेतुत्वेनापरमुक्तित्वादत्र पाशत्वेनानुपादानमित्यविरोधः ।

Page 83

(१) शिवशक्तेस्तु पाशाधिष्ठानेन आत्मनि तिरोधायिकत्वादुपचारेण पाशत्वमुक्तम् ।

(२) एक एव मलो जडत्वे सति नित्यत्वाज्जडानामनेकानां घटादिवदनित्यत्वं स्यात् ।

(३) निवृत्तिश्चास्य मलस्य चक्षुःपटलादेरिव द्रव्यत्वात् ईश्वराख्यवैद्यव्यापारसाध्यत्वेन तत्प्रवर्तनाय कमपि व्यापारमपेक्षते ।

Page 84

(१) आद्याननुगृह्य शिवो विद्येशत्वे नियोजयत्यष्टौ ।
मंत्रांश्च करोत्यपरान् ते चोक्ताः कोटयः सप्त ।।

(२) माया च तावद्वस्तुरूपा । न तु वेदान्तवादिनामिवासत्यरूपा ।

(३) मायीयतिरोधायकशिवशक्तिसमुद्भवौ चान्यौ ।

(४) मोहहेतुत्वाद्विपरीतप्रतिपत्तिहेतुना मायाख्येन बन्धेन भाव्यम् ।

(५) निर्हेतुकत्वे मुक्तस्यापि भवेत् । ततस्तत्कारणतयाऽनाद्यावारको मलोऽभ्युपगन्तव्यः ।

(६) कर्मणोऽनादित्वं प्रवाहानादितयेत्युक्तम् ।

(७) भोगस्य सुखदुःखादेर्भोगसाधनानां च शरीरेन्द्रियाणां प्रत्यात्मनियतत्वेन विचित्रत्वाद्वैचित्र्यकारणं कर्माप्यवश्यमभ्युपेयमिति ।

Page 85

(१) पाशत्वं तु तस्याः पाशधर्मानुवर्तनेनोपचारात् ।

(२) तिरोभावश्च पाशानुग्रहेणात्मनां यथानुगुणभोगभोजनम् ।

Page 86

(१) उत्तीर्णमायाम्बुधयो भग्नकर्ममहार्गलाः ।
अप्राप्तशिवधामानस्त्रिधा विज्ञानकेवलः ।।

Page 87

(३) एवंभूतमुपादानरूपं महामायाख्यं शिवतत्त्वमाचार्या जगदुरिति । नत्वियमार्या परमशिवविषयतया तच्छक्तिविषयतया वा व्याख्येया । शिवादिपृथिव्यन्ततत्त्वलक्षणप्रस्तावे तत्त्वातीतयोस्तयोरत्राप्रस्तुतत्वात् ।

(४) शिवतत्त्वं बिन्द्वात्मकमाद्यं प्रधानमुपादानं स्मरन्ति पूर्वाचार्याः । परमोपादानत्वेनैव चास्य मायावन्नित्यत्वं सिद्धमित्युक्तम् अतश्चान्यानि चत्वारि तानि तत्कार्याणीति भावः ।

(५) ज्ञानक्रिये स्वस्मिन् स्थिते आत्मनां भावयतीति ज्ञानक्रियास्वभावम् । अयमर्थः तत्तद्भुवनेश्वराराधनात् दीक्षया वा स्वकार्यभूतशुद्धाध्वभुवन—प्राप्तानां ज्ञानक्रिये प्रकटयतीति ।

Page 88

(१) न तु शक्त्यधिष्ठाननैरपेक्ष्येणास्वातन्त्र्यात् । अचेतनस्य चेतनाधिष्ठानं बिना कार्योत्पादनायोगात् ।

(२) किञ्च उपादानं हि परिणामेन वा कार्यमुत्पादयति यथा क्षीरस्य दधिभावः। वृत्तिरूपेण वा यथा पटस्य गृहादिभावः। शिवादीनामेषां तु वृत्तिपरिणामौ न संभवतः अविकारित्वात्, विकारित्वे जडत्वानित्यत्वादिदोष-प्रसङ्गात्।

Page 89

(१) विद्याशरीरो भगवाननन्तः क्षोभको मतः।
मायायाः सा च विद्वद्भिर्वैन्दवं तत्वमुच्यते॥

(२) अत्र आत्मनां चिच्छक्तिः येन नादात्मना परिणतेन अभिधेयबुद्धिबीजेन संपृक्ता मायेयसविकल्पार्थावलोकने प्रवर्तते।

(३) यस्य च प्रत्यात्मनियतैः नादाख्यैः विचित्रैः वृत्तिभेदैः उपहिता विचित्रैव प्रकाशते स बिन्दुः।

(४) एवं ज्ञानवैचित्र्यमपि नादसहकृतमेव करोति न केवलम्।

Page 90

(१) बुद्धेरध्यवसायहेतुत्वेऽपि बिन्दुकार्यशब्दसहकारादेव सविकल्पकज्ञानं जन्यते।

(२) केचिदाचक्षते बिन्दुः समवैति शिवे ततः।
इच्छाक्तिवत्क्रियाशक्तिरियं कुण्डलिनी परा॥

(३) स हि तादात्म्यसंबन्धो जडेन जडिमावहः।
शिवस्यानुपमाखण्डचिद्घनैकस्वरूपिणः॥

(४) ईश्वरस्याचेतनत्वाभ्युपगमे जगत्कर्तृत्वेन ईश्वरं साधयता अनुमानेन तस्य चेतनत्वादिस्वरूपप्रतिपादकैः आगमैश्च बाधः॥

(५) महामाया भवेत् त्रेधा तत्र स्थूला गुणात्मिका।
बुद्ध्यादिभोग्यजननी प्रकृतिः पुरुषस्य सा॥
सूक्ष्मा कालादितत्त्वानामविभागस्वरूपिणी।
जननी मोहिनी माया सर्वाशुद्धाध्वकारणम्।
मन्त्रयोनिः परा माया नित्या कुण्डलिनी तु या।
उपादानं शरीराणां विद्याविद्येश्वरात्मनाम्॥

Page 91

(१) ननु उक्तवद्वर्णानामर्थप्रतिपादकत्वासंभवात्तदन्यथानुपपत्त्या तदभिव्य-ङ्ग्योऽन्य एव अविनिर्भक्तो मायूराण्डरसवदनेकवर्णावभासकः क्रम एव पदात्मा पदव्यतिरिक्तश्च वाक्यस्वभावः समस्तस्य जगतो युगपत्क्रमेण वार्थप्रतीतिहेतुत्वाद्व्यापको नित्यश्चस्फोटोऽभ्युपगन्तव्यः। यतः स एव व्यवहर्तृणामर्थं स्फुटयतीति वैयाकरणाः।

Page 92

(२) पदवाक्यैकदेशभूतानां वर्णानां क्षणविध्वंसित्वेन परस्परोपकारकत्वाभावस्योक्तत्वात्तद्व्यतिरिक्तयोश्च पदवाक्ययोर्भेदेनादर्शनान्न तयोरपि अभिधायकत्वमिति प्रत्यक्षनिराकृतत्वेनानुमानेनापि न तयोः सद्भावः।

(३) गौरिति नामादिपदं श्रोत्रग्राह्यं सदस्ति चेन्नैवम्।
न गकारौकारविसर्जनीयबाह्यं यदतोऽन्यदत्रास्ति।
तेषां युगपद्भावाभावात् परोपलम्भे न पूर्वयोर्भावः।
प्राप्ताद्विसर्जनीयात् खुरकम्बललक्षणा न चिद्व्यक्तिः।।

Page 92

(१) स्मर्यमाणानुभूयमानवर्णसमूहात्मकं पदम् अभिधायकमिति चेत् तन्न।
स्मर्यमाणानां प्रदीपानां अर्थप्रकाशकत्वादर्शनात्।

(२) तत्र यत्तावदुक्तं वर्णव्यतिरिक्तः स्फोट इति तदयुक्तम्। न वर्णव्यतिरेकेण तस्य स्फोटस्य तद्ग्राहकयोर्मध्ये स्थितिरुपपद्यते। यतः स हि वर्णेभ्यो भिन्नो वा स्यादभिन्नो वा। न तावद्भिन्नः। वर्णव्यतिरेकेण तस्योपलब्धि लक्षणप्राप्तस्यानुपलब्धेः शशविषाणादेरिव। न चानुमानात्स्थितिरुपपद्यते। तस्य प्रत्यक्षनिराकृतत्वात्।

(३) व्यक्तं हि तावत्खुरकंबलादिलक्षणमर्थं बुद्ध्याऽध्यवस्य तदनुगुणं गौरित्यादि पदं चिन्तयैवानुसन्धाय ततः स्थूलशब्दं प्रयुङ्क्ते।

Page 93

(१) अयमेवास्य बुद्ध्याकारस्य वाचकस्य वाच्याद्बाह्याकाराद्विशेषः, यद्बाह्याकारपरामर्शरूपत्वाद्वाचकत्वम्, ततश्च वाचकैः परामर्शज्ञानभेदैर्गवादिलक्षणा बाह्याकारभेदा विमृश्यमाना वाच्या भवन्तीति विशेषः।

Page 94

(१) बुद्धिर्हि तावद्बाह्ये चक्षुरादिना विषयीकृत एवार्थेऽध्यवसायिनी दृष्टा नाविषयीकृते अतिप्रसङ्गात्। ततश्चान्तरे बुद्धिः केनापि विषयीकृत एवार्थे परामर्शं करोति। अन्यथा सर्वदा सर्वार्थपरामर्शप्रसङ्गात्। तस्माद्रूपरसादयोर्था: येन वक्तृबुद्धेः परामृश्यतां नीताः स एवात्र नादः।

Page 95

(१) स बिन्दुः परनादाख्यः नादबिन्द्वर्णकारणम्।
बिन्दुश्च तत्कार्यः मयूराण्डरसबिन्दुवदव्यपदेश्यः परामर्शज्ञानरूपः अक्षरबिन्दुः तत्रैव सूक्ष्मत्वेनोक्तः अर्णश्च वर्णः।

Page 96

(१) शब्दतत्त्वमघोषावाग्ब्रह्म कुण्डलिनी ध्रुवम्।
विद्याशक्तिः परा नादो महामायेति देशिकैः।
बिन्दुरेवं समाख्यातो व्योमानाहतमित्यपि।

(२) वैखर्या मध्यमायाश्च पश्यन्त्याश्चैतदद्भुतम् ।
अनेकतीर्थभेदायास्त्रय्या वाचः परं पदम् ।

page 97

(१) स्फोट एव हि पश्यन्ती तदन्या वा द्वयं भवेत् ।
तदन्यत्वे तदैक्ये वा तदङ्गुल्यग्ररूपया ।।

(२) आत्मस्वरूपविदस्तु शैवाः तां सूक्ष्माख्यां बिन्दुकार्यभूतां
शब्दवृत्तिमेव मन्यन्ते न तु पुरुषसमवायिनीम् ।

(३) अविभागेन वर्णानां सर्वतः संहृतिक्रमात् ।
स्वयंप्रकाशा पश्यन्ती मयूराण्डरसोपमा ।।
इयं च अक्षरबिन्दुरूपेत्युक्तम् ।

(४) स्वप्रकाशा संविद्रूपा वाक् सा पश्यन्तीत्युच्यते ।

Page 98

(१) यस्यां दृष्टस्वरूपायामधिकारो निवर्तते ।

(२) पुरुषे षोडशकले तामाहुरमृताह्वयाम् ।

3. See textual authority Page 97 , (२)

(४) अस्य बिन्दोर्य आद्य उन्मेषः प्रथमः परिणामः । शान्त्यादि—
भुवनात्मको नादात्मकश्च तच्छक्तितत्त्वमुच्यते ।

(५) ज्ञानक्रियाख्य शक्त्योरपकर्षोत्कर्षयोरभावेन ।
यः प्रसरस्तं प्राहुः सदाशिवाख्यं बुधास्तत्त्वम् ।।

Page 99

(१) न्यग्भवति यत्र शक्तिर्ज्ञानाख्योद्वृत्ततां क्रिया भजते ।
ईश्वरतत्त्वं तदिह प्रोक्तं सर्वार्थकर्तृ सदा ।

(२) न्यग्भवति कर्तृशक्तिर्ज्ञानाख्योद्रेकमश्नुते यत्र ।
तत्तत्वं विद्याख्यं प्रकाशकं ज्ञानरूपत्वात् ।

(३) पञ्चानामप्येषां न हि क्रमोऽस्तीह कालरहितत्वात् ।
व्यापारवशादेषां विहिता खलु कल्पना शास्त्रे ।

(४) सकलो बिन्दुःअक्षरबिन्द्वात्मको नादश्च स्थूलध्वनिरूपः ।
द्वौ च सदाशियतत्त्वान्तर्भूतौ ज्ञेयौ ।

Page 100

(१) शक्तय इहास्य करणं मायोपादानमिष्यते सूक्ष्मा ।
एका नित्या व्यापिन्यनादिनिधना शिवा ऽऽ सक्ता ।

(२) साधारणी नराणां कारणमपि चेयमखिलभुवनानाम् ।
निखिलजनकर्मखचिता स्वभावतो मोहसञ्जननी ।

(३) तुद्याादिप्रत्ययस्यार्थः कालो मायासमुद्भवः।
कलयन्नासमुत्थानान्नियत्या नियतम् पशुम्।

(४) नन्वेव कालो नैयायिकादिभिर्नित्योऽभ्युपगतः अत आह भावीति, तस्य भूतादिरूपेण त्रिविधत्वादचैतन्ये सत्यनेकत्वे-नास्यानित्यत्वं सिद्धमिति भावः।

Page 101

(१) नियत्यभावे अन्यैरुपार्जितान्यपि कर्माण्यन्ये भुञ्जीरन्।
राजनियमाभावे कृष्यादिफलानीव दस्यवः, अतस्तन्नि-यामकत्वेनेयं सिद्धा।

(२) मायातस्तदनुकला मलं नृणामेकतस्तु कलयित्वा।
व्यञ्जयति कर्तृशक्तिं कलेति तेनेह कथितेयम्॥

कला हि भोक्तृस्वरूपोपकारकत्वेनान्तरङ्गत्वात् प्रधानं कालादिस्तु बहिरङ्गत्वादप्रधानमिति भावः।

(३) उद्बुद्धकर्तृशक्तेः पुंसो विषयप्रदर्शननिमित्तम्।
विद्यातत्त्वं सूते प्रकाशरूपं कलैवैषा॥

(४) ननु विषयग्रहणे बुद्ध्यादीनि करणानि सन्ति, सत्यम्, यथा घटादिज्ञानं चक्षुरादिव्यतिरेकेण न संभवति तथा सुखादिविषय-ग्रहणं करणसापेक्षमत एवेयमात्मनः परममन्तरङ्गकरणम् तेषां बहिरङ्गत्वात्। एतदुक्तं भवति। अश्वेन पथा दीपिकया वा यातीत्या-दाविवात्रानेककरणसाध्येऽपि फले विद्यैव परमं करणमिति।

Page 102

(१) बुद्धिर्यदास्य भोग्या सुखादिरूपा तदा भवेत्करणम्।
विद्यैवं करणं स्याद्विषयग्रहणे पुनर्बुद्धिः॥

(२) अवैराग्यस्य च बुद्धिधर्मत्वेन वासनारूपत्वाच्च पुरुषोपकारः संभवति। अन्यथा बुद्धेरनन्तवासनायोगेन पुंसो युगपद्विरुद्धानन्तप्रतिपत्तिवैशस-प्रसङ्गात्।

Page 103

(१) पशुस्त्रिविधः। विज्ञानाकल प्रलयाकल सकल भेदात्। तत्र प्रथमो विज्ञान-योगसंन्याससंभोगेन वा कर्मक्षये सति कर्मक्षयार्थस्य कलादिभोगबन्ध-स्याभावात्केवलमलमात्रयुक्तो विज्ञानाकल इति व्यपदिश्यते।

(२) प्रलयकेवलाख्यो वर्गः प्रलये कलादेरुपसंहारात् मलकर्मयुक्तो भवति।

(३) मलमायाकर्मयुतः सकलस्तेषु द्विधा भवेदाद्यः।
सकलस्तु बन्धत्रययुक्तः तत्र च मायायाः साक्षात्संबन्धाभावात् माया-शब्देन तत्कार्यभूताः कलादयः कथ्यन्ते।

(४) तत्र पुर्यष्टकं नाम प्रतिपुरुषं नियतः सर्गादारभ्य कल्पान्तं मोक्षान्तं वाऽवस्थितः पृथिव्यादि-कलान्त-त्रिंशत्तत्त्वात्मकोऽसाधारणरूपः सूक्ष्म देहः ।

Page 104

(१) तत्त्वैरेभिः कलितो भोक्तृत्वदशां यदा पशुर्नीतः ।
पुरुषाख्यतां तदायं लभते तत्त्वेषु गणनां च ॥

(२) ननु गुणा एवाव्यक्तं बुद्ध्यादिकारणमिति साङ्ख्याः । तदयुक्तमित्याह गुणानामचैतन्ये सत्यनेकत्वात्कारणपूर्वकत्वमित्युक्तमतोऽनभिव्यक्तगुण-रूपकार्यत्वादेव तदव्यक्तमित्युच्यते ।

(३) अव्यक्ताद् गुणतत्त्वं प्रख्याव्यापारनियमरूपमिह ।

(४) ननु "अव्यक्तं मायातः" इत्यादिना प्रकृत्यधस्तनतत्त्वानां चतुर्विंशते-रुक्तत्वात्कथमत्र त्र्यधिका विंशतिरुच्यते अत आह "यस्मात्प्रकृतिगुणानाम्" इति.......... ततः कार्यकरणयोरभेदविवक्षयैवमुक्तमित्यविरोधः ।

Page 105

(१) अधिकारमलांशावशेषतोऽधिकारनिबन्धन एव । अत एव मायोत्तीर्ण-त्वान्मलरहितत्वाच्च विद्याविद्येश्वरप्राप्तेरपरमुक्तित्वम् ।

(२) न च तस्य मोक्षस्य 'आत्मा ज्ञातव्यः' इत्यादाविवायं पशुः कर्त्ता, पशो-रीश्वरसंस्कार्यत्वेन सर्वदा कर्मत्वात् ।

Page 106

(१) अतो विमुक्तास्सर्वज्ञा न तु चिन्मात्रवेदिनः । न तु स्वसंवेदनमात्रनिष्ठा अपि तु शिववत्सर्वज्ञा एवेति ।

(२) तेषां च सर्वज्ञत्वसर्वकर्तृत्वसंभवेऽपि प्रवृत्तिरित्याह ।
न ते विश्वस्य कर्तारः कर्तास्य शिव एव यत् । कुत इत्यत्राह—
न हि कर्तृबहुत्वस्य जनकं विद्यते क्वचित् ।

(३) नन्वात्मनां कैवल्यमेव श्रेय इति सर्वतन्त्र प्रसिद्धम् ।

(४) वेदान्ते तावत् सच्चिदानन्दलक्षणमात्मानमन्तरेण न वस्तु किञ्चि-दभ्युपगम्यते । विषयाभावेनास्य धर्मिधर्मात्मकस्वसंवित्परसंविद्रूप-भेदोऽनुपपन्नः सर्वस्यापि हि धर्मिणो धर्मः सर्वत्र स्वेतरविषयेष्वेव प्रकाशते । यथा वह्नेरुष्णत्वादि काष्ठादौ ।

Page 107

(१) आत्मधर्मत्वे तु तस्य नित्यत्वव्यापकत्वादेरिव निवर्तयितुमशक्यत्वेन अनिर्मोक्षः ।

(२) निवर्त्यत्वे न आत्मधर्मतेति वस्त्वन्तरमेवात्मनोऽनाद्युपरोधहेतुत्वात् अज्ञान-हेतुश्चक्षुष इव पटलादिः मलो वाच्यः। न च द्रव्यस्याज्ञानहेतोः पटला-देरन्यस्य वा ज्ञानान्निवृत्तिर्दृष्टा प्रतिपक्षत्वाभावात्। कथं तर्हि शुक्तिकारजतादौ ज्ञानान्निवृत्तिः।

Page 108

(१) पटलादेश्चक्षुर्वैद्यादिवत् ईश्वरादेव तन्निवृत्तिरिति ईश्वरकर्तृक एव मोक्षः नाऽत्मकर्तृकः।

(२) एकत्वदर्शनं मुक्तेः साधनं स्वात्मबाधितम्।
मोच्यमोचनकर्तृणां नाभेदे सा यतो भवेत्॥

(३) सर्वज्ञत्वादिगुणः परमेश्वरसम उत्पद्यत इति उत्पत्तिसमतापक्षः कैश्चिद-भ्युपगतः।

Page 109

(१) यैर्मुक्तावीश्वरसमता सर्वज्ञत्वादिगुणसाम्यमुत्पद्यते पुंस इति इष्यते तन्मते उत्पत्तिमदनित्यत्वात् अनित्यत्वं मुक्तेरिति।

(२) ईश्वरगुणा मुक्तौ सङ्क्रमन्त इति गुणसङ्क्रान्तिर्नैषा भवतां तावत्प्रत्यक्षसिद्धा। अतीन्द्रियत्वात्तेषाम्। अथानुमानादित्युच्यते। तदयुक्तम्। गुणसङ्क्रान्तिसाधनेऽनुमाने नोदाहरणस्य दृष्टान्तस्य सद्-भावोऽस्ति।

(३) अपरज्ञानिनस्तु अधिकारिण आचार्यास्सिद्धान्तव्यक्तचैतन्यत्वेनापर-मुक्ताः। त एव परमुक्त्यर्थमागमदृष्टातु क्रियायोगचर्यासु यथायोग्यं वस्तुत्रयं शिष्यैः सह विनियुञ्जते।

(४) तदेवं समधीतसामान्यविशेषशास्त्राणां समर्थानां समस्तसम्पत्सम्पन्नानां ब्राह्मणोत्तमानामेव सर्वपदार्थविनियोगभरणाय परमेश्वराधिकरणत्वा-परपर्यायमाचार्यत्वं व्यवस्थितमित्युपविशन्त्याचार्याः।

(५) वस्तुतस्तु गुरूणां स्वार्थतया विहितं सर्वं परार्थमेव। सिद्धिफलदाना-मेषां चरितस्य साधकादिमार्गदर्शनार्थत्वात्।

Page 111

(१) तथाहि शास्त्रान्तरे दुःखनिवृत्तिरेव दुःखान्तः इह तु परमैश्वर्यप्राप्तिश्च। तथाऽन्यत्राभूत्वा भावि कार्यमिह तु नित्यं पश्वादि। तथाऽन्यत्र कैवल्या-भ्युदयफलो योगः, इह तु परमदुःखान्तफलः। तथान्यत्रावर्त्तकः स्वर्गादि-फलो विधिरिह त्वनावर्तको रुद्रसमीपादिफल इति।

Page 112

(१) कारणं प्रधानमीश्वरश्च

Page 113

(१) मायां तु प्रकृतिं विद्यान्मायिनं तु महेश्वरम् ।
(२) योऽयमाकाशो मायाविशिष्टब्रह्मण उपादानकारणादुत्पन्नस्तस्मिन्ब्रह्मांशो मायांशश्चोभावनुगतौ ।
(३) यथा ब्रह्मतत्त्वस्य सच्चिदानन्दैकरसत्वं स्वभावस्तथा मायाविशिष्टस्य सृष्टिस्थितिसंहाराः स्वभावभूता अतो निःस्पृहस्य प्रयोजनविशेषो न कल्पनीय इत्यष्टमं मतम् । एतदेव सिद्धान्तरहस्यम् ।
(४) ननु कर्माण्येव स्वस्वफलदानाय प्राणिदेहानुत्पादयन्ति किमनेनेश्वरेणेति चेन्न । ईश्वर एव फलदातेति तृतीयाध्यायस्य द्वितीयपादे चिन्तितत्वात् ।
(५) किञ्च ब्रह्म सद्रूपं प्रवेष्टृत्वात् यथा गृहादौ प्रवेष्टा पुरुष इत्यभिप्रेत्य प्रवेशं दर्शयति---
(६) तदनुप्रविश्य । सच्च त्यच्चाभवत् । निरुक्तं चानिरुक्तं च । निलयनं चानिलयनं च । विज्ञानं चाविज्ञानं च । सत्यं चानृतं च सत्यमभवत् ।
(७) यस्मादेवं तस्मात्तद् ब्रह्म सुकृत मित्यनेन शब्देनोच्यते । सुशब्दोऽत्र स्वयं शब्दपर्यायः । कृतशब्दः कर्तृ शब्द पर्यायः । सुकृतं स्वयं कर्तृ ब्रह्मेत्येवं शास्त्रविद्भिरुच्यते ।

Page 114

(१) सर्वो वै रुद्रस्तस्मै रुद्राय नमो अस्तु । पुरुषो वै रुद्रः सन्महो नमो नमः । विश्वं भूतं भुवनं चित्रं बहुधा जातं जायमानं च यत् । सर्वोह्येष रुद्रस्तस्मै रुद्राय नमो अस्तु ।
(२) तस्या एवाम्बिकाया ब्रह्मविद्यात्मको देह उमाशब्देनोच्यते ।
(३) यतो वा इमानि भूतानि जायन्ते । येन जातानि जीवन्ति । यत्प्रयन्त्यभिसंविशन्ति । तद्विजिज्ञासस्व । तद् ब्रह्मेति ।
(४) अन्नमयादिभ्य आनन्दमयान्तेभ्यः पञ्चभ्यः कोशेभ्यो ब्रह्मतत्त्वं विवेक्तुकाम आदावन्नमयकोशं दर्शयति ।
(५) उत्तरवक्त्ररूपो वामदेवस्तस्यैव विग्रहविशेषा ज्येष्ठादिनामकाः । एते च महादेवपीठशक्तीनां वामादीनां नवानां पतयः पुरुषाः ।
(६) एष जिज्ञासुरेतस्मिन्सद्भावसाधनेन प्रवर्तते स्वानुभवगम्ये ब्रह्मणि प्रतिष्ठां स्वात्मत्वबुद्धिदाढ्यं यदा लभते. अथ तदानीं स विद्वान् अभयं जन्ममरणादिभयरहितं मुक्ति पदं प्राप्नोति ।
(७) संङ्क्रमणं नाम दृढसंयोगरूपप्राप्तिः । जलूका तृणे संक्रामतीत्यादौ तथा दृष्टत्वात् ।

Page 115

(१) सङ्क्रमशब्देनात्र भ्रान्तिविनाशलक्षणस्य विद्याफलस्य विवक्षितत्वात् ।

(२) ब्रह्मणः सायुज्यं सलोकतामाप्नोत्येतासामेव देवतानाँ–सायुज्यँ-सार्ष्टिताँ–समानलोकतामाप्नोति य एवं वेद इति ।

(३) तस्मात्साक्षात्कारात्तल्लोकवासिदेहपाताद्रूर्ध्वं हिरण्यगर्भलोकं गत्वा तत्र ब्रह्मणो हिरण्यगर्भस्य महिमानमैश्वर्यं प्राप्नोति । तत्रोत्पन्नब्रह्म-तत्त्वसाक्षात्कारस्तस्माज्ज्ञानाद् ब्रह्मलोकविनाशादूर्ध्वं सत्यज्ञानादि-लक्षणस्य ब्रह्मणो महिमानं महत्त्वं च प्राप्नोति ।

(४) तस्माद् गुहानिहितं प्रत्यक्त्वमेव ब्रह्मतया विद्यात् ।

Page 116

(१) अक्षात्पुरुषः ।

(२) योऽयमाकाशो मायाविशिष्टब्रह्मण उपादानकारणादुत्पन्नस्तस्मिन् ब्रह्मांशो मायांशश्चोभावनुगतौ ।

(३) भेदाभेदविरोधव्यवहारस्याऽऽकारभेदेनापि रहितेऽत्यन्तमेकस्मिन्नपि वस्तुनि सावकाशत्वात् । तस्माद् ब्रह्माकारेणाद्वैतं भोक्तृभोग्याकारेण द्वैतमित्याकारभेदाद् व्यवस्थासिद्धौ न कोऽपि बाधः ।

(४) सद्योजातनामकं यत्पश्चिमवक्त्रं तद्रूपं परमेश्वरम् प्रपद्यामि प्राप्नोमि । उत्तरवक्त्ररूपो वामदेवस्तस्यैव विग्रहविशेषा ज्येष्ठादिनामकाः । एते च महादेवपीठशक्तीनां वामादीनां नवानां पतयः पुरुषाः । अघोरनामको दक्षिणवक्त्ररूपः ।
प्राग्वक्त्रदेवस्तत्पुरुषनामकः ।
योऽयमूर्ध्ववक्त्रो देवः सोऽयं सर्वविद्यानां वेदशास्त्रादीनां चतुःषष्टिकला-विद्यानामीशानो नियामकः ।

Page 117

(१) अन्यत्र दुःखनिवृत्तिरेव दुःखान्तः इह तु पारमैश्वर्यप्राप्तिश्च । अन्यत्रा-भूत्वा भावि कार्यम् । इह तु नित्यं पश्वादि । अन्यत्र सापेक्षं कारणम् इह तु निरपेक्षो भगवानेव । अन्यत्र कैवल्यादिफलको योगः । इह तु पारमैश्वर्यदुःखान्तफलकः । अन्यत्र पुनरावृत्तिरूपसामीप्यादि-फलको विधिः । इह पुनरपुनरावृत्तिरूपसामीप्यादिफलकः ।

(२) तदेतद्वैष्णवमतं दासत्वादिपदवेदनीयं परतन्त्रत्वं दुःखावहत्वान्न दुःखान्तादी प्सितास्पदमित्यरोचयमानाः पारमैश्वर्यं कामयमानाः पराभिमता मुक्ता न भवन्ति परतन्त्रत्वात् पारमैश्वर्यरहितत्वादस्मदादिवत् । मुक्ता-त्मानश्च परमेश्वरगुणसंबन्धिनः पुरुषत्वे सति समस्तदुःखबीज-विधुरत्वात्परमेश्वरवत्—इत्याद्यनुमानं प्रमाणं प्रतिपद्यमानाः केचन माहेश्वराःपरमपुरुषार्थसाधनं पञ्चार्थप्रपञ्चनपरं पाशुपतशास्त्रमाश्रयन्ते ।

Page 118

(१) स्वतन्त्रस्याप्रयोज्यत्वं करणादिप्रयोक्तृता ।
कर्तुः स्वातन्त्र्यमेतद्धि न कर्माद्यनपेक्षता ।।

(२) आङिति कार्यकारणत्वं आत्मनो मुक्तानां च मर्यादा। तदुच्यते-उत्पाद्यानुग्राह्य (तिरोभाव्य) कल्पकत्वाभावकत्वेनापरिणामित्वम्, आत्मनो मुक्तानां च पुनर्दुःखैरसंयोजनमित्येषा कारणमर्यादा ।

Page 119

(१) यदेतत् पत्युः पतित्वं शक्तिः सामर्थ्यमैश्वर्यं स्वगुणः सद्भावः सतत्त्वं तत्त्वधर्मः तद् आसनम् न तु पद्मासनवदुपवेशनलक्षणमित्यर्थः । आसनं कस्मात् । आस्तेऽस्मिन् (इति) आसनम् । कार्यमनेन वा अध्यास्त इत्यासनमित्यर्थः ।

(२) के कारणगुणाः इति ? तदुच्यते पतित्वसत्त्वाद्यत्वाजातत्वोत्पादकानुग्राहकतिरोभावकत्व ....।

(३) ते देव पितरो रुद्रशक्त्यां हार्यधार्यकार्यत्वेन वर्तन्ते ।

Page 120

(१) अत्र सदिति नित्यत्वे । कस्मात् ? विनाशहेत्वभावात् । नित्यं ध्रुवमविनाशि पत्युः पतित्वं नान्येषाम् इत्यतोऽभिधीयते सदिति । आह किम् अयमादिमत्त्वे सति नित्यो मोक्षवत् ? उच्यते, न, यस्मादाह---आद्यः ।

(२) नम इत्यात्मप्रदाने पूजायां च । नमस्कारेणात्मानं प्रयच्छति, पूजां च प्रयुङक्त इत्यर्थः ।

(३) भव इति विद्याकलापशूनां समस्तानां ग्रहणम्·······अतिशयितभवेषु मा भवामीत्यर्थः ।

(४) भवोद्भवः ।।४४।। अत्र भव इति विद्याकलापशूनामेव ग्रहणम् । तस्योत्पत्तिकर्त्ता भगवानित्यतो भवोद्भव इति ।

Page 121

(१) क्रीडावानेव स भगवान् विद्याकलापशुसंज्ञकं त्रिविधमपि कार्यमुत्पादयन् अनुगृह्णाति तिरोभावयति चेत्यतो देवः

(२) अत्र परत्वाज्ज्येष्ठः केषां केन वा परः ? तदुच्यते सिद्धसाधकपशूनाम् च प्रवृत्तिनिवृत्तिस्थित्यादिफलानाम् इत्यतो ज्येष्ठः परतरः । परत्वमश्चेति । अकृतकं चास्यैश्वर्यम् । उक्तं हि---
दृक्क्रियालक्षणा शक्तिस्तत्त्वधर्मोऽस्य नित्यता ।
श्रेष्ठोऽतः सर्वभूतेषु तस्मादेष परः स्मृतः ।।

(३) नानाविधैः कृतैर्थस्माद् भयैश्च विविधैस्तथा ।
संयोजयति भूतानि तस्माद् रुद्र इति स्मृतः ॥
अत्रापि तद्धर्मित्वे षष्ठी ।

(४) तच्छन्दात् तेषां प्रवृत्तिनिवृत्तिः स्थितिरिष्टानिष्टस्थानशरीरेन्द्रिय-विषयादिप्राप्तिर्भवति ।

(५) ब्रह्मादि भूर्जपर्यन्तं जगदेतच्चराचरम् ।
यतः कलयते रुद्रः कालरूपी ततः स्मृतः ॥

(६) सिद्धेश्वरवर्जं चेतनेष्वेव सर्वभूतशब्दः ।

(७) कलविकरणाय नमः ।

(८) अत्र मनःशब्देनान्तःकरणम् तत्तन्त्रत्वादुदाहरणार्थत्वाच्च मनोग्रहणस्य उभयात्मकत्वाच्च मनसः सर्वकरणग्रहणानुग्रहणाच्च कार्यग्रहणमित्यतः कार्यकरणाधिष्ठातृत्वाच्च सकल इत्युपचर्यते । तथा चैतादृशमनसः प्रतिषेधादत्र कार्यकरणरहितो निष्कलो भगवान् अमन इत्युच्यते ।

Page 122

(१) अघोरेभ्यः ।

(२) विद्यादिकार्यस्य शरणाच्छर्व इत्युच्यते । सर्वं विद्यादिकार्यं रुद्रस्थम् ।

(३) महादेवाय धीमहि ।

(४) समस्तसृष्टिसंहारानुग्रहकारि कारणम् । तस्यैकस्यापि गुणकर्मभेदा-पेक्षया विभाग उक्तः पतिः साद्य इत्यादिना । तत्र पतित्वं निरति-शयदृक्क्रियाशक्तिमत्वं तेनैश्वर्येण नित्यसंबंन्धित्वम् । आद्यत्वमना-गन्तुकैश्वर्यसंबंन्धित्वम् इत्यादर्शकारादिभिस्तीर्थकरैर्निरूपितम् ।

(५) तत्र तावदीश्वरस्यैकैकशः परिमितेषु तेष्वेवबिभुत्वादपरिमितेषु तथा परिमितापरिमितेष्वर्थेषु अभिव्यक्तास्य शक्तिः ।

Page 123

(१) तत्पुरुषाय विद्महे ।
अत्र पूर्वं कारणत्वबहुत्वनानात्वेनोपदिष्टस्य परामर्शः तद् इति ।

(२) ऋषिः कस्मात् । ऋषिः क्रियायाम् । ऋषित्वं नाम क्रियाशंसनादृषिः, तथा कृत्स्नं कार्यं विद्याद्यमीशत इत्यतः ऋषिः ।

(३) यदेतद् दृक्क्रियालक्षणमस्ति अनागन्तुकमकृतकमैश्वर्यं तद्गुणसद्भावः सतत्त्वं तत्त्वधर्मः तदकृतकं पुरुषचैतन्यवत् ।

(४) यस्मादस्यैश्वर्यं निष्कलस्यापि स्वगुणसद्भावः सतत्त्वं तत्त्वधर्मः। तद-कृतकत्वं पुरुषचैतन्यवत्।

(५) सर्वस्येशानः। सर्वशब्दो विद्याप्रकृतेर्निरवशेषवाची दृष्टव्यः। विद्यानां धर्मार्थकामकैवल्यतत्साधनपराणाम् ईशानः।

(६) ब्रह्म च कस्मात्? बृंहणत्वाद् वृहत्त्वाद् ब्रह्म। बृंहयते यस्माद् विद्या-कलाभूतानि, वृहच्च तेभ्य इत्यतोऽधिपतिर्ब्रह्मा।

(७) शिवः कस्मात्? परिपूर्णपरितृप्तत्वाच्छिवः।

Page 124

(१) पश्यनात् पाशनाच्च पशवः। तत्र पाशा नाम कार्यंकरणाख्याः कलाः।

Page 125

(१) भवोद्भवः। अत्र भव इति विद्याकलापशूनामेव ग्रहणम्। तस्यो-त्पत्तिकर्त्ता भगवानित्यतो भवोद्भव इति।

(२) पालको नित्यः। पालकनित्यत्वाच्च पाल्यमपि नित्यम्। कस्मात्? नह्यसति पाल्ये पालक इत्येव। सति नित्यत्वे तान्येव पश्वादीनि संयो-जयति। मृल्लोहमयप्राकारादिवद् दृष्टान्तात्। वृत्तिलाभश्चो-त्पत्तिरित्युच्यते।

(३) कलितं शोभितं शब्दितं नभस्ताराभिरिवेत्यर्थः।
अतोऽव्ययोऽमृतो भगवान् कामतः स्वशक्तिस्थं कार्यं स्वशक्त्या अध्यास्ते। तस्मादासनस्थं कार्यं कारणं चेति।

(४) आह–कार्यकारणयोर्वृत्तिसङ्करदोषो गोजाविमहिषीक्षीरवत्। तदुच्यते–न। अङ्गुल्यग्ररूपादिवदित्यसङ्करः। दीपादित्यप्रकाशनयन-रश्मिवच्चासंकरः।

(५) एकोत्तरोत्कर्षेण व्याप्यव्यापकभावेनावस्थितानां तत्त्वादीनां नापरि-च्छेददोषः।

Page 126

(१) आह–वृत्त्यसङ्करग्रहणे दृष्टान्ताभावादयुक्तम्। तदुच्यते हरिद्रोदक-वद् व्याप्यंव्यापकं च। तद्यथा–हरिद्रोदके स्निग्धत्वशैत्यादिधर्मैरपां ग्रहणम्, गन्धवर्णघनक्षारत्वादिभिर्हरिद्रायाः।

(२) अस्वतन्त्रं सर्वं कार्यम्।

(३) विद्या पूर्वोक्ता स्वपरान्यप्रकाशिका प्रदीपवत्।

(४) विद्या नाम [सा] या ग्रन्थार्थवर्ति पदार्थानामभिव्यञ्जिका विप्रत्वलक्षणा। न्यायात् पदार्थानामधिगतप्रत्ययो लाभमलोपायाभिज्ञः (अधिगत प्रत्ययस्य?) विद्वानित्युच्यते।

(५) तत्र पञ्चपदार्थविषयं समासविस्तरविभागविशेषोपसंहारनिगमनत-स्तत्त्वज्ञानं प्रथमो विद्यालाभो ज्ञानमिति चोच्यते।

(६) तत्र प्रमाणाभासजं ज्ञानं मिथ्याज्ञानमुक्तं संशयविपर्ययादिलक्षणम् । शास्त्रान्तरेभ्योऽपि तर्हि संशयादिनिवृत्तेरविशेषप्रसङ्ग इति चेन्न, शास्त्रान्तरप्रणेतॄणामपि विपर्ययानिवृत्तिप्रतिपादनादाचार्यवैशे-

ष्यप्रकरणे । तत्र शास्त्रान्तरेभ्योऽपि संशयादिनिवृत्तिरिति कामक्रोध-द्वेषाः कलुषं तस्याप्यज्ञानेऽन्तर्भावः । कस्मात् ? अव्यक्तावस्थागमने प्रत्यनीकत्वात् । तदिदं संशयादिकलुषं चसहबीजेन मिथ्याज्ञानमित्युच्यते ।

Page 127

(१) (i) तत्र पशुगुणो विद्या । सापि द्विविधा--बोधाबोधस्वभावभेदात् । बोधस्वभावा विवेकाविवेकप्रवृत्तिभेदाद् द्विविधा । सा चित्तमित्यु-च्यते ।

(ii) तत्र पशुगुणो विद्या स्वशास्त्रदृष्ट्योक्ता । वैशेषिकदृष्ट्या द्रव्यवत् । सा द्विधा बोधाबोधस्वभावभेदात् । तत्राबोधस्वभावा धर्मादि-- लक्षणा । विद्यान्तर्भावकरणादविद्यात्मकस्य विद्यान्तर्भावे कलादेरप्यन्त र्भावः स्यादिति । बोधस्वभावा तु विषयभेदाच्चतुर्धापञ्चधा चोक्ता ।

(२) तत्र विवेकवृत्तिः प्रायेणोपदेशव्यङ्ग्या न च तत्र समाख्यान्तरमस्ति ।

Page 129

(१) चित्तेन हि सर्वः प्राणी बोधात्मकप्रकाशानुगृहीतं सामान्येन विवेचित-मविवेचितं चार्थं चेतयत इति ।

जीवो हि घटादीन्पदार्थांश्चित्तेन जानाति । चेतयते जानाति येन तच्चि-त्तम् । चित्तं चात्र दर्शने नान्तःकरणस्यावान्तरभेदः । किन्तु जीवस्य विषयज्ञानार्थं या प्रवृत्तिस्तद्रूपो जीवनिष्ठो गुणविशेषः । स च गुण : स्वयं बोधात्मकत्वाद् घटादीन् पदार्थान्बोधयति यथादित्यःस्वयंप्रकाश-रूपत्वाद्घटादीन्पदार्थान्प्रकाशयति तद्वत् ।

Page 130

(१) तत्र दृष्टमपि द्विविधं--पूर्ववच्छेषवच्च । तत्र पूर्वदृष्टोऽयं षडङ्गुलीयकः स एवेति पूर्ववत् ।

(२) चेतनानाश्रितत्वे सति निश्चेतना कला । साऽपि द्विविधा कार्याख्या करणाख्या चेति । तत्र कार्याख्या दशविधा पृथिव्यप्तेजोवाय्वाकाश-गन्धरसरूपस्पर्शशब्दलक्षणा, करणाख्या तु त्रयोदशविधा, पञ्च कर्मेन्द्रियाणि पञ्च बुद्धीन्द्रियाण्यन्तःकरणत्रयं चेति ।

Page 132

(१) अनैश्वर्यं बन्धः । कारणशक्तितन्निरोधलक्षणमस्वातन्त्र्यमनैश्वर्यं बन्धोऽनादिः ।

(२) पश्यनाच्च पशवः। यस्माद्विभुत्वेऽपि चित्समवेतत्वेऽपि च शरीर-मात्रमेव पश्यन्त्युपलभन्ति च न बहिर्द्धानि (?) कार्यकरणरहिताश्च न कार्यकरणं प्रतिपद्यन्ते त्यजन्ति वा। धर्माधर्मप्रकाशदेशकालचोद-नाद्यपेक्षित्वाच्च। अतः सुष्ठूक्तं पश्यनात् पाशनाच्च पशवः।

(३) आत्मा इति क्षेत्रज्ञमाह।

(४) तस्य सुखदुःखेच्छाद्वेषप्रयत्नचैतन्यादिभिर्लिङ्गैरधिगमः क्रियते।

Page 133

(१) ततोऽस्य योगः प्रवर्तते।
सर्वज्ञता।

मनोजवित्वम् कामरूपित्वम् विकरणधर्मित्वं च। सर्वे चास्य वश्या भवन्ति, सर्वेषां चावश्यो भवति। सर्वांश्चाविशति। सर्वेषां चाना-वेश्यो भवति। सर्वे चास्य वध्या भवन्ति। सर्वेषां चावध्यो भवति। अभीतः। अक्षयः। अजरः अमरः। सर्वत्र चाप्रतिहतगतिर्भ-वति।

(२) तत्र प्रमाणाभासजं ज्ञानं मिथ्याज्ञानमुक्तं संशयविपर्ययादिलक्षणम्।

(३) धर्माधर्मव्यतिरिक्तः प्रतिघातानुमेयः पुरुषगुणः पशुत्वम्। तस्य चतु-र्दशलक्षणोपेतस्य मलत्वम्। तानि च लक्षणान्यसर्वज्ञत्वादीन्यपति-त्वान्तानि सर्वज्ञत्वादिविपर्ययेणैव व्याख्यातानीति।

Page 134

(१) कैवल्यगतानामन्यमलाभावेऽपि पशुत्वादेव पुनः संसारापत्तिरिति।

2. **See textual authority** Page 133 (१)

Page 135

(१) ग्रहणधारणोहापोहविज्ञानवचनक्रियायथान्यायाभिनिवेशानां 'वास' इति संज्ञा।

(२) धर्मस्योपायः चर्या।

Page 137

(१) किन्तु प्रत्याहारद्वैविध्यमिहेष्टं परापरभेदात्। तत्रान्तःकरणपूर्वको-ऽपरः।

Page 138

(१) प्रातिपदावस्था खलु व्यक्तावस्थेत्युक्ता। कस्मात्? पाशुपत्येऽयमिति व्यक्तिनिमित्तत्वात् भस्मस्नानशयनानस्नानादिभिर्लिङ्गधारीत्युपदेशादिति

(२) सर्वस्वत्यागो दानावस्था।

(३) गुरुभक्तिः प्रसादश्च मतेर्द्वन्द्वजयस्तथा ।
धर्मश्चैवाप्रमादश्च बलं पञ्चविधं स्मृतम् ।

(४) अत्र विद्याकलापशुसंज्ञितं त्रिविधं कार्यं द्रव्यमित्युच्यते ।

Page 139

(१) तत्र पञ्चपदार्थविषयं समासविस्तरविभागविशेषोपसंहारनिगमनतस्तत्त्वज्ञानं प्रथमो विद्यालाभो ज्ञानमिति चोच्यते ।

(२) भस्मस्नानादिविधिजनितो धर्मस्तप इत्युच्यते ।

(३) यद्देवे भावाभ्यासलक्षणं नित्यत्वं तृतीयो लाभः स उच्यते ।

(४) विज्ञानम् इत्यत्रापि नस्त्रिकं चिन्त्यते । विज्ञाता विज्ञानं विज्ञेयमिति । तत्र विज्ञाता सिद्धः । विज्ञानमस्य सिद्धिर्ज्ञानम् । विज्ञेया वृत्तयः । तस्मादेका ज्ञानशक्तिरपरिमितेन ज्ञेयेनानेकविधोपचर्यते ।

(५) यादृङ् मनसो जवित्वमाशुकारित्वम् ईदृशमस्य सिद्धस्य कर्तृत्वे शीघ्रत्वम् । न चास्य प्रजापतिवत् तपोनिमित्तत्वाद् भावोत्तरा प्रवृत्तिः । किन्तु भावस्य बलीयस्त्वात् प्रवृत्तेरुत्पन्नस्वभावः, करोमीति कृतमेव भवति । विनाशयामीति विनष्टं वा कस्मात् ? दृक्क्रिययोरप्रतीघातत्वात् ।

(६) अथ किमयं सिद्धस्तेषां स्वकृतानां रूपाणां संहारे शक्तः, उत विश्वामित्रवदशक्तः इति ? उच्यते । यस्मादाह–"विकरणः" ।

Page 140

(१) सिद्धयोगी न लिप्यते कर्मणा पातकेन वा ।

(२) तत्र यतः प्रवर्तते ? विषयेभ्यः प्रत्याहृतचित्तस्य यत् प्रवर्तते तद्योगः । यथा प्रवर्तते ? क्रमशः । येन प्रवर्तते ? तपसा प्रवर्तते [यस्य प्रवर्तते] आत्मनः साधकस्य । यस्मिन् प्रवर्तते । योऽयमात्मन्यात्मभावः, स महेश्वरे प्रवर्तते इत्यर्थः ।

(३) अध्ययनध्यानादिलक्षणः क्रियायोगश्चरतः प्रवर्तत इत्यर्थः ।

Page 141

(१) यस्मात् सति विभुत्वे अनधिकारकृतत्वाद् वियोगस्य । वियुक्तस्यैव च संयोग उपदिश्यते । विषयरक्तविरक्तवत् क्रियायोगे । इह तु समाधिलक्षणे योगे संनियम इति ।

(२) शून्यागारगुहावासी । देवनित्यः । जितेन्द्रियः । षण्मासान्नित्ययुक्तस्य । भूयिष्ठं सम्प्रवर्तते ।

(३) भस्मना त्रिषवणं स्नायीत । भस्मनि शयीत । अनुस्नानम् निर्माल्यम् । लिङ्गधारी । आयतनवासी । हसितगीतनृत्तडुंडुंकारनमस्कारजप्योपहारेणोपतिष्ठेत् ।

(४) अहिंसा ब्रह्मचर्यं च सत्यासंव्यवहारकौ।
अस्तेयमिति पञ्चैते यमा वै संप्रकीर्तिताः॥
अक्रोधो गुरुशुश्रूषा शौचमाहारलाघवम्।
अप्रमादश्च पञ्चैते नियमाः संप्रकीर्तिताः।

Page 142

(१) हसितगीतनृत्तडुंडुंकारनमस्कारजप्योपहारेणोपतिष्ठेत्।

(२) न चैषां क्रमो नियम्यते। किन्त्वपमानादिनिष्पादकत्वं येन परिभवं गच्छेदित्युपदेशाद्द्वाग्नितुल्यत्वेनापमानादेरिष्टतमत्वादिति।

(३) इन्द्रो वा अग्रे असुरेषु पाशुपतमचरत्।

(४) अनेन विधिना रुद्रसमीपं गत्वा.........।

Page 143

(१) मांसमदुष्यं लवणेन वा।

Page 145

(१) स द्विविधोऽनात्मकः सात्मकश्चेति।

(२) एवं यत्सांख्यं योगश्च वर्णयति, असङ्गादियुक्ताः मुक्ताः शान्ति प्राप्ता इति, तदविशुद्धं तेषां दर्शनम्, तैमिरिकस्य चक्षुषश्चन्द्रदर्शनवत्। अयन्तु युक्त एव न मुक्त इति विशुद्धमेतद् दर्शनम् दृष्टव्यम्।

(३) नित्यत्वन्नाम सति विभुत्वे पुरुषेश्वरयोर्मनसा सह गतस्यात्मताभावस्य वृत्त्याकारस्य विषयं प्रति क्रमोऽक्षोपोऽवस्थानं वृक्षशकुनिवत्।

Page 146

(१) असङ्गित्वमप्यतीतानागतवर्तमानानां
विषयाणामननुचिन्तनम्।

(२) इच्छाद्वेषनिवृत्तोऽप्रवृत्तिमान् मैत्र इत्युच्यते।

Page 148

(१) शिवागमैकदेशे शिवस्य परब्रह्मणः केवलनिमित्तत्वमुपपादितम्। तत्परिहारार्थमिदमधिकरणमिति पूर्वाचार्याणां व्याख्या।

Page 149

(१) चिदात्मैव हि देवोन्तः स्थितमिच्छावशाद्बहिः।
योगीव निरुपादानमर्थजातं प्रकाशयेत्॥

(२) पशुपतिपाशादिवस्तुव्यवहाराणाम्।

(३) एवमेतानि परशक्त्यादीनि पृथिव्यन्तानि जडानि षट्त्रिंशत्तत्त्वानि ।

(४) मलत्रयसंबन्धोऽपैति ।

Page 150

(१) भेदाभेदकल्पनं विशिष्टाद्वैतं साधयामः । न वयं ब्रह्मप्रपञ्चयोरत्यन्तं भेदवादिनः घटपटयोरिव । तदनन्यत्वपरश्रुतिविरोधात् । न वाऽत्यन्ताऽभेदवादिनः शुक्तिरजतयोरिव । एकतरमिथ्यात्वेन तत्स्वाभाविकगुणभेदपरश्रुतिविरोधात् । न च भेदाभेदवादिनः, वस्तुविरोधात् । किन्तु शरीरशरीरिणोरिव गुणगुणिनोरिव च विशिष्टाद्वैतवादिनः ।

Page 152

(१) अश्मकाष्ठतृणादेरचेतनस्येव जीवस्याप्यज्ञत्वादिना सर्वज्ञत्वादियुक्तादीश्वरात् अत्यन्तविजातीयत्वश्रवणात् तयोरेकभावानुपपत्तेः ।

(२) चेतनाचेतनप्रपञ्चविशिष्टस्य शिवस्य तद्विशेषणयोश्चेतनाचेतनयोस्तस्य ताभ्याञ्चान्तर्गणिकभेदसत्वेऽप्युक्तरूपेण तत्समानजातीयवस्त्वन्तराभावोऽस्तीति स एव वस्तुपरिच्छेदराहित्यम् ।

Page 153

(१) बृंहणत्वं च सर्गकालोन्मिषत्सकलप्रपञ्चविस्तारयितृत्व–मुक्तिकालविलसन्मुच्यमानजीवगतधर्मज्ञानविकासकत्वादिसर्वविध बृंहयितृत्वरूपं वाच्यम् ।

(२) अनेनैवाभिप्रायेण कृत्स्नस्यापि शब्दराशेर्वेदवेदान्तादिरूपस्य शिव एव तात्पर्यमित्यमुमर्थम् "इमा रुद्राय शतधन्विने गिरः" इतिमन्त्रभागो दर्शयति ।

(३) ज्ञेयपरिच्छेदरूपत्वाज्ज्ञानस्य तदपरिच्छिन्नब्रह्मविषयं न सम्भवतीति तदज्ञानविलसितम् । ईदृगिदमिति ब्रह्मणः परिच्छेदासम्भवेऽपि लक्षणमुखेनेतरव्यावृत्ततामात्रेण परिच्छेदसम्भवात् ।

Page 154

(१) चेतनाचेतनसम्मेलनसमरसीभूतस्य ।

(२) चिदचित्प्रपञ्चरूपशक्तिविशिष्टत्वं स्वाभाविकमेव ब्रह्मणः कदाचिदपि न निर्विशेषत्वमित्यनेन सिद्धम्...... ।

अनन्तशक्तिमत्वाद् ब्रह्मणोऽपरिच्छिन्नप्रपञ्चसमवायिकारणत्वं सिद्ध्यति ।

(३) यथा सागरे पवनादिसंक्षोभ्योपरितनपरिणामो वीचीफेनबुद्बुदप्रपञ्चः, एवं ब्रह्मणि तदिच्छासंक्षोभ्यमाणतदाश्रितशक्तिपरिणामः सर्वोयं प्रपञ्च इति भावः ।

(४) अत एव भगवती शक्तिः शक्तिमदीश्वरस्वरूपाद् व्यतिरेकं पृथक् सिद्धिं न वाञ्छति नानुमन्यते । किन्तु चन्द्रचन्द्रिकान्यायेन ब्रह्मापृथक्सिद्धैव भवति ।

(५) स्वात्मनि संहृत्य यदा वर्तते परमेश्वरः तदा सर्वमिदं निरस्तचन्द्रसूर्यादिप्रकाशतया विध्वस्तरात्रिदिनादिकालविभागम् अपगतनामरूपविशेषतया स्थूलसूक्ष्मदेवमनुष्यादिव्यवहारशून्यतमोमात्रं वर्तते स एक एव परमेश्वरो निरङ्कुशप्रकाशः सर्वसाक्षी तदानीमपि परिशिष्यते ।

(६) इच्छाशक्तिभित्तौ निखिलजगच्चित्रमुन्मीलयति ।

Page 155

(१) परमेश्वरो हि जीवानां विचित्रं कर्म सर्वज्ञतयावलोक्य स्वशक्त्या तदनुगुणमेव भोगायतनं देवादिशरीरं सृजति । ततः कर्ममूलमेव सृष्ट्यादिवैषम्यम् । संहारश्च जीवानां संसारव्यापारखिन्नानां सुषुप्तिवद्विश्रान्तिहेतुतया परमेश्वरस्य न नैर्घृण्यापादकः ।

(२) अनाद्यज्ञानवासनावष्टम्भविजृम्भितविचित्रकर्मफलभोगानुगुणबहुशरीरप्रवेशनिर्गमव्यापारपरवशनिस्सीमतापसहिष्णुत्वं जीवत्वम् ।

(३) विस्फुलिङ्गदृष्टान्तोऽपि जीवोत्पत्त्यनुगुणः श्रूयते "यथाग्नेः क्षुद्रा विस्फुलिंगा व्युच्चरन्ति एवमेवैतस्मादात्मनः सर्वे प्राणाः सर्वे लोकाः सर्वे देवाः सर्वाणि भूतानि सर्व एवात्मानो व्युच्चरन्ति" इति ।

(४) ज्ञानैवायमात्मा .... मलत्रयसंबन्धोऽपैति ।

Page 156

(१) व्यतिरेको गन्धवत् तथा हि दर्शयति ।

(२) सिद्धान्तस्तु—आत्मा कर्तैव शास्त्रार्थवत्त्वात् । अन्यथा कुर्यान्न कुर्यादिति शास्त्रस्य वैयर्थ्यं स्यात् ।

(३) जीवः स्वेच्छया प्रवृत्तिनिवृत्तिहेतुं करोति स्वकर्मपाकवशेन, जीवकृतप्रयत्नं प्रवृत्तिनिवृत्तिहेतुमवेक्ष्य तदनुमतिदानेन परः प्रवर्तयतीति विधिनिषेधावैयर्थ्यं निग्रहानुग्रहादिभ्योऽवगम्यते ।

(४) सिद्धान्तस्तु—जीवात्मा परमेश्वरस्यांशो मूर्त्येकदेश एव...... यदुक्तम् "अयमात्मा ब्रह्म" इत्यादिना ब्रह्मण एव जीवत्वमिति । तत्राह—अन्यथा "तत्त्वमसि" "अयमात्मा ब्रह्म" इत्यादिकाद् व्यपदेशात् तयोर्जीवब्रह्मणोर्व्याप्यव्यापकभावेनानन्यत्वम् । अपि च तथैवानन्यत्वमधीयत एके "ब्रह्म दाशा ब्रह्म दासा ब्रह्मेमे कितवा उत" इत्यादिना ब्रह्मणोंऽशत्वेपि जीवस्य तद्व्याप्ततया तद्व्यपदेशो युक्तः ।

(५) जीवो देहान्तरप्राप्तये भूतसूक्ष्मैः परिष्वक्तो यातीति पञ्चाग्निविद्यायां प्रश्नप्रतिवचनाभ्यामवगम्यते ।

(६) मलत्रयसंबन्धोऽपैति ।
(मुक्तस्य तु मलमायाकर्मबन्धापायात्।)

Page 157

(१) मलतिरोधानापगमप्रकटितशक्तिमरीचिव्याप्तमुक्तजीवविषयम् ।
तस्मादणुरेवात्मा ।

(२) जीवानां जीवत्वापादकस्य सकलसंसारनिदानस्य मलावरणस्याग्राहकतया रोधशक्त्याख्यस्य पाशत्वव्यपदेशस्य शिवागमेषु तस्याप्रसिद्धत्वात् । यदाहुः
"तासां माहेश्वरी शक्तिःसर्वानुग्राहिका परम् ।
परानुवर्तनादेव पाश इत्युपचर्यते ।।

(३) तथा चाभियुक्तस्मृतिः "यस्यैते चत्वारिंशत्संस्काराः" इत्यादिना "स ब्रह्मणः सायुज्यं सालोक्यं च गच्छति" इत्यन्तेन गर्भाधानादिसकलकर्मणां पापमलापकर्षसंस्कारहेतुतां प्रकाशयति ।

(४) शिवस्य परब्रह्मणः प्रसादातिशयेनास्याधिकारिणः प्रध्वस्तपाशपटला प्रत्यक्षीभूतनिरतिशयज्ञानानन्दस्वरूपा तत्समानगुणसारा कैवल्य--लक्ष्मीः प्रयोजनं च भवति ।

Page 158

(१) वेदान्तविज्ञानोपलब्धया ब्रह्मात्मसामरस्यभावनया ब्रह्मभावमुपगतस्य विगलितमनुष्यादिदेहविषयकल्पिताहंभावसंकोचस्य संपन्नविश्वाकारपराहंभावस्य वामदेवस्य स्वात्मनः सर्वगतत्वावगमान्मनुसूर्यादिप्रपञ्चभावोक्तिः। एवमिन्द्रस्यापीति निरुच्यते ।

Page 159

(१) न हि मुक्तात्मनां प्राकृतप्रपञ्चो दर्शनविषयः। किन्तु निरतिशयानन्दस्वरूपं ब्रह्मैव प्रपञ्चाकारेणं दर्शनगोचरीभवति ।

(२) निरवधिकपरमानन्दमयनिष्कलङ्कशिवत्वप्राप्तिर्हि मुक्तिः ।

(३) ब्रह्मप्राप्तजीवस्य मलतिरोहितं ब्रह्मसदृशगुणं स्वरूपं पूर्वं सदेव मलावरणापगमादाविर्भवति ।

Page 160

(१) मुक्तस्य ब्रह्मणा सादृश्यमस्ति । कुतः "निरञ्जनः परमं साम्यमुपैति' "युक्तः शिवसमो भवेत्" इति मुक्तस्य ब्रह्मगुणस्वरूपाविभागेन ब्रह्मसदृशतया दृष्टत्वात् अतः "ब्रह्म वेद ब्रह्मैव भवति" इति ब्रह्मसादृश्यमेवोच्यते ।

(२) ततः जीवस्य जगद्व्यापाराद्यभावात् । वक्ष्यति "भोगमात्रसाम्यलिङ्गाच्च" इति ।

(३) मुक्तस्य परमेश्वरसाम्येऽपि जगत्सृष्ट्यादिव्यापारवर्जमेव स्वातन्त्र्यमस्य भोगवस्तुषु ।

(४) सायुज्यमिति । सादृश्यं विवक्षितम् ।

(५) घटादिपरिच्छिन्नस्य प्रदीपस्य परिच्छेदापाये स्वप्रभया यथा गृहादिव्याप्तिः, तथा मुक्तस्य स्वशक्तितिरोधायकमलापाये स्वशक्त्या विश्वव्याप्तिः आवेशः भवति ।

Page 161

(१) विश्च शेषश्च विशेषौ । विशेषयोरद्वैतं विशेषाद्वैतमिति निरुक्त्या तत्राद्वैतपदेन भ्रमरकीटवज्जीवस्य स्वाभाविकभेदनिवृत्तिरुपपाद्यते ।

Page 163

(२) नीलकण्ठ शिवाचार्यनाम्ना भाष्यमचीकरत् ।
विशिष्टाद्वैतसिद्धान्तप्रतिपादनमुत्तमम् ।।
मयापि तस्य तात्पर्यं श्रोतॄणां सुखसिद्धये ।
कारिकारूपतः सर्वं क्रमेणैव निबध्यते ।।
वक्ष्यमाणरीत्या शक्तिविशिष्टं ब्रह्म जगत्कारणमिति ।

(३) नीलकण्ठ शिवाचार्यभाष्यार्थमनुसंदधन् ।
वीरशैवैरभिमतमभिधास्ये श्रुतेर्मतम् ।।

(५) विशब्देनोच्यते विद्या शिवजीवैक्यबोधिका ।
तस्यां रमन्ते ये शैवाः वीरशैवास्तु ते मताः ।।

Page 164

(१) विशब्दो वा विकल्पार्थः र शब्दो रहितार्थकः ।
विकल्परहितं शैवं वीरशैवं प्रचक्षते ।।

(२) इह तु केचित् निष्प्रपञ्च–निर्धर्मिक––निर्गुण–निरवयव–निर्भेदनित्ये ब्रह्मणि प्रपञ्चकारणत्वायोगात् स्वप्न–प्रपञ्चदृष्टान्तेन जाग्रत्स्वप्नसुषुप्तिमूर्च्छावस्थानां चतसृणामपि मिथ्यात्वं साधयन्ति ।

Page 165

(१) ब्रह्मणः व्यावहारिकदृश्यत्वानङ्गीकारे निरधिष्ठानभ्रमप्रसङ्गः ।

Page 166

(१) व्यावहारिकसत्यत्वं नाम कालान्तरानवस्थायिवस्तुत्वं सदसद्विलक्षणत्वं वा, सत्त्वासत्त्वाभ्यां निर्वक्तुमशक्यत्वं वा । नाद्यः यत्किञ्चित्-

कालान्तरानवस्थायिवस्तुत्वस्य घटपटादौ अस्माभिरङ्गीकारादंशतः सिद्धसाधनात् "गौरनाद्यन्तवती" इत्युक्तायाः प्रकृतेः सर्वकालान्तराव-स्थायितया अव्याप्तेश्च। कालान्तरावस्थायित्वावच्छिन्नसामान्याभाव-विवक्षायां द्वितीयक्षणस्यापि कालान्तरतया तदनवस्थायित्वसाधनेन वैभाषिकाङ्गीकृतं क्षणिकत्वमेव साधितं स्यात्, न तु स्वदेशकालनिष्ठा-त्यन्ताभावप्रतियोगित्वं मिथ्यात्वमिति स्वसिद्धान्तविरोधः, प्रातिभा-सिके अतिव्याप्तेश्च ।

(२) न द्वितीयः सदसदात्मकस्य प्रतियोगिनोऽप्रसिद्धया तद्विलक्षणस्या-प्रसिद्धेः।

(३) नाभाव उपलब्धेः........ज्ञातुरात्मनोऽर्थविशेषव्यवहारयोग्यतापादनरूपेण ज्ञानस्योलब्धेः। एवमेव हि सर्वे लोकाः प्रतीयन्ति "घटमहं जानामि" इत्येवंरूपेण सकर्मकेण सकर्तृकेण ज्ञातात्वर्थेन (?) सर्वलोकसाक्षिक-मपरोक्षमवभासमानेनैव। ज्ञानमात्रमेव परमार्थ इति साधयन्तः सर्वलोकोपहासोपकरणं भवन्तीति व्याचक्षते ।

Page 167

(१) "मिथ्यात्ववादिवाक्यानि मिथ्येति परिगीयते" इति न्यायेन तन्मते वेदवेदान्तानां मिथ्याभूतत्वाङ्गीकारात्, तन्मिथ्याभूतवेदवेदान्तप्रति-पाद्यब्रह्मणः सत्यत्वं कथमुपपद्यते। निर्विशेषे वेदवेदान्तानां प्रतिपाद्य-त्वायोगात्, ब्रह्मसत्त्वे तदतिरिक्तप्रमाणाभावाच्च। तस्मात्तच्छा-स्त्रोक्तजगज्जीवेश्वरादिप्रपञ्चवत् तन्निर्विशेषब्रह्मणः मिथ्यात्वं दुर्निवारम्।

(२) निर्विशेषाद्वैतशास्त्रे स्वप्नशुक्तिरजतादिदृष्टान्तत्वेन प्रपञ्चस्य मिथ्या-त्वाङ्गीकारे निर्विशेषब्रह्मणः भावः विद्यमानत्वं नास्ति। कुतः? अनुपलब्धेः।

(३) तत्पदवाच्यमीश्वरचैतन्यं मायाप्रतिबिम्बरूपमिति केचित्। तेषामयमा-शयः जीवपरमेश्वरसाधारणं चैतन्यमात्रं बिंबम्, तस्यैव बिंबस्याविद्यात्मि-कायां मायायां प्रतिबिंबमीश्वरचैतन्यम्।

Page 168

(१) अत्र केचित्। अस्मिन्नानन्दमये ब्रह्मणि जीवस्यास्य तद्योगं शेषत्व-संबन्धं शास्ति शास्त्रं प्रतिपादयति इति विशिष्टाद्वैतमेव मुख्यमिति जल्पन्ति। तदवैदिकत्वान्न मुमुक्षुभिर्ग्राह्यम्। वैदिकमीमांसाकर्तृ-भिर्भट्टभास्करादिपूर्वाचार्यैः स्वसिद्धान्तस्थापनावसरे पूर्वपक्षस्या-प्ययोग्यत्वेनोपेक्षितत्वात्। विशिष्टमद्वैतमिति उक्तिविरोधात। विशिष्टस्य दुर्निरूप्यत्वेन मिथ्यात्वाच्च।

Page 169

(१) विशिष्टं नाम विशेषणविशेष्यसंबन्ध एव वा तदतिरिक्तं वा। नाद्यः त्रयाणामनेकत्वेन अद्वयत्वासंभवात्, एते "दण्डपुरुषसंबन्धाः" इति समूहावलम्बनस्य दण्डीति विशिष्टप्रत्ययत्वप्रसङ्गात्, विशिष्टप्रत्ययस्य अनतिरिक्तविषयत्वात्। न द्वितीयः। विशेष्यरूपपरमात्मनोऽन्यत्वेन विशिष्टाभिमतपरमात्मनो विशिष्टाद्वैतासिद्धेः।

Page 170

(१) न तावज्जीवपरयोः समवायसंबन्धः, युतसिद्धत्वात्। नापि स्वरूपसंबन्धः, स्वरूपद्वयात्मकस्य स्वरूपसंबन्धस्य संबन्धिरूपत्वात्। संबन्धसंबन्धिनोरेकत्वानुपपत्तेः स्वरूपद्वयात्मकसंबन्धस्य स्ववृत्तित्वे आत्माश्रयप्रसङ्गात्, स्वरूपद्वयस्य स्ववृत्तित्वासम्भवात्, अन्यवृत्तित्वासंभवाच्च। तस्मान्न जीवपरयोः स्वरूपसंबन्धः। नापि संयोगसंबन्धः।

(२) अत्र शैवाग्रगण्य–श्रीकण्ठ–शिवाराध्यकृतब्रह्ममीमांसाभाष्ये विशिष्टाद्वैतं स्वाभिप्रेतत्वेन प्रसाधितम्। तत्र मुक्तात्मनां गौरीपतित्व सर्वान्तर्यामित्वादिधर्मनिराकरणपूर्वकं तत्साम्यञ्चोपनिषन्मयदिव्यमङ्गलविग्रहात्मकसर्वैश्वर्यविशिष्टकल्याणविभूतिभिर्बहुधा प्रपञ्चितम्। यथा "नद्यः स्यन्दमानाः समुद्रे" इत्यादिश्रुतिनिष्ठत्रिपाद्विभूत्यधिककैवल्यविभूत्यात्मकशिवसायुज्यलक्षणा मुक्तिर्विरुध्यते तस्मात्तदेव युक्तमिति प्राप्ते ब्रूमः।

(३) तत्प्रणीतकामिकादिवातुलान्ताद्यागमविरुद्धमन्वादिस्मृतिपुराणानां मानाभावात्।

(४) वेदागमोभयवेदान्तप्रतिपादितस्वाभाविकानन्तशक्तिविशिष्ट–जगदुभय–कारणपशुपाशनियामकसकलनिष्कलस्थूलसूक्ष्मचिदचित्प्रकाशकसत्यज्ञानानन्तकल्याणगुणविभवाश्रयत्वं ब्रह्मत्वम्।

(५) मलत्रयविध्वंसाभावान्न साधनचतुष्टयानन्तर्यम्।

(६) मलत्रयात्मकमायापाशदुःखनिवृत्तिपूर्वकपरमपुरुषार्थपरशिवतत्त्वप्राप्तिदर्शनात्प्रयोजनम्।

(७) इत्यादिवाक्यानां प्रात्यक्षिकवेदवेदान्तेषु दर्शनात् पतिपाशपशु–पदार्थत्रयप्रतिपादकशैवागमानां वैदिकत्वं घण्टाघोषः।

Page 171

(१) स पुनस्तं होवाच कानि षट्त्रिंशत्तत्त्वानि इति। स तस्मा आह शिव-शक्ति-सदाशिव-ईश्वर-विद्येत्येतानि शुद्धानि पञ्च तत्त्वानि। माया कालो नियतिः कला विद्या रागः पुरुष इति शुद्धाशुद्धानि सप्त। चत्वारि ततः, प्रकृतिः प्रकृतेर्गुणत्रयम्। गुणत्रयान्नामरूपक्रियारपदानि परस्परविभिन्नानि धरण्यादीनि विंशतितत्त्वानि।

Page 172

(१) ननु स्वाभाविकस्य निम्बकषायवन्निवृत्तित्वं सर्वदा न संभवति । तदङ्गीकारेऽपि जलोष्णवदागन्तुकस्यानित्यत्वमेव स्यात् तस्मान्मोक्षस्याप्यनित्यत्वमेव स्यादिति चेन्न। भ्रमरकीट-शुक्तिसलिलादिषु स्वाभाविकस्य सर्वदा निवृत्तिदर्शनात् भेदाभेदमतमेव वैदिकं सिद्धम् ।

(२) ननु "एक एव रुद्रो न द्वितीयाय तस्थे" इत्यादि श्रुतिशतेषु सर्वप्रपञ्चनिषेधपूर्वकाद्वैतव्यवस्थापनात् "द्वासुपर्णा" इत्यादिमन्त्रगत-जीवब्रह्मणोर्भेद औपचारिक एवेति चेन्न । अद्वितीयप्रतिपादकश्रुतीनां निर्गुणत्वप्रतिपादकश्रुतीनाञ्च सृष्टेः पूर्वं मूर्तामूर्तोभयप्रपञ्चाभावात् तत्कालपरत्वम्। भेदश्रुतीनां सर्वासां सृष्ट्युत्तरकालपरत्वम् । ननु महेश्वरे सृष्टेः पूर्वं जगत्कारणप्रकृतिसद्भावात् कथमद्वैतत्वमिति चेन्न । "देवात्मशक्तिं स्वगुणैर्निगूढाम्" परास्य शक्तिर्विविधैव श्रूयते स्वाभाविकी ज्ञानबलक्रिया च" इत्यादि श्रुतिशतेषु तच्छक्तेस्तदभिन्नत्वदर्शनात् ।

(३) ननु भेदाभेदयोः तमःप्रकाशवत्परस्परविरुद्धस्वभावत्वात् तयोरेकः पक्षः परमसिद्धान्तत्वेन निर्णेतव्य इति चेन्न । श्रुत्यैकदेशप्रामाण्ये मानाभावात् पक्षैकस्वीकारे परस्परश्रुत्यप्रामाण्यप्रसङ्गाच्च।

(४) पृथ्वीवाय्वोरनुष्णाशीतत्वं महेश्वरस्य अर्धनारीत्वं लक्षणायां जहदजहत्वं योगसांख्याद्वैतमतेषु साक्षिरूपस्य सगुणनिर्गुणात्मकत्वं मानुषे पुण्यपापोभयविशिष्टत्वं खद्योतस्य प्रकाशाप्रकाशत्वं च दर्शनात् ।

Page 173

(१) अद्वैतमते सगुणब्रह्मत्वमीश्वरत्वं च रज्जुसर्पवत् कल्पितम् इति सिद्धान्तेन भक्तिशास्त्राणां विधिनिषेधव्यवस्थापकवेदशास्त्रागमपुराणादीनां दत्ताञ्जलिप्रसङ्गात् पूर्वोक्तमतद्वयं न विधेयम् ।

Page 174

(१) जन्मादिसृष्टिस्थितिलयतिरोधानानुग्रहात्मकं कृत्यपञ्चकम् अस्य चिदचित्प्रपञ्चविलासस्य यतो यस्मात् स्वाभाविकानन्तशक्तिविशिष्टब्रह्मणः सम्भवति तद् ब्रह्मेति सूत्रार्थः ।

(२) ब्रह्मणः शिवस्यैव स्वशक्तिसंकोचेन निर्गुणत्वं शक्तिविकासेन सगुणत्वं प्रसाधितम् ।

(३) यथाकाशः सर्वगतत्वेपि सर्वकारणत्वसर्वशरीरत्वसर्वान्तर्यामित्वेन व्यवस्थितोपि सर्वदोषकलङ्कविलक्षण इति सूत्राभिप्रायः ।

(४) प्रलयावस्थायां प्रपञ्चस्य संकुचितत्वं सृष्टिकाले विकासवत्वञ्च स्पष्टमुपदिष्टम् । जगत्सत्यत्वं प्रसाध्य इदानीं कार्यकारणयोरनन्यत्वे निदर्शनं सूत्रद्वयेन दर्शयति ।

(५) एवं परमेश्वरस्य स्वभावजीवत्वनिवृत्तिपूर्वकस्वात्मप्राप्तिप्रदायकशक्तिमत्वं प्रसाध्य तस्यैव मूर्तामूर्तोभयात्मकत्वमधिकरणान्तरेण दर्शयति ।

(६) लोके जीवानां सुखदुःखभोगदर्शनात् परमेश्वरस्य वैषम्यनैर्घृण्यादिप्रसक्तिर्नोपपद्यते । कुतः । सापेक्षत्वात्, जीवकृतपुण्यपापसापेक्षत्वात् ।

Page 175

(१) अनादिस्वाभाविकमायापाशबद्धघोरापारनिःसारसंसारव्यापारतापत्रयानलदन्दह्यमाननानाशरीरप्रवेशनिर्गमनवर्णाश्रमाभिमानविशिष्टकामक्रोधाद्यनुस्यूतसुखदुःखाश्रयत्वं जीवत्वम् ।

(२) जीवपरमेश्वरयोर्वैशेष्यम् । तस्माद्विशेषातिशयद्योतनाज्जीवपरमात्मनोश्चित्त्वैकत्वेऽपि विभुत्वाणुत्वसर्वज्ञत्वकिञ्चिज्ज्ञत्वनित्यतृप्तत्वसंसारभोक्तृत्वादिपरस्परविरुद्धधर्मस्वभावत्वात् तयोः स्वाभाविकं भिन्नत्वं श्रुतिसिद्धम् ।

(३) श्रुतियुक्त्यनुभवतया जीवेश्वरयोः स्वभावचित्त्वावगमाच्च ।

(४) तस्माज्जडजातिलोहादौ ताम्रसुवर्णादिवत् चिज्जातौ जीवब्रह्मणोः स्वाभाविकभेदो निर्दिष्टः ।

(५) बहुश्रुतिषु परमशिवत्रिपाद्विभूत्यात्मकसालोक्यसामीप्यसारूप्यसिद्धकल्याणविभूतिः स्वभावजीवभावनिवृत्तिपूर्वकशिवत्वप्राप्तिरूपकैवल्यविभूतिश्च दर्शनात् । चतुर्विधमुक्तिप्रतिपादकं सर्वं शास्त्रं प्रामाण्यमेव ।

Page 176

(१) "एषोऽणुरात्मा, चेतसा वेदितव्यम्" इति श्रुतिनिर्दिष्टाणुत्वमेव जीवस्याङ्गी करणीयम् ।

(२) यथा चन्दनस्यैकप्रदेशस्थितस्य सकलशरीरशैत्यजनकत्वम् एवं क्षेत्रज्ञस्यैकस्मिन् प्रदेशे स्थितस्यापि सर्वाङ्गसुखदुःखभोक्तृत्वमुपपन्नम् ।

(३) यथा पृथिव्या गन्धस्य गुणत्वेनोपलभ्यमानस्य ततो व्यतिरेकः तथा जानामीति ज्ञातृगुणत्वेन प्रतीयमानस्य ज्ञानस्य आत्मनो व्यतिरेकः सिद्धः दर्शयति च श्रुतिः ।

(४) प्रकाशादिवज्जीवः परमात्मनोंऽशः, यथाग्न्यादित्यादेर्भास्वतो भारूपः प्रकाशोंऽशो भवति ।

(५) See textual authority page 170 (६)

(६) See textual authority page 175 (५)

(७) यथा नद्यः स्यन्दमानाः समुद्रे ग्रस्तं गच्छन्ति नामरूपे विहाय ।
तथा विद्वान्नामरूपाद्विमुक्तः परात्परं पुरुषमुपैति दिव्यम् ।।

Page 177

(१) शिवोपासकजीवन्मुक्तानां प्रचण्डातपमध्यनिक्षिप्तकर्पूरदीपवदन्तः करण-सद्भावेऽपि सर्वशिवात्मकज्ञानसद्भावात् ।

(२) तथा घटनाघटनसामर्थ्यस्य सर्वशक्तिविशिष्टस्य भक्तवात्सल्यस्य भक्ताभीष्टफलप्रदायकस्य सर्वविद्याश्रयस्य सत्यकामस्य सत्यसङ्कल्पस्य परब्रह्मणः शिवस्य स्वभक्तस्वाभाविकजीवत्वनिवृत्तिपूर्वकं पुनरावृत्ति रहितस्वस्वरूपप्राप्तिप्रदायकत्वशक्तित्वे किं वक्तव्यम् ।

(३) श्रुतिसिद्धवर्णपदमन्त्रकलाभुवनतत्त्वात्मकषडध्वप्रतिपादकत्वेन ।

(४) हिरण्मयस्य सदाशिवस्य प्रभाकरमुख्यशरीरत्वमधिकरणान्तरमारभते .... । अन्तः य एषोऽन्तरमादित्ये स एषोऽन्तरक्षिणीत्यादित्याक्षणो-रन्तः श्रूयमाणः पुरुषः साक्षात् परमशिव एव ।

Page 178

(१) विद्याविद्याविलक्षण निरतिशयनिरञ्जन निर्विकार निरवयवपरमाकाश-रूप परिपूर्णशिवतत्त्व साक्षात्कारानुभवेन प्रचण्डातपमध्यनिक्षिप्त निर्वात-निश्चलित कर्पूरदीपवत् स्थितिं व्यपोह्य शरीरेन्द्रियमनःप्राणादि वाह्या-भ्यन्तरवस्तुपरिज्ञानशून्यमनोविलयात्मकोन्मन्यवस्थाप्राप्तिष्षट्को ह्यैक्य-स्थलेऽभिधीयते ।

(२) सिद्धान्ताख्ये महातन्त्रे कामिकाद्ये शिवोदिते ।
निर्दिष्टमुत्तरे भागे वीरशैवमतं परम् ।।

(३) वीरशैवास्तुषड्भेदाः स्थलधर्मविभेदतः ।
भक्तादिव्यवहारेण प्रोच्यन्ते शास्त्रपारगैः ।।
शास्त्रन्तु वीरशैवानां षड्विधं स्थलभेदतः ।
धर्मभेदसमायोगादधिकारिविभेदतः ।।
आदौ भक्तस्थलं प्रोक्तं ततो माहेश्वरस्थलम ।
प्रसादिस्थलमन्यत्तु प्राणलिङ्गि स्थलं ततः ।।
शरणस्थलमाख्यातं षष्ठमैक्यस्थलं मतम् ।

page 181

(१) सर्वतत्त्वजनकः स्वयं तत्त्वातीतः इति ज्ञापनार्थमेतत्सूत्रं चकारेत्याह "तत्त्वातीतः" इति। सर्वानुग्रहविग्रहः साक्षी तत्त्वातीतो हल् स्यामिति ढक्कानिनादव्याजेन सर्वेषां मुनिजनानां तत्त्वमुपदिशन् तिरोदधे इत्यर्थः।

(२) अकारो ब्रह्मरूपः स्यान्निर्गुणः सर्ववस्तुषु।
चित्कलामि समाश्रित्य... ... ... ॥
अकारः सर्ववर्णाग्र्यः प्रकाशः परमेश्वरः।
अकारं सन्निधीकृत्य जगतां कारणत्वतः।
इकारः सर्ववर्णानां शक्तित्वात्कारणं मतम्॥
अकारो ज्ञप्तिमात्रं स्यादिकारश्चित्कला मता।

Page 182

(१) स्वेच्छया स्वस्य चिच्छक्तौ विश्वमुन्मीलयत्यसौ।

(२) See textual authority Page 181 , (२)

(३) Ditto.

(४) चितिः प्रत्यवमर्शात्मा परा वाक् स्वरसोदिता।
स्वातन्त्र्यमेतन्मुख्यं तदैश्वर्यं परमात्मनः॥

Page 183

(१) See textual authority page 181 , (२)

(२) वृत्तिवृत्तिमतोरत्र भेदलेशो न विद्यते।
चन्द्रचन्द्रिकयोर्यद्वद् यथा वागर्थयोरपि॥

(३) See textual authority page 181 , (२) (last line).

(४) "चितिशक्तिरपरिणामिनी" "····तद् दृशेः कैवल्यम्"

Page 184

(१) ऋलृवर्णयोर्मिथः सावर्ण्यं वाच्यम्।

(२) सगुणनिर्गुणयोरैक्ये बोधिते।

(३) जन्यजनकत्वञ्च स्वस्यैव तद्रूपेण वर्तमानत्वादिति नाद्वैतहानिः

(४) प्राणादिपञ्चकं चैव मनो बुद्धिरहंकृतिः।
बभूव कारणत्वेन ख फ छ ठ थ च ट त व्।
प्रकृतिं पुरुषञ्चैव सर्वेषामेव सम्मतम्।
सम्भूतमिति विज्ञेयं कपय् स्यादिति निश्चितम्॥

(A variant reading of the above)

प्रकृतिः पुरुषश्चैव सर्वेषामपि सम्मतौ ।
सम्भूताविति विज्ञेयं कपय् स्यादिति निश्चितम् ।।
सत्त्वं रजस्तम इति गुणानां त्रितयं पुरा ।
तत्त्वातीतः परः साक्षी सर्वानुग्रहविग्रहः ।

Page 186

(१) अपरे माहेश्वराः परमेश्वरतादात्म्यवादिनोऽपि पिण्डस्थैर्ये सर्वाभिमता जीवन्मुक्तिः ।

(२) प्राभृते वातुले ब्राह्मे वैष्णवैन्द्रे च शाङ्करे ।
बृहस्पतिमते शौक्रे यत् सारं तदिहोच्यते ।।

(३) प्रमाणत्रयेण सिद्धं नृपञ्चाननाङ्गं कथमसत्स्यादिति सदादीनि विशेषणानि गर्भश्रीकान्तमिश्रैर्विष्णुस्वामिचरणपरिणतान्तःकरणैः प्रतिपादितानि ।

Page 187

(१) नागार्जुनः सुरानन्दो नागबोधिर्यशोधनः ।
खण्डः कापालिको ब्रह्मा गोविन्दो लम्पको हरिः ।।
सप्तविंशतिसङ्ख्याका रससिद्धिप्रदायकाः ।

(२) हरितालादिसिद्धिश्च रसपारदसाधनम् ।
नानारससमुद्भूतं रसभस्मादिसाधनम् ।।

(३) सूचिता सर्वतन्त्रेषु या पुनर्न प्रकाशिता ।
जीवन्मुक्तिरियं नाथ कीदृशी वक्तुमर्हसि ।।

(४) सप्ताहमम्लिताः सर्वे आयुधेनापि अर्चिषट् ।
शुल्वं कुर्वन्ति वापेन पाण्डरं गन्धवर्जितम् ।
नागार्जुनमुनिः श्रीमान् दृष्टयोगमिदं परम् ।

(५) रसार्णवादिशास्त्राणि निरीक्ष्य कथितं मया ।
रसोपयोगि यत्किञ्चिद् दिङ्मात्रं तत् प्रकाशितम् ।।

Page 189

(१) दीर्घमायुः स्मृतिं मेधामारोग्यं तरुणं वयः ।
प्रभावर्णस्वरौदार्यं देहेन्द्रियबलं परम् ।
वाक्सिद्धिं प्रणतिं कान्तिं लभते ना रसायनात् ।।

(२) रसवीर्यविपाके च सूतकस्त्वमृतोपमः ।
तेन जन्मजराव्याधीन् हरते सूतकः प्रिये ।।

(३) घोषं वा घण्टलोहं वा सहस्रांशेन बेधयेत् ।
एवं बिद्धं भवेद्धेमं जाम्बूनदसमप्रभम् ।।

Page 190

(१) लोहैरुपरसैश्चापि रसैस्तद्वन्महारसैः ।
मूलिभिः शुष्कबीजैश्च लोहं रञ्येत नैकधा ।

(२) पीतरोहितवर्णा ये द्रुमाःकाञ्चनिकाः स्मृताः।
अन्ये च सितपुष्पाश्च द्रुमा रजतकारकाः ।।

(३) यत्र कूर्पासमुत्पन्नो भूमिभागश्च पीतकम् ।
कृष्णाश्च बालुकाः स्निग्धाः काञ्चनं तत्र जायते ।।
मत्स्यगन्धोग्रगन्धाश्च मृत्तिकाश्च गुरूणि च ।
कृष्णाश्च सितवर्णाभा रजतं तत्र जायते ।।

(४) देवैः संभाव्यतां याति विद्युज्ज्वलनसप्रभः ।
न च शस्त्रं क्रमेद् देहे नाग्निर्दहति न क्षुधा ।।

(५) तस्य मन्त्रं प्रवक्ष्यामि त्रिदशैरपि दुर्लभम् ।
प्रणवो भुवनेशी बीजं लक्ष्मीबीजं ततः परम् ।।

(६) रसदीक्षाविधानन्तु तस्मान्निगदितं श्रृणु ।

(७) रसलिङ्गं न्यसेत् तत्र हेम्ना च सहितं प्रिये ।

(८) यावन्न शक्तिपातस्तु न यावत् पाशकृन्तनम् ।
तावत्तस्य कुतो बुद्धिर्जायते मृतसूतके ।।

(९) आदौ परीक्षयेद् देवि साधकान् सुसमाहितान् ।
ब्राह्मणान् क्षत्रियान् वैश्यान् शूद्रांश्चानुक्रमेण तु ।।

(१०) गुरुसेवां विना कर्म यः कुर्यान्मूढचेतनः ।
स याति निष्फलं कर्म स्वप्नलब्धं धनं यथा ।
यः कर्म कुरुते दृष्टं तस्य लाभः पदे पदे ।

page 191

(१) वेदो ह्याथर्वणो दानस्वस्त्ययनबलिमङ्गलहोमनियमप्रायश्चित्तो-
पवासमन्त्रादिपरिग्रहात् चिकित्सां प्राह ।

(२) सर्वदा सर्वभावानां सामान्यं वृद्धिकारणम् ।
ह्रासहेतुर्विशेषश्च प्रवृत्तिरुभयस्य तु ।।
सामान्यमेकत्वकरं विशेषस्तु पृथक्त्वकृत् ।
तुल्यार्थता हि सामान्यं विशेषस्तु विपर्ययः ।।
खादीन्यात्मा मनः कालो दिशश्च द्रव्यसंग्रहः ।

सेन्द्रियं चेतनं द्रव्यं निरिन्द्रियमचेतनम् ॥
सार्था गुर्वादयो बुद्धिः प्रयत्नान्ताः परादयः।
गुणाः प्रोक्ता प्रयत्नादि कर्म चेष्टितमुच्यते ॥
समवायोऽपृथग्भावो भूम्यादीनां गुणैर्मतः ।
स नित्यो यत्र हि द्रव्यं न तत्रानियतो गुणः ॥
यत्राश्रिताः कर्मगुणाः कारणं समवायि यत् ।
तद् द्रव्यम्.......... ॥

(३) आप्तोपदेशः प्रत्यक्षम् अनुमानं युक्तिश्चेति ।

(४) प्रत्यक्षपूर्वं त्रिविधं त्रिकालं चानुमीयते ।
वह्निर्निगूढो धूमेन मैथुनं गर्भदर्शनात् ॥
एवं व्यवस्यन्त्यतीतं बीजात्फलमनागतम् ।
दृष्ट्वा बीजात्फलं जातमिहैव सदृशं बुधाः ॥

(५) पुनश्च धातुभेदेन चतुर्विंशतिकः स्मृतः ।
मनो दशेन्द्रियाण्यर्थाः प्रकृतिश्चाष्टधातुकी ॥

(६) खादयश्चेतनाषष्ठा धातवः पुरुषः स्मृतः ।
चेतनाधातुरप्येकः स्मृतः पुरुषसंज्ञकः ॥

(७) आत्मा ज्ञः करणैर्योगाज्ज्ञानं त्वस्य प्रवर्तते ।

(८) अव्यक्तमात्मा क्षेत्रज्ञः शाश्वतो विभुरव्ययः ॥

Page 192

(१) रजस्तमोभ्यां युक्तस्य संयोगोऽयमनन्तवान् ।
ताभ्यां निराकृताभ्यां तु सत्त्वबृद्ध्या निवर्तते ॥

(२) एतैरविमलं सत्त्वं शुद्ध्युपायैर्विशुद्ध्यति ।
मृज्यमान इवादर्शस्तैलचेलकचादिभिः ॥
ग्रहाम्बुदरजोधूमनीहारैरसमावृतम् ।
यथार्कमण्डलं भाति भाति सत्त्वं तथाऽमलम् ॥

(३) शुद्धसत्त्वस्य या शुद्धा सत्या बुद्धिः प्रवर्तते ।
यया भिनत्त्यतिबलं महामोहमयं तमः ॥
सर्वभावस्वभावज्ञो यया भवति निःस्पृहः ।

(४) याति ब्रह्म यया नित्यमजरं शान्तमव्ययम् ।

(५) See textual authority Page 191 (८)

(६) चतुः पले तु रुद्रत्वमीशः पञ्चपले भवेत् ।
षट्पले भक्षिते देवि सदाशिवतनुर्भवेत् ॥

(७) सद्योजातं तस्य जानु वामदेवन्तु गुह्यकम् ।
अघोरं हृदयन्तस्य वक्त्रं तत्पुरुषं स्मृतम् ।

निष्कलं निर्मलं नित्यं निस्तरङ्गं निरामयम् ॥
निष्प्रपञ्चं निराधारं निर्गुणं गुणगोचरम् ।

(८) गुञ्जामात्रन्तु देवेशि महाकल्पायुषो भवेत् ।
माषमात्रं वरारोहे मम तुल्यगुणो भवेत् ॥

Page 193

(१) सर्वज्ञः सर्वकर्त्ता च सूक्ष्मरूपो निरञ्जनः ।
इच्छया कुरुते सृष्टिमिच्छया संहरेज्जगत् ॥

(२) यस्मिन्सर्वं यतः सर्वं यः सर्वं सर्वतश्च यः ।
यश्च सर्वमयो नित्यं तस्मै सर्वात्मने नमः ॥

३. See textual authority page 186 (१)

४. See textual authority page 190 (८)

(५) तत्संयोगजनितस्य नित्यशरीरस्य प्राप्तौ न षाट्कौशिकस्य पूर्वशरीरस्य त्यागः। प्रत्युत हरगौरीसृष्टिजशरीरसंबन्धेन तत्र दिव्यत्वं दार्ढ्यं च संपाद्यते तेन तस्य मृत्युभयं नास्तीति सिद्धं भवति।

(६) अजरामरदेहस्य शिवतादात्म्यवेदनम् ।
जीवन्मुक्तिर्महादेवि देवानामपि दुर्लभा ॥

(७) यदि मुक्तिर्भगक्षोभे किन्न मुञ्चन्ति गर्दभाः ।
अजाश्च वृषभाश्चैव किन्न मुक्ता गणाम्बिके ॥
तस्मात्संरक्षयेत्पिण्डं रसैश्चैव रसायनैः ।
शुक्रमूत्रपुरीषाणां यदि मुक्तिर्निषेवणात् ।
किन्न मुक्ता महादेवि श्वानशूकरजातयः ॥

Page 194

(१) See textual authority page 192 H, (८)

(२) वज्रदेहः स सिद्धः स्यात् दिव्यस्त्रीजनवल्लभः ।
क्रीडते खेचरैर्भोगैः स्वेच्छया शिवतां व्रजेत् ॥

(३) एवं जीवेन्महाकल्पं प्रलयान्ते शिवं व्रजेत् ।

(४) तस्मिन्नेकार्णवे घोरे नष्टस्थावरजङ्गमे ।
देवा यत्र विलीयन्ते सिद्धस्तत्रैव लीयते ॥

(५) रुद्रतुल्यो महादेवि अजरामरकारिणि ।

INDEX

A

A, 181, 182, 183, 184.
Ābhāsa, 196, 201, 202.
Ābhāsavāda, 200, 206.
Abhāva, 129, 166.
Abhāvādhikaraṇa, 157, 166.
Abhidhāyaka, 92.
Abhidheyabuddhibīja, 89.
Abhinavagupta, 6, 16, 17, 18, 20, 21, 22, 23, 33, 43, 48, 51, 57, 83, 149, 158, 170, 178, 180, 183, 185, 195, 197.
Abhinavagupta (An Historical and Philosophical study) 195, 201.
Abhivyakta, 158.
Abhivyakti, 118.
Abhivyakti Pakṣa, 23.
Abhyudaya, 25.
Abodhasvabhāva, 127, 128.
Absolute, 163.
Absolute unity, 154, 158.
Abstract Monism, 205.
Ācārya, 30, 38.
Acit, 32, 46, 124, 126.
Acquinas, 75.
Acquisition, 126.
Action, 7, 48, 77, 78, 90, 101, 103, 104, 105, 109, 118, 121, 141, 145, 155, 159, 162, 171, 174, 175, 191, 198, 202, 203, 204, 205.
Activity, 97, 129, 146, 184.
Actor, 194.
Actualisation, 196.
Adharma, 127, 128, 133, 138.
Adhikārimala, 83, 90.
Adhyāsa, 164.
Ādinātha, (Śiva) 54.
Advaita, 6, 32, 35, 157, 161, 168.
Advaita Vedāntin, 167.
Advaitin, 167.
Ādya, 220, 222.
Aesthete, 158, 159.
Aesthetic, 57.
Aesthetic experience, 153, 158, 159, 160.
Aesthetic object, 158.
Aesthetician, 59.
Āgama, 7, 18, 27, 33, 45, 62, 63, 73, 130, 148, 178, 187.
Āgamādhikāra, 197, 206.
Āgama Viveka, 23.
Āgamic, 15, 41, 153.
Āgantuka, 171.
Agasti, 12.
Agastya, 39, 40, 170, 179.
Aghora, 6, 77, 114, 116, 123, 192.
Aghora Pantha, 193.
Aghora Śiva, 5, 16, 17, 18, 19, 21, 24, 63, 96, 98, 110.
Āgneya, 62.
Agni, 53, 59.
Aham, 181.
Ahaṅkāra, 68, 171.
Aikyasthala, 178.

Aindra, 186.
Aitihya, 129.
Aja, 146.
Ajita, 62, 63.
Ajitāgama, 8.
Ajñāna, 107.
Akala, 121.
Ākāra, 116.
Ākāśa, 10, 66, 78, 88, 96, 113, 116, 156, 168.
Akṣapāda, 12,13, 64.
Akṣarabindu, 94, 95, 96, 97, 98, 106.
Alaṅkāra, 23.
Alchemy, 189.
Alexandar, 55.
All-inclusive, 162, 201, 282.
All-pervasive, 43, 91, 92, 100, 125, 132, 139, 140, 162, 168, 171, 178.
All-transcending, 76, 79, 114, 117, 181.
Āmalaka, 55.
Amanas, 121.
Amaratva, 189.
Amoghā Vāk, 96.
Aṁśa, 156.
Aṁśumān, 62.
Anādi Avidyā, 164.
Anāhata, 96.
Anāhatavyoma, 96.
Analogy, 4, 35, 45, 77, 90, 109, 114, 156, 158, 183.
Ānanda, 7, 114.
Ānandagiri, 64.
Anandagirīya, 10, 13.
Ānanda Kanda, 54.
Ānanda Laharī, 36.
Ānanda Tīrtha, 117.
Ānanda Vardhana, 158.
Ananta, 86, 83, 88, 89, 99, 113.
Anātmaka, 145.
Āṇava, 48, 103.
Āṇavamala, 83, 106, 109, 157.
Anavasthā, 165.
Āndhra, 3, 27.
Anger, 133.
Aṇimādyaiśvarya, 118.
Anna, 144.
Annihilation, 153, 174.
Anslem, 75.
Antaḥ Karaṇa, 128, 129, 168, 176.
Antaḥ sañjalp, 93, 94.
Āntara Spandana 204.
Antithesis, 58, 59.
Anubhāva, 158.
Anugraha, 177, 195.
Anugraha Śakti, 82.
Anuvāka, 112, 116.
Apāna, 178.
Apara, 82, 85, 105, 109, 137.
Aparakuśika, 12.
Apara-mukti, 86.
Apavarga, 111.
Apitadbhāṣaṇa, 142.
Apitatkaraṇa, 142.
Apohana, 201.
Appayya Dīkṣita, 7, 8, 33, 36, 149, 150, 157.
Ārādhya, 43.
Architecture, 7.
Argumentum-ad-infinitum, 165.
Aristotle, 75, 86.
Art, 58, 95.
Artha, 119, 126.
Arthāpatti, 129.
Artistic conception, 59.
Āsāḍha, 29.

Āsana, 9, 125, 141.
Asat, 120.
Asatkāryavāda, 64, 66, 112, 117.
Asatkāryavādin, 124.
Āścaryasāra, 24.
Ascetic, 14.
Asceticism, 44, 141.
Ashoka, 3.
Ashokeśvara, 3.
Āśmarathya, 158.
Aspirant, 143.
Aspirate, 91.
Aṣṭādhyāyī, 159.
Aṣṭavarṇa, 38.
Astikāya, 64.
Aśuddha, 170.
Aśuddhādhva, 83.
Āśvamedhika Parva, 20.
Asvatantra, 125, 126, 155.
Atharvaśiras, 148.
Atharvaveda, 2, 55, 191.
Atheism, 204.
Atītāgama, 8.
Ātman, 66, 106, 132, 192, 197.
Ātmapratyakṣa, 129.
Ātma Samarpaṇa, 26.
Atom, 67, 149.
Atomic theory, 17.
Ātreya, 15.
Atri, 12.
Atrigupta, 23.
Attachment, 67, 121, 127, 138, 140.
Aṭṭahāsa, 142.
Attribute, 35, 47, 151, 168, 169.
Auḍulomi, 48.
Aulūkya Darśana, 13.
Avairāgya, 102.
Avantivarman, 21.
Avasthā, 138.
Averice, 133.
Aversion, 106, 146.
Āveśapakṣa, 23, 108.
Avidyā, 47.
Avīta, 129.
Avivekapravṛtti, 127.
Avyakta, 104, 138, 191.
Āyasa, 55.
Āyurveda, 189, 191.

B

Bādarāyaṇa, 9, 14, 32, 39, 40, 48, 56, 65, 163, 166, 173.
Bādari, 48
Baindava śarīra, 105
Bala, 138
Bālagovinda, 54
Balakrishana Shastri, 50
Balapramathana, 116
Balavikaraṇa, 116
Balehonnur, 38
Bāsa, 135
Basava, 4, 12, 37, 38, 39, 56
Base emotions, 133.
Basic emotions, 158
Basic mental state, 158
Basic view 35
Bauddha, 11, 21, 33, 40, 49, 102, 145, 166, 186, 197, 198, 199, 202, 204, 205.
Beginning, 120
Beginningless, 83, 120, 141.
Being, 84, 163, 165.
Berkeley, 200
Bhagavadgītā, 21

Bhagavad Govinda Pāda, 53, 54, 187, 188.
Bhairava, 6
Bhajasva, 120
Bhaktaprakāśa, 24
Bhaktasthala, 178
Bhakti, 161, 195
Bhāmatī, 10, 13
Bharata, 12
Bhartṛhari, 20, 71, 96, 97.
Bhāsa, 29, 30
Bhāsarvajña, 26, 91
Bhāskara, 54, 149
Bhāskarācārya, 32
Bhāskara Kaṇṭha, 17, 35.
Bhāskarī, 17, 33, 35, 195, 202
Bhāṣya, 33, 47
Bhaṭṭa Bhāskara, 47
Bhava, 153
Bhavodbhava, 9, 120
Bhedābheda, 48, 62, 76, 149, 150, 151, 152, 161, 171, 172, 173, 178.
Bhedābhedavāda, 32, 34, 48, 116, 119, 148.
Bhīmanātha, 47.
Bhoga, 67, 68.
Bhoga Kārikā, 16, 21, 25, 98.
Bhoga Malleśa, 41.
Bhoja, 7, 18, 24. 25, 63, 74.
Bhoktā, 104.
Bhṛṅgī, 176.
Bhṛṅgiriṭa, 39.
Bhūta, 59, 123.
Bhūtanātha, 59.
Bhūta Vijjā, 2.
Bhūtirāja, 22.
Bhuvana, 177.
Bijjala, 4, 37.
Bilhaṇa, 37.
Bindu, 8, 19, 73, 74, 75, 77, 78, 79, 80, 81, 82, 83, 85, 87, 88, 89, 90, 95, 99, 104, 105, 109, 192.
Black Yajurveda, 26
Blanket, 12
Bliss, 108, 159, 177.
Blissful, 153.
Blue, 35.
Blueness, 34
Bodhasvabhāva, 127, 128, 129
Bondage, 82, 106, 121, 141, 153, 155, 170, 174.
Bound, 76, 121.
Brahmā, 54, 77, 123, 180.
Brahmakāṇḍa, 71.
Brahmamīmāṁsā, 47.
Brahmamīmāṁsā Bhāṣya, 47, 148.
Brahman, 32, 34, 35, 40, 42, 69, 96, 106, 107, 108, 112, 113, 114, 115,120, 122, 123, 151, 152, 153, 159, 160, 162, 164, 165, 166, 167, 168, 171, 172, 173, 175, 176, 177, 181, 182, 183, 184.
Brāhmaṇa, 45, 190.
Brāhmaṇa Gītā, 20.
Brāhmaṇa Vaiṣṇava, 47.
Brāhmaṇic literature, 55.
Brahmanism, 27, 58, 148, 157.
Brahmarākṣasa, 71.
Brahma-randhra, 177.
Brahmarśi, 49.
Brahmasūtra, 32, 47, 63, 163, 173.
Brahmatattvam, 49.
Brahma Vidyā, 27.
Bṛddhajāvālopaniṣad, 170.
Breath-control, 141, 142.
Bṛhadācārya, 12.
Bṛhadvṛtti, 30.
Bṛhajjāvāla, 147.
Bṛhaspati, 16, 21.

Bṛhaspatimata, 186.
Bṛhati, 10.
Bṛhaṭṭīkā, 20.
British period, 61.
Buddha, 2, 196.
Buddhādvaita, 164.
Buddhaghoṣa, 2.
Buddhi, 67, 68, 69, 78, 84, 89, 90, 92, 93, 94, 100, 101, 102, 105, 113, 125, 171.
Buddhism, 3, 5, 42, 51, 54, 58, 64, 196, 198, 200.
Buddhist, 52.
Buffoon, 58.
Buhler, 30.
Bulb, 12.
Bull, 3, 142.

C

Caesar, 85.
Caitanya, 103.
Cakra, 48, 187.
Cāmuṇḍā, 53.
Caṇḍiśvara, 39.
Candrācārya, 71.
Candrāṁśu, 62.
Candrasena, 54.
Caraka, 55, 189, 191.
Caraka Saṁhitā, 191.
Caraṇāmṛtakuṇḍa, 1.
Cārumati, 3.
Cārvāka, 21, 58, 67.
Caryā, 7, 135, 137, 143.
Caste, 34, 148.
Caste system, 190.
Category, 8, 11, 13, 14, 16, 48, 51, 61, 65, 72, 87, 90, 98, 104, 110, 111, 115, 119, 120, 160, 161, 170, 171, 173, 175, 181, 182, 185.
Causal, 174, 197.
Causal efficiency, 107, 204.
Causal law, 113, 119.
Causal state, 163.
Cause, 10, 34, 74, 113, 120, 122, 124, 125, 126, 182, 206.
Causeless cause, 122.
Cave, 137, 143.
Celebacy, 141.
Certainty, 43.
Cetana, 132, 191.
Chalukya, 4, 30, 37.
Chalukya dynasty, 37.
Chandragupta, 28.
Characteristic, 9, 13, 39, 106, 107.
Cheda, 138.
Chemical, 52.
Chemistry, 53, 188, 189.
Chola, 56.
Chola kings, 4.
Cidghana, 77.
Cintya, 62.
Cit, 7, 32, 46, 67, 76, 119, 124, 126, 162.
Citi, 79, 182, 183, 184.
Citkalā, 182, 183, 184.
Citkalāmaya, 178.
Cit-śakti, 182.
Citta, 128, 129, 146.
Cognition, 196, 197, 199.
Cognitive activity, 68, 127, 154.
Cola, 24.
Concentration 140, 141, 143.
Conception, 11, 13, 23.
Conclusion, 39, 195.

Concrete Monism, 205.
Configuration, 191.
Consciousness, 32, 68, 79, 80, 84, 91, 92, 93, 94, 129, 139, 176, 201.
Contact, 109.
Contemplation, 26, 27, 107, 113, 115, 117, 120, 142, 153.
Contemplator, 107, 115.
Contradiction, 32, 116.
Controller, 117.
Copper, 55, 83, 149, 157, 175, 189.
Cosmological, 75, 118.
Created, 184.
Creation, 11, 14, 77, 78, 84, 85, 110, 112, 116, 118, 121, 122, 140, 153, 172, 174.
Creative activity, 9, 80, 105, 118, 155.
Creative power, 82, 106.
Creator, 78, 106, 118, 184, 196.
Cremation ground, 137, 143.
Croce, 59.
Cronstedt, 55.
Culture, 188.
Cyuti, 133.

D

Dakṣiṇāmūrti stotra, 8.
Damaru, 47, 49
Dāna, 137.
Dance, 141.
Daṇḍin, 169.
Dantidurga, 4.
Dāruka, 38.
Dāsatva, 117.
Dāsya, 195.
Dasyavaḥ, 100.
Dedication, 120.
Deep sleep, 44, 164.
Dehapramātā, 132.
Dehasiddhi, 53.
Deindividualisation, 159.
Demerit, 109, 121, 129, 132, 133, 167.
Dependent, 73, 125, 156.
Dependent category, 99, 100, 104.
Deśa, 137.
Descartes, 75.
Desire, 137.
Detachment, 141, 145.
Determinacy, 80, 88, 128.
Determinate, 113, 129, 197, 200.
Determinate knowledge, 79, 89, 106, 128.
Determinative Judgment, 93.
Deva, 16.
Devabala, 16, 18.
Devakula, 30.
Devanityatā, 143.
Devotee, 15.
Devotion, 43, 138, 161, 172, 176, 190, 195.
Ḍhakvā. 4, 195.
Dhāraṇā, 135, 137, 141, 143.
Dhāraṇāpūrvaka, 137.
Dharma, 9, 125, 126, 127, 128, 135.
Dhātu, 191.
Dhyāna, 137, 141, 143.
Dīkṣā, 139.
Dīkṣākāri, 138.
Dīpikā, 25.
Dīpta, 42.
Dissolution, 81, 121, 140, 153.
Diversity, 7, 72.
Divine perfection, 111.

Doer, 69.
Doṣa, 146.
Doubt, 127, 164.
Drākṣārāma Kṣetra, 38.
Draviḍa, 27.
Dravya, 16, 138.
Dream, 164, 166, 167, 201, 202.
Drśi, 183.
Drṣṭa, 129.
Drṣṭa pūrvavat, 130.
Dualism, 6, 15, 23, 43, 44, 57, 62, 65, 88, 99, 151, 161, 162, 163, 172, 173, 197, 205.
Dualism-cum-monism, 7, 116, 162, 163.
Dualism-cum-non-dualism, 6, 32, 44, 180.
Dualist, 17, 22, 107, 170, 200.
Dualist Śaiva, 100, 104, 106, 133.
Dualistic, 7, 9, 16, 40, 61, 63, 65, 99, 111, 158, 192, 194, 197.
Dualistic-cum-non-dualistic, 6, 26.
Dualistic Pāśupata, 14, 40, 42, 61, 64.
Dualistic Śaivāgama, 14, 15, 62, 63.
Dualistic Śaivaism, 16, 19, 56, 63, 192.
Dualist Siddhānta Śaiva, 78.
Dualistic Siddhānta Śaivaism, 66, 149, 150.
Duality, 44, 98, 107, 194.
Duality-cum-non-duality, 150.
Duḥkhānta, 9, 10, 65, 70, 74, 111, 117, 120, 145.
Duṇḍukāra, 142.
Dūradarśana, 139.
Durvāsā, 42, 47, 48.
Durvāsīya, 47.
Dvaita, 6, 11, 62.
Dvaitādvaita, 6, 9, 11, 28, 34, 44, 48, 62, 162, 191.

E

Earth, 59, 65, 66, 104, 105.
Eastern face, 117
Ecstacy, 181.
Effect, 10, 34, 111, 113, 117, 120, 123, 124, 125, 126, 128, 130, 132, 134, 206.
Efficient, 65, 69, 70, 74, 99, 112.
Efficient cause, 65, 75, 79, 125, 154, 171.
Ekanetra, 83.
Ekarudra, 83.
Ekorāma, 38, 39, 42, 43, 44.
Ellora, 4.
Emanation, 87, 201.
Emancipation, 7, 10, 11, 42, 62, 112, 115.
Emergence, 105.
Emotion, 159.
Empirical, 57, 72, 133, 143.
Empirical knowledge, 89, 128.
Empirical level, 84, 89.
Empirical multiplicity, 151, 152.
Empirical world, 65, 86, 87, 100.
Empiricism, 196, 202, 205.
Encyclopaedic, 57.
End, 108, 120.
Enjoyer, 69.
Enjoyment, 106, 109.
Enmity, 133, 140.
Epigraphical, 26, 28.
Epistemic, 186, 204.
Epistemology, 7.

Equilibrium, 98.
Essence, 36, 116,
Essential identity, 52.
Essential nature, 9, 10, 25, 101, 118, 121, 183.
Eternal, 66, 78 ,91, 100, 104, 111, 120.
Eternal being, 67.
Eternal cause, 120.
Eternal substance, 100.
Eternal world, 92.
Eternalism, 196.
Eternality, 89, 120, 172.
Ether, 10, 156.
Ethical, 204.
Ethics, 7, 126, 128, 204.
Evolute, 99.
Evolution, 11, 58, 80, 87, 100, 124, 134, 154, 171, 174.
Evolutionistic, 78.
Example, 195.
Existence, 34, 106, 156.
Exorcism, 2.
Experiencer, 198.
Expression, 96.
External, 69, 81, 106, 141, 196.
External body, 109.
External means, 102.
External senses, 132, 146.

F

Faith, 37.
Final emancipation, 45, 137, 186, 194.
First category, 100.
Five faced, 120.
Formal limitation, 152.
Fourteen Sūtras, 49.
Free, 126, 174, 195, 201, 205.
Freedom, 18, 102, 107, 109, 118, 134, 138, 190, 196, 201, 202, 205.
Free Will, 124, 182.
Fruition, 118, 191
Function, 98
Fundamental doctrine, 35.

G

Gaṇa Kārikā, 24, 111, 112, 127, 128, 135, 137.
Gāṇapatya, 47.
Gaṅgā, 54
Gangaikonda Cholapuram, 4.
Garbhaśrīkānta Miśra, 186.
Garga, 29.
Gārgya, 12, 30.
Gauḍa, 3.
Gauḥ, 91.
Gautama, 11, 60, 91, 145, 197.
Ghaṇṭānātha, 47.
Ghaṭākāśa, 145.
Ghora, 114, 123.
Ghoratara, 114, 123.
Ghṛtakīṭanyāya, 66.
Gītā, 50.
Goal, 7.
Goal of humanity, 123, 126.
God, 2, 5, 12, 15, 47, 64, 75, 108, 165, 166, 167, 168, 197, 198, 202, 205.
Gold, 53, 55, 175, 186, 189.
Gomukha, 54.
Gourd, 12.
Govinda, 54.

Govindarāja, 45.
Grace, 77, 78, 80, 82, 84, 98, 109, 120, 121, 122, 137, 140, 145, 153, 157, 158, 174, 177, 181, 190, 193.
Graceful, 75.
Graha, 23, 108, 109.
Grammar, 49, 50, 71.
Grammarian, 91, 184.
Great Lord, 117.
Gross body, 103.
Gross elements, 103.
Gross expression, 97.
Gross Nāda, 99.
Gross word, 93.
Grossification, 97, 153.
Guhā, 115.
Guṇa, 9, 81, 103, 104, 125, 149, 171, 181, 184.
Guṇa Ratna, 13.
Guṇa Ratna Sūri, 10, 13. 30.
Guṇa Tattva, 104.
Gupta era, 28.
Gupta years, 28.
Guru, 32.

H

Hand-drum, 49.
Harappa, 1.
Hari, 54.
Haribhadra, 10, 11, 12, 13, 14.
Haribhadra Sūri, 5, 61, 64.
Harṣa, 3, 188.
Heart, 113.
Hegelian, 58, 205.
Helārāja, 20, 22.
Herb, 189.
Highest Lord, 52, 192.
Highest Self, 169.
Highest Subject, 196.
Himālaya, 38.
Himavat Kedara, 38.
Hindu Chemistry, 189.
Hiraṇyagarbha, 117.
Historical evidence, 28.
Historical reality, 39.
History of Philosophy, 61, 195.
Hitler, 85.
Hiuen Tsang, 54.
Hume, 196, 197, 198.
Huvishka, 3.

I

I 182.
I-consciousness, 118.
Icchā, 7, 77, 88, 98.
Icchāśakti, 98.
Idea, 119, 196, 197.
Idealism, 119, 200.
Idealistic, 201, 204.
Idealistic Monism, 200.
Idealistic voluntarism, 124.
Identification, 84, 49, 187.
Identity, 39, 114, 116, 151, 154, 157, 173, 184, 186, 193, 194, 201, 203.
Identity in difference, 159.
Ignorance, 106, 107, 138, 164, 176, 177, 178, 192, 196.
Illuminative, 128.
Illusion, 15, 47, 115, 150, 152, 135, 167, 168, 174, 182, 201, 205.
Illusory, 48, 107, 164, 166.

Image, 3, 7, 29, 31, 46, 96.
Imaginary, 97, 106.
Immanent, 181, 184, 201.
Immortality, 53, 54, 55, 189.
Implication, 152.
Impure, 72, 87, 100, 110.
Impure creation, 80, 89, 102.
Impure world, 88.
Impurity, 48, 67, 79, 82, 83, 84, 85, 101, 103, 105, 106, 109, 110, 126, 133, 135, 138, 149, 155, 157, 160, 174, 175, 176, 192, 193.
Inaction, 121.
Incarnation, 12, 29.
Independent, 117, 118, 125, 156.
Independent categories, 77.
Indeterminacy, 79, 90, 106, 178.
Indeterminate, 76, 113, 129, 197.
Indeterminate object, 94.
Indian Philosophy, 5, 10, 66, 70.
Individual, 32, 45, 82, 95, 105, 119, 121, 141, 150, 155, 156, 157, 159, 160, 162, 163, 165, 166, 174, 178, 185, 186, 194, 197, 200, 201, 202, 203, 204, 206.
Individual self, 100, 121, 140, 153, 156.
Individual soul. 69, 84, 100, 167, 168, 175.
Individual subject, 89, 101, 127, 129, 133, 167.
Individuality, 86, 115, 145, 157.
Indo-Grecian dynasties, 55.
Indra, 50, 142.
Indrada, 54.
Indriya, 121.
Indriyajaya, 138.
Indriya pratyakṣa, 129.
Indus Valley, 1.
Inference, 91, 92, 109, 118, 129, 130, 167, 191, 204.
Infinite regress, 102.
Inherence, 89, 151, 169, 191.
Inner sense, 168.
Inner speech, 94.
Inscription, 28, 30, 44.
Insentiency, 88, 162.
Insentient, 69, 88, 90, 91, 98, 104, 108, 113, 124, 126, 130, 132, 152, 162, 164, 173.
Instrumental cause, 11, 13, 34, 75.
Instrumentality, 102.
Intellect, 133.
Intercalary month, 28, 29.
Internal means, 102.
Internal senses, 132, 176.
Internal Stir, 204.
Introduction, 195.
Iron, 53, 55, 175, 185, 188, 189.
Irrational, 205.
Īśa, 77, 192.
Īśāna, 12, 116, 117, 192.
Īśānadevi, 3.
Isolation, 34, 134.
Īśvara, 11, 14, 22, 32, 46, 47, 74, 75, 82, 83, 85, 86, 87, 89, 99, 104, 107, 112, 113, 117, 119, 123, 132, 140, 141, 165, 170, 182, 184, 185.
Īśvara Pratyabhijñā, 195, 197, 202, 206.
Īśvara Pratyabhijñā Kārikā, 33, 149.
Īśvara Pratyabhijñā Vimarśinī, 17, 195, 200, 201, 204, 205.
Īśvara Tattva, 99.
Īśvara Vimarśini, 50

J

Jaḍa, 130.
Jagatāmpati, 60.
Jaiminīya, 11.
Jain, 11, 21, 37, 40, 47, 102.
Jainism, 42, 47, 51, 58, 64.
Jalauka, 3.
Japa-Dhyāna, 135, 137.
Japapūrvaka, 137.
Jaṭādhārī Śaiva mata, 13.
Jayaratha, 16, 17.
Jīva, 32, 100, 109, 114, 115, 162, 168, 171, 172, 175.
Jīvanmukti, 52, 193, 194.
Jña, 191.
Jñāna, 7, 67, 68, 77, 98, 107, 126, 139, 156, 166, 172, 176, 196, 199, 200, 201.
Jñānādhikāra, 202.
Jñāna Śakti, 77, 121.
Jñānasvarūpa, 67.
Jñāpaka, 92.
Jñapti, 183.
Jñaptimātra, 183.
Jñātā, 155, 198.
Judgement, 94.
Jyeṣṭha, 114, 116.
Jyotirliṅga, 5.

K

Kadphises, 3.
Kailāśa, 4.
Kaivalya, 106, 134, 140, 143.
Kaivalyagata, 134.
Kaivalya Prakāśa, 157.
Kaiyaṭa, 50, 71.
Kākatīya, 44.
Kakṣāpuṭa, 54.
Kalā, 9, 14, 65, 66, 73, 90, 100, 103, 104, 111, 117, 119, 120, 121, 122, 123, 125, 126, 130, 132, 170, 177, 185.
Kāla, 73, 100, 103, 104, 116, 138, 170, 185.
Kālāgni, 148.
Kālamukha, 13, 14.
Kalavikaraṇa, 116.
Kālidāsa, 4.
Kallaṭa, 180, 188.
Kālottara Āgama, 25.
Kalpa, 2.
Kalpavṛkṣa, 40.
Kaluṣa, 133.
Kalyāṇa Nagarī, 24.
Kalyāṇa vibhūti, 178.
Kāma, 126.
Kāmaja, 62.
Kambali, 54.
Kāmika, 39, 99, 110, 178.
Kaṇāda, 11, 13, 44, 64, 197.
Kanishka, 3, 16, 55.
Kant, 196, 197.
Kantian terminology 75.
Kaṇṭha, 57.
Knave, 58.
Kānyakubja, 21, 22, 23, 24.
Kapāli, 54.
Kāpālika, 63, 47, 54.
Kapila, 29.
Kapilācārya, 31.
Kapilāṇḍa, 12.
Kapileśvara, 29.
Karaṇa, 121.

Kāraṇa, 8, 9, 62, 63, 64, 65, 70, 74, 111, 118, 119, 120, 124, 126.
Kāraṇapadārtha, 26.
Karma, 66, 69, 73, 74, 75, 80, 82, 83, 84, 85, 86, 99, 100, 101, 103, 105, 106, 109, 110, 113, 116, 117, 118, 140, 156, 170, 172, 174, 175, 176, 196.
Kārma, 48, 149.
Karmakāṇḍa, 27.
Karma mala, 103.
Karṇāṭaka, 27.
Kartā, 75, 156, 198, 202, 204.
Kārtikarāśi, 30.
Kāruṇika, 13.
Kārvān, 29, 31.
Kārya, 9, 10, 14, 64, 65, 70, 74, 111, 118, 119, 120, 123, 124, 125, 126, 132.
Kāśakṛtsna, 48.
Kashmir Śaiva, 8, 81, 188.
Kāśī, 38.
Kauṇḍinya, 9, 119, 120.
Kauruṣa, 12.
Kauruśya, 29.
Kauśika, 12, 29, 30.
Kāyārohaṇa, 29.
Kāyāvatāra, 29.
K. B. Pathak, 28.
Khaṇḍa, 54.
Kheṭakanandana, 16, 21.
Kheṭapāla, 16.
Khila, 27.
Kiraṇa, 25, 62, 63.
Kīrtivarman, 2, 4.
Knowledge, 7, 77, 78, 101, 102, 104, 105, 107, 108, 111, 117, 121, 126, 145, 151, 153, 155, 157, 159, 163, 164, 165, 166, 167, 177, 176, 178, 191, 192, 194, 197, 199, 200, 201, 202, 204, 205, 206.
Knower, 197, 198.
Kośa, 114, 115.
Kramamukti, 176, 194.
Krāthana, 142.
Krishna, 4.
Kriyā, 7, 77, 121, 204.
Kriyādhikāra, 205.
Kriyālakṣaṇa, 141, 142.
Kriyā Sāra, 163, 164.
Kriyā Śakti, 77, 98, 204, 205, 206.
Kṛṣṇa Āyasa, 55.
Kṛṣṇa Yajurveda, 2, 5.
Kṣaṇa, 203.
Kṣatriya, 45, 46.
Kṣemarāja, 18, 180, 183.
Kṣetrajña, 102, 132.
Kulārṇava Tantra, 45, 55.
Kumāradeva, 24.
Kumbhodbhava, 39, 45.
Kuṇḍalinī, 88, 96.
Kuṇḍina Kula, 24.
Kuśa, 128.
Kuśika, 30.

L

L, 185.
Lābha, 126, 139.
Laghvī, 10.
Lakṣmaṇa, 22.
Lakulī, 29, 30, 31.
Lakulīśa 9, 11, 27, 30, 31, 34, 60, 113, 117, 119, 143, 145, 180.
Lakulīśa Kṣetra, 30.

Lukulīśa Pāśupata, 5, 6, 9, 10, 14, 16, 22, 23, 26, 29, 40, 56, 60, 61, 62, 65, 108, 111, 112, 113, 115, 116, 117, 118, 119, 120, 124, 125, 126, 127, 128, 129, 133, 134, 139, 140, 141, 145, 149, 150, 152, 158.
Lakulīśa Pāśupata system, 28, 143, 150.
Lalita, 62.
Lalitāditya, 21, 22.
Lalitavistara, 64.
Lampaka, 54.
Laṅkeśa, 54.
Lāṭa, 24.
Latent, 158.
Leibniz, 75, 95.
Liberation, 23, 26, 76, 80, 82, 85, 101, 105, 106, 108, 109, 111, 112, 115, 120, 134, 145, 149, 150, 153, 157, 158, 159, 161, 163, 168, 170, 172, 177, 192, 193, 194.
Light, 129.
Limitation, 104.
Limited subject, 108.
Limiting condition, 107.
Liṅga, 9, 12, 29, 31, 37, 38, 39, 179.
Liṅgadhāraṇa Chandrikā, 38.
Liṅga Purāṇa, 28, 29.
Liṅgāyat, 38, 163.
Liṅgāyat School, 4.
Logical evolution, 60.
Lohasiddhi, 53.
Lokāyatika, 40, 58.
Lord, 48, 64, 65, 69, 75, 78, 80, 84, 85, 87, 89, 100, 105, 107, 108, 109, 111, 112, 114, 118, 119, 120, 122, 123, 124, 125, 126, 127, 130, 132, 134, 139, 140, 141, 142, 143, 146, 149, 150, 152, 154, 156, 161, 171, 174, 177, 182, 183, 186, 199, 204, 205.
Lordship, 10.
Luminosity, 199.

M

Madgīta, 62.
Mādhava, 10, 14, 26, 34, 52, 54, 60, 61, 111, 127, 128, 186, 187.
Madhva, 43, 44, 45, 47.
Madhyamā, 71, 96, 97, 98, 110.
Magaḍavya, 54.
Mahābhārata, 20.
Mahābhāṣya, 49, 50.
Mahādeva, 116, 117, 122, 153.
Mahākāla, 5.
Mahāmantratattva Prakāśikā, 50.
Mahāmāyā, 72, 73, 81, 85, 86, 87, 95, 96, 97, 98, 100.
Mahān, 13, 14, 65, 123, 124.
Mahānārāyaṇopaniṣad, 39.
Mahāpralaya, 77, 81.
Mahat, 125.
Mahāvrata, 13.
Mahāvratadhara, 13, 14.
Maheśvara, 9, 13, 29, 52, 139, 140, 143, 146, 192, 196.
Māheśvara, 52.
Māheśvaram Yogaśāstram 59.
Māheśvarasthala, 178.
Māheśvara Sūtra, 181.
Maheśvaratattvāvirbhāva, 177.
Mahimā, 115.
Mahimna Stotra, 153.
Maintenance, 77, 122, 153.
Maitra, 146.
Maitrya, 12.

Mala, 16, 73, 74, 82, 83, 84, 85, 99, 101, 103, 105, 107, 110, 133, 156, 157, 170, 175, 176.
Mālava, 55.
Mallikārjuna 38.
Maṁjūṣā, 96.
Manana, 40.
Manas, 102, 114, 121, 123, 145, 155, 171, 178.
Mānasollāsa, 8.
Mandana, 142.
Maṇi Bhadra Sūri, 10.
Manifestation, 91, 101, 121, 184, 196, 201, 205.
Manonmana, 116.
Manovṛtti, 182.
Mantra, 5, 27, 72, 73, 83, 86, 112, 116, 117, 177.
Mantra Maheśa, 72, 73, 82, 86.
Mantra Maheśvara, 105.
Mantra Viveka Ṭīkā, 23.
Mantreśa, 72, 73, 82, 83, 86.
Mānuṣyaka, 12.
Marula, 39, 41, 42, 44, 48, 50.
Marut, 59.
Mataṅga, 8, 22, 25.
Material cause, 9, 17, 35, 65, 77, 79, 99, 100, 108, 113, 125, 154, 171, 173.
Materialist, 102.
Maṭha, 38.
Mathurā, 31.
Mathurā Pillar, 28, 30.
Matta, 54.
Matted hair, 12, 14.
Matter, 32, 119, 126, 163, 197, 204, 205.
Māyā, 8, 17, 28, 66, 72, 73, 74, 76, 79, 80, 81, 84, 85, 86, 88, 89, 90, 95, 99, 100, 103, 104, 105, 106, 109, 110, 113, 155, 156, 164, 168, 170, 175, 176, 182, 183, 185.
Māyāviśiṣṭa, 28, 113.
Māyin, 113.
Māyīya, 48, 83, 149.
Māyīyamala, 84.
Meaning, 4, 91, 92, 96, 97.
Means, 108, 126, 134, 166, 172, 201, 202.
Means of knowledge, 126, 134.
Meat, 143.
Medical system, 188.
Medicine, 52.
Meditation, 137.
Meghadūta, 5.
Memorial, 30, 31.
Memory, 92, 128, 199.
Mercy, 155.
Mercurial, 188.
Mercurial body, 194.
Mercurial science, 186, 187, 191.
Mercury, 52, 53, 55, 186, 187, 188, 189, 190, 193.
Mercury-well, 53.
Merit, 109, 121, 129, 132, 135, 138, 142, 167.
Metal, 46, 189, 190.
Metallography, 188.
Metallurgy, 188.
Metaphysical categories, 11, 84.
Metaphysical concept, 119.
Metaphysical Reality, 181.
Metaphysical theory, 11, 35, 66, 70.
Metaphysics, 7, 57, 78, 201.
Meykaṇḍadeva 110.
Mica, 52, 193.
Microcosm, 95.

Mīmāṁsā, 21, 42, 112.
Mīmāṁsaka, 67.
Mimetic changes, 158.
Mind, 119, 127, 145, 146, 163, 181, 182, 183, 197, 200, 201, 202, 203, 204, 205, 206.
Mine, 190.
Mineralogy, 188.
Miseries, 111, 112, 145.
Misra, 53.
Miśra, 37.
Misraka, 53.
Mithyā, 166, 171.
Mithyādvaita, 40, 51.
Mithyājñāna, 126, 133.
Modification 68.
Moha, 106.
Mohenjo-daro, 1.
Mokṣa, 10, 11, 13, 14, 16, 25, 70, 105, 106, 107, 108, 114, 117, 120, 126, 149, 170.
Mokṣa Kārikā, 15, 16, 23.
Momentariness, 204.
Momentary, 80, 91, 102, 197.
Momentary being, 197, 203.
Monad, 95.
Monarchy, 80.
Monism, 6, 15, 23, 42, 48, 51, 99, 107, 108, 124, 151, 162, 163, 164, 172, 173, 180, 205.
Monism-*cum*-dualism, 119, 124, 148, 151.
Monist, 22, 86.
Monistic, 6, 7, 8, 20, 24, 35, 36, 48, 49, 96, 165, 184, 197.
Monistic-*cum*-dualistic, 28, 150.
Monistic Idealism, 107.
Monistic Kashmir Śaivaism, 51.
Monistic Śaiva, 33, 35, 43, 51, 180.
Monistic Śaivaism, 6, 57, 149.
Monistic system, 49, 62, 184.
Monistic tendency, 36.
Monistic Vedānta, 115.
Monistic Voluntarism, 18.
Mother of pearl, 107, 150.
Mṛcchakaṭika, 188.
Mṛgendra, 2, 8, 19, 21, 25, 63.
Mṛgendra Vṛtti, 20, 25.
Mukhabimba, 62.
Mukta, 75, 108, 115.
Muktākaṇa, 21.
Muktāpīḍa, 22.
Mukti, 22, 85.
Mūlavigraha, 46.
Multiplicity, 7, 32, 34, 35, 123, 151, 152, 161, 162, 164, 166, 170, 171, 172, 203, 204, 205.
Music, 95.
Mystic, 159, 160, 166, 167, 181, 201, 203.
Mysticism, 85, 86, 175, 181.

N

Nāda, 8, 89, 90, 93, 94, 95, 96, 97, 98, 99.
Nāda-Brahma-Vāda, 95.
Nāda Kārikā, 17, 19, 23, 25, 51, 72.
Nāḍi, 178.
Nāga, 53.
Nāgabodhi, 54.
Nāgārjuna, 52, 54, 139, 186, 187, 188, 196.
Nāgasena, 197.
Nāgeśa Bhaṭṭa, 49, 50, 71, 96, 183.
Naiyāyika, 11, 13, 67, 102.
Nakleśvara, 31.

Nakulīśa, 12.
Nānā, 3.
Nandī, 3.
Nandikeśvara, 4, 38, 48, 49, 50, 51, 56, 57, 180, 183, 184.
Nandikeśvara, Kāśikā, 4, 48, 49, 50, 180.
Nandikeśvara Śaivaism, 6, 49, 56, 57, 62, 181, 184, 185.
Narasiṁha, 186.
Nārasiṁhaka, 62.
Naravāhana, 54.
Nārāyaṇa, 21, 22, 23, 27.
Nārāyaṇa Kaṇṭha, 19, 21, 22, 25.
Nārāyaṇopaniṣad, 27, 28.
Nareśvaraparīkṣā, 22.
Nāṭaka, 25.
Naṭarāja, 5.
Navāhnika, 50.
Negation, 166, 167.
Nepal, 3.
Netra, 8.
Nickel, 55.
Nididhyāsana, 40.
Nihilism, 196.
Nihilistic monism, 42, 51.
Nimbārka, 151.
Nimitta, 34, 100.
Niradhiṣṭhānabhrama, 165.
Nirañjana, 134, 192.
Nirātmaka, 145.
Niravayava, 98.
Nirguṇa, 174, 184.
Nirguṇa Brahman, 40, 113.
Nirguṇa-Brahmavāda, 161.
Nirodha 77, 83.
Nirodhaśakti, 74, 81, 82, 83, 85, 94.
Nirvāṇa, 64.
Nirviśeṣa, 154, 173.
Nirviśeṣa Brahman, 167.
Nirviśeṣādvaita, 44, 47, 161, 166, 167.
Niṣkala, 123.
Niṣprapañca-Brahmādvaita, 45.
Niṣṭhā, 138.
Niṣṭhāyoga, 143.
Niṣṭhāyogayukta, 134.
Niśvāsa, 62.
Niyama, 141.
Niyati, 73, 100, 103, 104, 170, 185.
Noesis, 86.
Noeta, 86.
Non-difference, 34, 154.
Non-dualism, 44.
Non-dualistic, 63.
Non-duality, 44, 169, 170.
Non-eternal, 100.
Non-existence, 151, 197.
Non-idea, 119.
Non-illusory, 167.
Non-recognition, 107, 148.
Non-violence, 141.
Noose, 3.
Northern face, 116.
Not-being, 124, 165, 166, 174, 182.
Not-free, 126.
Not-self, 84, 100, 200, 201.
Nous, 86.
Nyāya, 5, 11, 12, 13, 14, 17, 21, 26, 47, 56, 64, 67, 75, 100, 117, 119, 124, 125, 129, 130, 132, 140, 191, 192, 197.
Nyāya Sūtra, 111, 145.

O

Object, 68, 102, 166, 200, 201, 202, 204, 206.
Objective, 106.
Objective categories, 11.
Objective relation, 106.
Objective world, 10, 74, 78, 80, 81, 114, 146, 154, 155.
Objectivity, 106, 115, 176, 177.
O.B. Lepeshinskaya, 189.
Obscuration, 77, 80, 81, 103, 122, 153.
Oesho, 3.
Omnipotence, 14, 23, 77, 78, 80, 82, 105, 106, 108, 133, 134, 149, 198, 202, 204, 205.
Omnipotent, 195.
Omniscience, 14, 23, 77, 82, 99, 105, 106, 108, 123, 133, 134, 149, 198, 202.
Omniscient, 99, 107, 109, 123, 132, 162, 175, 195, 197.
Oneness, 108.
Organs of action, 163.
Organism, 115.
Original image, 156.
Outcaste, 46.
Owl, 13.

P

Pāda, 177.
Padakāṇḍa, 71.
Padārtha, 119.
Paddhati, 21, 24.
Padma, 7.
Pain, 10, 11, 13, 14, 102, 155.
Pākhaṇḍāpajaya, 24.
Pānaka Rasa, 154.
Pañcaka, 135.
Pañcakṛtya, 153.
Pañcaratnavyākhyā, 41.
Pañcarātrāgama, 46, 58.
Pañcarātra Vaiṣṇava, 32.
Pañcārtha Bhāṣya, 119.
Pañca vaktra, 6, 77, 115.
Paṇḍita, 153.
Paṇḍitāradhya, 38, 43.
Pāṇini, 4, 49, 56, 71, 180.
Para, 82, 85, 105, 109, 138.
Parā, 71, 96, 97, 110.
Para Bindu, 72.
Para Brahman, 47.
Pārada, 52.
Pārada sādhana, 187.
Paragārgya, 12.
Parā Kuṇḍalinī, 90.
Pāramaiśvaryāvāpti, 10.
Paramārtha satya, 161.
Pāramārthika, 165.
Paramaśakti, 202.
Parama Śiva, 40, 42, 51, 81, 87, 88, 98, 100, 105, 159, 185.
Paramaśivārādhya 47.
Paramātman, 169.
Paramavyoma, 192.
Parameśvara, 62, 153.
Paramokṣa Nirāsa Kārikā, 16, 23, 70, 109, 150.
Para mukti, 86.
Para Nāda, 95, 96.
Parāpekṣā, 76.
Parārdha, 7.
Parasaṁvid, 106.
Pārāśara, 29.

Para Śiva, 148, 149, 173, 174, 175, 176, 177, 178, 184.
Parigraha Śakti, 88.
Paripāka, 83.
Partial liberation, 82.
Particular, 5, 86.
Pārvatī, 3, 53.
Pāśa, 70, 72, 73, 74, 77, 85, 99, 110, 149, 154, 160, 170, 173, 192.
Passion, 141, 142.
Passive resistence, 37.
Paśu, 9, 10, 40, 62, 64, 65, 70, 72, 73, 74, 77, 81, 82, 95, 97, 99, 100, 102, 103, 110, 111, 118, 119, 122, 125, 126, 132, 133, 134, 149, 155, 159, 160, 170, 173.
Pāśupata, 11, 13, 14, 26, 30, 60, 61, 64, 65, 70, 111, 112, 139, 145, 148, 197.
Pāśupatādhikāraḥ, 9, 34, 42, 148.
Pāśupata Dualism 6, 57, 61, 64, 70, 74, 75.
Pāśupata ritual, 117.
Pāśupata Śāstra, 141.
Pāśupata School, 56, 57.
Pāśupata section, 26.
Pāśupata Sūtra, 9, 11, 14, 26, 27, 28, 30, 34, 111, 112, 113, 117, 119, 124, 135, 142, 152, 180.
Pāśupata system, 10, 34, 56.
Paśupati, 3, 5, 13, 60, 64, 153.
Paśupatinātha, 3.
Paśutva, 105, 133, 134, 149, 155, 156, 160.
Paśutva mala, 82, 83, 85, 86, 103, 105, 157, 158, 159.
Paśyantī, 96, 97, 98, 110, 182.
Patañjali, 7, 49, 50, 56, 71, 140, 141, 180, 183.
Patent, 158.
Pati, 9, 60, 62, 64, 65, 70, 73, 74, 75, 77, 78, 80, 81, 82, 87, 88, 98, 99, 100, 110, 113, 118, 119, 120, 121, 122, 124, 125, 126, 132, 133, 149, 161, 170, 173.
Pauṣkarāgama, 8.
P.C. Ray, 189.
Peace, 192.
Pearl, 34.
Pentad, 135, 137, 138.
Perceiver, 113.
Perception, 10, 91, 128, 129, 145, 171, 191, 206.
Perdurable, 52.
Perdurable body, 186, 194.
Personality, 39, 128, 145, 146, 169, 176, 198.
Pervasion, 78.
Pervasive, 113, 126.
Phallic, 1, 37.
Phallus, 1.
Phallus worshipper, 5.
Phenomenal multiplicity, 34.
Phenomenological, 11.
Phenomenon, 59, 200, 201.
Philosophy, 7, 28, 37, 44, 56, 58, 87.
Philosophy of grammar, 20, 71, 91, 96, 183.
Philosophy of Kashmir, 204.
Piety, 141.
Pinākin, 2.
Piṅgalākṣa, 12.
Piśāca, 59.
Place, 129.
Plaster, 55.
Plato, 86.
Playfulness, 121.
Pleasure, 102, 155.

Plotinus, 86, 87, 181, 201.
Pluralism, 62.
Pluralist, 200.
Plurality, 103.
Portrait, 31.
Portugal, 30.
Possessor, 35.
Posture, 141.
Post-Vedic, 2.
Potential, 196.
Potentiality, 72, 78, 119, 184.
Power, 35, 118, 154, 162, 171, 174, 182, 201.
Power of action, 122, 139.
Power of cognition, 199.
Power of creation.
Power of differentiation, 199, 201.
Power of knowledge, 90, 122, 123, 133, 139, 162, 200.
Power of remembrance, 199, 201.
Power of will, 154.
Prābhrata, 186.
Prācārya, 19.
Pracchanna Bauddha, 47, 166.
Practical, 7.
Practical life, 199, 201, 205.
Practical reality, 161.
Pradhāna, 13, 65, 70, 75, 101, 103, 104, 105, 112, 125, 130.
Prafulla Chandra Ray, 54.
Prajāpati, 139.
Prajñālaṅkāra, 17.
Prajñā Pāramitā sūtra, 196.
Prakāśa, 182, 201.
Prakāśasvarūpa, 101.
Prakṛti, 81, 104, 124, 134, 143, 156, 166, 171, 172, 173, 191.
Pralaya, 103.
Pralayākala, 73, 74, 103, 132.
Pramā, 13.
Pramātā, 206.
Prāṇa, 37, 97, 114, 177, 178, 184.
Prāṇaliṅga, 12, 38.
Prāṇaliṅgisthala, 178.
Prāṇāyāma, 141, 142.
Prasāda, 137, 138.
Prasādisthala, 178.
Pratibhā, 129.
Prātibhāsika, 165.
Pratimā Nāṭaka, 29, 30, 59.
Pratiṣṭhā, 114.
Pratyabhijñā, 35, 71, 196, 206.
Pratyabhijñā Hṛdaya, 183.
Pratyāhāra, 135, 137, 141, 180.
Pravṛtti, 127.
Preceptor, 12.
Preta, 59.
Pride, 133.
Primary categories, 70, 73, 81, 87.
Prime Mover, 75.
Priority, 100.
Prompter, 75, 82.
Protector, 117.
Pṛthivī, 59.
Psycho-epistemic, 57.
Psycho-physical limitation, 130.
Purāṇa, 29, 30, 39, 45.
Pure, 72, 110.
Pure being, 106.
Pure bliss, 175.
Pure creation, 88, 89, 100.
Pure Dvaitādvaita, 161.
Purification, 138.
Purified mercury, 186.
Purpose, 204.
Puruṣa, 8, 67, 68, 72, 73, 74, 75, 81, 102, 104, 105, 113, 116, 120, 123, 124, 143, 170, 177, 191.

Puruṣa Sūkta, 40, 42.
Pūrvavat, 129.
Puryaṣṭaka, 103.
Puṣpadanta, 153.
Puṣpaka, 12.
Puṣyabhūti, 3.

Q

Qualified Monism, 148, 149, 151.
Qualified Non-dualism, 167.
Qualified non-duality, 169.
Quality, 151, 198.

R

Rāga, 67, 73, 100, 101, 102, 103, 104, 105, 170, 185.
Raghuvaṁśa, 4.
Rāhula Sankṛtāyana, 54.
Rājarāja, 4.
Rājarājeśvara, 31.
Rajas, 104, 114, 116, 185.
Rājaśekhara, 5, 10, 11, 12, 14, 28, 30, 38, 61.
Rājendra, 4.
Rāma, 42, 43.
Rāmakaṇṭha,-I 18, 19, 20, 22, 25, 51.
Rāmakaṇṭha-II 17, 19, 21, 22, 23, 25, 72, 150.
Rāmanātha, 38.
Rāmānuja, 32, 33, 44, 45, 46, 117, 148, 149.
Raṅgarāja, 45.
Rasa, 54, 158, 188.
Rasa Bhairava, 192.
Rasa Hṛdaya, 53, 188.
Rasaliṅga, 190.
Rasamahodadhi, 187.
Rasa Ratnākara, 54.
Rasa Ratna Samuccaya, 187, 188.
Rasārṇava, 54, 187, 192.
Rasasaṅāketa Kalikā, 53.
Rasasiddha, 53, 54.
Rasa Tantra, 54.
Rasāyana, 189.
Rasendra (Pārada), 53, 189, 194.
Rasendra Maṅgala, 54.
Raseśvara, 52.
Raseśvara Śaivaism, 6, 62.
Raseśvara system, 56, 186, 189, 190, 192.
Rāśikara, 12.
Rasopaniṣad, 186, 187.
Rāṣṭrakūṭa, 4.
Rational foundation, 106.
Rationalism, 118.
Rationalistic Voluntarism, 112, 199.
Ratnaghoṣa, 54.
Ratna Prabhā, 10, 13, 70, 112.
Ratna Ṭīkā, 111.
Ratna Traya, 18, 19, 20, 22, 23, 25, 51, 72, 76, 96.
Ratnatrayollekhinī, 96.
Ratnāvalī, 188.
Raudra, 47, 59.
Rauravāgama, 15, 16, 61, 62.
Rāvaṇa, 71.
Real, 7, 44, 84, 164, 165, 166, 167, 174, 203, 204.
Realisation, 98, 108, 114, 195, 196.
Realism, 200.
Realist, 171.
Realistic, 201, 203.

Realistic Idealism, 200, 205.
Reality, 7, 101, 108, 113, 124, 161, 171, 173, 181, 184, 195, 196.
Reason, 106, 191, 195.
Recension, 27, 50.
Recognition, 206.
Reflection, 68, 93, 168, 171, 175, 189, 205.
Region, 27.
Relation, 168, 169, 173, 198.
Religion, 1, 10, 15, 39, 58, 116, 148, 188, 190.
Religio-philosophic tradition, 2.
Religious ceremony, 37.
Religious festival, 46.
Religious revolution, 37.
Religious sect, 38, 43.
Religious tradition, 38, 39, 46.
Remembrance, 198, 199, 200, 205.
Reṇuka, 41, 44, 179.
Renunciation, 40.
Representation, 49.
Residual traces, 91, 92, 102, 164, 198, 199.
Revaṇa, 39, 40, 41, 42, 44, 48, 50, 51.
Revaṇārya, 40, 41.
Revelation, 105.
Ṛgveda, 1, 55, 59.
Ritual, 7, 40, 117, 120, 133, 148.
Rock-cut shrine, 4.
Rodhaśakti, 73, 81, 85.
Rudra, 1, 2, 5, 6, 59, 114, 116, 117, 119, 122, 137, 148, 153.
Rudrākṣa, 15.
Rudrāmbā, 44.
Rudra sāyujya, 139.
Rudra Yāmala, 8, 187.
Ruru, 15, 61.
Russian scientist, 189.

S

Śabda, 66, 89.
Śabda Brahman, 95.
Śabdabrahmavādin, 98.
Śabda Tattva, 96.
Saccidānanda, 113.
Ṣaḍadhva, 48.
Sadānandopaniṣad, 38.
Sadārudrasmṛti, 137.
Sadāśiva, 13, 39, 82, 85, 86, 87, 98, 99, 104, 117, 170, 177, 185, 192.
Sadāśiva Tattva, 99.
Ṣaḍ-darśana Samuccaya, 5, 10, 12, 13, 28, 30.
Sādhāraṇa Vṛtti, 128.
Sadvṛtti, 18, 19, 20.
Sadyojāta, 6, 77, 116, 120, 192.
Sadyojyoti, 15, 16, 17, 20, 21, 23, 25, 61, 63, 70, 109, 110, 150.
Saguṇa, 28, 42, 113, 184.
Saguṇa Brahman, 40.
Saguṇa Brahmavāda, 119, 161.
Sahasra, 62.
Śaiva, 4, 12, 13, 14, 15, 17, 34, 37, 52, 60, 63, 64, 95, 118, 148, 164, 186, 187, 197, 202, 203, 204.
Śaiva Bhāṣya, 39.
Śaiva categories, 8, 16, 17, 170.
Śaiva Dualism, 18, 23, 26, 37, 62, 63, 67, 95, 96, 101, 105, 156, 157.
Śaiva Dualist, 96, 101, 108, 109.
Śaiva Dualistic Philosophy, 5.
Śaivāgama, 5, 6, 7, 8, 14, 15, 16, 22, 27, 34, 39, 42, 44, 50, 51, 58, 60, 62, 66, 76, 77, 78, 110, 148, 149, 152, 170, 177, 183, 186.
Śaiva Monism, 16, 18, 159.
Śaiva Philosophy, 1, 4, 5, 6, 7, 15, 21, 32, 36, 49, 56, 57, 58, 59, 60,

61, 62.
Śaiva religion, 11, 12, 34, 39.
Śaiva sect, 38.
Śaiva systems, 5, 52, 60, 186.
Śaiva temple, 141.
Śaiva theory of inference, 206.
Śaiva Viśeṣādvaita, 60.
Śaiva Viśiṣṭādvaita, 47, 60, 156, 170.
Śaivaism, 2, 3, 5, 7, 16, 18, 26, 27, 33, 37, 40, 59, 60, 62, 66, 99, 116, 143, 148, 158, 163, 186, 198, 199, 202, 203.
Śaivaism of Kashmir, 182, 195, 196, 197, 201.
Sajātīya, 173.
Sakala, 73, 74, 103, 121.
Śāka years, 28.
Śākhā, 40.
Sākṣātkāra, 177.
Śākta, 157.
Śakti, 1, 4, 8, 9, 24, 40, 42, 72, 73, 75, 76, 77, 81, 87, 88, 96, 99, 104, 112, 119, 124, 150, 151, 154, 163, 170, 171, 172, 174, 183, 184, 185, 192.
Śaktidhara, 39.
Śaktihetu, 133.
Śaktipāta, 192.
Śakti Tattva, 98.
Śakti Viśiṣṭādvaita, 163.
Śaktyadvayavādin, 76.
Salokatā, 115.
Sālokya, 175, 176, 194.
Samādhi, 135, 141, 143, 174.
Sāmajaigīśīya Sākhā, 38.
Sāmānya, 37.
Sāmānyatodṛṣṭa, 129.
Sāmānya vṛtti, 127.
Samarāṅgaṇa Sūtradhāra, 7.
Samatā Saṅkrānti Pakṣa, 23, 108.
Samavāya, 81, 169.
Sāmaveda, 2.
Sāmavidhāna, 2.
Sambhava, 129.
Śambhu, 54, 153.
Saṁhāra śakti, 81.
Saṁhitā, 2, 58.
Saṁhiti, 26.
Saṁhṛta, 134.
Śamī, 44.
Samīpa, 142.
Sāmīpya, 117, 175, 176.
Sāmīpya mokṣa, 142.
Saṁskāra, 129.
Saṁskāra Kārikā, 138.
Samudragupta, 28.
Saṁvid, 90, 106.
Saṁvidrūpā, 97.
Sāmya, 149, 160, 175.
Sāmya mokṣa, 158.
Saṁyoga, 169.
Sāndīpa, 57.
Sāñjana, 134.
Śaṅkara, 8, 9, 11, 12, 14, 15, 32, 34, 44, 45, 47, 53, 55, 61, 64, 70, 112, 148, 153, 161, 164, 166, 188.
Śāṅkara, 186.
Śāṅkara Bhāṣya, 9, 10, 13, 26.
Śāṅkara Vedānta, 164, 165, 166.
Śaṅkaranandana, 16, 17.
Śaṅkarārādhya, 44.
Śaṅkha, 7, 46.
Sāṅkhya, 11, 14, 21, 47, 65, 66, 67, 81, 84, 102, 103, 104, 105, 120, 121, 124, 125, 129, 130, 132, 133, 142, 145, 170, 172, 184, 185, 191, 200.
Saṅkramaṇa, 114.

Saṅkrānti, 16, 118, 150, 158.
Śānta, 8, 114.
Santāna, 12, 62.
Saptacakra, 178.
Sāraṅgadeva, 30.
Sarvabhūtadamana, 116.
Sarva Darśana Saṅgraha, 26, 34, 60, 63, 111, 177, 186, 187, 188.
Sarvaśrutisāramata, 48, 161, 162.
Sarvathānupapatti, 47.
Sarvātma Śiva, 24.
Sarvatobhadra, 21.
Sarveśa Deśika, 40.
Śaśāṅka, 3.
Śāśvatavāda, 196.
Sat, 113, 120.
Ṣaṭcakra, 177.
Ṣaṭka, 177.
Satkāryavāda, 66.
Sātmaka, 145.
Ṣaṭsthala, 38.
Sattva, 104, 114, 116, 171, 172, 177, 184, 185, 191, 192, 206.
Sāttvika, 54.
Satya, 165, 203.
Satya buddhi, 192.
Śaukra, 186.
Saundarya Laharī, 8.
Saura, 47.
Saurabheya, 62, 63.
Saviśeṣa, 173.
Sāyaṇa, 27, 112, 113, 114, 115, 116, 117, 120.
Sāyujya, 134, 143, 145, 160, 161, 170, 175.
Sāyujya mokṣa, 115.
Science, 186, 188, 189, 190, 191.
Scientific process, 53.
Script, 60.
Self, 7, 52, 83, 106, 107, 115, 122, 145, 181, 183, 184, 186, 193, 197, 200, 201.
Self-awareness, 7.
Self-consciousness, 106, 163, 196.
Self-control, 40.
Selfhood. 145.
Self-realisation, 26.
Self-shining, 76.
Self-sufficient, 196.
Self-surrender, 157.
Sense, 102, 146.
Senses of perception, 103.
Sensuous object, 146.
Sensuous perception, 129.
Sentiency, 126, 127, 128, 168, 173, 175, 191.
Sentient, 75, 76, 113, 124, 130, 139, 152, 156, 173, 174.
Sentient principle, 134.
Sentient self, 69.
Sentient Subject, 104, 132.
Servitude, 117.
Seṣavat, 129.
Śeśvarādvaita, 48, 161.
Siddha, 40, 41, 52, 62, 121, 123, 132, 133, 139, 140, 145, 186, 188.
Siddhānta, 15, 16, 18, 24, 76, 170.
Siddhānta Dualist, 152,
Siddhānta Śaiva, 60, 72, 73, 83, 88, 170.
Siddhānta Śaiva Dualism, 6, 57, 61, 66, 67, 68, 70, 74, 75, 85, 86, 87, 89, 109, 110.
Siddhānta Śaivaism, 24.
Siddhānta School, 7, 8, 25, 38, 63, 76, 109, 149.
Siddhānta Śikhāmaṇi, 40, 41, 163, 179.

Siddhāntavādin, 22.
Siddhāntin, 93, 95, 107.
Siddhi, 139.
Śikhaṇḍin, 83.
Śilāda, 39.
Silver, 34, 55, 107, 150, 189.
Similarity, 105, 107, 149, 158, 159, 160, 170, 176, 192, 199, 203.
Simuka, 3.
Śiva, 1, 2, 3, 4, 5, 6, 8, 11, 12, 13, 22, 24, 31, 34, 37, 38, 45, 46, 47, 48, 49, 52, 53, 56, 59, 60, 61, 70, 72, 73, 76, 77, 78, 79, 87, 88, 90, 98, 99, 104, 105, 108, 112, 116, 118, 120, 123, 140, 142, 143, 149, 150, 151, 152, 153, 154, 155, 156, 157, 159, 160, 161, 162, 163, 170, 171, 173, 177, 181, 184, 190, 192, 193, 194.
Śiva Dṛṣṭi, 5, 35, 96.
Śivādvaita, 158, 161, 162.
Śivādvaita Nirṇaya, 36.
Śivāgama, 34.
Śivāgamaikadeśa, 148.
Śivajñānabodha, 110.
Śivajñāna Candrodaya, 47.
Śiva Liṅga, 1, 46, 47.
Śivaratnapañcaratna, 41.
Śivārcana Candrikā, 7.
Śiva-Śaktisaṁyoga, 177.
Śivasāmya 86, 105, 155, 159.
Śivatāgamana, 194.
Śivatattvaprakāśikā, 41.
Śiva Vijjā, 2.
Śivayoga, 177.
Śivottama, 83.
Six systems, 11.
Skandha, 196.
Sleep 154, 167.
Smṛti, 201.
Soma, 59.
Somānanda, 5, 20, 35, 71, 96, 97, 180, 188.
Somanātha, 28, 30.
Someśvara, 38.
Sosali-Vīraṇārādhya, 151.
Soul, 43, 47, 76, 79, 80, 82, 89, 95, 101, 105, 107, 121, 141, 151, 168, 169, 171, 174, 176, 177, 194, 197.
Southern face, 116.
Southern Gujarāta, 24.
Space, 116, 154.
Spanda Kārikā, 18, 19, 22, 180.
Spandana 142.
Spatial, CLII.
Speech-organ, 98.
Sphoṭa, 91, 92, 97.
Sphoṭavāda, 23.
Spirit, 86.
Spiritual discipline, 88, 121.
Spiritual insight, 145.
Spiritual level, 7.
Spiritual perception, 86, 129.
Spiritual world, 86, 87.
Śravaṇa, 150.
Śreṣṭha, 116.
Śrīkaṇṭha, 5, 18, 19, 20, 23, 25, 32, 33, 34, 35, 36, 47, 51, 56, 60, 62, 63, 65, 72, 83, 96, 97, 98, 148, 149, 150, 152, 157, 160, 163, 170.
Śrīkara Bhāṣya, 33, 39, 42, 43, 44, 50, 63.
Śrīpati, 41, 46, 47, 48, 165, 166, 167, 168, 170, 171, 172, 173, 177, 179.
Śrīpati Paṇḍita, 38, 40, 41, 42, 43, 44, 45, 46, 50, 51, 60, 62, 63, 65.
Śrīpati Paṇḍitārādhya, 33, 37, 39, 161, 164, 168.

Śrīperuṁbudūr, 32.
Śrīśaila, 38.
Śṛṅgāraḥ, 142.
Śrotavyaḥ, 42.
Śruti, 40, 42, 44, 48, 162, 167.
Śrutyarthapradīpikā, 151.
Sthala, 178.
Sthāyin, 158.
Sthiti, 139.
Storm, 60.
Stotrāvalī, 22.
Subject, 68, 102, 137, 157, 161, 167, 196, 197, 198, 199, 200, 201, 202, 204, 206.
Subjective, 203.
Subjective individuality, 133.
Subjectivism, 200.
Subjectivist, 33, 200.
Subjectivity, 177.
Substance, 17, 77, 107, 108, 116, 151, 159, 168, 169, 191, 198.
Substratum, 34, 203, 204.
Subtle, 76, 100.
Subtle elements, 103.
Subtle inner word, 93.
Subtle state, 104, 153.
Succession, 7, 39, 43, 99, 203.
Śuddha, 37, 72.
Śuddhādhva, 79.
Śuddhādvaita, 164.
Śuddha Śaivaism, 37.
Śuddhāśuddha, 170.
Śuddhavidyā, 170.
Śuddhi, 138.
Śūdra, 190.
Śūdraka, 188.
Suffering, 15.
Sukeśa, 39.
Śukla, 5.
Śukla Yajurveda, 2.
Sukṛta, 113.
Sūkṣma, 62, 63, 83, 97, 98.
Sūkṣmarūpa, 192.
Sūkṣmā Vāk, 98.
Sūkta, 42.
Śūla, 47.
Śūnyādvaita, 40, 44, 51, 164.
Superimposition, 84, 164, 165.
Supersensible nature, 87.
Suprabheda, 8, 62, 63.
Suprabhedāgama, 38.
Supremacy, 111.
Supreme, 117, 193.
Supreme Lord, 80.
Surānanda, 54.
Sūrasena, 54.
Sureśvarācārya, 8, 15.
Surgeon, 108.
Surgical instrument, 82.
Surgical operation, 83.
Śuṣkādvaita, 164.
Suśruta, 55.
Suṣumṇā, 177, 178,
Sūta Saṁhitā, 24, 28, 30.
Sūtra, 4, 9, 42, 45, 49, 120.
Svabhāva, 113.
Svābhāvika, 171.
Svacchanda, 8.
Svacchanda Tantra, 18.
Svara Vimarśinī, 50.
Svarūpasambandha, 169.
Svatantra, 118, 126, 132, 174, 205.
Svātantrya, 182, 183, 201.
Svātantryavāda, 205.
Svāyambhuva, 25, 62.
Svāyambhuvāgama, 16, 22.

Svāyambhuvodyota, 22.
Swami Kannu Pillai, 29.
Syllogism, 195.
Synthesis, 58, 197, 199.
Synthetic activity, 199.
System of medicine, 189.

T

Tadananyatva, 150.
Tādātmya, 171.
Taila, 37.
Taittirīya Āraṇyaka, 5, 26, 27, 28, 56, 76, 112, 113, 114, 115, 117, 120, 142, 152, 153.
Taittirīya Saṁhitā, II.
Tamas, 104, 114, 116, 171, 172, 185, 191, 206.
Tamil, 41.
Tamil Śaiva Siddhānta, 109.
Tamil Siddhānta Śaivaism, 110.
Tanmātras, 67, 121.
Tantra, 25, 50, 187, 189.
Tantrāloka, 6, 16, 17, 48, 51, 83.
Tantra Pāśupata, 47.
Tantrarāja, 50.
Tantrasārapañcaratna, 41.
Tantrasāraprakāśikā, 41.
Tantrāvatāra, 8.
Tāntric, 188.
Tapas, 139.
Tarka, 42.
Taṭastha Lakṣaṇa, 175.
Tatpuruṣa, 6, 77, 116, 117, 123, 192.
Tatpuruṣa Samāsa, 152.
Tattva, 87, 177, 191.
Tattvamasi, 156.
Tattva Prakāśikā, 18, 23, 24, 25, 63, 74.
Tattva Saṅgraha, 16, 20, 25, 63, 206.
Tattva Saṅgrahādhikāra, 197.
Tattvatraya Nirṇaya, 16, 21, 25.
Tattva Vimarśinī, 49, 50.
Teacher, 12, 31, 39, 141.
Teleological argument, 75.
Temple, 4, 7, 137.
Temporal, 152.
Terrific, 59, 122.
Theism, 197.
Theistic, 197.
Theory of knowledge, 126.
Theory of Meaning, 20.
Theory of reflection, 168.
Thesis, 58, 59, 148.
Thinker, 57.
Thirty-six categories, 51, 184, 206.
Thought, 184, 196.
Ṭīkā, 1.
Time, 66, 129, 132, 138, 154.
Tin, 189.
Tirobhāva, 81.
Tirobhāvaśakti, 81.
Tirodhāna, 157.
Tirodhānaśakti, 81, 83.
Tirodhāyaka, 83.
Ṭīrthakara, 13.
Tirupati, 46.
Top-face, 117.
Transcendental, 72, 88, 181, 201.
Transcendental Bliss, 153.
Transcendental experience, 57.
Transcendental level, 45.
Transcendental Philosophy, 196.
Transient, 89, 100, 104, 171.

Transient emotion, 158.
Transitory, 78.
Transmigratory existence, 116, 117, 118, 153.
Transmigratory states, 52.
Triad, 9.
Trident, 3.
Trika, 139, 177.
Trikūṭa, 71.
Triliṅga, 71.
Trimūrti, 83.
Tripuṇḍra, 15, 148.
Tripurāntaka, 30.
Truth, 113, 141.
Tryambaka, 2.
Turaimaṅgalam Śiva Prakāśasvāmin, 41.

U

Ucchedavāda, 196.
Udbhaṭārādhya, 48.
Uditācārya, 29, 30, 31.
Udyota, 49.
Ugly, 155.
Ugrajyoti, 16.
Ujjain, 5, 38.
Ujjayinī, 5.
Ultimate, 108, 181, 195, 196, 205.
Ultimate Reality, 27, 97, 112, 123, 127, 128, 150, 152, 153, 161, 162, 164, 170, 178.
Ultimate Śiva, 58.
Ultimate Unity, 34.
Umāpati, 114.
Umeśa, 3.
Undifferentiated, 94.
Undifferentiated mass, 32.
Undifferentiated unity, 95.
Unification, 153, 199.
Uniformity, 82.
Union, 111, 123, 134, 139, 140, 141, 143, 161, 170, 172, 175, 176, 177.
Unity, 32, 34, 124, 154, 158, 162, 164, 170, 171, 203, 204, 205.
Unity in multiplicity, 7, 123, 124, 159.
Universal, 22, 45, 69, 92, 114, 115, 119, 158, 159, 160, 162, 178, 191, 194, 196, 197, 200, 204.
Universal annihilation, 72, 81, 100, 103, 116, 137, 154, 160.
Universal being, 162.
Universal Consciousness, 178.
Universal Mind, 124, 196, 201, 202.
Universal nescience, 168.
Universal Self, 69, 156.
Unmana, 192.
Unmanyavasthāprāpti, 178.
Upamanyu, 48, 49, 50, 51, 180.
Upamita, 29.
Upamitācārya, 29, 31.
Upmiteśvara, 29.
Upaniṣad, 2, 45, 50, 58, 148.
Upāsanā, 107, 173.
Upasaṅkrāmati, 114.
Upāya, 126.
Ūrdhva-Vaktra, 117.
Uṣas, 59.
Utpala, 22, 33, 180, 183.
Utpalācārya, 18, 22, 32, 33, 35, 149, 195, 197, 199.
Utpatti samatā pakṣa, 23, 108.
Uttuṅga Śiva, 24.

V

Vācaka, 93.
Vācaspati, 64.
Vāgbhaṭa, 187.
Vāgbhaṭa Saṁhitā, 53, 54.
Vaikharī, 71, 96, 97, 110.
Vairāgya, 102.
Vaiśeṣika, 5, 10, 11, 13, 14, 17, 21, 26, 47, 56, 59, 64, 65, 66, 67, 75, 89, 100, 111, 112, 117, 119, 124, 125, 140, 145, 177, 191, 197, 198.
Vaiṣṇava, 46, 149, 186.
Vaiṣṇava doctrines, 48.
Vaiṣṇava thought, 32.
Vaiṣṇava Viśiṣṭādvaita, 46.
Vaiṣṇavaism, 28, 32, 33, 46, 58, 148, 186.
Vaiṣṇavaite, 148.
Vājasaneya Saṁhitā, 2.
Vaktra, 116.
Vākyakāṇḍa, 71.
Vākyapadīya, 22, 71, 96.
Vālmīkirāśi, 30.
Vāma, 6, 76, 114.
Vāmadeva, 39, 116, 192.
Vāmamārga, 193.
Varadarāja, 45.
Varma, 46.
Varṇa, 92, 96, 177.
Varuṇa, 27.
Vāruṇī, 26, 27.
Vaśiṣṭha, 47, 49.
Vāstu Śāstra, 23.
Vāsudeva, 3.
Vasurāta, 71.
Vātāpi, 4.
Vaṭa Vṛkṣa Siddheśvara, 38.
Vātsyāyana, 111, 130.
Vātula, 178, 186.
Vātulāgama, 33.
Vāyu, 29.
Vāyu Purāṇa, 28.
Veda, 5, 26, 34, 38, 45, 47, 55, 56, 58, 59, 75, 77, 112, 117, 148, 170, 172, 173.
Vedānta, 14, 21, 48, 69, 84, 120, 145, 163, 164, 166, 182.
Vedānta Sūtra, 9, 23, 24, 39, 42, 43, 44, 45, 47, 48, 56, 63, 64, 65, 148, 150, 164, 166, 176.
Vedāntic, 40, 106.
Vedāntin, 69, 82, 102, 106, 107, 108, 112, 125, 128, 156, 167.
Vedic, 15, 40, 56, 174.
Vedic period, 5, 60.
Vedic ritualism, 58.
Vedic Saṁhitā, 27.
Vedic system, 5.
Vedic text, 5, 69.
Vemana, 40.
Vemanārādhya, 48.
Veṅkaṭeśvara, 46.
Verbal testimony, 129, 130, 191.
Vibhāva, 158.
Vibhu, 140, 141.
Vidhi, 9, 62, 65, 70, 74, 111, 120, 195.
Vidyā, 8, 9, 10, 65, 73, 79, 81, 82, 85, 86, 87, 89, 96, 99, 100, 101, 102, 103, 104, 111, 117, 119, 120, 122, 123, 125, 126, 127, 128, 129, 138, 163, 170, 185.
Vidyā Bodhasvabhāvā, 128.
Vidyā Bodhasvabhāvā Sāmānya vṛtti, 129.
Vidyāguru, 12.
Vidyākaṇṭha, 19, 20.

Vidyāraṇya Yatīndra, 24.
Vidyā Tattva, 99.
Vidya Tilaka, 10.
Vidyeśa, 99.
Vidyeśvara, 79, 80, 103.
Vijātīya, 173.
Vijaya, 62.
Vijjana, 37.
Vijñāna, 90, 92, 93.
Vijñānākala, 73, 74, 82, 103.
Vijñānākevala, 85.
Vijñānātma, 27.
Vikalpa, 164.
Vikaraṇa, 140.
Vikramāditya, 4.
Vikramāṅka, 37.
Vikramāṅkadeva Carita, 37.
Vikṛti, 124.
Vimala, 62.
Vimarśa, 182
Vimarśātmaka, 93.
Vimarśinī 33, 195, 197.
Vipra, 123.
Vīra, 163, 164.
Vīrabhadra, 46, 62.
Vīraṇārādhya, 40, 41.
Vīra Śaiva, 6, 39, 42, 44, 163, 164.
Vīra Śaivaism, 4, 12, 37, 38, 39, 41, 43, 44, 56, 177, 178.
Vīreśvara, 46.
Visara, 62.
Viśārada, 54.
Visarjanīya, 91.
Viśeṣa, 48.
Viśeṣādvaita, 6, 154, 158, 62, 161, 162, 164, 166.
Viśiṣṭādvaita, 32, 33, 35, 44, 45, 62, 151, 152, 168, 169, 170.
Viśiṣṭādvaita Śaivaism, 6, 34, 56, 63, 149, 154, 157, 159, 163.
Viśiṣṭādvaitin, 28.
Viśiṣṭādvaitavādin, 34.
Viśiṣṭādvaitism, 37.
Viṣṇu, 37, 150, 156.
Viśuddha Muni, 26.
Viśvamaya, 201.
Viśvāmitra, 140.
Viśvanātha, 38, 40.
Viśvārādhya, 38, 40, 43.
Viśvottīrṇa, 201.
Vita, 129.
Vital air, 52, 59, 97, 98, 133, 155.
Viṭhaleśvara, 46.
Vivekapravṛtti, 127, 128.
Vocal music, 141.
Voluntarism, 183, 203.
Voluntaristic, 181, 183, 192, 201, 203, 204.
Vluntaristic metaphysics, 51.
Voluntaristic monism, 57.
Voluntaristic philosophy, 180.
Vṛṣabhendra Paṇḍita, 39.
Vṛtti, 19, 45, 127.
Vṛttilābha, 125.
Vṛttisaṅkara, 10, 125.
Vṛtyākāra, 145.
Vyabhicāribhāva, 158.
Vyāḍi, 54, 71.
Vyāghrapāt, 49.
Vyākaraṇa, 42.
Vyākaraṇāgama, 71.
Vyakta, 138.
Vyāpyavṛtti, 169.
Vyāvahārika, 165.
Vyāvahārika Satya, 161, 164.
Vyomavyāpi, 99.

W

Wakeful, 166, 167.
Wakefulness, 44, 164.
Western face, 116, 120.
Western Philosophy, 86.
Wheeler, 1.
Will, 7, 77, 78, 118, 121, 129, 132, 134, 162, 182, 193, 194, 203, 204, 205.
Wolff, 65.
Wrong knowledge, 126.

Y

Yādavaprakāśa, 32, 149.
Yājñikī, 26, 27.
Yajurveda, 55, 60.
Yama, 141.
Yama Prakaraṇa, 26.
Yaśodhana, 54.
Yauga, 12.
Yoga, 7, 9, 21, 47, 52, 62, 65, 70, 74, 75, 111, 112, 120, 140, 141, 142, 145, 177, 194.
Yogaja, 8, 62, 63.
Yoga Sūtra, 7, 140, 183.
Yoga system, 52.
Yogic discipline, 7.
Yogic practices, 7.
Yogin, 42, 140, 174.
Yoni, 1.
Yuan Chwang, 3.
Yukta, 146.
Yukti, 191.